Tax Simplification

Series on International Taxation

VOLUME 53

Series Editors

Prof. Ruth Mason, University of Virginia School of Law
Prof. Dr Ekkehard Reimer, University of Heidelberg

Introduction & Contents

The Series on International Taxation deals with a wide variety of topics in the global tax arena. The authors include many of the field's leading experts as well as talented newcomers. Their expert views and incisive commentary has proven highly useful to practitioners and academics alike.

Objective

The volumes published in this series are aimed at offering high-quality analytical information and practical solutions for international tax practitioners.

Readership

Practitioners, academics and policy makers in international tax law.

Frequency of Publication

2-3 new volumes published each year.

The titles published in this series are listed at the end of this volume.

Tax Simplification

Edited by
Chris Evans
Richard Krever
Peter Mellor

Wolters Kluwer
Law & Business

Published by:
Kluwer Law International
PO Box 316
2400 AH Alphen aan den Rijn
The Netherlands
Website: www.wklawbusiness.com

Sold and distributed in North, Central and South America by:
Aspen Publishers, Inc.
7201 McKinney Circle
Frederick, MD 21704
United States of America
Email: customer.service@aspenpublishers.com

Sold and distributed in all other countries by:
Turpin Distribution Services Ltd
Stratton Business Park
Pegasus Drive, Biggleswade
Bedfordshire SG18 8TQ
United Kingdom
Email: kluwerlaw@turpin-distribution.com

Printed on acid-free paper.

ISBN 978-90-411-5976-2

Printed and Bound by CPI Group (UK) Ltd, Croydon, CR0 4YY.

Editors

Chris Evans is a professor in the School of Taxation and Business Law (incorporating Atax), UNSW Australia; an Extraordinary Professor in the Department of Taxation at the University of Pretoria; an International Fellow at the University of Exeter and at the University of Oxford; an adjunct research fellow in the Taxation Law and Policy Research Group of the Monash Business School, Monash University; and editor of the *Australian Tax Review*. He has researched and published extensively in comparative taxation, capital and wealth taxation, tax law and administration (and particularly tax compliance costs), tax policy and reform.

Richard Krever is a professor in the Monash Business School, Monash University and director of the University's Taxation Law and Policy Research Group. He is the author of many research volumes, textbooks and journal articles. Richard has been seconded to international agencies such as the IMF and provided tax and law design assistance for organizations such as the World Bank, Asian Development Bank, as well as many ministries of finance and Treasury departments in Asia, Africa, the Pacific, the Caribbean, Eastern Europe and Australasia.

Peter Mellor is an adjunct research fellow in the Taxation Law and Policy Research Group of the Monash Business School, Monash University.

Contributors

Jacqueline Coolidge is a consultant for the World Bank Group (WBG) and former Lead Investment Policy Expert in the Investment Climate Department of the WBG, where she led the development of tax compliance cost surveys for businesses in developing countries. She holds degrees in economics and international studies from University of Michigan, Ann Arbor, Princeton University and Johns Hopkins University.

Michael D'Ascenzo AO is an adjunct professor in the School of Taxation and Business Law (incorporating Atax), UNSW Australia and a professorial fellow at Melbourne University. He is currently a member of Australia's Foreign Investment Review Board and Clean Energy Regulator, and is also a non-executive director of Australia Post. He was previously Australia's Federal Commissioner of Taxation.

J. Clifton Fleming Jr is the Ernest L. Wilkinson Chairholder and Professor of Law at Brigham Young University and an adjunct research fellow, Taxation Law and Policy Research Group, Monash Business School, Faculty of Business and Economics, Monash University. In 2011, he held the Fulbright Distinguished Chair at the Vienna University of Economics and Business and in 1985–1986 he was Professor-in-Residence in the IRS Chief Counsel's Office in Washington, DC. He is a Life Member of the American Law Institute.

Judith Freedman CBE is Pinsent Masons Professor of Taxation Law at Oxford University, Director of Legal Research at the Oxford University Centre for Business Taxation, adjunct professor in the School of Taxation and Business Law (incorporating Atax), UNSW Australia and joint editor of the *British Tax Review*. She was a member of the Office of Tax Simplification Small Business Consultative Committee and the Aaronson Study Group, which proposed the UK GAAR, and is currently a member of the Tax Law Review Committee of the Institute for Fiscal Studies.

John Hasseldine FCCA is a professor of accounting at the University of New Hampshire and an International Fellow at the University of Exeter. His PhD is from Indiana University and he has served on several UK government tax advisory committees. He is the journal editor of *Advances in Taxation* and consults widely.

Kristin Hickman is the Harlan Albert Rogers Professor of Law at the University of Minnesota Law School. She held the Donald C. Alexander Visiting Professorship in Tax Law at Harvard Law School in 2012–2013. Her academic work focuses principally on tax administration issues.

Neville Howlett is a tax director responsible for external and government relations for the UK tax practice of PwC. He is involved in developing tax research projects and disseminating the results, and leads various pieces of work in connection with the PwC Total Tax Contribution framework including the Paying Taxes study which is undertaken with the World Bank Group as part of their *Doing Business* project.

Gareth Jones is the head of digital design and delivery within HM Revenue & Customs' Business Customer and Strategy unit. Prior to that he was a policy adviser for the Office of Tax Simplification (OTS) in 2013, where he was responsible for managing the partnerships and competitiveness reviews.

Philip Lignier is a lecturer in taxation in the Tasmanian School of Business and Economics at the University of Tasmania. He has published and researched in the areas of tax compliance costs and environmental taxation.

Marco Lugo co-authored his chapter in this volume while an M.Sc. (Economics) student at the Université de Montréal and research assistant at the Center for Interuniversity Research and Analysis on Organization (CIRANO). He is now an economist at the Canada Mortgage and Housing Corporation.

Gregory Morris is a lecturer at the University of Exeter Business School. He worked for many decades in business and professional practice. Most recently he was head of the UK and EMEA tax practice of a large international law firm. His research interests are in the area of business, society and taxation.

Kudakwashe M.M. Muli is a lecturer at the African Tax Institute in the Faculty of Economic and Management Sciences at the University of Pretoria. She obtained her M.Com. (Tax), B.Com. (Hons) (Tax) and B.Compt. degrees from the University of Pretoria. Her research focus is mainly on tax compliance and administration.

Lynne Oats is a professor of taxation and accounting, University of Exeter Business School, Deputy Director of the Tax Administration Research Centre and Vice Chair of the UK Tax Research Network. Lynne is Assistant Editor (Accounting) of the *British Tax Review*, Managing Editor of the *Journal of Tax Administration* and editor of *Taxation: A Fieldwork Research Handbook*.

Andrew Packman is a senior tax partner with PwC in the United Kingdom. He is responsible for the work that PwC undertakes globally on Tax Transparency and Total Tax Contribution, engaging with clients and governments on how tax systems impact on business and on what companies contribute to the public finances. In this connection he leads the PwC team working with the World Bank Group on the Paying Taxes indicator as part of their *Doing Business* project.

Frank Høgholm Pedersen is a research fellow at the University of Southern Denmark. He previously worked as Head of the Tax Simplification Unit, Danish Ministry of Taxation. He has been a visiting researcher at New York University and Harvard Law School. Frank also works as an independent consultant for government organizations and consulting firms, specializing in new ways to improve assessment of compliance and psychological cost, and ways to use an understanding of issues facing taxpayers as the key to facilitating their tax compliance.

Alex Raskolnikov is Wilbur H. Friedman Professor of Tax Law at Columbia Law School. Prior to joining Columbia faculty he practised tax law at Davis Polk & Wardwell. Alex's research interests include tax policy, economic analysis of deterrence, social norms and relational contracts. He has testified in the US Congress at several hearings focused on taxation of financial instruments.

Jeremy Sherwood has been the head of the Office of Tax Simplification (OTS) secretariat since 2010. Prior to that he held a range of policy and operational roles in HM Treasury and HM Revenue & Customs. He joined the civil service as a tax inspector in 1990.

Joel Slemrod is the Paul W. McCracken Collegiate Professor of Business Economics and Public Policy at the Stephen M. Ross School of Business at the University of Michigan, and professor of economics in the Department of Economics. He also serves as Director of the Office of Tax Policy Research and consultant to many overseas governments and institutions. In 2012 Joel received from the National Tax Association its most prestigious award, the Daniel M. Holland Medal for distinguished lifetime contributions to the study and practice of public finance.

Sharon Smulders is an independent tax consultant and researcher and was the Head of Tax Technical Policy & Research at the South African Institute of Tax Professionals (SAIT) until July 2014 where she was primarily responsible for liaising with the South African Revenue Service (SARS), National Treasury, Parliament and international organizations on tax matters. Prior to joining SAIT, Sharon was an associate professor in taxation at the University of Pretoria and a tax manager at Deloitte.

Theuns Steyn is a chartered accountant (South Africa) and an associate professor in the Department of Taxation at the University of Pretoria. He obtained his PhD from the University of Pretoria. His research interests include the imposed tax burden and how taxpayers perceive their tax burden.

Binh Tran-Nam is a professor at the RMIT Asia Graduate Centre in Vietnam and associate professor in the School of Taxation and Business Law (incorporating Atax), UNSW Australia and an adjunct research fellow in the Taxation Law and Policy Research Group of the Monash Business School, Monash University. He has published widely in tax journals around the world and acted as a consultant to many projects in China and Vietnam. He is a founding editor of the *eJournal of Tax Research*.

David Ulph is a professor of economics at the University of St Andrews, and Director of the Scottish Institute for Research in Economics (SIRE). Previously he was Chief

Economist and Director of Analysis at HM Revenue and Customs. Prior to that, he was professor of economics at University College London.

François Vaillancourt is Emeritus Professor (economics) at the Université de Montréal and Fellow at the Center for Interuniversity Research and Analysis on Organization (CIRANO). He has published extensively and often been a national/international consultant on the topics of intergovernmental finance (Finance Canada; Finance Québec; Council of the Federation; OECD; UNDP; World Bank), compliance cost of taxation (Canadian Tax Foundation, Fraser Institute) and language policy (Office et Conseil de la langue française, Québec, New Zealand Treasury).

Michael Walpole is a professor and the Deputy Head of School in the School of Taxation and Business Law (incorporating Atax), UNSW Australia and an adjunct research fellow in the Taxation Law and Policy Research Group of the Monash Business School, Monash University. He is currently editor of *Australian Tax Forum*. Michael is an active contributor to the profession via involvement in the Tax Institute Education Committee, Technical Committee, Tax Practitioners' Board meetings; and the New South Wales Law Society Specialist Accreditation Committee.

John Whiting OBE is the (part-time) tax director of the Office of Tax Simplification (OTS), a role he has held since the OTS's formation in 2010; he is also a non-executive director of HM Revenue & Customs. John was a tax partner with PricewaterhouseCoopers for twenty-five years and has also been Tax Policy Director of the Chartered Institute of Taxation.

Fatih Yılmaz is an assistant professor of economics in the School of Business at ADA University in Baku, Azerbaijan and has worked as a consultant for the World Bank Group providing econometric analysis on different tax policy issues in developing countries.

Summary of Contents

Table of Contents

CHAPTER 14
Some Cautions Regarding Tax Simplification
J. Clifton Fleming Jr   227

CHAPTER 15
The Office of Tax Simplification and Its Complexity Index
John Whiting, Jeremy Sherwood & Gareth Jones   235

Preface and Acknowledgements

The chapters in this volume derive from a three year, multi-university research project entitled 'Assessing and Addressing Tax System Complexity', funded by the Australian Research Council (ARC) together with the Institute of Chartered Accountants in Australia (ICAA) under the ARC's Linkage Grant scheme. The project investigated the causes and costs of complexity in tax law with the aim of identifying paths forward to simplification and consequent reduction of tax compliance and administration costs.

The volume derives from the last stage of the research project, a critical research forum to explore the key issues of tax simplification that brought together a number of the world's leading international academics in the fields of tax administration, tax complexity and tax simplification. Contributors and commentators included Professors Joel Slemrod (Michigan), Judith Freedman CBE (Oxford), Alex Raskolnikov (Columbia), François Vaillancourt (Montréal), Sharon Smulders (Pretoria), Kristin Hickman (Minnesota), John Hasseldine (New Hampshire), Michael Walpole and Binh Tran-Nam (UNSW Australia), Lynne Oats and Ann Hansford (Exeter), Pasquale Pistone (IBFD and WU, Vienna), Julian Alworth and Giampaolo Arachi (Bocconi), Cliff Fleming (Brigham Young), David Ulph (St Andrews) and Yang Bin (Xiamen), as well as emerging scholars from Europe, Australia, Asia and South Africa.

Members of the judiciary, tax policy-makers, tax administrators and tax professionals contributing to the research program included an Australian Federal Court Judge (Hon. Justice Tony Pagone, also Professorial Fellow at the University of Melbourne); eminent UK tax counsel Philip Baker OBE QC (also Senior Visiting Fellow, University of London); the former head of the Danish Office of Tax Simplification (Frank Pedersen); the Director of the UK Office of Tax Simplification (John Whiting OBE, who is also a Non-Executive Director of HM Revenue and Customs); a senior representative from the World Bank (Jacqueline Coolidge); the former Australian Commissioner of Taxation (Michael D'Ascenzo AO, who is also an Adjunct Professor at UNSW Australia and Professorial Fellow at the University of Melbourne); and partners/former partners from major accounting/tax firms, including Andrew Packman and Neville Howlett from PwC, Patricia Billingham from Ernst & Young, and Gordon Cooper AM (also an Adjunct Professor at UNSW Australia) from tax practice.

We would like to thank both the ARC and ICAA for their invaluable support during the life of the research project. Additional financial support for the research program was provided by PwC and the Tax Administration Research Centre at Exeter University as well as Monash Business School at Monash University and the Business School at UNSW Australia. The support of Kluwer Law International and in particular, Lijntje Zandee, our Editor at Wolters Kluwer Law and Business, was crucial in making the publication process so straightforward.

We hope that the contents of this volume will provide an enduring legacy which will be of assistance to other tax scholars, policy-makers, legislators and administrators.

Chris Evans, Richard Krever & Peter Mellor
June 2015

List of Figures

List of Tables

CHAPTER 1
Why'd You Have to Go and Make Things So Complicated?*

Joel Slemrod

§1.01   INTRODUCTION

Simplicity is one of the classic triad of tax system *desiderata*, along with efficiency and equity. Although complexity of tax systems is commonly proclaimed and decried, comprehensive, successful simplification initiatives are rare. This paradox has attracted attention from scholars of different stripes, the latest initiative being the chapters presented in this volume. In this opening chapter I collect some thoughts about how to measure complexity and why it persists but, alas, have little to say about how to address it.

§1.02   MEASURING COMPLEXITY

For many years I have argued that the most useful summary measure of the cost of tax complexity, and of complexity itself, is the total resource cost of collecting the revenue.[1] The cost of collection is the sum of the tax collection agency's budget, plus the value of the time and money spent by the taxpayers, plus any costs incurred by third parties to the collection process, such as employers that withhold tax liability and submit information reports on behalf of their employees. It is a useful measure because

---

* From the song of the same name by Avril Lavigne, 2002. This chapter draws on ideas discussed in Joel Slemrod, 'Which is the Simplest Tax System of Them All?', in Henry J. Aaron & William G. Gale (eds), *Economic Effects of Fundamental Tax Reform* 355 (Brookings Institution, 1996); and Joel Slemrod & Christian Gillitzer, *Tax Systems* (MIT Press, 2014).
1. See, for example, Joel Slemrod, 'Which is the Simplest Tax System of Them All?', in Henry J. Aaron & William G. Gale (eds), *Economic Effects of Fundamental Tax Reform* 355 (Brookings Institution, 1996).

it naturally weights aspects of tax systems by their consequences so that, for example, lines on tax forms or pages in the tax code that affect few taxpayers in a trivial way are automatically ignored. Having a sufficient statistic for complexity sidesteps the fact that complexity is a multi-dimensional concept, and knowing about its anatomy can point to where policy changes aimed at reducing complexity should be targeted. Indeed, Ulph argues that 'the primary purpose of measuring tax complexity is to guide decisions as to where to direct efforts to reduce complexity'.[2] Ulph goes on to argue that it is important to distinguish costs of complexity from measures of complexity per se; I agree, but do not see why the latter is of interest conditional on a comprehensive measure of cost – why does a measured aspect of complexity matter if it has no cost? – unless it sheds light on social costs not well measured by collection costs.

Note that this measure does not distinguish between involuntary costs, which must be expended in order to comply with the law, and discretionary costs, which are incurred in an effort to reduce tax liability, whether through legal or illegal means. For many high-income individuals and businesses, the discretionary costs can be a substantial portion of total costs, due to the incentives created by the tax system to engage in particular transactions which would not otherwise make sense, and some alternative tax systems would drastically reduce the cost related to this. On the tax collection agency's side, the administrative cost does not distinguish between the cost of running the tax collection process and the cost of enforcing it equitably. Although these distinctions seem important to make in any analytical treatment of simplification, all are resource costs of operating the tax system and should be considered in an assessment of how simply it operates.

The measure refers to the social, rather than the private, cost of collection. Because monetary costs of compliance are deductible for businesses and many individuals, the private cost is in these cases less than the social cost. This is also true because employers that withhold taxes for employees need not remit the tax to the Internal Revenue Service immediately, thus earning interest in the interim period; that is a private gain, but not a social one because the present value of tax collections falls commensurately with the private saving.

In some situations a collection-cost-based measure of complexity provides results that may conflict with intuition. As an example, consider that the record-keeping and calculation requirements of a particular credit are loosened so that only half as many resources as before are required to qualify for the deduction. Suppose that, as a result, there is a quadrupling of the number of households who apply for and receive the credit, and that any changes needed to make up the lost revenue have no collection-cost implications. According to the cost-based measure, the tax system has become more complicated. I believe that, all things considered, this is an accurate character-ization of the change. The credit procedure itself has become simpler to understand, but the system as a whole is more complex. Whether this increased complexity is worthwhile depends on whether the apparently beneficial equity impact of inducing households which 'deserve' the credit to take it, plus any accompanying efficiency

---

2. See David Ulph, *Measuring Tax Complexity*, this volume, §4.04[B].

effects, are judged to be of overriding import. This is another example of why it is critical that the complexity of a tax change, especially as measured by the change in the cost of collection, be considered in conjunction with other implications of the policy. It also highlights why, although simplicity is generally placed beside efficiency and equity as tax system *desiderata*, it is not actually a separate criterion. Simplicity matters only to the extent that it enhances efficiency (by, for example, reducing collection costs) or equity (by, for example, ensuring that the incidence of a tax system is what is intended).

The collection-cost measure of complexity confronts researchers with a dilemma. Because it is difficult to measure, comparable cross-country data, or even time-series data, do not exist, preventing empirical analysis of its causes and effects. More readily available data, such as the number of lines on tax forms or the number of pages in the tax code, are much more easily compiled and therefore analysed, but they are highly imperfect indicators of impact-weighted complexity. They might be correlated with impact-weighted complexity, although this is impossible to verify. Indeed, Lugo and Vaillancourt find no correlation between a form-based measure of tax complexity and total compliance costs.[3] We can certainly study the effect of, say, the political system on the number of lines on tax forms, but we cannot infer anything about impact-weighted complexity as embodied in collection costs.

§1.03   WHY SO COMPLEX?

Some of the complexity of the current tax system stems from the inherent structural difficulties of any tax system based on a comprehensive (Haig-Simons) measure of income. Although, in practice, income tax systems compromise that objective in many ways, there inevitably remain difficult issues of income measurement, especially with respect to capital income.[4] Part of the cause is the fundamental incoherence of a realization-based income tax system in a world where financial innovations, including derivative securities, can exploit the incoherence to create tax arbitrage gains (e.g., buying and selling equivalent but differentially taxed streams of income). Attempts by the government to patch these tax arbitrage gaps – for example, by attempting to distinguish form from economic substance – may create even more complexity.

Using the income tax system to achieve non-revenue, non-progressivity objectives also complicates the tax system. The presence of many extraneous elements that are implicit subsidies for programmes that could never survive on their own, or are simply sops to politically powerful groups, make an income tax system more complicated, and costly, to administer. Subsidizing charitable giving by allowing a deduction requires documentation and occasional verification of donations, subsidizing research requires the same for research expenses, and so on. Fine-tuning tax liability to improve horizontal equity also engenders tax complexity, giving rise to a classic trade-off between one type of equity and the resource cost of achieving it.

---

3. See Marco Lugo & François Vaillancourt, *Measuring Tax Complexity: Analytical Framework and Evidence for Individual Income Tax Preferences for Canada*, this volume, §9.05.
4. See David Bradford, *Untangling the Income Tax* (Harvard University Press, 1986).

The desire for vertical equity, or progressivity, is another reason for complexity. After all, a poll tax, for which the tax liability is the same for all persons, is relatively simple because the base is clearly and easily defined, say being a resident over the age of 21, the levy itself is clearly and easily defined, and neither the rate nor base is easily manipulable by taxpayer actions. In principle, anyway. But a poll tax fails to assign the burden of taxes across individuals in what most people would see as an equitable manner. Moreover, as the British attempt to replace local property taxes with a poll-tax-like 'community charge' in 1989 showed, its enforcement is not trivial. Indeed, the widespread non-compliance with the British poll tax raises a fundamental point: the simplicity of a tax system can only be assessed with respect to a stated degree of enforcement. What if an announced, but loosely and therefore inexpensively enforced poll tax, was remitted by the dutiful 70% of the population, but that to achieve 99% compliance would require an expensive and highly intrusive enforcement bureaucracy? Does that make the poll tax cheap and unintrusive, or expensive and intrusive, to collect?

Musgrave has stressed that, if a society were willing to settle for having the tax burden be approximately *proportional* to income or consumption, then taxes could be impersonal (e.g., a value-added or retail sales tax), and no personal information, including annual income or consumption, need be collected or verified.[5] This would greatly simplify the tax system, at the cost of constraining the progressivity of the tax burden.

Politicians have an incentive, and often the ability, to take advantage of taxpayers' behavioural quirks and cognitive limitations. McCaffery,[6] and Krishna and Slemrod,[7] argue that the US income tax has many features that take advantage of taxpayers' cognitive biases to reduce the perceived tax burden, and it does so by applying well-known features of what in marketing science is known as 'price presentation', such as the use of discounts (as in deductions from a broad measure of income) and of small frequent disbursements (as in employer withholding). The laboratory experiments of McCaffery and Baron provide some support that such a strategy can be successful, as they demonstrate that people tend to underestimate the total tax burden when it is spread among multiple taxes.[8] An incumbent government may try to, and may be able to, take advantage of framing difficulties to benefit themselves by reducing the perceived burden of what they do. Note that, in the process, the more sophisticated of taxpayers may actually benefit.

Hettich and Winer argue that complex tax structures emerge as a by-product of the struggle for political office, in the course of which political parties are forced to propose and implement policies that discriminate or distinguish as carefully as possible

5. See Richard A. Musgrave, 'Progressive Taxation, Equity, and Tax Design', in Joel Slemrod (ed.), *Tax Progressivity and Income Inequality* 341 (Cambridge University Press, 1994).
6. Edward J. McCaffery, *Cognitive Theory and Tax*, 41(7) UCLA L. Rev. 1861 (1994).
7. Aradhna Krishna & Joel Slemrod, *Behavioral Public Finance: Tax Design as Price Presentation*, 10(2) Int'l Tax & Pub. Fin. 189 (2003).
8. Edward J. McCaffery & Jonathan Baron, *The Humpty Dumpty Blues: Disaggregation Bias in the Evaluation of Tax Systems*, 91(2) Org. Behav. & Hum. Dec. 230 (2003).

among heterogeneous voters.[9] This story suggests an entirely different perspective on tax collection costs, as they limit the ability of governments to discriminate fully among taxpayers.

The incentives for government to obfuscate became, in 2014, an incendiary political issue in the US when Massachusetts Institute of Technology Professor Jonathan Gruber, who was a major 'player' in the design of the Affordable Care Act, known familiarly as ObamaCare,[10] was revealed to have suggested that many lawmakers and voters did not know what was in the law or how its financing worked, and that this helped it win approval. 'Lack of transparency is a huge political advantage', Gruber stated, '[a]nd basically, call it the stupidity of the American voter or whatever, but basically that was really, really critical for the thing to pass'.[11] He suggested that voters would have rejected ObamaCare if the penalties for going without health insurance were interpreted as taxes, either by budget analysts or the public. His views were quickly disavowed by the Obama administration, but it is certain that Republican Party candidates will revive the issue in the 2016 presidential election in which ObamaCare is likely to figure prominently.

Of course, the people in government are also 'just' people and so may themselves be subject to cognitive limitations. One important and understudied issue is how to model the behaviour of policy-makers subject to cognitive limitations: are they subject to the same kind of heuristic biases as taxpayers and voters?

Why some taxes levied in some jurisdictions become complex, while others do not, has not been widely studied, hampered by the absence of reliable, comparable measures of complexity across jurisdictions. One exception is my 2005 study,[12] in which I use the variation in US state income tax systems, and their differential change over time, to examine what engenders tax complexity, measured by the number of lines in the income tax forms and the number of pages in the instruction booklets, and some intriguing patterns are revealed. The analysis shows that in 2000, states with more professional legislatures, as measured by the salaries paid, tended to have more complex tax systems, as did states with a less active voting population. The former relationship suggests that complexity – specifically form-line and instruction-book-page complexity – is one of the things that professional legislatures *do*, although it may also be that, in the case of states in which voters want more activist policy, those voters will also want professional legislatures and choose more complex tax systems. The latter relationship suggests that a more politically involved citizenry acts as a deterrent to this aspect of tax complexity.

9. Walter Hettich & Stanley L. Winer, *Democratic Choice and Taxation: A Theoretical and Empirical Analysis* (Cambridge University Press, 1999).
10. Patient Protection and Affordable Care Act 2010, 124 Stat. 119-1024; Health Care and Education Reconciliation Act 2010, 124 Stat. 1029-1083.
11. Jonathan Gruber, comments in the plenary conference session 'The Role of Economics in Staging the ACA and How Economics Can Inform Inevitable Mid-Course Corrections', 24th Annual Health Economics Conference, University of Pennsylvania Leonard Davis Institute of Health Economics, Philadelphia, 17–18 October 2013; webcast available at: http://ldi.upenn.edu/ahec2013/agenda.
12. Joel Slemrod, *The Etiology of Tax Complexity: Evidence from U.S. State Income Tax Systems*, 33(3) Pub. Fin. Rev. 279 (2005).

§1.04   CONSEQUENCES OF COMPLEXITY

Although simplicity is put alongside equity and efficiency in the usual list of tax system criteria, it is not a parallel concept. Simplicity is good because it saves wasteful costs and thereby makes people better off and because it facilitates the intended distribution of tax liability.

The collection cost is the most obvious manifestation of its resource cost, but there are other potential costs. Tax complexity may affect individuals' perceptions of their choice set and the (relative) prices among alternative choices, and therefore their decisions. There is a long strand of research about taxpayer misperceptions of their average and marginal income tax rate. Sheffrin reviews studies of American, British, and Canadian taxpayers that find that taxpayers generally underestimate both their total tax liability and marginal tax rates.[13] What is not clear is the connection between knowledge of one's marginal tax rate and the complexity of the tax system. One hypothesis is offered by Liebman and Zeckhauser,[14] who suggest that because of cognitive limitations taxpayers presume that their marginal tax rate is the easier-to-calculate average tax rate. One striking conclusion is that such a perception eliminates some of the deadweight loss from high marginal taxes. Thus, if tax complexity fools people into acting as if the marginal disincentive of taxation is lower than it really is, economic efficiency might actually improve. Whether that implies that complexity should be actively encouraged takes me beyond the scope of this chapter into the nascent field of behavioural welfare economics.

That taxpayers have cognitive limitations has many implications for tax analysis. One is that the distribution of the tax burden may depend on, in addition to the intended characteristics, cognitive ability. Another is that taxpayers who are not so good at addressing tax matters may avoid certain employment statuses, such as self-employment, that require or reward this kind of 'savvy', and punish its absence.

The burden of compliance costs also becomes part of the cost of certain activities, and may affect the allocation of resources, as emphasized in Tran-Nam;[15] the efficiency costs of this are not captured in a measure of collection costs. Thus, while relative to being an employee, the relative facility of tax evasion may make self-employment more attractive to those willing to evade, the higher relative burden of tax compliance makes it relatively less attractive to the dutiful.[16]

---

13. Steven M. Sheffrin, 'Perceptions of Fairness in the Crucible of Tax Policy', in Slemrod (ed.), above n. 5, at 309.
14. Jeffrey B. Liebman & Richard J. Zeckhauser. 'Schmeduling', Harvard University Working Paper (October 2004), available at http://www.hks.harvard.edu/jeffreyliebman/schmeduling.pdf.
15. Binh Tran-Nam, *An Integrated Approach to the Economic Measurement of the Costs of Tax Complexity*, this volume, §5.04.
16. For discussion of this issue, see Joel Slemrod, 'Small Business and the Tax System', in Henry J. Aaron & Joel Slemrod (eds), *The Crisis in Tax Administration* 69 (Brookings Institution Press, 2004).

§1.05   WHY IS IT SO HARD TO SIMPLIFY?

There are substantially less complex, and therefore less costly, ways to raise money than most current tax systems. Whether one should adopt one of these alternatives depends on what the extra complexity is now 'buying' us. Some of the complexity is buying us the capacity to fine-tune tax liability – to 'personalize' it – according to family characteristics, to deliver progressivity and justifiable incentives for activities that provide positive externalities. But some of the complexity is buying us nothing of social value, and is caused by misguided attempts to 'encourage' particular activities, attempts that end up distorting the economy in addition to causing complexity.

One political barrier to tax simplification is that there is no such thing as a pure tax simplification. Any change in the tax law in the apparent direction of simplification will also have some equity and efficiency implications. Consider doubling the standard deduction. Because this change would reduce the number of households that itemize deductions and its attendant record-keeping requirements, it may be advocated as a simplifying measure. Of course it would also reduce the tax liability of those households for whom the value of their potentially itemized deductions lies between the previous and new zero-bracket amount. In order to maintain the same level of tax revenue, tax rate increases must be incurred by other households. In addition, the net after-tax price of those activities which give rise to itemizable deductions would be increased for those who no longer itemize, and decrease for those who continue to itemize but now face a higher marginal tax rate. These additional implications are present even in a tax system change more narrowly addressed to simplification, such as rendering the instructions about how to compute a particular credit more easily understandable, while leaving the law itself unchanged. Although this reform sounds like the kind of change that is likely to command broad support on grounds of simplification, it nevertheless has a re-distributional element. In particular, those households who did not receive the credit, because formerly the instructions were too complicated, now do get it. With a given revenue requirement, tax revenue must be raised through some other change in the system. Some households are clearly better off, but, in addition, other households are likely to end up worse off.

This aspect of simplification is amplified by the fact that, while just about everyone supports simplification in principle, when policy 'push comes to shove', the simplification benefits are generally dwarfed by the direct tax liability implications of particular changes. Attempts to institutionalize attention to complexity into the tax policy process, by for example requiring complexity analyses to accompany policy proposals, have not yielded any apparent success.

§1.06   CONCLUSION

Tax complexity can be quite costly and causes unintended and probably undesirable impacts on the distribution of the tax burden. Reducing it substantially is politically difficult because the private simplification benefits are often dwarfed by the direct tax liability implications of particular simplifying changes. As social scientists we can contribute to the formulation of good policy by calculating, as best as we can, the overall costs of complexity. Even more important, we can help by quantifying the benefits and costs of concrete simplifying tax reform initiatives and explaining the inevitable trade-offs that any policy change entails.

CHAPTER 2

A Contemporary Approach to Tax Complexity: Polycentrism in an Increasingly International Tax Environment

Frank H. Pedersen

§2.01 INTRODUCTION

Our society is experiencing an unprecedented level of complexity, but nevertheless succeeds in muddling through.[1] For example, today tax experts cannot achieve full comprehension of the entire tax system[2] in which they work; however, as a group, they still manage to reach useful, functional solutions. This chapter attempts to advance the field of tax complexity by presenting a theoretical frame of reference for contemporary tax complexity which can better encapsulate tax systems' current condition, and which may provide a stronger basis from which scholars and policy-makers can address the challenges of present-day tax complexity.

The way in which complexity appears today, as well as how it is managed by society in general, have changed radically compared with, for example, the 1970s or, to an even greater extent, the 1930s. For instance, nowadays it is more common for

---

1. Lars Qvortrup, *The Hypercomplex Society*, at, e.g., 3, 34 (Peter Lang, 2003) [hereinafter, *The Hypercomplex Society*]. Regarding complexity growth in society in general, see, e.g., Eric Beinhocker, *The Origin of Wealth: Evolution, Complexity, and the Radical Remaking of Economics* (Harvard Business School Press, 2007). Regarding the difficulties in general in measuring complexity, see, e.g., Melanie Mitchell, *Complexity: A Guided Tour* (Oxford University Press, 2009).
2. This chapter uses the term 'tax system' in a broad and generic sense (as it pertains to countries with comprehensive and mature tax systems) which includes the confluence of tax statutes, regulations, and the like along with the authorized administrative organs, without reference to any particular country or limitation to any country's system.

agents[3] managing a high-level task to depend on advice and assistance from other professionals; this has become common for tax professionals as well. Another example is how information and communication technology (ICT) so clearly has changed how agents – including taxpayers and tax professionals and officials – manage complexity, leaving much of the 'handling' to the software. The enhanced capabilities of ICT and developments in modes of cooperation are examples of changes in what is referred to as the 'coupling capacity'[4] of agents. Hence, agents' ability to cope with complexity is much improved from what it was forty or eighty years ago. Further, if the level of tax complexity is much higher today, but agents' 'coupling capacity' has developed (or can develop) in tandem with the increasing complexity, does this imply that a related development could, or has already begun to, occur in our mindset and our conception of what to aim for? In other words, is it possible that within the academic field of tax complexity, a new approach to managing complexity, different from previous understandings, is emerging?

The sociologist Lars Qvortrup's monograph entitled *The Hypercomplex Society* deals with the topic of how the growing level of complexity represents the basic challenge of our current society.[5] The essence of his thesis is that our ability to manage complexity increases when we have a correspondingly up-to-date understanding and acceptance of the basic structures of contemporary society, including how complexity arises. Otherwise, 'we become mistrustful, and complain that things are less and less like the expectations we have for them – instead of trying to comprehend where we are heading'.[6] This chapter's proposed interpretation of contemporary tax complexity is based on Qvortrup's concept of *hypercomplexity* as the phenomenon which most fundamentally characterizes our society.[7]

The tax literature has, from its early years to the present, offered warnings and discussions about the alarming increase in tax complexity.[8] For example, in 1936 William H. Crow and U.S. Greene noted 'the increasing complexity and importance of tax laws',[9] and in 1950 Henry Simons presaged, more colourfully, '[i]f [present legislation] is not simplified, half of the population may have to become tax lawyers and tax accountants'.[10] In 1979, Sidney Roberts issued the apocalyptic warning that

---

3. This chapter uses the term 'agents' broadly to include taxpayers, privately as well as publicly employed tax professionals, and any other individuals or entities working with taxation.
4. See also §2.02 below.
5. Qvortrup, *The Hypercomplex Society*, above n. 1. The Danish version, which is more comprehensive, was first published in 1998 as *Det Hyperkomplekse Samfund: 14 fortællinger om informationssamfundet*. [hereinafter *Det Hyperkomplekse Samfund*] (2nd ed., Gyldendal, 2000).
6. Qvortrup, *Det Hyperkomplekse Samfund*, above n. 5, at 11 (this author's translation).
7. Qvortrup's thesis is inspired by the German sociologist Niklas Luhmann and his work in systems theory, see Qvortrup, *The Hypercomplex Society*, above n. 1, at viii. However, it is beyond the scope of this chapter to review systems theory and its characteristic terminology. A useful general introduction to systems theory and its terminology is provided in Hans-Georg Moeller, *Luhmann Explained: From Souls to Systems* (Carus Publishing Company, 2006).
8. The first report on tax simplification in the United States was issued in 1927 by the Joint Committee on Internal Revenue Taxation. See generally Edward J. McCaffery, *The Holy Grail of Tax Simplification*, [1990] 5 Wis. L. Rev. 1267, 1269.
9. William H. Crow & U.S. Greene, *Planning for Tax Economy* (Waldrep-Tilson,1936).
10. Henry C. Simons, *Federal Tax Reform*, 28 (University of Chicago Press, 1950).

'we cannot reach agreement on a solution unless we agree, with only a marginal difference in intensity, on the proposition that the present course of development of the tax law, if not reversed, will result in a breakdown of the self-assessment system'.[11] A contemporary example can be found in Lawrence Zelenak's essay *Complex Tax Legislation in the Turbo Tax Era*: '[W]hat is needed is not structural reform, but a basic change in attitudes – in hearts and minds – among the members of Congress. This may be too much to hope for – but if it is, then there is no hope'.[12]

Throughout the decades, then, there has been no lack of pessimism in the tax literature regarding complexity. And however critically one might view the tax system's current stage of development, it would be difficult to maintain that the outcome has been as dire as predicted. Drawing on the concept of hypercomplexity, this chapter offers an explanation as to why one might misjudge where the tax system, like the rest of society, is heading, and become overly sceptical – and run the risk of overlooking possible options for improvement of the status quo.

This chapter examines different meanings of 'complexity'.[13] Moreover, it discusses how the fact of complexity growth (an increasing number of elements in the observed system, such as a tax system, or a rise in the extent of possible actions available to an agent)[14] cannot by itself support a conclusion that the management of tax-related tasks has become more difficult for agents. A previous work by this author has examined the reason therefor: how well a task is managed is a concrete and context-dependent empirical phenomenon, and thus is distinguishable from a description of the level of complexity in, for instance, a tax statute.[15] For this reason, increasing levels of complexity do not inevitably result in more resource expenditure, frustration, and other undesirable effects; rather, the ways in which various agents actually carry out their tax-related tasks – for instance, the use by taxpayers of tax-preparation software – largely influences the success of their outcomes. However, the growth of complexity does lessen the possibility that anyone can actually be in control of the system or fully comprehend it; in addition, complexity growth redefines accepted definitions and norms regarding rationality.[16] Finally, with national sovereignty in a process of de facto erosion[17] it is becoming less clear to whom expectations

---

11. Sidney I. Roberts, *The Viewpoint of the Tax Adviser: An Overview of Simplification*, The Tax Adviser 32, 33 (January 1979).
12. Lawrence Zelenak, *Complex Tax Legislation in the TurboTax Era*, 1(1) Colum. J. Tax L. 91, 93 (2010).
13. See §2.02 and §2.03[A] below.
14. See §2.03[A] below.
15. Frank H. Pedersen, *Advancing the Study of Tax Complexity with the Usability Model*, 12(2) Hous. Bus. & Tax L.J. 282 (2012) [hereinafter *The Usability Model*]. For the distinction noted, see *The Usability* Model, at 314. See also §2.02 below.
16. See §2.03[C] below.
17. See generally Angus Cameron, *Turning Point? The Volatile Geographies of Taxation*, 38(2) Antipode 236, 244 (2006) ('What might have seemed to be a normal and self-defining fiscal space ... in the early 19th century... is so compromised by changes in the economic praxis barely a century later as to need shoring up through a proliferation of domestic and international legal structures'); John Braithwaite & Peter Drahos, *Global Business Regulation*, Pt. I (Cambridge University Press, 2000) (addressing 'how the regulation of business has shifted from national to global institutions').

of being in control can be directed,[18] and consequently to whom demands for simplification in the traditional sense can be made.

According to the concept of hypercomplexity, industrial society's overarching presumption – that control can be achieved by making a supreme effort – is retreating. Industrial society's self-understanding was embedded in anthropocentrism, with its belief in human rationality and control. During the twentieth century, however, a new perspective – that of polycentrism – has emerged.[19] A polycentric approach implies a different understanding and different goals. It finds attempts to attain control merely through rules and regulations illusory, and instead places its confidence in achieving solutions through modes of decision-making that can adjust more rapidly to the concrete demands of the surrounding society.[20]

The transition period between these two mindsets, the anthropocentric and the polycentric, is difficult when a new structure has emerged in society to accommodate the contemporary level of complexity, but the prevailing mindset and accompanying expectations continue to be marked by ideals befitting the former time.[21] Qvortrup calls such a transition period 'the complexity of complexity', a sign of which is a high level of frustration that things are not the same as they were in the past.[22] This chapter suggests that some of the overly sceptical predictions made through the decades regarding the tax system's condition due to complexity might be explained by our being in the midst of such a prolonged transition period. Furthermore, it suggests that awareness and acceptance of changes in society's level of complexity are necessary to allow freedom to organize the tax system differently, where such alteration would be beneficial.

In §2.02, I explain that complexity growth does not necessarily have to result in more resource expenditure, frustration, or other undesirable effects. In §2.03, I present Qvortrup's concept of hypercomplexity and link it to the tax system. In §2.04, I illustrate how the scholarly tax literature may be in the midst of a period of transition between anthropocentric and polycentric mindsets. Section §2.04 also presents the example of the advance tax ruling as a legal instrument which provides an alternative to traditional rules and regulations as a means of providing certainty. The chapter ends with a brief conclusion (§2.05).

---

18. With intensified international engagement, tax law and administration are becoming less monopolistic and more polycentric: see generally OECD, *Explanatory Statement*, OECD/G20 Base Erosion and Profit Shifting Project (2014), www.oecd.org/tax/beps-2014-deliverables-explanatory-statement.pdf; OECD, Global Forum on Transparency and Exchange of Information for Tax Purposes, *Tax Transparency, 2014, Report on Progress*. See also e.g., Georg Kofler & Pasquale Pistone, 'General Report', in Georg Kofler, Miquel Poiares Maduro & Pasquale Pistone (eds), *Human Rights and Taxation in Europe and the World* 3, 3 (IBFD Publications, 2011); Daniël S. Smit, 'General Report', in Michael Lang, Pasquale Pistone, Josef Schuch, Claus Staringer & Alfred Storck (eds), *Tax Rules in Non-Tax Agreements* 1 (IBFD Publications, 2012); Hans Gribnau, *Soft Law and Taxation: EU and International Aspects*, 2(2) Legisprudence 67 (2007).
19. See §2.03[C] below.
20. See §2.04[B] below.
21. See §2.04[C] below.
22. See §2.04[C] below.

§2.02 NOTIONS OF TAX COMPLEXITY

This section outlines various conceptions of tax complexity. Moreover, it explains the principle that how well a task is managed is a concrete and context-dependent empirical phenomenon, independent of and distinguishable from the level of complexity in, for example, a tax statute or some other part of a tax system.[23] This distinction is central because it underlies the proposition that complexity growth in a tax system can take place without any necessary decline in how well tax-related tasks are managed. Consequently, complexity growth does not inevitably have implications for society's welfare.[24]

Although the tax literature is rich with warnings regarding tax complexity,[25] broad references to 'tax complexity' without further clarification do not in themselves reveal much about what is considered to be the problem in question.[26] Various underlying phenomena which have been referred to in the tax literature as tax complexity can be characterized as: (1) linguistic difficulty ('plain English' discussions);[27] (2) mere compliance costs;[28] and (3) specific characteristics of tax statutes, e.g., the degree of differentiation in a statute's rules.[29] Particularly in the US literature, references to 'compliance complexity', 'transactional complexity', and 'rule complexity' are common, although which concrete phenomena these terms might include is often unclear.[30]

How well a tax-related task is managed can be assessed only on the basis of the empirical occurrences that derive from it: cost, time consumption, uncertainty, frustration, and the like. The resulting resource expenditure, level of psychological well-being, and extent of actual accomplishment in managing the task are the empirical occurrences that have welfare implications.[31] Important to the argument in this chapter

---

23. As mentioned in §2.01, this argument was set forth in my previous article, *The Usability Model*, above n. 15. For the distinction noted, see *The Usability Model*, at 314.
24. See Pedersen, *The Usability Model*, above n. 15, at 284 and 314–316 (explaining that empirical occurrences, such as resource-spending derived from managing a tax-related task, imply welfare propositions, whereas descriptions of levels of complexity in a legal authority, such as a tax statute, involve a static account of the attributes of the object in question).
25. See §2.01.
26. Pedersen, *The Usability Model*, above n. 15, at 301–308.
27. Pedersen, *The Usability Model*, above n. 15, at 303.
28. Pedersen, *The Usability Model*, above n. 15, at 295–297 and 302.
29. See Pedersen, *The Usability Model*, above n. 15, at 302. Definitions of complexity encompassing degrees of differentiation and/or numbers of elements in the observed object, such as a statute, are common general definitions. See §2.03[A] below.
30. See Pedersen, *The Usability Model*, above n. 15, at 304–306. Another notion of tax complexity in the literature encompasses situations in which the underlying empirical occurrences that derive from a tax-related task, such as resource expenditures (of time and money) and the degree of accomplishment of the task, are appraised as unsatisfactory. *The Usability Model*, at 303–304 and 352–353.
31. In *The Usability Model*, I recommend that when the interest lies in what taxpayers and tax professionals encounter empirically when managing compliance-related tasks, and the focus concerns empirical occurrences beyond mere resource-spending, the terminology 'low or high usability level' is preferable as providing more clarity than 'complexity' and its cognates: *The Usability Model*, at 350. For an outline of the above-mentioned notions of tax complexity and the underlying phenomena which are their real focus, see *The Usability Model*, at 326, fig. 4.

is that all management of a task occurs within a context, and this context very much influences the resulting empirical occurrences. Context is comprised of the physical and social environment in which an agent is actually performing the activities[32] required to complete the task at hand. Elements of this environment include how well the agent cooperates with other people and the equipment to which the agent has access, such as information and communication technology.[33] These elements are part of what this chapter refers to as the agent's 'coupling capacity'. Other elements of coupling capacity, which are also part of the context influencing how well a task is managed, include the agent's skills and other abilities.[34]

Inquiries as to what occurs for taxpayers and tax professionals in their management of tasks thus always concern empirical occurrences,[35] which must be assessed based on their real-world settings. By contrast, a description of a part of the tax system, such as its level of complexity as ascertained by the degree of differentiation in a tax statute, cannot be used to make inferences regarding expected empirical occurrences and outcomes,[36] as those occurrences are not intrinsic to the degree of complexity in the tax statute[37] but are heavily influenced by specific settings.[38] Depending on specific agents' coupling capacities, complexity growth in the tax system therefore need not result in more resource expenditure, frustration, or other undesirable effects.

§2.03   THE CONCEPT OF HYPERCOMPLEXITY

This section introduces Qvortrup's concept of hypercomplexity and links the comprehension of tax complexity to the society's development in accordance with this concept. Qvortrup intends his hypercomplexity concept to be an 'exploratory guide into the complexities of our current society',[39] such that hypercomplexity may help to

---

32. The management of a task, such as a taxpayer's preparation of a tax return for filing, requires a number of activities, such as information retrieval and computation. See *The Usability Model*, at 300–301. Tax professionals such as those working for the tax authority have other tasks, which involve other kinds of activities.
33. Pedersen, *The Usability Model*, above n. 15, at 312–313.
34. Pedersen, *The Usability Model*, above n. 15, at 310–311.
35. Pedersen, *The Usability Model*, above n. 15, at 354 (explaining that this also holds for references to 'tax complexity' which pertain to what occurs for taxpayers).
36. Pedersen, *The Usability Model*, above n. 15, at 315 (explaining that assessment of empirical occurrences can be characterized as *process-oriented* because it is taxpayers' multiplicity of encounters from carrying out activities for tax-related tasks that is being assessed. By contrast, a *product-oriented* description of a legal authority, such as a tax statute, is a static account of the attributes of that statute).
37. Pedersen, *The Usability Model*, above n. 15, at 314.
38. Assessment of empirical occurrences by estimating the level of complexity in a tax statute is an assessment through a proxy. The well-known example of referring to the size of the tax code as a symbol for complexity – whether its size is assessed by number of sections, word count, or dimensions of the complete set of volumes – is also an application of a proxy, if the reference is meant to imply welfare implications; and it requires an explanation as to why the size of the code is appropriate for illuminating the empirical occurrences that derive from how taxpayers and tax professionals carry out tax-related tasks. See *The Usability Model*, at 318.
39. Qvortrup, *The Hypercomplex Society*, above n. 1, at 10.

explain a growing number of phenomena in contemporary[40] as well as emerging society.[41] The basic thesis of his book is that the fundamental challenge of our society is complexity: 'namely the situation of there being more points of connection in the world than we are able to connect to as a society. What is special about this challenge is that complexity cannot be removed or neutralized'.[42] An application of this thesis to taxation – which Qvortrup himself does not discuss – might mean that the focus for improvement should be on enhancing agents' coupling capacity, and that attempts to eradicate tax complexity may have a lesser chance of success.

[A] Complexity

In Qvortrup's conception, complexity, and the growth of complexity, can be defined by two factors: space and time.[43] Space is understood to entail both the number of elements in the observed system and the extent of possible actions for an agent.[44] Qvortrup explains our current society's environment as 'complex in the sense of space because we live in a global society'[45] and 'complex in the sense of time because we live in a society that changes at an ever-increasing rate',[46] constituting a situation in which there are more points of connection than any agent is able to connect with. Hence, complexity growth refers to individuals and society being able to engage in as well as experience more and more possibilities – many more than individuals living in earlier societies.[47]

Linking these factors to an observed tax system might aid in an examination of its complexity growth. (The observed system might be a national tax system or a small or large part of it, or it might span multiple national tax systems.) Has the number of elements increased in the observed system?[48] Has the number of potential actions increased, due to an increase in agents' ability to engage in possible actions (e.g., through sophisticated tax planning offered by tax professionals)? Has the rate of change itself increased – either within the system, through accelerated change in statutes, regulations, and the like, or for taxpayers, through more rapid change in the sources of income that is subject to taxation? Affirmative answers to these questions seem likely.

---

40. Qvortrup, *The Hypercomplex Society*, above n. 1, at 14.
41. Qvortrup, *The Hypercomplex Society*, above n. 1, at 10.
42. Qvortrup, *The Hypercomplex Society*, above n. 1, at 34. Qvortrup clarifies that he is not contending that current society 'is' a hypercomplex society – rather, that hypercomplexity constitutes a framework for analysis: *The Hypercomplex Society*, at 14.
43. Qvortrup, *The Hypercomplex Society*, above n. 1, at 38.
44. Qvortrup, *The Hypercomplex Society*, above n. 1, at 5, 10 ('… and it is a question not only of the number of elements in the observed system…').
45. Qvortrup, *The Hypercomplex Society*, above n. 1, at 5.
46. Qvortrup, *The Hypercomplex Society*, above n. 1, at 5.
47. Qvortrup, *The Hypercomplex Society*, above n. 1, at 10.
48. Ascertaining complexity growth based on this factor alone is comparable to applying the designation 'complexity denoting some characteristic of a tax statute, e.g., its degree of differentiation in the rules', as referred to in §2.02 above. Such a definition can be characterized as product-oriented, since it provides a static account of the attributes of the observed statute.

Qvortrup finds it palpable that current society is becoming 'more complex' than earlier societies.[49] However, he clarifies that complexity is neither simply a quantitative phenomenon, nor something that should be conflated with answers to the question of whether current society is more challenging for its agents as they attempt to manage complexity than earlier societies were for their inhabitants:

> For me, "complexity" is a relative, not an absolute, concept, and it is a question not only of the number of elements in the observed environment, but also of the coupling capacity [meaning the context in which the task is managed, including tools and resources for management] of the observer.[50]

The point Qvortrup makes here is similar to what was established in §2.02 above: that there is no intrinsic relationship between the complexity of a particular statute or regulation and how well a task subject to that statute or regulation is handled, since the entire context – or 'coupling capacity' – influences the outcome to such a significant extent.

To sum up, one aspect of the concept of hypercomplexity is the observation of complexity growth based on the factors of space and time. These factors also appear useful for analyses of tax system complexity, and are likely to demonstrate that tax systems have experienced a significant growth in complexity. Thus, it would not be unique to tax systems, but merely indicate that those systems have developed in the same way as society more generally. It is important to note, however, that how well taxpayers, tax professionals, and tax officials manage their tasks is a separate question from the extent of complexity growth, and hence that complexity growth does not in and of itself support an inference that agents working on tax-related tasks within a more complex tax system necessarily face greater challenges.

[B]   Differentiation and Complexity Management

A related use of the term 'complexity' describes degrees of social differentiation, where a society's level of complexity is rising with increasing functional differentiation.[51] An illustration of such differentiation could be the structure of an early modern tax system, which might have consisted of an income tax, a property tax, a wealth tax, and an inheritance tax. Each of these types of tax contained sub-differentiations: for the income tax, for example, between taxation of income from work and taxation of income from capital.[52] Current tax systems' comparatively higher levels of differentiation are one example of increased complexity. Depending upon the perspective (e.g., of

---

49. Qvortrup, *The Hypercomplex Society*, above n. 1, at 10.
50. Qvortrup, *The Hypercomplex Society*, above n. 1, at 10.
51. Qvortrup, *The Hypercomplex Society*, above n. 1, at 21. See also e.g., Moeller, *Luhmann Explained: From Souls to Systems*, above n. 7, at 40–41.
52. See generally Frank H. Pedersen, *Skatteaversion: en retssociologisk og skattepolitisk analyse med hovedvægten på indkomstopgørelsen*, 98 (Jurist- og økonomforbundets forlag, 2000) [hereinafter *Skatteaversion*].

business or of a tax authority), this can be construed as either external or internal complexity.[53]

Qvortrup's explanation for this aspect of hypercomplexity is that development of society arises from continuously more detailed functional differentiation. As a result, agents, including individuals as well as organizations, must develop an internal complexity – a coupling capacity – to correspond to the level of external complexity.[54] The external complexity has thus been broken down into smaller pieces, so to speak, in order for the internal structure to succeed in coupling with it.[55]

How this internal complexity has developed is one of the core diagnostics in the concept of hypercomplexity. Qvortrup describes twentieth century internal complexity-building in this way:

> In the world of organizations the first reactions to the growth in complexity in the world was to meet external complexity with bureaucracy. Private enterprises developed horizontal specialization and vertical lines of command based on a strict hierarchy, and public institutions created detailed rules and procedures, based on the belief that surrounding complexity could be met and balanced by a similar amount of internal bureaucracy-based complexity.[56]

For the tax system, this meant growth in the number of tax statutes and also in their differentiation, in an attempt both to cover the expansion in the number of types of underlying enterprises subject to taxation, and to do this with greater differentiation between kinds of income or expenses. In terms of tax authorities' organization, it meant establishment of manifold offices, with specializations matching the various subject matters (property taxation, taxation of corporations, inheritance taxation, and the like).[57] Correspondingly, businesses established internal tax departments, and among tax professionals, in addition to smaller companies, the 'Big Eight' (now the 'Big Four') grew into massive enterprises offering highly sophisticated audit and tax services.[58]

One of the most important causes of increased internal complexity, and thus of agents' coupling capacity, is the use of tax software.[59] By all appearances, the development of tax software and the electronic services offered by tax authorities have

---

53. See, e.g., George Ritzer & Jeffrey Stepnisky, Contemporary Sociological Theory and Its Classical Roots, 102–103 (4th ed., McGraw-Hill, 2013).
54. Qvortrup, *The Hypercomplex Society*, above n. 1, at 171.
55. Qvortrup, *The Hypercomplex Society*, above n. 1, at 101–102.
56. Qvortrup, *The Hypercomplex Society*, above n. 1, at 41.
57. See, e.g., Mikael Venge, 'Skatter på Slotsholmen før 1975', 22–23, in *Festskrift: Glimt fra 25 år 1975–2000* (Skatteministeriet, 2000).
58. For references to 'Big Eight'/'Big Four' see e.g., Mark Stevens, *The Big Six*, 13–14 (Simon & Schuster, 1991) and Thomas D. Tolleson & Kalpana Pai, *The Big 4 Accounting Firms: Too Big to Fail*, 5(1) Int'l J. Bus. Acct. & Fin. 56 (2011).
59. Qvortrup depicts information and communication technology as having a paradoxical role with regard to the complexity challenge. On the one hand, they are a cause of complexity growth, as they broaden the range of possible actions as well as speeding them up. On the other hand, they represent the necessary tools for handling the problem. *The Hypercomplex Society*, above n. 1, at 10 (Qvortrup discusses 'electronic proximity' with reference to renowned Professor in Computer Science, Michael Dertouzos); see also *The Hypercomplex Society*, at 45–46.

been the most significant developments in managing tax complexity.[60] As a result, access to and mastery of such tools has become a de facto necessity for managing tax-related tasks.[61] Alternatively, some taxpayers can rely on the revenue authority's preparation and assessment, when such services are offered.[62] Confidence in the revenue authorities' work then becomes crucial.

[C]   Society's Development Away from Anthropocentrism and toward Polycentrism

A separate aspect of the concept of hypercomplexity is that in society, specific historical periods are characterized by different epistemes,[63] i.e., systems of understanding or bodies of ideas which give shape to the knowledge base of the time.[64] Modern society – which in technological terms can be called industrial society[65] – has been characterized by an episteme of anthropocentrism.[66] Since the twentieth century, however, a new phase has emerged, characterized by an episteme of polycentrism, which moves contemporary society in the direction of a hypercomplex society.[67] Currently, anthropocentrism and polycentrism overlap as the bases for discourse and the expansion of knowledge in our society.[68] A main difference between these epistemes relates to their understanding of rationality. A characteristic of anthropocentrism is the belief in unlimited rationality: that society can control its environment by pushing the limits of rationality to their extremes. In contrast, polycentrism is associated with bounded rationality and polycontextual observations.[69]

---

60. See §2.02 above.
61. See e.g., Zelenak, above n. 12, at 92–95 (describing the development of the use of return preparation software in the United States, and its necessity for satisfying the computational demands of tax returns).
62. See e.g., OECD, *Tax Administration 2013: Comparative Information on OECD and other Advanced and Emerging Economics*, 236 (2013). 'In its most advanced form, pre-filling services and related facilities have just about fully automated return preparation and assessment; some seven revenue bodies reported having capability to prepare fully completed tax returns for the majority of their PIT [Personal Income Tax] clients'.
63. Qvortrup, *The Hypercomplex Society*, above n. 1, at 6.
64. Dictionary.com, 'episteme', in *Dictionary.com's 21st Century Lexicon*. Source location: Dictionary.com, LLC. http://dictionary.reference.com/browse/episteme. Available: http://dictionary.reference.com (accessed on 1 August 2014).
65. Qvortrup, *The Hypercomplex Society*, above n. 1, at 23.
66. The historical period before modern society is designated 'traditional society'. Traditional societies have had an episteme of theocentrism, which characterizes a society with God or destiny as the focus of the knowledge horizon. *The Hypercomplex Society*, at 14. The decisive cultural change from traditional to modern society was the replacement of the belief that God was the structural and semantic centre of the world by the belief that man, i.e., human reason and creativity, was the central force of the world. *The Hypercomplex Society*, at 23.
67. Qvortrup, *The Hypercomplex Society*, above n. 1, at 6.
68. Qvortrup, *The Hypercomplex Society*, above n. 1, at 48–49.
69. Qvortrup describes how '[t]oday, the belief in unlimited rationality has been replaced by the concept of bounded rationality [by Herbert A Simon], reflecting the social fact that in every decisional situation the number of possibilities, not only for observation-based conclusions, but also for determining the premises of observation, exceeds the capability to make decisions'. *The Hypercomplex Society*, at 13.

Hypercomplexity is inextricably linked to polycentrism. Qvortrup explains how the concept of hypercomplexity represents a way to express a developmental characteristic of present-day society: 'The ground structure in society is not a relationship between a center of control and rationality and a world of disorder that is to be brought into control'.[70] Qvortrup further explains how the fundamental challenge is the growth in external complexity, which renders it impossible for any entity to attain control: 'It is not a realistic project to build up an even greater capacity, devise far more rules and regulations, and employ even more bureaucrats, as it was believed in the twentieth century. This marks a break with industrial society's self-understanding'.[71] For taxation, this development might mean that it is becoming increasingly difficult to prepare 'off-the-shelf' answers, so to speak, in advance.

Because industrial society's self-understanding was embedded in anthropocentrism, the emergence of polycentrism challenges industrial society's entire mode of reasoning. A way to portray this change is through the notions of *complex simplicity* and *organized complexity*.[72] Complex simplicity stands for the notion that while a system or organization might be quite comprehensive, each small unit functions according to simple principles. This was the industrial society's mode of organization. The archetype is a watch or other mechanical device. An organizational example is the Ford Motor Company, which had, enthroned at its pinnacle, reason personified: the paragon of industrial leadership, Henry Ford.[73] Such companies, like large public bureaucracies, worked by breaking down all elements into their smallest units.[74] In organized complexity, by contrast, rather than an arrangement of small, simple pieces, there are multifarious interactions by each unit, each of which is also complex.[75] A contemporary tax system – which frequently deals with tax issues across national borders – might best be understood using the notion of organized complexity.

The concept of hypercomplexity implies that current society is not necessarily more complex in some quantitative sense.[76] Hypercomplexity represents 'complexity inscribed in complexity'.[77] General anti-avoidance rules (GAARs) and doctrines might

---

70. Qvortrup, *The Hypercomplex Society*, above n. 1, at 35.
71. Qvortrup, *The Hypercomplex Society*, above n. 1, at 34. Qvortrup emphasizes that society's self-identification as hypercomplex has yet to be fulfilled. *The Hypercomplex Society*, at 7, 14.
72. Qvortrup, *The Hypercomplex Society*, above n. 1, at 101–105.
73. In the Charlie Chaplin film *Modern Times* (1936), a comic look at complex simplicity, one finds in the centre the President of Electro Steel Corp., the anthropocentrically rational leader who has indirect insight and control over the whole complicated organizational machine.
74. Qvortrup, *The Hypercomplex Society*, above n. 1, at 101–102.
75. Qvortrup, *The Hypercomplex Society*, above n. 1, at 103–104 (also explaining that the question of how organized complexity should be interpreted, beyond being a new type of complexity, is one that science is still working on). The originator of the notion of organized complexity is Warren Weaver: see Warren Weaver, *Science and Complexity*, 36(4) Am. Scientist 536 (1948). For a version with foreword by Ross Wirth, see http://philoscience.unibe.ch/documents/uk/ (accessed on 15 August 2014).
76. Qvortrup, *The Hypercomplex Society*, above n. 1, at 10. See also discussion in §2.03[A] above.
77. Qvortrup offers this short definition of hypercomplexity: 'hypercomplexity is complexity inscribed in complexity, e.g., second-order complexity. As an example, hypercomplexity is the result of one observer's description of another observer's descriptions of complexity, or it is the result of a complex observer's description of its own complexity'. *The Hypercomplex Society*, at 6. Based on this, Qvortrup argues that for contemporary society it 'is not that rationality must be

be an example of such hypercomplexity, i.e., complex, ambiguous rules about the meaning and application of the underlying complex rules.[78]

§2.04   IN THE MIDST OF A PERIOD OF TRANSITION

This section expounds upon the difference between anthropocentric and polycentric approaches to the income tax system. Moreover, it illustrates the possibility that the tax environment may currently be in the midst of a period of transition between the two mindsets, and that one's understanding of the condition of the current tax system depends on whether one uses an anthropocentric or polycentric approach.[79] This section first briefly illustrates the two approaches, using examples from the taxation context: (1) the anthropocentric mindset, with its general desire for tax experts (if no one else) to be capable of attaining full comprehension of the tax system that is their subject of expertise; and (2) the polycentric mindset, which is able to relinquish the possibility of achieving clarity by means of the tax code alone. This relinquishment, however, can be balanced by other factors; one example is the introduction of procedural devices such as advance tax rulings. The advance tax ruling is a legal instrument through which a taxpayer, if in doubt, can request an answer from the tax authority about the taxable consequences of a future disposition which the inquirer is considering.[80]

[A]   'Ought to Know'

Should professors of taxation and top officials at the tax authorities, if no one else, be expected to fully comprehend the tax system? An answer based on an anthropocentric understanding of society would be 'yes'. And according to this mindset, something is wrong if that is not the case. An example of this perspective might be Kenneth Ryesky's references to certain confessions by IRS executives:

---

given up, but that the ideal of unlimited rationality must be replaced by the concept of bounded rationality, i.e., that the state of hypercomplexity is constituted by the mutual observations and self-observations of complex systems'. *The Hypercomplex Society*, at 13–14.

78. Another example might be the mutual agreement procedure in the OECD Model Tax Convention on Income and on Capital. Article 25(3) reads as follows: 'The competent authorities of the Contracting States shall endeavour to resolve by mutual agreement any difficulties or doubts arising as to the interpretation or application of the Convention. They may also consult together for the elimination of double taxation in cases not provided for in the Convention'. This procedure, like a GAAR, can be said to be a complex rule about underlying complex rules. See also generally, Pedersen, *The Usability Model*, above n. 15, at 327 (discussing 'complexity experience'). For a discussion of the UK general anti-abuse rule and the role of the 'GAAR Panel', see also Judith Freedman, *Creating new UK institutions for tax governance and policy making: progress or confusion?*, [2013] 4 Brit. Tax Rev. 373, 378.

79. Applying a different theoretical framework Oats and Morris describe in their chapter the notion of 'doxa' and the fight to influence the form of the primary experience of the social world. In their terminology, one can say that what is ongoing is a contest between anthropocentrism or polycentrism as the foundation for 'the way in which we all understand the game'. See Lynne Oats & Gregory Morris, *Tax Complexity and Symbolic Power*, this volume, §3.03.

80. See §2.04[B], with reference to Carlo Romano, *Advance Tax Rulings and Principles of Law: Towards a European Tax Rulings System?*, 119 (IBFD Publications, 2002).

The Internal Revenue Service ('IRS') itself has had occasion to hesitate and waver in its interpretation and application of the tax statutes, and indeed, several IRS officials have admitted to retaining professional assistance to prepare their personal income tax returns. . . . [including] Carol Landy, Director of [an] Internal Revenue Service Center. . .: 'I don't do my own tax return. I'm afraid to make a mistake.'. . . [and] Internal Revenue Commissioner Fred Goldberg [, who] reportedly admitted... to engaging an accountant to prepare his personal income tax returns.[81]

This quote illustrates the anthropocentric ideal that, at a minimum, those at the top of a hierarchy should be capable of comprehending the full component of available knowledge. Within a polycentric mindset, however, accounts of executives managing their personal tax affairs in the same way they are expected to run their organizations – by delegating tasks to experts – seem quite acceptable.[82] Under a polycentric approach, no single person is expected to be able to interpret all obtainable information.[83]

[B]   Procedural Leeway

According to the anthropocentric ideal, the tax code should be a manifest example of unlimited rationality. Optimally, it would be a centre of control and scientifically based order, articulated through rules and regulations.[84] A polycentric approach, by contrast, renounces such ideals, finding them illusory. Instead, a polycentric approach sees the tax code as contextually joined with the outcomes of procedural operations – which themselves are elements of the tax code's authority.

The legal instrument known as the advance tax ruling,[85] and the development of other such procedural devices, can serve to illustrate the differences between these approaches. Advance ruling procedures have been an issue for debate since at least the 1960s.[86] Since then, the prevalence of such devices has steadily increased

---

81. Kenneth H. Ryesky, *Tax Simplification: So Necessary and So Elusive*, 2(2) Pierce L. Rev. 93, 93–94 and 94, n. 7 (2004). This is not to say that Ryesky adheres exclusively to an anthropocentric viewpoint.

82. However, ordinary taxpayers nowadays might expect not to need paid professional assistance, because tax software makes it manageable to submit tax returns themselves. See generally Pedersen, *The Usability Model*, above n. 15, at 348.

83. See Qvortrup, *The Hypercomplex Society*, above n. 1, at 42 (explaining how a single person is unable to interpret all the information with which an organization is bombarded).

84. The 'plain English' literature and corresponding sub-specialty in the field of tax complexity, which attempts to improve taxpayers' welfare through the rewriting of tax legislation, might originate in such an anthropocentric mindset. For a general, brief discussion of the 'plain English' tax complexity literature, see Pedersen, *The Usability Model*, above n. 15, at 303 and 318–319. See also Erich Kirchler, *The Economic Psychology of Tax Behaviour*, 7–8 (Cambridge University Press, 2007) (noting that 'plain English' projects in New Zealand and Australia have not been successful).

85. Romano offers this definition: 'an advance tax ruling may be generally defined as any advice, information or statement provided by the tax authorities to a specific taxpayer or group of taxpayers concerning their tax situation in respect to future transactions and on which they are (to a certain extent) entitled to reply'. See Romano, above n. 80, at 119.

86. Romano, above n. 80, at 118. The 1965 resolution from the Congress of the International Fiscal Association reads as follows: 'The Congress points out that the complexity of fiscal legislation is

worldwide.[87] Today the common view among scholars is that advance tax ruling procedures are essential procedures to taxpayers.[88]

However, this procedural device has also had its opponents. An example of such criticism comes from Danish Professor Svend Gram Jensen, who finds it difficult to see the introduction of advance tax rulings[89] as progress, and instead advocates replacement of the current Danish tax code with a new, rewritten version.[90] From an anthropocentric viewpoint, Gram Jensen's criticism is quite sound, since it sees the introduction of advance tax rulings as an abandonment of attempts to provide clarity purely through the tax code. By contrast, from a polycentric viewpoint, supplementing traditional rules- and regulations-based navigation with optional procedural devices might be viewed as a more realistic and pragmatic way to proceed.[91]

Maintenance of an adequate level of confidence in the tax system and between its agents becomes essential in a tax environment without a central source of order, transparency, or control of the system. As a consequence, institutions, procedures, and policies to safeguard a well-founded confidence become a necessity.[92]

[C]   Tax in 'the Complexity of Complexity'

The Danish debate about advance tax rulings, as well as Ryesky's references to IRS executives' admissions, illustrates how the tax environment remains in transition between the anthropocentric and polycentric epistemes. Such a transition period between two phases, when a new episteme has emerged but expectations and ideals continue to be marked by the previous episteme, is disturbing in its discrepancies. Qvortrup even has a name for such a period: 'the complexity of complexity'.[93]

---

constantly increasing in all countries and for this reason it has become increasingly difficult for the taxpayers to obtain reliable information concerning the application of tax law...Therefore, it is important that taxpayers be provided with an opportunity to obtain an authoritative opinion on the meaning of the law before taking measures, the fiscal consequences of which are uncertain....'. See Romano, above n. 80, at 118.

87. See Yehonatan Givati, *Resolving Legal Uncertainty: The Unfulfilled Promise of Advance Tax Rulings*, 29(1) Va. Tax Rev. 137, 139–140 (2009) (discussing reasons for infrequent use of advance tax rulings in the United States). See also LexMundi World Ready, Global Practice Guide, *Tax Rulings*, http://www.lexmundi.com/lexmundi/Tax_Rulings_Guide.asp (accessed on 15 November 2014).

88. See Givati, above n. 87, at 147–149.

89. The advance tax ruling was introduced in Denmark in 1983 (Lov nr. 143 af 13/4 1983).

90. Svend Gram Jensen, *Skattemyndighedernes kompetence*, 104–107 (3rd ed., GadJura, 1997).

91. See Qvortrup, *The Hypercomplex Society*, above n. 1, at 42 (discussing how the use of collective, decentralized functions allows organizations to make evaluations and adjust themselves to the demands of the surrounding society).

92. See, e.g., generally, Bogumił Brzeziński, 'Taxpayers' Rights: Some Theoretical Issues', in Włodzimierz Nykiel & Małgorzata Sęk (eds), *Protection of Taxpayer's Rights: European, International and Domestic Tax Law Perspective*, 17, 17 (Wolters Kluwer, 2009) (explaining how the rights of taxpayers became the subject of discussion in the last quarter of the twentieth century); OECD, *Taxpayers' Rights and Obligations: A Survey of the Legal Situation in OECD Countries* (1990). For a review of the internal and external oversight mechanisms established in the case of the US tax system, see John Hasseldine, *Oversight Mechanisms and Administrative Responses to Tax Complexity in the United States*, this volume, §17.04 and §17.05.

93. Qvortrup, *The Hypercomplex Society*, above n. 1, at 48–49.

§2.05 CONCLUSION

The growth of tax complexity has for almost 100 years caused concern and fear that the tax system will eventually cease to function properly under its burden of complexity. Are we witnessing a century-long downward spiral, or is something else going on? In this chapter, I have suggested that the tax system – like the rest of society – is in the midst of a transition period. By means of this transition, society is moving away from the order and related ideals of industrial society and towards an emerging period of increased cross-border activity and polycentrism, in which it is no longer possible to create absolute order in any system or institution, including the tax system. Things certainly are not as they used to be, but nonetheless the tax system, like society as a whole, continues to function. How well tax-related tasks can be managed in the face of increasing complexity is influenced not only by the level of complexity itself, but also by the extent to which taxpayers' and tax professionals' coping capacity has been enhanced, particularly through the use of ICT such as tax software.

A fresh examination of the tax system through the lens of hypercomplexity is not intended to demonstrate that the current system is free of problems; rather, it suggests that attempts to return to an expectation that the system should be fully comprehensible by someone, if only the experts, will provide fewer solutions than will a polycentric approach. Acceptance of a more contemporary approach, polycentric in character, would allow for some optimism that our ability to cope with tax complexity can continue to develop. In the field of tax complexity, such a shift in mindset might reduce pessimism and liberate creative thinking, and as a result enhance the ability of the field to contribute to improvements in the tax system, which continues to pose real challenges. Not the least of these challenges will be that of sustaining confidence in a tax system which, while not out of order, has shed the perceived order of earlier, less complex times.

CHAPTER 3

Tax Complexity and Symbolic Power

Lynne Oats & Gregory Morris

§3.01 INTRODUCTION

Much has been written about the vested interests associated with tax complexity, and the manner in which such interests inhibit simplification projects. Much less has been written about the ideological underpinnings of tax simplicity, although there is some acknowledgement of this nested within critiques, for example, of optimal tax theory. Using insights from French sociologist Pierre Bourdieu, the latter form of vested interests and ideologies are explored in this chapter as a field analysis, in which the tax field is conceived of as a site of struggle and in which symbolic power plays an important role.

As Cooper astutely notes, '[t]here are no developed theories to explain why the cause of simplification is at the same time so lauded by government, practitioners and taxpayers, and yet so universally disregarded in practice'.[1] Much of the literature dealing with the suggested undesirability of tax complexity starts from the premise that simplicity has inherent 'goodness' and is something worth striving for; for example, '[o]ne of the practical design rules that comes out of standard welfare analysis of taxation is that, other things being equal and in very general terms, simplicity is a goal of tax policy'.[2] Yet complexity has been a feature of tax system design and its practical operation for a very long time.

Approaches to tax complexity take on a variety of guises and can be addressed from different perspectives. This chapter aims to provide an alternative reading of the simplicity/complexity debate, in an attempt to provide a note of caution in relation to uncritical adoption of the 'simple is good' discourse. It does so by invoking concepts

---

1. Graeme Cooper, *Themes and Issues in Tax Simplification*, 10(4) Austl. Tax F. 417, 420 (2003).
2. William Congdon, Jeffrey R. Kling & Sendhil Mullainathan, *Behavioral Economics and Tax Policy*, NBER Working Paper 15328, 6 (2009).

developed by French sociologist Pierre Bourdieu, whose insights have to date been used only sparsely in tax scholarship.[3]

A Bourdieusian lens allows us to construct an interdisciplinary understanding and critically question the actions and motives of agents or actors involved in the tax field, both those that advocate more simplicity and those for whom a simplification of the tax code is less compelling. As will be explained below, '[t]he work of Bourdieu is particularly useful ... because of its understanding of practice as emerging from the relational interaction of subjective experiences and the objective social structures that frame those experiences'.[4]

The chapter begins with a brief overview of the various dimensions of tax complexity before identifying key Bourdieusian concepts and illustrating how the concepts are crucially interrelated, offering a framework of significant explanatory power. These concepts are then applied to the tax field more broadly and to the complexity debates within that field. It concludes that great care is needed when assessing attempts that seek to provide solutions to the (perceived) problems associated with tax complexity, and that it is important firstly to identify and recognize and then understand the significance of, and the workings of symbolic power (§3.05 and §3.06, below) in driving the simplification agenda.

§3.02   DIMENSIONS OF TAX COMPLEXITY

Tax simplicity and complexity has been a topic of vigorous debate for many years, most vociferously in the US, partly perhaps as a result of the dogged dominance at the Federal level of income taxes, but also in other countries where it has manifested in overt attempts to simplify the tax system, for example Australia, New Zealand and the UK. The complexity debates are wide-ranging, and emanate from a variety of disciplinary perspectives including economics, law and psychology. Numerous commentators have articulated the various dimensions of complexity in the tax context, some of whom are noted in this section below (in no particular order).

Cooper, for example, notes that 'complexity is evident at four levels in the tax system, in the choice of tax base, in the design of the rules applied to that base, in the expression of those rules and in the administrative requirements imposed on those who must comply'.[5]

Harris, in dealing with the notion of simplicity as the obverse of complexity, divides it into three broad categories: policy simplicity – that is, the type of tax and its

---

3. The following works have used a Bourdieusian approach in relation to taxation: Louise Gracia & Lynne Oats, *Boundary Work and Tax Regulation: A Bourdieusian View*, 37(5) Acct., Org. & Soc'y 304 (2012); Diane Kraal, *Paul Keating, tax alchemist? A study proposing the interpretive tools of Pierre Bourdieu*, 8(1) J. Australasian Tax Teachers' Ass'n 77 (2014); and Ann Mumford, 'Inheritance Taxation, Notions of Legitimacy and Bourdieu', in Guido Erreygers & John Cunliffe (eds), *Inherited Wealth, Justice and Equality* 173 (Routledge, 2012).
4. Gracia & Oats, above n. 3, at 306.
5. Cooper, above n. 1, at 459.

incidence, form simplicity – referring to how the intentions of government appear in statute form, and action simplicity – specifically the administration of the tax system.[6]

Donaldson identifies at least seven components of complexity that he argues will always be present.[7] These are as follows: using tax laws to affect behaviour, frequent change, socio-economic complexity, the 'certainty trade off', judicial gloss, the income tax base definition and the legislative process.

In presenting an argument that the US tax code be divested of trivial provisions, Veliotis identifies from prior literature four aspects of complexity – judgmental complexity (resulting, for example, from attempts to mirror 'economic reality' in the design and application of tax rules), computational complexity ('numerous and tedious calculations … required to determine tax liability'), density complexity (relating to the wording of the code), and compliance complexity.[8]

Schenk, in an analysis of tax salience, suggests that categories of complexity used by previous scholars overlap, but are, broadly, compliance, transactional, and rule complexity, the last of these, difficulty in understanding the law, being most obviously related to salience.[9]

As a modest adaption of the above categorizations, the following elements of complexity within the tax field can be distinguished with a view to subsequent analysis in light of Bourdieu's notion of symbolic power. These categories are not intended to provide clean distinctions; they overlap to some extent and influence each other in subtle ways.

[A] Code Complexity

[1] Language of Legislation: Type and Number of Words

Several studies seek to measure complexity in terms of the specific wording of the tax code. Katz & Bommarito, for example, propose an empirical framework based on computational linguistics for the measurement of relative legal complexity.[10] The framework uses a hypothetical individual engaging with acquiring tax knowledge through a process that entails identification of the appropriate rules, assimilating their information content coping with any latent uncertainty, assessing the cost of complying and weighing the costs and benefits of compliance. Based on this process, the authors produce a composite measure of three qualitative features of the tax code: structure (in terms of layers or density of provisions), language (including the length

---

6. Peter Harris, *Corporate/Shareholder Income Taxation and Allocating Taxing Rights Between Countries*, 8 (IBFD Publications, 1996).
7. Samuel Donaldson, *The Easy Case against Tax Simplification*, 22(4) Va. Tax Rev. 645, 660 (2003).
8. Stanley Veliotis, *Sweating the Small Stuff: The Cost of Immaterial Tax Law Provisions*, 3(1) Wm. & Mary Pol'y Rev. 36, 59 (2011).
9. Deborah H. Schenk, *Exploiting the Salience Bias in Designing Taxes*, 28(2) Yale J. on Reg. 253 (2011). See also Ann Mumford, *Tax Complexity, Tax Salience and Tax Politics*, paper presented at the Political Power of Tax Complexity colloquium, Birmingham, 19 September 2013.
10. Daniel Martin Katz & Michael J. Bommarito II, *Measuring the complexity of the law: the United States Code*, 22(4) Artif. Intell. & L. 337 (2014).

and diversity of the words) and interdependence between various provisions (the more cross-references, the greater the complexity).

[2]   Anti-avoidance Rules

Many commentators point to the incremental complexity of the tax code that arises from successive attempts to tackle tax avoidance.

In a historical investigation of attempts by the Australian government to distinguish private companies with a view to treating them differently, and which in turn led to various tax avoidance practices, Oats notes:

> The definition of private company for tax purposes was not intrusive when rates of tax were not high, but when circumstances changed, during WWII and subsequently when rates of tax were pushed higher, the definition took on much greater significance.[11]

The importance of this is the diachronic dimension, which is sometimes overlooked. However, changes to a tax code prompted by a desire to deal with the prevention or deterrence of tax avoidance do not always create additional complexity. In the recent hearings before the UK Public Accounts Committee, this issue was discussed in oral evidence by Edward Troup (Tax Assurance Commissioner, HM Revenue & Customs), who said:

> Yesterday we announced the closure of four specific loopholes. Three of those were not simplifying measures. They are having to close off some complicated loopholes that have arisen. One of them, interestingly, abolished a relief that is now outmoded. It was something introduced many years ago, which was deduction [sic.] for patent royalty payments by individuals who weren't carrying on a trade. That we found was being used just for avoidance now. For once, the Government have introduced an anti-avoidance measure that is simplifying.[12]

[3]   Rules or Principles

Tax complexity arises also in the context of the structure of the tax code and the extent to which the rules are codified. There is a large body of literature dealing with the question of the relative merits of principles over rules in the drafting of tax legislation. However in seeking to understand the distinction between rules and principles and how the adoption of one approach rather than another is relevant to the tax simplicity/complexity debate, a number of important distinctions must be made in

---

11. Lynne Oats, *Distinguishing Closely Held Companies for Taxation Purposes: The Australian Experience 1930–1972*, 15(1) Acct. Bus. & Fin. Hist. 35, 38 (2005).
12. Edward Troup, in Transcript of Evidence to the House of Commons Public Accounts Committee inquiry into Tax Avoidance Marketed Schemes, 6 December 2012, Evidence 21 (question 303) in relation to the Office of Tax Simplification. Available at: http://www.publications.parliament.uk/pa/cm201213/cmselect/cmpubacc/uc788-i/uc78801.htm (accessed on 21 November 2014).

order to clarify the framework and content of the discussion. For example, Freedman has suggested that an understanding of the rules or principles debate requires a recognition that a purposive interpretation of the tax code and even the enactment of purpose clauses which in some manner seek to explain the relevant legislation are not necessarily the same as adopting a principle based approach (in contrast to a rules based approach) to structuring a tax code, although both might be relevant to the complexity/simplicity debate.[13] Before such distinctions are made and a robust understanding of the differences between rules or principles can be demonstrated, little clarity can be achieved on the relevance that the rules or principles debate has for assessing the relative complexity or simplicity of a tax system.

[B] Structural Complexity

[1] Number of Rates

Some scholars focus in particular on the number of different rates of tax, arguing that the more rates within a given rate schedule, the more complex the tax computation will be. While this may well have been problematic in times gone by, modern computational capability means that such concerns are no longer paramount, although there is evidence that taxpayers have difficulty, for example, in determining the marginal tax rates they face when making investment or other financial decisions.

[2] Number of Provisions

The number of provisions in a tax code is frequently cited as indicative of complexity and attempts are also frequently made to eliminate or at least reduce outdated provisions on this basis, as in the work of the UK Office of Tax Simplification.[14] In a US study, Veliotis decries incremental change increasing complexity and recommends, drawing on institutional (transaction cost) economics, incremental elimination of 'trivial' or 'immaterial' provisions in the US tax code, including tax expenditures that could be converted to direct subsidies, as a means of reducing 'clutter'.[15] Arguably this analysis overlooks the political imperatives associated with the use of tax expenditures including a desire to disguise the extent of support given to particular sections of society and the difficulties associated with administering direct spending provisions.

---

13. Judith Freedman, *Improving (Not Perfecting) Tax Legislation: Rules and Principles Revisited*, [2010] 6 Brit. Tax Rev. 717.
14. Office of Tax Simplification https://www.gov.uk/government/organisations/office-of-tax-simplification.
15. Veliotis, above n. 8, at 59.

[C]   Policy (System) Complexity

[1]   Socio-Economic Imperatives

It goes without saying that tax policy is at the mercy of prevailing, and changing, socio-economic imperatives. The current worldwide discussions related to base erosion and profit shifting (BEPS)[16] reflect this. Interestingly, these discussions also highlight the different understandings of how the tax code should work in practice. As noted by Lin Homer (Permanent Secretary and Chief Executive, HM Revenue & Customs):

> ...there is a complexity to the system, which sometimes separates the outcomes from the common-sense view of what should happen. That is not the same as saying that it is a mess. The law is rarely involved in areas that are simple and this is an area where I think there is a complexity – the last debate about permanent establishment illustrates that – which sometimes creates a gap between what people would like to happen and what is possible within the law.[17]

This view of a tax code is also reflected by Edward Troup, again when giving oral evidence to the Public Accounts Committee (§3.02[A][2] above):

> But if you look at the cases that we have litigated, and if you look at the example of film schemes that you were talking about with the previous witnesses, it was not so much the complexity of the tax system, it was abuse of a genuine purpose that Government had in making a change to the tax system. So, while simplification is part of where we should tackle this, I think to believe that somehow a simpler tax system would cure all these problems is not going to work.[18]

[2]   Tax Expenditures

There is a substantial literature also on the role of, and necessity for, tax expenditures. Tax expenditures not only create complexity when considered in isolation, but also the complexity is magnified when they are considered in aggregate. In the context of tax complexity, the OECD survey of country practices in relation to tax expenditures observes that:

> ... aspects of tax expenditures can cause the resulting complexity of the whole to exceed the sum of the complexity of the parts, in public perception as well as reality. As legal provisions, regulations, instructions and forms are piled upon one

---

16. See, for example, the description of BEPS and the OECD/G20 BEPS Project at: http://www.oecd .org/tax/beps-about.htm.
17. Lin Homer, transcript of evidence on 16 May 2013 (in response to Question 246 from Guto Bebb, Welsh Conservative Party Member for Aberconwy), in House of Commons Committee of Public Accounts, *Tax Avoidance – Google, Ninth Report of Session 2013-14, together with formal minutes, oral and written evidence*, Ev. 28 (13 June 2013). Available at: http://www. publications.parliament.uk/pa/cm201314/cmselect/cmpubacc/112/112.pdf (accessed on 21 November 2014).
18. Edward Troup, in transcript of evidence to the House of Commons Public Accounts Committee inquiry into Tax Avoidance Marketed Schemes, 6 December 2012, Evidence 21 (question 303) in relation to the Office of Tax Simplification, above n. 12.

another, the body of tax wisdom needed to navigate the system can grow beyond the capacity of many non-experts. The marginal added provisions, even if they do not apply to a particular taxpayer, obscure that taxpayer's field of vision of what he or she needs to know. From a simple systems perspective, the potential interactions among additional tax expenditures could grow geometrically as more are added.[19]

Donaldson makes the distinction between mass complexity and specific complexity.[20] The former relates to provisions that are of universal application. The latter is complexity that arises for taxpaying entities that are affected by specific aspects of the tax code, for example tax expenditures. Such provisions, however, create mass complexity also, in the sense that even if not directly affected by specific provisions, taxpayers, their advisors and tax administrators all have a need to be apprised of specific provisions to assess their potential applicability.

[3]   Political Goals

The raw politics of tax legislation is often neglected when tax policy is discussed,[21] although some scholars do acknowledge it as a constraint in achieving simplification. Slemrod examined variations in US state income tax systems in terms of compliance complexity and the correlation with political ideology, among other things, in attempt to identify the aspects of a state's political system that engender tax complexity.[22] Given the usual caveats about statistical significance, he found some evidence that complexity is higher in states with a more liberal ideology, when proxied by the number of pages in the instruction book.

[D]   Administration and Compliance Complexity

[1]   Compliance Complexity

Filing and information provision requirements arise because of the need to provide information to the tax authority to enable them to evaluate tax liabilities. In some cases this can involve the creation of bespoke information sets for the tax authority.

The relationship between complexity and compliance is not entirely clear. Forest and Sheffrin, for example, challenge the notion that simplifying the system will increase compliance in an empirical study, based on a US 1990 Taxpayer Opinion Survey, that seeks to examine the relationship between taxpayer perceptions of

---

19. OECD, *Tax Expenditures in OECD Countries*, 29 (OECD, 2010).
20. Donaldson, above n. 7, at 660–661.
21. As observed in Mark A. Covaleski, Mark W. Dirsmith & Katrina L. Mantzke, *Institutional destabilisation and the new public management: the case of tax incremental financing*, 1(1/2) Int'l J. Pub. Pol'y 122 (2005).
22. Joel Slemrod, *The Etiology of Tax Complexity: Evidence from U.S. State Income Tax Systems*, 33(3) Pub. Fin. Rev. 279 (2005).

fairness and compliance with the tax rules.[23] Their results suggest that simplification may not in fact deter tax evasion as taxpayers do not necessarily equate complexity and unfairness, i.e., complexity and non-compliance are not consistently linked. Here, though, the authors equate non-compliance and evasion; they do not consider the concept of creative compliance with the tax rules.

[2]   Administrative Complexity

The flipside of the practical operation of the tax system is complexity as experienced by the tax administration. The following further observation by Lin Homer (see §3.02[C][1] above) illustrates that the functioning of the tax system is not rule-bound; that tax administrations are adaptable organizations capable of improvization to achieve their goals:

> Truthfully, there are other things that we can do in this space without having to wait for legislative changes, which is to be much better and clearer about informing people about tax regimes. Some of our improved data analytics, which we have talked to you about, also allow us to be more challenging in the area where people use that complexity to be mischievous with us, so I do not think that we in any sense wait until the complexity goes away; I think there are things we can do. I do not believe that there are many places in the world with simple tax systems, so ways of making the complexity less of a barrier to good, effective administration is the alternative.[24]

What is evident from this discussion of the various aspects of what can be considered to be tax complexity is that the practice of taxation (considered in all its aspects) has to operate in a social world that is, of itself, remarkably complex.

There is evidence to suggest that the *complexity v. simplicity* debate is one that does not focus on issues that might also be important. As the Office of Tax Simplification recognizes, clarity and understandability are key attributes of a tax code. This suggests that an important dimension of any discussion as to the content, application and administration of a tax code is that it be framed in terms of clarity and understandability (which together encourage certainty), and to assume that simplicity is some form of synonym for these characteristics is a mistake.

In the next section, we present an overview of Bourdieu's theory of social practice, prior to applying it specifically to the tax field, and to simplification debates in particular.

§3.03   BOURDIEU'S THEORY OF SOCIAL PRACTICE

Throughout Bourdieu's work there is a 'common thread' which seeks 'to uncover the specific contribution that symbolic forms make to the constitution and perpetuation of

---

23. Adam Forest & Steven M. Shefrin, *Complexity and Compliance: An Empirical Investigation*, 55(1) Nat'l Tax J. 75 (2002).
24. Lin Homer, transcript of evidence on 16 May 2013, above n. 17, at Ev. 29, in response to another question (Q. 251) from Guto Bebb.

structured inequality by masking its economic and political moorings'.[25] He does this primarily by using three key concepts: field, capital and *habitus*, each described here, in brief overview, in turn.

'Field' is the term used to describe the various social spaces which comprise the social world. Fields are neither discrete nor static, rather they overlap and intertwine and their boundaries are constantly shifting. The actors that inhabit these social fields challenge each other to acquire various forms of capital, the most dominant actors being those with the most capital in the particular configuration valued by the particular field. The capital, over which field actors struggle, is not capital as understood in an economic sense, but embraces a range of things of value, and of which economic capital, money and property, is but one. Other forms of capital that may be valued in a particular social field are cultural capital, referring to attributes recognized as important in society such as educational credentials, and social capital, which refers primarily to networks of personal and professional social contacts.[26] Other forms of capital identified by Bourdieu and those who draw on his work, include informational capital[27] and political capital.[28]

The third key feature (in addition to that of field and capital) of Bourdieu's thinking brings into play a subjective notion that interweaves with the structural elements; specifically *habitus*. Individual actors in social fields carry with them a *habitus* which is a 'set of attitudes, values and behaviours that dispose agents to behave in particular ways'.[29] *Habitus* is durable and deeply internalized, although not completely incapable of adaptation; a product of life chances – upbringing, education, early exposure to facets of social life including class etc. *Habitus* is central to the 'continual reproduction of belief in the game, interest in the game and its stakes'.[30]

Together, these three interconnected concepts, field, capital and *habitus*, help us to better understand aspects of social practice.

Another important feature of social fields is the *doxa*, a term which Bourdieu adapts from the Greek term for common belief. Swartz describes it as 'the taken-for-granted everyday life realities that form the primary experience of the social world'.[31] In Bourdieu's description of fields as analogous to a 'game', he states that fields follow rules, or regularities, and the field actors, as players in the game, 'concur in their belief (*doxa*) in the game and its stakes; they grant these a recognition that escapes

25. Loïc J.D. Wacquant, *On the Tracks of Symbolic Power: Prefatory Notes to Bourdieu's 'State Nobility'*, 10(3) Theory, Culture & Soc'y 1 (1993); Pierre Bourdieu, *Pascalian Meditations* ([1997], tr. Polity Press, 2000).
26. See Pierre Bourdieu, 'The Forms of Capital', in John G. Richardson (ed.), *Handbook of Theory and Research for the Sociology of Education* 241 (Greenwood, 1986).
27. Pierre Bourdieu, *Practical Reason*, Ch. 3 ('Rethinking the State: Genesis and Structure of the Bureaucratic Field') ([1994], tr. Polity Press, 1998).
28. Bourdieu also refers to 'political' capital as a subset of social capital; '[h]eads of political machines, parties, unions and lobbies are powerbrokers of institutionalised political capital', as described in David L. Swartz, *Symbolic Power, Politics, and Intellectuals: The Political Sociology of Pierre Bourdieu*, 65 (University of Chicago Press, 2013).
29. Gracia & Oats, above n. 3, at 307.
30. Pierre Bourdieu, *The Rules of Art: Genesis and Structure of the Literary Field*, 227 ([1992], tr. Susan Emanuel, Polity Press, 1996).
31. Swartz, *Symbolic Power, Politics, and Intellectuals*, above n. 28, at 80.

questioning'.[32] Indeed, Bourdieu suggests that each field has its own unique *doxa* and 'is characterised by the pursuit of a specific goal'.[33] To continue the analogy of a game, the purpose of rugby union as a game is to win through scoring tries, conversions and penalties in accordance with the laws of rugby union; in contrast, football (soccer) as a game provides a set of rules in accordance with which teams play to score goals. Rugby union and football (soccer) are different 'fields' with different '*doxa*'; each field and the players on the field abide by 'different rules of the game'.

How then can we use these ideas to conceptualize a tax 'field', as a way of exploring its dynamics, including, for the purpose of this chapter, the dynamics of tax complexity?

§3.04 THE TAX FIELD

In the context of taxation, both tax scholars and tax practitioners frequently refer to the operation of the tax system as akin to a 'game', which, as noted above (§3.03), is a metaphor used by Bourdieu in his explanations of fields, reflecting the competitive element of the struggles that occur within and between them.[34] Gracia and Oats present a view of tax regulation as a relational process that sees it in terms of 'struggles between groups within the tax field where participants shape, and are shaped by, the game being played'.[35]

We can all describe a number of the main players in the tax game: the taxpayer called upon to pay the tax, the tax authority charged with collecting it, the politicians who construct the tax code, the legislative drafters who translate the politicians' will into statute, the advisors who help taxpayers navigate the code's requirements, the judges who are called upon to adjudicate different interpretations of the code and the media which disseminate views of the field for the wider public. Less prominent (and maybe less influential), perhaps, but nonetheless important, are tax academics and researchers, who are able to influence the development of the tax system and the tax code in more subtle ways.

Applying Bourdieu's conceptual 'toolbox' or framework to the tax arena allows us to conceive of it as overlaid and intertwined with various other social and professional fields and, in part, shaped by a series of constantly changing questions about the design and operation of the tax system. The tax field has economic, social, political, legal and bureaucratic dimensions. Consequential upon the *habitus* of each actor:

> [e]ach protagonist in the game attempts to impose the definitions that are favourable to their own interests. The game in this sense is not one of benign play,

---

32. Pierre Bourdieu and Loïc J.D. Wacquant, *An Invitation to Reflexive Sociology*, 98 (tr. Loïc J.D. Wacquant, Polity Press, 1992).
33. Bourdieu, *Pascalian Meditations*, above n. 25, at 11.
34. See, for example, Bourdieu, *Practical Reason*, above n. 27, at 65.
35. Gracia & Oats, above n. 3, at 305.

but rather a constant and competitive struggle for power in which tensions are most acutely present at the boundaries of practice.[36]

The purpose of such struggle is the maintenance and acquisition of one or more of the various forms of capital. The nature of the capital sought in this struggle will depend on the *habitus* of the player and the role undertaken or position occupied within the tax field.

The tax administration is a prominent player in the tax field, and as part of the government is also an actor in a 'bureaucratic' field. Such matters as a reputation for efficiency, objectivity, and fairness might be important forms of capital for the tax administration. The tax administration may provide guidance to taxpayers, or may withhold guidance, creating what Osofsky calls 'strategic uncertainty'.[37] Lawyers and judges obviously also belong to the 'juridical field' and import into the tax field a legal *habitus*; approaching the tax system as primarily a legal text to be interpreted.

In relation to the tax field, we can also think, for example, of a taxpayer *habitus* as emerging 'from their experiences and interactions with the tax field'.[38] Arguably, 'the dense complexity of tax law puts its requirements beyond the grasp of many taxpayers, strengthening the cultural capital of the tax authority'.[39] Complexity creates an important role for advisors: '[s]ome taxpayers therefore choose to acquire the expertise of professional advisors to help not only with compliance, but also with strategies to minimise future tax obligations through judicious planning'.[40]

The tax field *doxa* can be thought of as the way in which we all understand the game; taxpayers can be reluctant to pay taxes, professional advisors act in the interests of their clients and possibly also in the interests of maintaining the integrity of the tax system. The tax administration is politically neutral in its work of collecting revenue, although through a 'desire' to be approved of by government it might seek taxation in accordance with its own *habitus* which, on a Bourdieusian understanding, cannot be neutral. The tax system is complex, imposing burdens (economic and psychological) on all concerned.

A Bourdieusian analysis allows for an unravelling of the relational struggle for the stakes in the game, including the power to name and define boundaries within the tax field, for example, boundaries between tax compliance and non-compliance.[41] Another important concept in Bourdieu's work is that of symbolic power, which is now explored in more detail.

---

36. Gracia & Oats, above n. 3, at 307.
37. Leigh Osofsky, *The Case against Strategic Tax Law Uncertainty*, 64(4) Tax L. Rev. 489 (2011).
38. Gracia & Oats, above n. 3, at 309–310.
39. Gracia & Oats, above n. 3, at 309–310.
40. Gracia & Oats, above n. 3, at 309–310.
41. Gracia & Oats, above n. 3, at 308.

§3.05   SYMBOLIC POWER

The question of power is a thread that runs through Bourdieu's sociology. Bourdieu uses the notion of symbolic power, in particular, to signify a power to make facets of social life appear to be natural, given, inevitable and, importantly, apolitical.[42]

'Symbolic power' emerges from 'the recognition of authority as legitimate which confers its carrier with an additional "value added" power above and beyond the specific form and amount of power upon which that authority is originally based'.[43] Bourdieu's use of the concept of symbolic power is a feature of his work that distinguishes him from other sociologists. Symbolic power is 'the capacity that systems of meaning and signification have of shielding, and thereby strengthening, relations of oppression and exploitation by hiding them under the cloak of nature, benevolence and meritocracy'.[44]

Symbolic power can be thought of as the means whereby the 'rules of the game' possess their power, significance and influence. The 'rules of the game' are assumed as given and yet, it is actors with power (which arises as a result of their *habitus* and the capital they possess) in the pursuit and maintenance of capital within a field that 'unconsciously' arrange the 'rules of the game' in their favour; the dice are loaded through the operation of symbolic power.

Swartz observes that:

> Bourdieu's sociology makes no distinction between the sociological approach to the study of the social world and the study of political power...[indeed he] sees *all* of sociology as fundamentally dealing with power...not as an independent domain that can be separated from culture or economics but a force that pervades all human relations.[45]

Bourdieu did not pay explicit attention to law, but in one paper[46] described the juridical field, in which he explains how powerful actors have the capacity to manipulate interpretation of legal texts as a mechanism for controlling field practices.[47]

Loveman distinguishes Bourdieu's symbolic power from other forms of power,[48] such as Mann's four sources of power (ideological, economic, military and political),[49] noting that symbolic power may be based on any or all of these or other forms of social power. Loveman describes it as a form of metapower, that 'accrues to carriers of specific forms of power to the extent that their particular basis of power is recognised

42. Pierre Bourdieu, *Language and Symbolic Power*, 170 ([1977–1984], tr. Polity Press, 1991); see Mara Loveman, *The Modern State and the Primitive Accumulation of Symbolic Capital*, 110(6) Am. J. Sociology 1651, 1655 (2005).
43. Loveman, above n. 42, at 1655.
44. Wacquant, *On the Tracks of Symbolic Power: Prefatory Notes to Bourdieu's 'State Nobility'*, above n. 25, at 1–2.
45. David Swartz, *Culture and Power: The Sociology of Pierre Bourdieu*, 87 (University of Chicago Press, 2006).
46. Pierre Bourdieu, *The Force of Law: Toward a Sociology of the Juridical Field*, (tr. Richard Terdiman), 38(5) Hastings L.J. 805 (1987).
47. Gracia & Oats, above n. 3, at 315.
48. Loveman, above n. 42, at 1655–1666.
49. Michael Mann, *The Sources of Social Power* ([1st ed.] Cambridge University Press, 1986).

as legitimate'.[50] Symbolic power can also be distinguished from ideology, which also relies on symbols, but arguably lacks a cultural dimension.

Bourdieu conceives of the state as being the primary, but not exclusive, repository of symbolic power, accumulated, as noted by Loveman, over time: '[b]ureaucratic administration is at the heart of the modern state's ability to exercise symbolic power... [and] also enables the state to define more effectively the parameters of individual identities and existence', through the accumulation of informational capital.[51]

Having outlined various aspects of tax complexity, and the Bourdieusian conceptual framework, we now bring together the two issues and ask the question, in what way is symbolic power present in debates that seek to minimize tax complexity?

§3.06   VESTED INTERESTS AND SYMBOLIC POWER

Symbolic power is used to create a framework within which the 'rules of the game' operate in favour of one or more actors. Such actors participate in the exercise of such symbolic power with a view to enhancing their opportunities to retain and obtain capital. One way of identifying vested interests, and the potential for symbolic power to come into play, is to think about the related fields which actors or groups of actors occupy and the relative importance of different forms of capital therein.

Using such an analysis, it is possible to categorize various groupings of interested parties on each side of the simplicity/complexity debate and, by offering descriptions of capital which are of value to these groupings, to also identify opportunities for the exercise of symbolic power.

Cooper suggests that both administrators and legislators may not actually want complexity to disappear;[52] the former benefit from complexity as a source of power within government and the latter create and maintain complexity as a mechanism for securing votes. As we saw earlier (§3.04), the tax administration is also part of the bureaucratic field, where value is attached to impartiality and procedural fairness. Notwithstanding this, the tax authority in the tax field is powerful in the sense of being able to promulgate authorized (by virtue of symbolic capital bestowed through state sanction) interpretations of the tax code and its application even though on occasion such interpretations might spring from the *habitus* of the tax administration.

The question of expertise is pervasive here. Tax knowledge is a valuable form of (informational) capital in the practical operation of the tax field. It is a feature of the tax field that generates considerable struggle between field actors.

This leaning towards complexity arises, in part, out of the *habitus* of such actors. For example, as an agent of government, a tax administration is concerned with ensuring that tax policy is reflected in the tax code as accurately as possible; there is a need to identify that set of circumstances in which tax will crystallize and also that set of circumstances in which a relief is available. In the exhibition of objective, impartial, bureaucratic virtue, complexity is allied to accuracy. In contrast, the *habitus* of tax

---

50. Loveman, above n. 42, at 1656.
51. Loveman, above n. 42, at 1660.
52. Cooper, above n. 1, at 449.

advisors values professionalism, expertise and knowledge, virtues more naturally linked to dealing with the complex rather than the simple. Knowledge is also relevant elsewhere in terms of tax policy design. Here it is a different form of knowledge that dominates debates, specifically economic knowledge. Philipps demonstrates, in a Canadian setting, how the presentation of tax rules as objective and 'scientific' can have the effect of delegitimizing value-based critiques.[53]

Symbolic power is evident in the work of optimal tax theorists, who present compelling arguments for policy simplification, for example the removal of tax preferences, consistent with the 'simplification is good' discourse, while disguising the neoliberal agenda that underpins such policy prescriptions.

The power of the simplification discourse is further illustrated in the World Bank publication *A Handbook for Tax Simplification*,[54] which is designed for use by policy-makers and tax practitioners. This highlights another player in the tax game, with an increasingly significant role, the supra-national organization. Bodies such as the World Bank, OECD, European Commission, relying as they do on the symbolic power associated with the 'virtue' of expertise and of being a supra-national organization, produce texts that are designed to promulgate best practice in tax system design as well as tax administration. They provide legitimacy for courses of action and proposals for change in countries where this may otherwise be difficult to achieve. However, little attention is paid to the *habitus* of the individuals that constitute such organizations, each of whom, on a Bourdieusian analysis, is operating within their fields of work seeking economic, social and cultural capital. The tax system in these texts is invariably treated as an economic issue, reaching out to the tax field *doxa* that efficiency is of paramount importance, although to be balanced against equity, and administrative ease. The World Bank Handbook also states: '[t]ax experts agree that a good tax has a low rate and a broad base. This principle captures, to a large extent, the goals of equity, efficiency, and administrative feasibility'.[55] Note here the appeal to expertise, which has the effect of diminishing objections to the 'low rate, broad base' efficiency mantra and also that the nature of efficiency within the tax field might be very different from efficiency as a *doxa* within the field of economics.

§3.07   CONCLUSION

How we understand tax complexity, and the call for simplification, is partly a result of our own *habitus*. Systems of education, which we would argue includes professional education, naturalize 'principles of vision and division',[56] that is, ways of categorizing the world that shape how we understand the society in which we live. Symbolic power

53. Lisa Philipps, *Discursive Deficits: A Feminist Perspective on the Power of Technical Knowledge in Fiscal Law and Policy*, 11(1) Can. J.L. & Soc'y 141 (1996).
54. World Bank, *A Handbook for Tax Simplification* (World Bank Group, 2009). The Handbook acknowledges (at iii) that it was published with 'the generous support of the UK Department for International Development (DFID) under the partnership program between DFID and the Investment Climate Advisory Services of the World Bank Group'.
55. World Bank, *A Handbook for Tax Simplification*, above n. 54, at 6.
56. Bourdieu, 'Rethinking the State: Genesis and Structure of the Bureaucratic Field', above n. 27.

attaches to the ability to make arbitrary distinctions appear as imperatives. There are many aspects of the call for tax complexity that illustrate symbolic power at work. Two of these will, in conclusion, be discussed further here.

The first relates to compliance complexity, and paternalistic calls for simplification to reduce the administrative burden of taxation and hence improve its economic efficiency. Such arguments are grounded in a small state ideology, the idea that we should roll back the state.[57] Symbolic power rests with those who are able to make people believe it is in their interests to 'cut red tape'. The promulgation of a small state ideology has the effect on actors (in many fields) of simply accepting such a principle to be relevant and 'better' than any alternative. When considered in Bourdieusian terms, the actors who promote such ideology do so in order to enhance their capital (in its various manifestations) and fix 'the rules of the game' to their advantage. The aim of the exercise of such symbolic power is for such a principle to be part of the *doxa* of the field. By failing to recognize such calls for simplicity as the exercise of symbolic power, the 'rules of the game' of the tax field are surreptitiously changed. The exercise of symbolic power means that unfortunately such changes are not challenged but instead accepted by all and yet, what is important, the changes benefit (initially) only the vested interests.[58]

By way of example, cash accounting for small business has recently been introduced in the UK and is presented as if helping struggling budding entrepreneurs. An alternative view, however, is that such processes actually engender bad practice – businesses should keep proper books of account for a whole range of reasons. Many small businesses would go to accountants for help regardless of how simple the system is. Another example, which illustrates the principle of unexpected consequences, is the 'Check the Box' election possible in the US as discussed by Dean.[59] This was introduced to satisfy administrative and compliance simplicity, but created considerable dysfunctional behaviour potentially damaging to wider society particularly outside the US. For example, it has resulted in complex anti-arbitrage legislation in the UK which is not as clear or as certain as would have been ideal.

The second illustration of symbolic power relates to the stubborn persistence of tax expenditures. Calls for reductions in tax expenditures are largely based on welfare economics thinking: broadly, that tax should not interfere with decision-making more than is absolutely necessary, and tax expenditures should be removed to make the code simple, and make tax economically efficient. But arguably this overlooks the very important social role of tax and risks harming those in need of special treatment. It also potentially denies the possibility of using differential taxes to accommodate social differences.

---

57. In the 21st century this is exemplified by the 'Tea Party' in the US but can be traced back to the work of the Chicago School as taken up by former UK Prime Minister Margaret Thatcher and President Ronald Reagan.
58. As time passes, the rules of the game will be accepted by actors other than the ones who initially exercised and sought the exercise of symbolic power. Such new actors, through their evolved *habitus*, will also benefit and thereby enhance and maintain their capital.
59. Steven A. Dean, *Attractive Complexity: Tax Deregulation, the Check-the-Box Election, and the Future of Tax Simplification*, 34(2) Hofstra L. Rev. 405.

In this case, what is important within the field is that consideration is given to the relationship between efficiency, objectivity, knowledge and even the desire for truth. The field of economics (out of which comes optimal tax theory) claims to itself the virtues of being objective, neutral and, perhaps above all, scientific. In the modern age of evidence based policy-making, significant credence is given to these virtues. Proponents of optimal tax theory are exercising symbolic power by associating their proposals with virtues that are highly valued. If adopted, the status (and hence capital) of those that propose such theory will be enhanced.

However, when the calls for the adoption of the principles of optimal tax theory as a means of simplification of the tax system are recognized as being reliant upon the exercise of the symbolic power that resides in the vision of economics as a neutral and objective science, then the debate on simplification can be assessed in a more useful manner.

This chapter set out to offer an alternative reading of the tax complexity debates. By thinking with Bourdieu's concepts, in particular that of symbolic power, it is possible to probe the various dimensions of tax complexity and ask some difficult questions. How is the tax field constituted, and what is the relationship between the various actors; individuals, organizations and institutions? What forms of capital are valued in the tax field, and what capital do field participants bring with them from other social fields that they inhabit? Who are the successful field actors who demonstrate mastery of the rules of the game?

In closing we reiterate the need for caution in embracing uncritically the 'simplicity is good' discourse. History has shown in many instances that measures adopted to simplify either tax policy or its practical operation have unforeseen consequences. This is particularly so when tax is treated as being primarily an economic phenomenon and the social dimensions of its operation are neglected. Tax complexity is a reflection of the complexity of wider society, including, but most definitely not limited to, its economic dimensions.

CHAPTER 4

Measuring Tax Complexity[*]

David Ulph

§4.01   INTRODUCTION

The aim of this chapter is to try to provide a conceptual framework within which to think about issues relating to measuring tax complexity, and to pose questions rather than come up with definitive answers. Put differently, rather than plunging in and trying to produce a measure or number for the sake of having a measure or number, I want to stand back a bit and ask some more ground-clearing questions about what one is trying to measure and why, and using the answers to these questions to shape how a measure could or should be constructed.[1]

To give some greater substance to these reflections I conclude by offering some views on the particular measure of tax complexity produced by the Office of Tax Simplification (OTS) in the UK.

Since I am trying to provide a more over-arching view, I will simply sketch out my thoughts rather than pursue any one issue in considerable depth. The chapter should

---

[*]   This chapter was prepared for the Tax System Complexity Symposium held in Prato, Italy, 29–30 September 2014, and has subsequently been revised for inclusion in this volume. An earlier version of this chapter was prepared for the Office of Tax Simplification (OTS), HM Treasury, and appears on the OTS website (www.gov.uk/government/organisations/office-of-tax-simplifica tion) as one of the papers published under the Tax Complexity Project, 28 February 2014. I am grateful to Joel Slemrod for his comments as discussant in Prato and to John Whiting, Jeremy Sherwood and Phillip Rice of HM Treasury for their comments on the earlier version.
1. The chapters by Binh Tran-Nam, *An Integrated Approach to the Economic Measurement of the Costs of Tax Complexity*, this volume, and Marco Lugo & François Vaillancourt, *Measuring Tax Complexity: Analytical Framework and Evidence for Individual Income Tax Preferences for Canada*, this volume, are very closely related to this chapter and make a number of very similar points.

be thought of as providing a basis for discussion of how to measure tax complexity rather than an exhaustive treatment of the topic.

The chapter proceeds in the following four sections:

§4.02: What is Tax Complexity?
§4.03: What are the Consequences/Costs of Tax Complexity?
§4.04: Measuring Tax Complexity; and
§4.05: Assessing One Particular Measure.

§4.02   WHAT IS TAX COMPLEXITY?

Although the concept of tax complexity is widely used and much discussed, with the complaint always being made that the tax system is 'too complex' – no one ever complains that the system is 'not complex enough' – the concept turns out to be a little more elusive when one tries to pin it down.

Certainly it is a concept that does not figure in standard economic analysis of tax systems,[2] and has not been given any very precise definition. I think that much of the popular discussion of tax complexity uses the term 'complexity' as a catch-all term that might encompass a number of different features such as lack of transparency rather than complexity per se.

In thinking about what might be meant by tax complexity the first issue to address is what do we mean by 'the tax system'?

By a 'tax system' we have in mind the set of tax laws/rules that define the various rates and duties that apply to the various transactions that individuals and companies might undertake, and the set of administrative procedures that individuals and companies have to go through in order to comply with the rules relating to providing information; completing tax returns; paying tax; and undergoing investigations where tax returns are challenged.

But right away one has to recognize that there are in fact many different 'tax systems' that could be relevant for UK taxpayers. For very many individuals and quite a lot of companies with rather simple tax affairs, the relevant tax system will be the UK tax system. But for a large number of individuals and companies the relevant 'tax system' will be some part of the international tax system that involves the tax rates and the rules and administrative conditions applying in many different countries. Which countries might matter will vary from taxpayer to taxpayer depending on the variety of countries in which they actually conduct transactions or might contemplate conducting transactions.

The complexity of these international systems lies largely beyond the control of the UK government, but one should at least be aware that for a significant number of UK taxpayers adjusting various features of the UK tax system may have little impact on the overall complexity of the 'tax system' they actually face, and indeed that some 'simplifications' of the UK tax system – by, say, bringing some tax rates in line with one

---

2. This point is made clearly in Tran-Nam, *An Integrated Approach to the Economic Measurement of the Costs of Tax Complexity*, this volume, §5.02.

another – may increase the complexity of the international system if they move rules or tax rates in the UK out of line with those in other parts of the world.

Now, in thinking about the complexity of any given system, I think it is helpful to distinguish two different features of a tax system and its consequent complexity in each case.

[A] Design Complexity

The first is what I call the *tax design* features of a tax system. This is something that reflects the number of different commodities that are taxed but also the number of different tax rates that apply to those commodities. This latter issue encompasses a number of different dimensions:

(1) Whether, for any given commodity, the rate at which it is taxed varies with the amount of that commodity that the taxpayer supplies/consumes.[3] The classic case where this happens is income tax – though there has been much discussion of flat rate income tax schedules.

(2) Whether, for any given commodity, the tax rate paid by some taxpayers might be different from that of others purely because of the nature of the taxpayer (rather than, as in (1) above, the amount consumed/supplied) – e.g., whether incorporated businesses pay tax at a different rate of tax on their profits than unincorporated businesses.

(3) Whether the unique tax rate on commodity j differs from that imposed on commodity k.

It might be thought that one way to measure complexity is to count the number of different tax rates – but this is potentially misleading.

To fix ideas, suppose you had an economy where there were N different commodities, H different types of household, and F different types of firm, where, realistically, N is a very large number and H and F are also likely to be large. There will be many households of each type and many firms of each type. Ignore externalities, and assume a closed economy.

One tax system of which you could conceive is one that taxes all N commodities at exactly the same constant proportional rate irrespective of household and firm type. It might be argued that this is the most minimally complex system, and give it a complexity index of 0.

Now when you tax commodities you essentially raise the price of things that consumers buy – e.g., bread – and lower the price of things they sell – e.g., labour. The net result is that consumers get less bread for every hour they work. But if you tax *everything* at exactly the same rate (e.g., have 20% income tax and 20% consumption or value added tax (VAT) on everything) then, in a very simple context, you are

---

3. The distinction here is between what economists call a linear tax schedule and a non-linear tax schedule.

essentially doing the same thing (reducing the amount of bread people get per hour of work) twice over. You could achieve the same outcome by having a higher rate of tax on income (40%) and a zero rate of VAT; or a zero rate of income tax and a 40% rate of VAT, or any combination in between.

This introduces the important idea of *tax equivalence*: there can be tax systems that appear to be nominally/formally different from one another but yet have exactly the same impact on the economy. In this simple example an economy with a 20% rate of income tax and 20% rate of VAT is *tax equivalent* to an economy with a tax rate of 40% on income and no VAT.

What this very simple example suggests is that:

(1) A tax system in which there is a single rate of tax – in the example, 20% – applied to *all* commodities (consumer goods and income) may to all intents and purposes be *equivalent* to one in which there are two different tax rates – 40% on income and 0% on VAT. In this case can we say that one is more complex than the other, or should we say that they are equally complex?

(2) Indeed it might be argued that a system in which there is a single rate of tax applied to all commodities is *more* complex than that in which there are two different tax rates – in the example, a single rate of tax of 40% on income, coupled with a zero rate of tax on all consumer goods – simply because in the second case there are far fewer things that are effectively being taxed.

At the other extreme you could think of a tax system that not only taxes all commodities at different rates but also has non-linear taxes with multiple bands and rates for various commodities, and these tax rates and/or bands can vary by household and firm type. We might all agree that this will have an extremely high level of complexity.

All this serves to illustrate why economists have not spent a great deal of effort trying to define and measure the complexity of tax systems, and why a simple counting of different tax rates may be rather misleading.[4]

Now any given tax system has multiple aims:

(1) The first is to raise revenue to fund public expenditure.

(2) The second is to promote economic efficiency (growth and productivity) by raising this revenue in a way that minimizes what economists call distortions – the difference between the allocation of resources that arises with taxes and that which would have happened without taxes. This involves:

(a) taxing 'bads' such as pollution rather than 'goods' such as work and savings;

(b) where 'goods' must be taxed, taxing more heavily those things that are more 'sticky' (less mobile).

---

4. Economists have been much more concerned about the efficiency and equity of a tax system – the amount of unwarranted distortions it creates and the degree of progressivity.

(3) The third is to promote fairness by having progressive income taxation and taxing less heavily those things that are consumed heavily by the poor and more heavily those things that are consumed heavily by the rich.

The traditional treatment of tax design by economists focuses on these three objectives, and assumes that taxpayers are fully compliant. However, in the current climate of concern about tax avoidance it is important to recognize another objective:

(4) To reduce opportunities for non-compliance through avoidance and evasion.

To some extent this is covered by the efficiency objective since avoidance often arises when similar things are taxed at different rates[5] – which creates a distortion – but nevertheless this objective would tend to point to a flatter tax system than might emerge from the first three objectives alone.

The theory of tax design helps us understand how to optimally design a tax system that achieves these objectives.[6] Associated with this 'optimal' system will be some level of complexity – in the sense that different commodities are taxed at different rates and so there are multiple tax rates. But the fundamental point is that some degree of complexity is an inevitable consequence of any tax system that has the aims of raising revenue, redistributing income and doing so in the least distortionary fashion possible.

Now any given tax system will typically have a design that is far from optimal as defined above. This may not always be associated with excessive complexity – it may just be that the tax rates are wrongly set. For example, the rate of tax on some 'bads' may be too low while that on some 'goods' is consequently too high. Re-balancing the system may not reduce its complexity as measured by the number of different things that are taxed at different rates.

But often tax systems do end up having too many different tax rates/reliefs as politicians pursue additional objectives which may have a strong political imperative at a particular moment of time, but which then recedes as the economic and political climate changes, leaving the rate/relief in place. This results in the need for periodic overhaul and reform. So the issue is whether, in reducing complexity, one is aiming to reduce what one might call this unnecessary complexity – which involves having some

---

5. See, for example, the research paper by Wojciech Kopczuk, 'Tax simplification and tax compliance: An economic perspective', available at: http://www.columbia.edu/ ~ wk2110/bin/epi.pdf (accessed on 15 November 2014) (reproduced in Max Sawicky (ed.), *Bridging the Tax Gap: Addressing the Crisis in Federal Tax Administration* 111 (Economic Policy Institute, 2006)), where the author states (at 19) that '[c]omplexity in the tax code should be thought of as the extent of variation in possible tax treatments of economically related activities. This kind of complexity naturally creates opportunities for tax avoidance, and it also causes difficulties for otherwise honest taxpayers'. This reference is also cited in Lugo & Vaillancourt, *Measuring Tax Complexity: Analytical Framework and Evidence for Individual Income Tax Preferences for Canada*, this volume, §9.02.
6. Since the different objectives can conflict with one another, the precise design depends on what weights are given to these objectives.

view of what the right degree of complexity is and where differences in tax rates are warranted.

So a major issue which has to be confronted is whether, in trying to measure complexity, the aim is to measure the extent to which the tax system is *unnecessarily complex*, or whether one is trying to measure just its total/absolute level of complexity without differentiating fundamental complexity from unnecessary complexity.

In order to measure unnecessary complexity one first has to ask what is the policy purpose behind various tax measures and whether the resulting system of rates is well-crafted to achieve those measures.

It will also be important to recognize that policy purposes can change over time. Here is an example. When vehicle excise tax was first introduced it was imposed as a revenue-raising measure. Since, over time, car ownership had become a necessity rather than a luxury, and so had become relatively price-insensitive, taxing vehicle ownership was quite a sensible policy from the point of view of raising revenue in a way that minimizes distortions, since it chimes with the objective of taxing most heavily those commodities that are in inelastic demand. But more recently vehicle duty has been seen as a tool to help achieve environmental objectives and, as a result, the rate of duty has been differentiated by emissions standards. So the *total* complexity of vehicle excise duty could be said to have increased. However, the change in policy objective could be thought to have raised the level of *fundamental* complexity, and so there may have been no change in the level of *unnecessary complexity*.

[B]   Operational Complexity

The second feature of a tax system is what might call its *operational complexity*, which essentially reflects how easy/costly it is for an honest taxpayer to comply with the informational, filing and payment requirements/obligations of the tax system.

It is important to recognize that, while there are many such costs, they do not all have to do with complexity. For example, for taxpayers with cash-flow issues there may be costs of meeting the payment obligations; there is an inevitable fixed cost in time/money in filling out one's tax return – however complex the system.

But there are aspects that I think can be said to relate to complexity, and what I have in mind is how easy it is for a taxpayer to map the various transactions they undertake and the terms in which they understand these transactions into the categories used by the tax system and the language in which these are described. To some extent this aspect of complexity will relate to the tax design complexity discussed above – other things being equal, the more distinctions that there are between different categories of transaction and the tax rates these attract, the more costly it may be for taxpayers to complete their returns.

But compliance complexity could arise for other reasons:

(1) The first is that the fit between the terms in which the taxpayer conducts their affairs and the way the tax system treats different transactions could be low. The tax system may treat as different types of transaction those that the

taxpayer treats as identical, or treat as identical transactions those that the taxpayer regards as different.

(2) Second, the language that is used to define transactions may be difficult for taxpayers to understand. There is an understandable desire by HM Revenue & Customs (HMRC) to write tax law and guidance in a language that reduces legal ambiguity and will survive challenge by lawyers and courts. But this can often sound rather stilted, and may not be the language in which individuals understand or describe their affairs. There may be more effective ways of combining the two objectives – using the legally tight terminology but giving an illustration in more common language which will be accurate in the vast majority of cases.

(3) Inconsistencies in tax law/guidance. At one point there were five different definitions of a 'child' in the US tax code.[7]

(4) Taxpayers may not fully perceive/understand the logic behind the various steps through which they have to go to complete tax returns. The complexity can be reduced by giving taxpayers as many opportunities as possible to answer a simple question and then skip a great number of steps that do not apply to them.

While these factors can contribute to what may be called *operational complexity* there is an extent to which this complexity will fall over time as taxpayers learn about the tax system, and become more familiar with its definitions. So a fifth aspect of *operational complexity* has to do with:

(5) Frequency of changes. In discussing *tax design* complexity (§4.02[A] above), I distinguished between *fundamental complexity* and *unnecessary complexity*. The same distinction could apply to *operational complexity*. There may be certain irreducible information requirements that a tax authority needs from taxpayers. But over time informational requirements can change – because, for example, of changes in technology that allow HMRC to capture information provided in one context and apply it in many others, thus reducing the need to capture essentially the same information repeatedly.

So drawing all this discussion together, when one talks of reducing tax complexity there are a number of different things that could be meant:

(1) Retaining the existing tax design but delivering it in a less complex way – essentially by reducing operational complexity, by, for example, writing legislation/guidance in a form that is easier to understand or removing unnecessary informational complexity.

(2) Retaining the given aims of the tax system but trying to achieve these in a less complex way – by reducing the *design* complexity which is *unnecessary*.

---

7. See, for example, Patricia Strach, *All in the Family: The Private Roots of American Public Policy*, 112, nn. 57–58 (Stanford University Press, 2007) who cites five prior to standardization in 2004, and also points out that, in the tax authority's instruction manual for the relevant forms (at the time), 'the explanation of who qualifies as a child spans a total of 17 pages'.

§4.03 WHAT ARE THE COSTS/CONSEQUENCES OF TAX COMPLEXITY?

Even if we could provide a tight definition and reliable measure of what I will call *tax complexity* per se as discussed in §4.02 above, there is the 'so what?' question of why it matters.

There are a number of reasons why tax complexity could matter.

(1) *Distortions.* If the design of the tax system is unnecessarily complex it could create unwarranted distortions, and this has costs that can, in principle, be measured as lost gross domestic product (GDP). However, I stress again that there is no automatic link between complexity and the distortionary costs of the tax system.

(2) *Non-Compliance.* Tax complexity can create opportunities for tax avoidance that can create significant costs to the economy in terms of both reduced efficiency and fairness. The efficiency losses arise for a number of reasons, amongst which are: (a) in the presence of avoidance, tax rates have to be higher than otherwise in order to raise given revenue, and (b) very bright people are being employed to both devise and then to detect and counter elaborate schemes of essentially paper transactions to move money around and reduce tax liabilities. Equity losses arise because these schemes are expensive and so it is typically the better off who can avail themselves of them. Nevertheless it is important to recognize that tax avoidance may actually be a way of reducing some of the potential distortionary costs induced by excessive complexity.

(3) *Compliance Costs.* Since the pioneering work in the UK of Cedric Sandford,[8] economists have put a lot of effort into measuring the costs to taxpayers of complying with the tax system. These costs can be measured in terms of the amount of resources – particularly time – that are incurred by taxpayers in meeting their obligations. In cases where taxpayers use professional advisers to undertake some of the tasks required in fulfilling compliance obligations, compliance costs can be measured by the financial costs incurred in using such professionals. While, as stressed above, not all compliance costs arise because of complexity, nevertheless the factors giving rise to what I called *operational complexity* will give rise to compliance costs.

(4) *Legal Uncertainty. Operational complexity* can potentially give rise to legal uncertainty.[9] This arises when taxpayers do not fully understand what their true tax liabilities are – how certain transactions should be treated for tax purposes – and/or when they do not understand the basis on which the tax

---

8. See, for example, Cedric Sandford, Michael Godwin & Peter Hardwick, *Administrative and Compliance Costs of Taxation* (Fiscal Publications, 1989).
9. The issue of legal uncertainty is discussed in many contexts, but has not been subject to any systematic analysis in the context of tax policy. In the joint paper, Yannis Katsoulacos & David Ulph, *Legal uncertainty, competition law enforcement procedures and optimal penalties*, Eur. J.L. & Econ. (Online, 2015), we formalize the concept and analyse its implications in the context of Competition Policy.

authority comes to a different view on how they should be treated, if the authority challenges the tax return.

It is important to get a sense of which taxpayers are affected by which degrees of complexity. The Pay As You Earn (PAYE) system in the UK is very complex because it has to cope with the full complexity of the vast range of individual circumstances that can conceivably arise. Yet the vast majority of PAYE taxpayers have very simple affairs and, if it is easy to identify which parts of the system apply to them, may be largely unaffected by this complexity. On the other hand the complexities of the international tax system have to be mastered by multinational corporations – who also need to invest resources to master the complexities of many other systems of international legislation – e.g., competition law, environmental regulation, intellectual property law. In both cases what appear to be very complex tax systems may have relatively low *marginal* costs on taxpayers.

§4.04   MEASURING TAX COMPLEXITY

Having discussed what might be meant by tax complexity and its implications, in this section I turn to consider some general issues relating to how one might measure it.

[A]   What to Measure

Following the previous discussion there are in principle two things that one might want to measure:

(1) The first is what one might call the *complexity of the tax system* per se - the factors referred to in §4.02. Here one might try to develop a measure of *design complexity* and of *operational complexity*. Both would raise significant conceptual and practical problems – certainly to construct direct measures. This would be particularly true if one was trying to measure what I called the *unnecessary* complexity of the tax system.

(2) The second is to measure the *costs of complexity* – the factors referred to in §4.03. While economists do have some measures of the distortionary costs of a tax system and of the compliance costs, it is more difficult to measure those parts that are directly attributable to complexity.

In principle one might want to measure both – and so know both how intrinsically complex the tax system is, *and* the costs of this complexity (how much it matters).

Of course, trying to measure these various dimensions of complexity directly raises formidable conceptual and practical problems. Some of the issues to be considered are as follows:

(1) One problem is that both the complexity of the tax system per se and the costs of the tax system involve multiple components. So even if one could come up

with satisfactory measures of the individual components, there remains the problem of combining these to get some overall measure. It is not at all clear where these weights would come from, so one may end up with a wide range of numbers depending on what weights are applied.

(2) Given the problems of getting direct measures of some of the components of complexity, there may be some indirect/proxy measures that could be used. For example one might think of measuring the number of pages of tax legislation as a proxy for design complexity.

(3) An alternative approach to getting indirect/proxy measures is 'crowdsourcing'. A carefully structured questionnaire covering the various dimensions of tax complexity could be sent to a variety of people with a professional interest in the tax system asking them to assess its complexity on a scale. By combining these scores one might get a fairly reliable measure of the various components and dimensions of complexity.

(4) Indeed in measuring some of the costs/consequences of complexity it is interesting to ask whether one is doing this because one is interested in these costs (as I have argued we should be) or whether one sees this as an indirect way of measuring the complexity of the tax system per se.

[B]   Why Measure?

In thinking about what might be a good measure of tax complexity it is worth asking what the measure is going to be used for. A measure might serve one purpose quite well but be a very poor measure for another purpose.

To give an example, one reason one might want to measure tax complexity is the fairly academic one of trying to compare tax complexity either over time or across countries. Using the number of pages of legislation may be a pretty blunt measure of tax design complexity, but it may do not too bad a job of tracking changes in complexity over time. However, it is unlikely to be anything like robust enough to serve as a cross-country measure of complexity.

My understanding is that the primary purpose of measuring tax complexity is to guide decisions as to where to direct efforts to reduce complexity.

But in that case it is far from clear why one would want to construct some aggregate measure. In thinking about the complexity of the tax system per se it would seem to be really quite important to separately measure *tax design complexity* from *operational complexity*, and to measure the costs of tax complexity separately from the measure of tax complexity per se. That way one can tell not just whether tax complexity is high but whether this is imposing a considerable cost, but can also tell whether to direct efforts to reforming the design of the tax system or the guidance/information that is given to taxpayers.

Given that, as I said above, there is a considerable degree of arbitrariness in the weights applied to combining various sub-measures into an overall measure of tax complexity, it seems far better to just keep track of all the sub-measures and use these to make decisions about where to direct reform.

However, I recognize that there is an attraction in having some overall measure, not least because it provides an indicator of whether there is a significant problem of complexity that needs to be addressed and whether steps that are taken to reduce complexity are effective.

§4.05   ASSESSING ONE PARTICULAR MEASURE

In this section I want to put all these considerations and reflections to work by considering a particular measure of Complexity produced by the Office of Tax Simplification (OTS).

My comments are based on the version of the measure that appears in the paper by Gareth Jones, Phillip Rice, Jeremy Sherwood and John Whiting, 'Developing a Tax Complexity Index for the UK' (February 2014).[10] As the authors acknowledge, this version of the index has been considerably modified from an earlier version, in part to take account of some comments I made on the earlier version in the previous version of this chapter that also appears on the OTS website:

(1) The index is interesting in that it tries to distinguish the measurement of the intrinsic or underlying complexity of the tax system from the impact that this complexity has on taxpayers. This distinction essentially captures the discussion in §4.02 and §4.03 respectively of this chapter. The OTS therefore produces two separate indices – one for each component of complexity. My view is that this is a very sensible procedure, not least because it enables one to distinguish between measures to reduce complexity through legislative changes to the underlying tax system and measures to improve the administration of a given tax system. The authors acknowledge that there is a temptation to try to combine these into a single index. My view is that, as the methodology is developed and improved, this may ultimately be possible, but in our current state of knowledge it is better to keep the two components separate.[11]

---

10. This is available on the OTS website as one of the papers published under the Tax Complexity Project, 28 February 2014: see https://www.gov.uk/government/publications/tax-complexity-project (accessed on 15 November 2014). See also John Whiting, Jeremy Sherwood & Gareth Jones, *The OTS and its Complexity Index*, this volume.
11. It may help to give an analogy. In the literature relating to the economics of inequality one can distinguish between various essentially statistical measures of the degree of inequality in a given distribution of income – corresponding to measures of the intrinsic/underlying degree of complexity – and concerns about the welfare consequences/costs of inequality. These latter ultimately rest on value judgments that reflect one's degree of inequality aversion. There are of course some sophisticated measures of inequality, such as the Atkinson measure of inequality that combine the two. But that requires a well-developed social welfare function and a whole apparatus for developing an understanding of the 'appropriate' degree of inequality aversion. Ultimately one may have a similarly well-developed welfare framework that encompasses all the various dimensions of tax complexity and so produce a single index that captures both the underlying degree of complexity and its welfare costs.

(2) In measuring tax complexity per se – or underlying complexity - there are elements that reflect *tax design complexity* - number of pages of legislation, number of reliefs, etc. - and others that measure some components of compliance complexity – e.g., readability. As indicated above, I think it would be better to separate these out more clearly and track them separately.

(3) I am not sure that the readability index adequately captures the factors in compliance complexity that I identified above (§4.02[B]).

(4) In measuring tax design complexity, a number of different measures are used – number of pages of legislation, number of reliefs, etc. There are a couple of points to make:

    (a) I am not persuaded that the number of pages of legislation is an appropriate measure of complexity. The authors themselves seem somewhat ambivalent about it, saying (at 10) that it 'can contribute towards an impression of complexity, but it can also make legislation easier to understand' and noting that '[f]or the present we have retained length as a measure of complexity partly because it is a simple and objective measure but mainly because most people do seem to view length as an indicator of complexity'.

    (b) There may some element of double-counting involved since the number of reliefs may also have a bearing on the length of legislation.

(5) Turning to the component of the index that measures the impact or costs of complexity, one factor that is included is the average ability of the taxpayer. I understand the rationale for including this factor but have the following observations:

    (a) The rationale has to do with the extent to which the costs of complexity fall on relatively sophisticated or relatively unsophisticated taxpayers. But since this seems to be a distributional matter it is not clear why the average distribution of ability is the relevant thing to measure. Maybe we need a more sophisticated measure of the distribution of taxpayer ability.

    (b) While less sophisticated taxpayers may take longer to come to terms with a given level of complexity than do more sophisticated taxpayers, the value of time may be higher for sophisticated than for unsophisticated taxpayers.

    (c) However, counteracting this is the consideration that, to the extent that sophisticated taxpayers are cash-rich but time-poor, they have the option of paying others to handle complexity on their behalf.

    (d) I am far from persuaded that HMRC operating costs should be included in a measure of tax complexity. Of course, just as complexity can have implications for the costs incurred by taxpayers in complying with the tax system, so, other things being equal, increased complexity could lead to increased costs of administering the tax system. But other things are not equal. If the Chancellor (Minister of Finance) decides to cut public expenditure and so reduces HMRC's operating costs, that does not mean that the tax system has become less complex.[12]

So my overall view is that there are some interesting elements in this measure of complexity but, as the authors recognize, this is still a very preliminary measure that has considerable scope for further development.

---

12. Indeed, over time, such a cut in expenditure might lead to increased complexity to the extent that less resources were devoted to drafting and checking legislation etc.

CHAPTER 5

An Integrated Approach to the Economic Measurement of the Costs of Tax Complexity[*]

Binh Tran-Nam

§5.01   INTRODUCTION

Taxation represents perhaps the most important relationship between the private sector (individuals, households and firms) and the government in modern societies. Tax revenue is the most significant source of finance for the provision of essential services such as education, healthcare, transport and social security. In his three-function framework of the public sector, Musgrave identified the role of taxation in influencing resource allocation, macroeconomic stabilization and income redistribution.[1] Good tax policy is thus essential for good government, personal welfare and economic growth.

Tax simplicity was formally recognized as an integral part of good tax policy at least from as early as the birth of modern economics.[2] Despite that early theoretical

[*] This chapter is a revised version of the paper presented at the Tax System Complexity Conference jointly organized by Monash University and the University of New South Wales Australia, Prato, 29–30 September 2014. It is derived from an Australian Research Council (ARC) Linkage project being conducted by the author in conjunction with Professor Chris Evans (UNSW Australia), Professor Richard Krever (Monash University) and Dr Philip Lignier (University of Tasmania) together with the Institute of Chartered Accountants in Australia (ICAA). The views expressed in this chapter are the author's and not necessarily those of the ARC or ICAA. Useful comments by Professor Joel Slemrod (as the discussant of the paper) and participants at the Conference are grateful acknowledged.

1. Richard A. Musgrave, *The Theory of Public Finance – A Study in Public Economy*, 5-6 (McGraw-Hill, 1959).
2. Adam Smith, *An Inquiry into the Nature and Causes of the Wealth of Nations*, Bk. 5, Ch. II ([1776] Dent, London, 1947).

recognition and repeated calls for tax simplification around the world in the last thirty years,[3] tax systems in developed countries have evolved into complex ones. In Australia, a Federal Court judge remarked that tax 'legislation in general is simply far too complex'.[4] In the same year, a US report noted that 'taxpayers and businesses spend 7.6 billion hours and incur significant out of pocket expenses each year complying with federal income tax filing requirements' as a direct result of tax complexity.[5] This has prompted tax scholars to remark that 'simplification is the most widely quoted but least widely observed of the goals of tax policy'.[6]

Before proceeding further, it is helpful to note that the two fundamental issues facing any economy are efficiency (the 'size of the cake') and equity (how it is 'divided between mouths'). In this sense, the ultimate aim of any tax system is to ensure that the economy functions as efficiently and equitably as possible. Thus, tax simplicity is desirable as a property rather than an ultimate goal of the tax system.[7] Since fewer economic resources are diverted from productive use in a simpler tax system, simplicity can, in some sense, be regarded as a part of efficiency. However, the relationship between simplicity and equity appears to be more complicated. Policy equity is often cited as a cause of tax complexity yet a complex tax system can also reduce the progressivity of the tax system.[8]

The present chapter is motivated by the observation that any first step toward much needed tax simplification necessarily involves the measurement and monitoring of the adverse impact of tax complexity. There is now a substantial body of literature on the 'collection costs'[9] (defined as the sum of tax compliance and administrative costs) of the tax system.[10] While the estimation of tax collection costs is important as the first step in the process of tax simplification, these costs alone do not seem to fully capture the costs of tax complexity. A more systematic and integrated approach seems to be needed.

---

3. See, for example, the Tax Reform Act of 1986 (US); Australian Treasury (circulated by Treasurer Hon. P. Costello), *Not a New Tax, a New Tax System* (August 1998); Australia's Future Tax System Review Panel (K. Henry, chair), *Australia's Future Tax System: Report to the Treasurer* (2009) (Henry Review); Stuart Adam, Tim Besley, Richard Blundell, Steve Bond, Robert Chote, Malcolm Gammie, Paul Johnson, Gareth Myles & James Poterba (eds) for the Institute for Fiscal Studies, *Dimensions of Tax Design: The Mirrlees Review* (Oxford University Press, 2010) (Mirrlees Review).
4. Justice Nye Perram, *The perils of complexity: Why more law is bad law*, 39(4) Austl. Tax Rev. 179, 184 (2010).
5. President's Economic Recovery Advisory Board (PERAB), *Report on Tax Reform Options: Simplification, Compliance and Corporate Taxation*, 3 (2010).
6. Stanley S. Surrey & Gerard M. Brannon, *Simplification and Equity as Goals of Tax Policy*, 9(4) Wm. & Mary L. Rev. 915, 915 (1968).
7. The author is grateful to Joel Slemrod for suggesting this line of argument.
8. Binh Tran-Nam, 'Tax compliance costs methodology: A research agenda for the future', in Chris Evans, Jeff Pope & John Hasseldine (eds), *Taxation Compliance Costs: A Festschrift for Cedric Sandford* 51, 65 (Prospect, 2001).
9. Alternatively known as 'administrative costs' (see Joseph Stiglitz, *Economics of the Public Sector*, 464 (3rd ed., Norton, 2000)) or 'operating costs'.
10. For a comprehensive review of these studies, see Chris Evans, 'Taxation compliance and administrative costs: An overview', in Michael Lang, Christine Obermair, Josef Schuch, Claus Staringer & Patrick Weninger (eds), *Tax Compliance Costs for Companies in an Enlarged European Community* 447 (Linde Verlag & Kluwer Law International, 2008).

The principal aim of this chapter is to contribute to the growing literature on the measurement of tax complexity by exploring different types of costs of tax complexity in a systematic fashion. In particular, it attempts to examine the relationship, if any, of the various measures of costs of tax complexity. In this sense, the chapter intends to provide a conceptual basis for future empirical studies in this area. Its scope is primarily confined to the costs of tax complexity that arise from tax compliance. Thus, the costs related to other aspects of taxpayers' behavioural responses (such as tax lobbying, evasion and avoidance) lie outside the scope of the chapter. Similarly, the potentially adverse effect of tax complexity on tax equity is also beyond the scope of the chapter.

The remainder of the chapter is organized as follows. Section §5.02 presents a brief examination of the relative neglect of tax system complexity by economists, especially public finance economists. This section explores the rationale for the lack of attention given to tax compliance cost research by economists and the recent rise of interest in tax compliance costs from both private researchers and government agencies. Section §5.03 then provides a succinct but thorough overview of the concept of tax complexity including its meaning, causes and indicators. This section is intended to serve as a contextual and conceptual framework for the subsequent discussions. In §5.04, a simple model of tax compliance is presented and the various types of tax complexity costs are discussed. In addition to the familiar tax collection costs, the indirect costs (efficiency costs induced by tax complexity) and the macroeconomic costs of tax complexity are also considered and linked. It is suggested that the conventional approach to measuring the costs of tax complexity underestimates the true costs of tax complexity. Section §5.05 concludes.

§5.02 THE RELATIVE NEGLECT OF TAX SIMPLICITY/COMPLEXITY

As suggested in §5.01 above, tax simplicity (or its mirror, tax complexity) was explicitly mentioned in Adam Smith's 1776 path-breaking classic. In fact, among his four principles for good tax policy, 'Certainty' and 'Convenience' were wholly concerned with tax simplicity, while 'Economy' was concerned with both collection and efficiency costs of taxation. Despite this early promising start, tax simplicity has been neglected as a criterion for good tax policy for different reasons. Sandford, Godwin and Hardwick suggested that tax simplicity was largely ignored by early nineteenth century classical economists such as John Stuart Mill in favour of tax equity and, to a lesser extent, tax efficiency.[11] In fact, the first empirical study of tax compliance costs only appeared about eighty years ago.[12]

---

11. Cedric Sandford, Michael Godwin & Peter Hardwick, *Administrative and Compliance Costs of Taxation*, 25–26 (Fiscal Publications, 1989).
12. Robert M. Haig, *The Cost to Business Concerns of Compliance with Tax Laws*, 24(11) Mgmt. Rev. 323 (1935) (this is Haig of the Haig-Simons definition of income fame).

Interestingly enough, according to Slemrod and Yitzhaki,[13] almost all public finance textbooks, until the mid-1950s, devoted considerable attention and space to tax administration, compliance and enforcement. However, beginning in the 1960s, such issues almost disappeared from the literature, except in the case of developing economies. As a result of the development of the optimal theory of taxation in the early 1970s, economists have further shifted their interests away from tax system complexity and tax administration.

This disregard has, to a lesser extent, persisted until today, especially in public finance, and is evident from a quick examination of leading textbooks and academic journals in this field. For example, Boadway and Wildasin[14] and Rosen and Gayer[15] contained nothing on tax simplicity. Stiglitz provided in Chapter 25 of his book a short section on collection costs of the US tax system.[16] Groenewegen devoted about one page to tax simplicity and compliance costs, and referred to some Australian studies.[17] Leading public finance journals such as the *Journal of Public Economics*, *National Tax Journal*, *Public Finance*, *Fiscal Studies*, etc. publish a very small proportion of articles relating to tax simplicity or tax collection costs. Most tellingly, the *Journal of Economic Literature* (JEL) classification H2 (Taxation, Subsidies, and Revenue) contains efficiency, incidence and even tax evasion, but nothing on tax simplicity/complexity.

A similar situation exists at the tax policy-making level. In the various tax reform reports in the English-speaking world, simplicity has typically ranked well below efficiency/neutrality and equity as a goal of tax reform. For example, the Meade Report on direct taxation reform ranked simplicity as fourth among six characteristics of a good tax structure.[18] Similarly, in a chapter on the political economy of taxation prepared for the Mirrlees Review, Alt, Preston and Sibieta did not even mention 'tax simplicity' or 'tax simplification' once.[19] These views have influenced the wave of substantial tax reforms around the world in the past thirty years. While these reforms have exhibited many efficiency-enhancing features (such as lower income tax rates, broader tax bases and more uniform and neutral tax structure), more often than not only lip service has been paid to the need for tax simplification.

The reasons for this neglect are many-fold:[20]

- it is extremely difficult to quantify tax complexity and incorporate it in formal normative models of taxation;

---

13. Joel Slemrod & Shlomo Yitzhaki, *The costs of taxation and the marginal efficiency costs of funds*, 43(1) Intl. Monetary Fund Staff Papers 172, 172 (1996).
14. Robin Boadway & David Wildasin, *Public Sector Economics* (2nd ed., Little, Brown & Co., 1984).
15. Harvey S. Rosen & Ted Gayer, *Public Finance* (8th ed., McGraw-Hill Irwin, 2008).
16. Stiglitz, above n. 9.
17. Peter Groenewegen, *Public Finance in Australia: Theory and Practice*, 121 (3rd ed., Prentice Hall, 1990).
18. Institute for Fiscal Studies, *The Structure and Reform of Direct Taxation*, 7 (George Allen and Unwin, 1978).
19. James Alt, Ian Preston & Luke Sibieta, 'The Political Economy of Tax Policy', in Adam, Besley, Blundell, Bond, Chote, Gammie, Johnson, Myles & Poterba (eds), above n. 3, at 1204.
20. See Binh Tran-Nam, Chris Evans, Michael Walpole & Katherine Ritchie, *Tax Compliance Costs: Research Methodology and Empirical Evidence from Australia*, 53(2) Nat'l Tax J. 229, 230 (2000).

- there are unresolved problems in defining and measuring tax compliance costs (to be further discussed in §5.04);
- tax compliance cost estimates typically require painstaking research involving the collection of large amounts of data that is not available from published sources;
- there are problems with quality of survey data arising from low response rates and memory recollection; and
- tax compliance costs are thought to be inevitable or trivial.

The difficulty of incorporating the complexity of tax laws into the optimal theory of taxation represents perhaps the most discouraging feature of tax complexity to public finance theorists. As pointed out by Slemrod,[21] the modern – now standard – theory of taxation is a typical example of high-level abstract economic models. It is highly stylized and makes a simplifying assumption that emphasizes certain aspects of taxation at the expense of others. More specifically, the optimal theory of taxation assumes that both the government can administer its tax instruments and individual taxpayers can comply with their tax obligations costlessly. Assuming away tax system complexity in this way allows tax researchers to focus on efficiency and equity aspects of taxation, but it hampers addressing many key, practical issues of tax policy.

There are hardly any theoretical models of taxation that formally incorporate tax complexity/compliance costs into their analysis. Slemrod's work is a rare and interesting exception.[22] In this model of tax compliance behaviour based on utility maximization, a typical individual taxpayer (in the US) chooses how much time and money to spend on tax compliance to maximize that taxpayer's utility subject to a modified financial constraint on consumption. Slemrod's analysis focuses on the computational rather than planning aspect of tax compliance. Further, it is not clear how his model can be extended to the more relevant case of business taxpayers.

The neglect of tax complexity drove Sandford in the early 1970s to label tax compliance costs the 'hidden costs of taxation'.[23] Nevertheless, there has been a steady growth in international interest, particularly among OECD countries, in tax compliance costs, both by academic researchers and by governments. Sandford subsequently identified a number of reasons for the growth in interest in tax compliance costs.[24] These include:

- changes in technology (facilitating large-scale computer-driven surveys);
- the introduction of value added tax (VAT) regimes in many countries (with high and visible compliance costs);

21. Joel Slemrod, *Optimal Taxation and Optimal Tax Systems*, 4(1) J. Econ. Persp. 157 (1990).
22. Joel Slemrod, 'Complexity, Compliance Costs, and Tax Evasion', in Jeffrey A. Roth & John T. Scholz (eds), *Taxpayer Compliance, Volume 2: Social Science Perspectives* 156 (University of Pennsylvania Press, 1989).
23. Cedric Sandford, *Hidden Costs of Taxation* (Institute for Fiscal Studies, 1973).
24. Cedric Sandford (ed.), *Tax Compliance Costs Measurement and Policy*, 5–7 (Fiscal Publications, 1995).

- the growth of enterprise cultures involving the small business sector (where compliance costs are particularly onerous); and
- the increasing complexity of tax systems.

It is possible to add to the above list government's commitments to reduce business 'red tape' in the developed world. Specific examples include the European Union's Action Programme for reducing administrative burdens stemming from European Union legislation,[25] the establishment in the UK of the Office of Tax Simplification (OTS) charged with the responsibility of addressing existing complexity of the tax system,[26] and New Zealand's *Better Public Services* programme which aims to reduce business costs from dealing with government by 25% within five years.[27]

Over the past three decades, tax compliance cost studies have spread from 'initial' countries (US, Canada, Germany and UK) to virtually all parts of the globe, including Western Europe (Ireland, Netherlands, Spain, Portugal, Sweden and Switzerland), Australasia (Australia and New Zealand), Asia (Singapore, Malaysia, Hong Kong, India, South Korea, Thailand), Eastern Europe (Croatia and Slovenia), Africa (Tanzania, Ethiopia and South Africa) and South America (Brazil).[28] In 1998–1999, the Organisation for Economic Co-operation and Development (OECD) undertook a study on the administrative and regulatory burdens (including tax compliance burden) faced by small and medium enterprises (SMEs) in eleven selected countries, including Australia, Austria, Belgium, Finland, Iceland, Mexico, New Zealand, Norway, Portugal, Spain and Sweden.[29] More recently, the World Bank has sponsored various surveys of business tax compliance costs in many developing countries including Armenia, Burundi, Georgia, India, Kenya, Lao PDR, Nepal, Peru, South Africa, Ukraine, Uzbekistan, Vietnam and Yemen.[30]

To summarize, the past thirty years have witnessed the transformation of tax compliance costs from the 'hidden costs of taxation' into an established field of study, owing to the work of many tax scholars around the world, particularly the studies of Sandford and Slemrod.

---

25. European Commission, *Europe Can Do Better – Best Practices for Reducing Administrative Burdens*, 2 (2012).
26. HM Treasury, *Office of Tax Simplification Framework Document*, 1 (2010), https://www.gov.uk/government/uploads/system/uploads/attachment_data/file/193545/ots_framework_document_jul10.pdf (accessed on 26 July 2014).
27. Ministry of Business, Innovation and Employment (NZ), *Better Public Services for Business*, 1 (2012).
28. Most of these studies have been reviewed in Evans, 'Taxation compliance and administrative costs: An overview', above n. 10. Note that the South Korean study on tax compliance costs is in Korean.
29. OECD, *Businesses' Views on Red Tape: Administrative and Regulatory Burdens on Small and Medium Sized Enterprises* (2001).
30. See Jacqueline Coolidge, *Findings of tax compliance cost surveys in developing countries*, 10(2) eJournal of Tax Research 250 (2012).

§5.03 REVIEW OF TAX COMPLEXITY

Despite its widespread usage, the term tax complexity is capable of a variety of different interpretations. It is thus useful to consider the meaning, causes and indicators of tax complexity.

[A] Meaning of Tax Complexity and Tax Simplification

To begin with, tax complexity is a multi-dimensional and multi-disciplinary concept that cannot be adequately captured by a single definition or measure. It means different things to different people depending on their perspectives or interests. For example, to a businessperson, tax complexity means the time and monetary costs spent in complying with the requirements of business tax laws. To a tax accountant, tax complexity refers to the time that accountant needs to expend in order to prepare an income tax return or to provide tax advice (including tax planning, objections or appeals). To a tax lawyer, tax complexity may refer to the difficulty with which a body of tax legislation can be read, understood and applied in practice.

There are two principal approaches in characterizing tax complexity. The first is to describe tax complexity by a set of collectively exhaustive, fundamental attributes. In his early and authoritative analysis (referred to in §5.02 above),[31] Slemrod defined tax complexity in terms of four core attributes: 'predictability' (certainty of tax law), 'enforceability' (tax administrative costs), 'difficulty' (computational tax compliance costs) and 'manipulability' (tax planning costs). Predictability and enforceability essentially pertain to the tax law while difficulty and manipulability refer to taxpayers' responses to the tax law.[32] Slemrod's pioneering approach has been adopted by other tax researchers, admittedly with different expressions or more elaboration.[33]

An alternative is based on the process approach which classifies tax complexity by where it occurs during different stages of the operation of the tax system.[34] According to this approach we can distinguish between policy complexity, statutory complexity, administrative complexity and compliance complexity. Policy complexity and compliance complexity have been referred to by Ulph as design complexity and operational complexity, respectively.[35]

---

31. Slemrod, 'Complexity, Compliance Costs, and Tax Evasion', above n. 22, at 157.
32. Strictly speaking, difficulty and manipulability are not truly primary attributes as they can be regarded as functions of (or at least highly correlated with) predictability.
33. See, for example, Edward J. McCaffery, *The Holy Grail of Tax Simplification*, [1990] 5 Wis. L. Rev. 1267, 1269–1273; Graeme S. Cooper, *Themes and issues in tax simplification*, 10(4) Austl. Tax F. 417, 424 (1993); Peter Harris, *Corporate Shareholder Income Taxation and Allocating Taxing Rights between Countries*, 8–10 (IBFD Publications, 1996).
34. Chris Evans & Binh Tran-Nam, *Managing tax system complexity: Building bridges through pre-filled tax returns*, 25(2) Austl. Tax F. 245, 249 (2010).
35. David Ulph, 'Measuring Tax Complexity', this volume.

In the same vein, it is also possible to make a distinction between legal and effective complexity.[36] Legal simplicity (complexity) refers to the ease (difficulty) with which a particular tax law can be read, interpreted and applied in various hypothetical or actual situations. The principle of certainty is perhaps the most important single requirement of legal simplicity. Certainty means that a taxpayer's 'true' tax liability can be uniquely determined from a minimal supply of relevant data with reasonable efforts. Effective (or economic) complexity refers to the time and effort (value of resources) expended by society in raising a given amount of tax revenue. In shifting from comprehensibility to applicability, effective complexity emphasizes the interaction of the tax law and the economy.[37] While the definition of effective complexity encompasses legal complexity, the two measures do not always move in the same direction. For example, effective complexity may fall (as a result of an improvement in information technology) while legal complexity stays constant or increases slightly. Similarly, when a particular tax is replaced by a legally simpler tax, effective complexity may nevertheless rise if many more taxpayers have to comply with the new tax.

A number of secondary attributes of tax complexity emerge from the above discussion. First, in the absence of a universally accepted, cardinal measure, tax complexity is essentially a comparative concept. It is more meaningful to say that a proportional income tax schedule 'A' is less complex than a progressive income tax schedule 'B', rather than saying that the proportional income tax schedule A is simple. Second, when comparing the complexity of two alternative taxes, it is important, especially from an effective perspective, to ensure that the two taxes yield potentially the same level of revenue. Third, tax complexity is an interactive concept in the sense that the observed level of complexity in a tax system depends not only on government policy intentions and tax administrative procedures, but also on behavioural responses of taxpayers. As elaborated in the next sub-section (§5.03[B]), for any given tax system and economy, there is a wide range of possible levels of tax complexity.

Because tax complexity has several different meanings, so has tax simplification. To simplify a tax law/system could mean any combination of the following:

- to improve the tax legislation/system in the linguistic and structural sense; or
- to make the tax legislation/system simpler in the content or conceptual sense; or
- to lower the burden of tax administrative requirements; or
- to reduce the collection costs (in an absolute or relative sense) of the tax law/tax system.

Thus, one of the fundamental difficulties with tax simplification is that the above objectives are not always jointly compatible.

---

36. Binh Tran-Nam, *Tax reform and tax simplification: Some conceptual issues and a preliminary assessment*, 21(3) Syd. L. Rev. 500, 508 (1999).
37. In this sense, the relationship between statutory complexity and effective complexity is somewhat analogous to that between local income tax progression and overall tax progressivity.

[B] Causes of Tax Complexity

Various causes of tax complexity have been identified in the literature. In this chapter I choose to continue the previous approach in my study with Evans in 2010[38] which breaks down the sources of tax complexity by reference to the interaction between the government and taxpayers. Since these sources have been well discussed, they are only briefly mentioned here.

[1] Within the Direct Control of Government

Sources of complexity that are directly within the control of the government include protection of revenue, use of tax law for non-policy objectives, the distinction between taxes and transfers,[39] tax base broadening (that increases the number of taxpayers and third parties), the frequency of tax law changes, tax law drafting, minimization of cash flow losses by tax administrators, and judicial traditions.[40]

[2] Partly within the Direct Control of Government

Sources of complexity which are partly within the direct control of the government include tax culture[41] and the growing complexity of the domestic and global economy (e.g., the use of complex business structures, increase in the number of people owning equity investments, globalization, etc.).

[3] Outside the Direct Control of Government

Finally, there are a number of sources of complexity which the government cannot directly control, though various policy interventions may be able to 'nudge' taxpayers in more favoured directions. These include household and business preferences for tax liability minimization (e.g., the 'tax refund' culture in Australia), tax practitioner preference for complexity (more chargeable hours) and aggressive planning (partnership between high-risk tax practitioners and high-risk taxpayers).

For very large taxpayers (e.g., high wealth individuals or multinational firms), the complexity of the tax system can be viewed as the outcome of a non-cooperative, taxpayers-versus-tax authorities game. A complication of this game is that the behaviour of taxpayers is unlikely to be independent (e.g., successful tax planning activities

---

38. Tran-Nam & Evans, *Managing tax system complexity: Building bridges through pre-filled tax returns*, above n. 34, at 251–252.
39. Joel Slemrod, 'Complexity in the Australian Tax and Transfer System', in *Melbourne Institute Australia's Future Tax and Transfer Policy Conference: Proceedings of a Conference* 257, 263–264 (Melbourne Institute of Applied Economic and Social Research, 2010).
40. Richard Krever, *Taming complexity in Australian income tax*, 25(4) Syd. L. Rev. 467 (2003).
41. The term 'tax culture' in this chapter is narrowly interpreted to mean the extent to which taxpayers engage in tax avoidance and tax evasion and the extent of the tax administrators' efforts to combat these schemes.

by some taxpayers may induce other taxpayers to engage in similar activities). For any given tax law, the equilibrium complexity depends on the factors discussed in this section (§5.03[B][1]-[3]) and ranges from most complex and wasteful outcome (high-tax planning, high-auditing costs) to least complex and wasteful outcome (low-tax planning, low-auditing costs).

[C]   Indicators of Tax Complexity

As a multi-dimensional concept, tax complexity has been captured by a variety of measures. The various, alternative indicators of tax complexity that have been considered in the literature include:[42]

- the number of all taxes at various levels of government in a country (policy complexity);
- the length of the tax code in terms of words or pages (statutory complexity);
- the readability of the tax legislation, e.g., Flesch readability index or Cloze testing[43] (statutory complexity); note that these are measures of readability in the linguistic sense, not in the content sense;
- the extent of use of professional tax advisers by taxpayers (compliance complexity);
- tax collection costs, i.e., the sum of tax administrative and compliance costs (administrative and compliance complexity); and
- the extent of tax disputes (legal and effective complexity).

There appears to exist a trade-off in the sense that more (less) meaningful indicators tend to be less (more) precisely measured. For example, the number of taxes is not a particularly meaningful indicator of tax complexity but it can be exactly measured. Conversely, tax collection costs are the most relevant measure of tax complexity but they cannot be precisely measured.

§5.04   COSTS OF TAX COMPLEXITY

To a certain extent, the complexity of a tax system is unavoidable (due partly to the growing complexity of commercial transactions in the increasingly globalized world) and may even be desirable (e.g., to protect the integrity of the tax base). However, excessive complexity has many adverse effects on the economy and all stakeholders. To study the costs of tax complexity in a systematic fashion, it seems useful to start by

---

42. As noted in §5.03[A], strictly speaking, tax complexity is a comparative concept so that it is more meaningful to say 'tax A is more complex than (a revenue-equivalent) tax B' than 'tax A is complex'.
43. The Flesch index, available from Microsoft Word, has been used extensively to measure the readability of accounting and finance information, tax legislation and business communication textbooks. It is based upon the average number of syllables per word and words per sentence. The Cloze test is a procedure in which a passage of text is chosen, then every fifth word is deleted and participants are required to insert the missing words.

considering how taxpayers respond to the requirements imposed upon them by the tax system.

[A] A Simple Model of Tax Compliance

Tax compliance/non-compliance has been widely discussed in the tax literature.[44] Figure 5.1 below illustrates a simple model of tax compliance in which the taxpayer compliance/non-compliance behaviour can be viewed as the outcome of the interaction of three building blocks: internal factors, external factors and the tax system.

Internal factors refer to two basic attributes of taxpayers: their tax morale[45] (intrinsic willingness to pay taxes) and understanding of legal and administrative requirements of the tax system (own knowledge, ability to hire paid tax intermediaries, etc.). External factors refer to relevant environmental attributes such as: (a) social norms/tax culture (ethical values, perception of tax cheating as a crime, etc.); (b) occupational characteristics (opportunities to evade taxes due to cash payments, lack of third party reporting and auditing trail, etc.); (c) accounting rules and practices (how accounting profit is defined relative to taxable profit); and (d) tax intermediary attitudes and practices (especially related to tax planning). The tax system can be represented by tax laws, how tax bases are defined (exemptions, deductions, etc.), tax rates, tax administrative practices including tax remittance, audits, enforcement and dispute resolution, and tax decisions made by tribunals and courts.

The relationship between any two building blocks can be bi-directional although the effects of external factors or the tax system on internal factors are expected to be much stronger than the corresponding effects in the opposite direction. The strength of the influence is indicated by whether the line is dark or dotted. For example, social norms and tax culture (external factors) or taxpayers' perceptions of tax policy equity and procedural justice (tax system) may affect their tax morale (internal factors). While taxpayers (personal or business) cannot in general individually affect external factors or the tax system, high-profile wealthy individuals or large corporate taxpayers may be able to influence social norms, tax culture or tax laws.

As a result of the interaction between internal factors, external factors and the tax system, various behavioural outcomes are conceivable. They include:

---

44. See, for example, Günter Schmölders, *Fiscal Psychology: A New Branch of Public Finance*, 12(4) Nat'l Tax J. 340 (1959); Burkhard Strümpel, 'The contribution of survey research to public finance', in Alan T. Peacock (ed., with assistance of Dieter Biehl), *Quantitative Analysis in Public Finance* 13 (Praeger, 1969); Michael G. Allingham & Agnar Sandmo, *Income Tax Evasion: A Theoretical Analysis*, 1(3-4) J. Pub. Econ. 323 (1972); Betty R. Jackson & Valerie C. Milliron, *Tax compliance research: findings, problems and prospects*, [1986] 5 J. Acct. Lit. 125; James Andreoni, Brian Erard & Jonathan Feinstein, *Tax Compliance*, 36(2) J. Econ. Lit. 818 (1998); Nigar Hashimzade, Gareth D. Myles & Binh Tran-Nam, *Applications of Behavioural Economics to Tax Evasion*, 27(5) J. Econ. Surv. 941 (2013).
45. A concept which was first introduced in 1968 by Strümpel and has become increasingly popular in recent years. It is important to recognize that tax morale is applicable to individuals, partnerships and small businesses but less so to incorporated businesses.

- attempting to change tax laws through means such as lobbying;
- complying with the tax system, whether voluntarily or involuntarily (e.g., via tax audits, penalties and fines);
- not complying unintentionally (e.g., due to lack of knowledge of the tax system);
- not complying intentionally (and succeeding).

Figure 5.1   A Simple Model of Tax Compliance

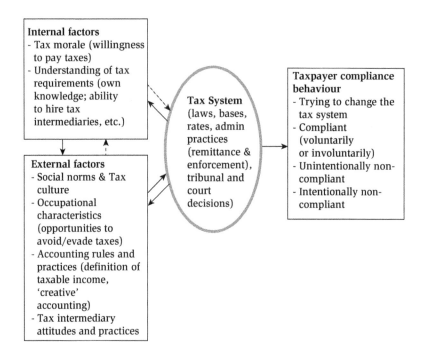

Each of the compliance behavioural outcomes leads to different types of costs to the economy. Attempting to change tax laws can potentially give rise to lobbying costs, corruption and rent-seeking losses. Trying to comply with tax system requirements can give rise to efficiency costs, compliance costs, administrative costs and other indirect costs (to be further discussed, §5.04[B]-[D] below). Attempting not to comply with the tax system requirements leads to tax avoidance costs, tax evasion costs, tax revenue losses, etc. As stated at the outset (§5.01), the focus of this chapter is to examine the costs of tax complexity associated with tax compliance. These include tax collection, indirect and macroeconomic costs, and they will be further discussed below (§5.04[B]-[D]). The costs of tax system complexity associated with non-compliance are beyond the scope of this chapter.

It also seems worthwhile to comment on the interaction between tax complexity and taxpayer compliance behaviour, and between tax complexity and equity. There is empirical evidence that tax complexity gives rise to both intentional and unintentional non-compliance – 'studies suggest that non-compliance is higher among filers faced with complex eligibility rules and recordkeeping requirements'.[46] As discussed previously in this sub-section, this relationship can be bi-directional, i.e., intentional non-compliance (e.g., aggressive tax planning or evasion) may itself further complicate the tax system. A similar interaction exists between tax complexity and tax equity. Concerns for equity may complicate tax laws, and, conversely, tax complexity can have an adverse impact upon equity. Thus, while tax complexity may arise as a result of policy concerns for equity, regressive tax compliance costs can reduce the progressivity of the income tax system.[47] Moreover, complexity 'reduces the system's transparency and undermines trust in its fairness'.[48] The interactive relationships lie beyond the scope of this chapter.

In the remainder of this section, three separate but related measures of costs of tax complexity are examined in turn: direct, indirect and macroeconomic costs.

[B]   Direct Costs

The direct costs of tax complexity refer to the value of resources taken away from productive activities to operate the tax system. Direct costs of tax complexity are conventionally measured as the sum of tax administrative and compliance costs. Tax administrative costs are defined as the costs incurred by the tax authorities in collecting tax revenue, whereas tax compliance costs are those incurred by taxpayers or third parties in satisfying the requirements of the tax system.[49] This chapter focuses on tax compliance costs because: (i) compliance costs are conceptually more problematic than administrative costs, and (ii) the magnitude of tax compliance costs far outweighs that of tax administrative costs.[50]

Tax administrative costs are typically measured as the costs incurred by tax administrators in collecting tax revenue. However, the operation of a tax system involves the government at different stages and in various capacities: tax policy design and planning, tax law drafting and enactment, administration and enforcement, and tax dispute resolution.[51] In principle, all the resources expended in carrying out the above activities should be counted toward the collection costs of the tax system. As a minimum, the recurrent costs of resolving tax disputes (incurred by tribunals and courts) should be included in measuring tax administrative costs as the extent of tax disputes is an indicator of tax system complexity.

---

46. President's Economic Recovery Advisory Board, above n. 5, at 3.
47. Tran-Nam, 'Tax compliance costs methodology: A research agenda for the future', above n. 8, at 63–66.
48. President's Economic Recovery Advisory Board, above n. 5, at 3.
49. Sandford, Godwin & Hardwick, *Administrative and Compliance Costs of Taxation*, above n. 11, at 3, 10.
50. Evans, 'Taxation compliance and administrative costs: An overview', above n. 10, at 457.
51. Tran-Nam, *Tax reform and tax simplification: Some conceptual issues and a preliminary assessment*, above n. 36, at 511.

Tax administrative and compliance costs are transferable, e.g., a government may place responsibility for some aspects of tax collection either on the private sector or its own tax administration; or personal income tax may be partly or wholly self-assessed or revenue authority-assessed. Similarly, it may be argued that the costs of tax policy planning, drafting and enactment on the one hand and the costs of tax administration, tax compliance and tax dispute resolution on the other are also transferable. For example, if the drafting of a sophisticated piece of tax legislation is underfunded, this may lead to more costly tax disputes later. This endorses the need to consider the collection costs of a tax system in totality rather than by reference to its isolated components.

Despite its seemingly clear-cut definition, the measurement of tax compliance costs is anything but straightforward. A brief review of estimating issues is outlined below.

At the conceptual level, there has been a debate about what legitimately constitute tax compliance activities? A distinction has been drawn between avoidable (voluntary) and unavoidable (involuntary) tax compliance activities, where tax computation is regarded as unavoidable and tax planning as avoidable. This distinction, first introduced by Johnston,[52] gave rise to an ongoing debate which can never be fully resolved. A related debate is the distinction between preventable and inevitable costs of tax compliance. Inevitable costs refer to those resulting when a taxpayer employs the least combination of inputs and technology to achieve a given level of tax compliance, whereas preventable costs refer to the excess of actual over the least costs due to poor practice or lack of knowledge in meeting tax legislative requirements (e.g., poor record-keeping or not using 'e-filing'). Empirically observed tax compliance costs include both of these costs, although it is the inevitable costs of tax compliance that are of interest to tax policy-makers.[53]

Further, there are benefits associated with tax compliance and these should be deducted from tax compliance costs to arrive at net tax compliance costs in assessing the impact of tax complexity. The complication is that some benefits exist at the societal level, e.g., managerial benefits (more stringent record-keeping requirements help businesses to make better and more informed decisions), whereas other benefits accrue only to taxpayers, e.g., cash flow benefits (the mismatch in timing that allows businesses to hold on to tax revenue for a period before remitting it to the tax office), tax deductibility benefits (many tax compliance activities are tax deductible) or one-off or recurrent cash subsidy. The cash flow and tax deductibility benefits represent transfers from the government to the private sector so that they vanish at the societal level.[54]

---

52. Kenneth S. Johnston, 'Corporations' Federal income tax compliance costs; A study of small, medium-size, and large corporations', Ohio State University Bureau of Business Research Monograph No. 110, 67 (1963).
53. This author subscribes to the comprehensive view adopted by the majority of tax researchers, who consider all costs (whether avoidable or unavoidable, and whether preventable or inevitable), are tax compliance costs.
54. Even if one is only interested in the resource costs of tax compliance (so that all transfers between sectors are disregarded) one still has to contend with managerial benefits (true compliance benefits). Further, in the case of business taxpayers, by netting out all the benefits from the recourse costs of tax compliance, one can arrive at an estimate of the increase in production cost due to tax compliance.

At the practical level, there are issues associated with psychological costs, accounting/tax overlap, implicit costs and transitional/recurrent costs. Psychological costs refer to the stress and anxieties experienced by business owners and individuals in having to satisfactorily deal with taxation. They are problematic because there is no objective and consistent way to monetize these costs across taxpayers or over time. One plausible approach is to capture psychological costs (or the change in such costs) by the use of a suitable Likert scale.[55]

There is clearly an overlap between accounting and taxation costs in most business situations. This overlap is particularly pronounced for SMEs as, for these businesses, tax and accounting functions cannot be easily separated and internal staff members (e.g., an account clerk) are often employed to do both accounting and taxation activities. In the presence of multiple outputs (taxation and accounting), it is difficult to accurately attribute the joint costs to tax compliance alone. However, without reasonably precise attribution, it is conceivable that tax compliance costs can be overestimated.

Many important components of tax compliance activities involve implicit costs, e.g., time spent by a sole trader in dealing with business tax affairs. The accounting approach only recognizes explicit costs and will underestimate the true tax compliance costs. While the opportunity cost concept provides an appropriate approach, it is not always easy to implement it in practice. In the absence of market information, estimating the labour cost component of tax compliance can be difficult. As a result, quantitative estimates of tax compliance costs can be sensitive to the valuation of non-market time spent on tax compliance.

There is a distinction between transitional and recurrent compliance costs where transitional costs refer to the start-up and learning costs that tend to vanish over time, whereas recurrent costs refer to the positive costs incurred by taxpayers on a regular basis. Ideally it is useful to observe transitional and recurrent costs separately although this is unlikely in practice. In relation to transitional costs, capital costs are problematic to deal with, especially if the capital investment can be used for a variety of purposes (e.g., a laptop computer can be used for tax and other purposes).

It is useful to summarize the above discussion by two definitional equations:

(1)   *Tax compliance costs = Tax computation costs + Tax planning costs*

   = Inevitable costs + Preventable costs

   = Monetary costs + Psychological costs

   = Transitional costs + Recurrent costs

(2)   *Net tax compliance costs = Tax compliance costs – Tax compliance benefits to taxpayers*

   = Tax compliance costs – (Managerial benefits + Cash flow benefits + Tax deductibility benefits + Cash subsidies from the government)

---

55. Binh Tran-Nam & John Glover, *Estimating the Transitional Compliance Costs of the GST in Australia: A Case Study Approach*, 17(4) Austl. Tax F. 499, 533 (2002).

In terms of empirical studies, the large-scale survey approach tends to dominate the field, principally using what has come to be known as the 'Sandford' methodology or refinements of it.[56] Under this approach, tax compliance costs are estimated from large-scale survey data using the following definition:

(3)   *Tax compliance costs = Internal labour costs + External labour costs + Non-labour costs*

> where internal labour costs include implicit or explicit costs of time spent by owners, employees, contractors or unpaid spouses/friends on tax affairs, and external labour costs include payments to tax advisers and for other tax services. Non-labour costs are often omitted in many empirical studies.

Since the mid-2000s, there has been a growing popularity in the use of estimating/simulating techniques such as the Standard Cost Model (SCM). The SCM – also known as the Dutch model – applies a base formula as follows:

(4)   *Activity cost = Price (Tariff × Time) × Quantity (Population × Frequency × Rate)*

Note that equation (4) can be shown to be consistent with equation (3) above. Further, the resulting estimate of costs by (4) is only a partial measure of full compliance costs (e.g., it does not seek to measure voluntary compliance costs and non-labour costs) but nonetheless has shown itself to be a further useful methodology for benchmarking purposes. There are a number of largely government endorsed or developed estimating models, some based upon SCM, currently in use.[57]

Despite different research methodologies and data collection strategies, international empirical studies of tax compliance costs have come up with a number of consistent results.[58] First, tax compliance costs around the world are large, whether in absolute monetary terms or relative to relevant tax revenue collected or GDP (ranging from 2% to 10% of tax revenue and up to 2.5% of GDP). Second, internal labour costs dominate the composition of tax compliance costs (about two-thirds). Third, tax compliance costs are regressive in the sense that, as the size of taxpayer (by taxable income for individuals or annual turnover for business taxpayers) increases, tax compliance costs become a smaller fraction of taxpayer income or turnover. Fourth, tax compliance costs show no sign of decreasing over time despite commitments to tax simplification by governments around the world.

The regressivity of tax compliance costs deserves elaboration. First, tax complexity works against the principle of progressive income taxation, which is the hallmark characteristic of tax policy in most countries in the world. Second, it is interesting to note that net tax compliance costs of personal taxpayers were more regressive than

---

56. European Commission, 'A review and evaluation of methodologies to calculate tax compliance costs', Taxation Papers: Working Paper N. 40-2013, 3 (2013).
57. European Commission, 'A review and evaluation of methodologies to calculate tax compliance costs', above n. 56, at 9, 22.
58. Evans, 'Taxation compliance and administrative costs: An overview', above n. 10, at 457.

gross tax compliance costs in Australia for the 2011–2012 tax year.[59] This is mainly due to the cash flow costs suffered by the lowest taxable income group in Australia and the substantial cash flow benefits to the highest taxable income group in that year. This finding is not peculiar to 2011–2012 as the same phenomenon was observed in a much earlier Australian study.[60]

Perhaps the most ironic characteristic of tax compliance costs is that, while these costs are the best indicator of tax complexity, the estimates of the amount of these costs cannot easily be used across countries and over time to make inferences about either the changing levels of tax complexity within one country over time, or between two or more countries during the same time period. A recent study involving the proposed construction of a tax system complexity index attempts to overcome this problem.[61]

[C] Indirect Costs

Tax complexity gives rise to two main types of indirect costs which may not be apparent to a casual observer. The first is the potential loss in tax revenue and the second involves the complexity-induced efficiency costs. The focus of this chapter is on the latter type of costs. Suffice it to note that the combined direct and indirect effects of tax complexity on total output may result in slower economic growth.[62]

It has been long recognized that tax complexity may give rise to losses in tax revenue collection. Unintentional non-compliance may cause taxpayers to pay the wrong amount of taxes but if the errors are unintentional then they are likely to be a random variable with negative and positive values cancelling one another out. As a result, the aggregate error would be close to zero or negligible. However, if tax non-compliance is intentional (e.g., aggressive tax planning or tax evasion) and not caught by the auditing process, then it may result in losses in tax revenue. Tax complexity may give rise to aggressive tax planning/tax evasion which results in higher direct costs of non-compliance and losses in tax revenue. As far as this author is aware, there exists no formal model that links tax complexity and losses in tax revenue. Although some estimates of the extent of tax evasion (tax gap) are available, there are no reliable estimates of tax losses due to aggressive tax planning.

The efficiency costs of taxation are well-established in public finance literature. Taxation can distort economic agents' behaviour because of changes in the relative prices of factors of production, commodities and economic choices. The changes in relative prices give rise to the substitution effect resulting in losses of total output and lower level of welfare. The direct costs of tax complexity, discussed above (§5.04[B]), give rise to social wastages that are similar to the efficiency costs of taxation.

---

59. Binh Tran-Nam, Chris Evans & Philip Lignier, *Personal taxpayer compliance costs: Recent evidence from Australia*, 29(1) Austl. Tax F. 135, 155 (2014).
60. Tran-Nam, Evans, Walpole & Ritchie, *Tax Compliance Costs: Research Methodology and Empirical Evidence from Australia*, above n. 20, at 247.
61. See Binh Tran-Nam & Chris Evans, *Towards the Development of a Tax System Complexity Index*, 35(3) Fiscal Stud. 341 (2014).
62. Andrew Sentance, *Tax and growth - Supply and demand*, Tax Adviser 23 (January 2013).

In addition, tax complexity may also cause indirect losses of total output because it can adversely affect economic incentives. As a result of perceived or actual direct costs of tax complexity, a business taxpayer may be less motivated to engage further in entrepreneurial activities, which results in reduced total output being produced. There is some evidence suggesting that these complexity-induced efficiency costs do exist in practice. For example, a UK Open University Business School report claimed that nearly 18% of small, non-VAT-registered companies surveyed in Britain were deliberately avoiding sales to stay below the GBP 50,000 threshold for VAT registration.[63] This complexity-driven 'sales avoidance' strategy can give rise to both reduced total output and lower aggregate consumption.

Another example[64] also involved the UK's VAT, which has many different rates for different types of goods and services. It was observed that small shopkeepers deliberately reduced the variety of their stocks in order not to have to deal with too many different VAT rates. Again this complexity-driven 'variety reduction' strategy can give rise to a lower level of economic activities.

However, perhaps the most significant form of complexity-induced efficiency costs is related to foreign investors' perceptions of costs of doing business in a host country. This is because foreign investors are likely to be sensitive to the actual or perceived complexity of the host country's tax system. For any given effective income tax rate, foreign investors look for predictability, certainty, consistency and timeliness in the application of the tax rules.[65] A body of consistent international evidence has emerged on the negative effect of tax complexity (however defined) on foreign direct investment (FDI) inflows. While the findings of such a negative effect are theoretically plausible, they should nevertheless be regarded as preliminary and require further, more rigorous verification.

In a pioneering study, Edmiston, Mudd and Valev examined the effects of tax law uncertainty and complexity on FDI inflows to transition countries of the former Soviet Union and Eastern and Central Europe during the period from 1993 to 1998.[66] The key independent variable 'tax complexity' was measured in five different ways: number of different tax rates; number of lines in the description of the tax base (as a proxy for special provisions, conditions, restrictions); presence of indefinite phrases (proxy for ambiguity); number of changes in tax parameters (frequency of tax changes); and number of changes in tax parameters in the opposite direction. Negative effects were established for 'complex tax structure' (number of tax rates), 'tax law ambiguity', and 'tax rate change in the opposite direction', with varying degrees of statistical significance.

Müller and Voget subsequently investigated the effect of tax complexity on FDI at firm level, using the location choice of 4,474 new German FDI projects in OECD

---

63. Small Business Research Trust, *VAT and compliance burdens*, 14(1) NatWest SBRT Quarterly Survey of Small Business in Britain 18, 19 (1998).
64. See Sandford, Godwin & Hardwick, *Administrative and Compliance Costs of Taxation*, above n. 11, at 163–165.
65. OECD, *Policy Brief, Tax Effects on Foreign Direct Investment*, 4 (2008).
66. Kelly Edmiston, Shannon Mudd & Neven Valev, *Tax Structures and FDI - The Deterrent Effects of Complexity and Uncertainty*, 24(3) Fiscal Stud. 341 (2003).

countries from 2005 to 2009.[67] Tax complexity was defined as the time taken by a firm to prepare, file and pay a variety of business taxes. It was derived from the World Bank's *Doing Business* survey data. Their study found that reducing tax complexity is a fairly potent instrument for raising a country's attractiveness for new FDI projects. It was estimated that on average reducing tax complexity by 1% leads to an increase of about 0.8% in the expected number of new investments. Further, the effect of tax complexity reduction was particularly powerful for countries with a low statutory corporate income tax rate.

Lawless has also analysed how various levels of tax complexity affect the existence and level of bilateral FDI relationships for 16 OECD source countries with fifty-seven host countries in the year 2002.[68] Data from the World Bank's *Doing Business* surveys was employed to construct two tax complexity variables: amount of time a representative firm takes to process its taxes, and the number of tax payments per year. The econometric analysis suggested that the main impact of both complexity measures is to inhibit FDI flows from occurring. This finding implies an analogy between a high-level of tax complexity and a fixed cost that a firm must incur before establishing an FDI flow, i.e., the setup decision is affected but not the subsequent flows. Her study also indicated that reducing tax complexity by 10% is roughly equivalent to a 1% reduction in the corporate tax rate, causing total FDI to increase by about 6%.

In summary, the indirect costs of tax complexity can be non-trivial, especially in view of the rapid international integration of the world economy in recent years. There is no reason why econometric analyses of the effect of tax complexity on FDI flows cannot be extended to domestic investment. There exists, however, a fundamental difference between direct and indirect costs of tax complexity. While the direct costs of tax complexity can in principle be estimated for any tax system, the indirect costs of tax complexity can only be estimated by reference to a benchmark tax system. It is thus most important to develop a conceptual framework that integrates both direct and indirect costs of tax complexity as additive components of tax complexity.

[D]   Macroeconomic Costs

It has long been recognized that tax complexity is itself a tax. This chapter has to this point considered how tax complexity as a tax affects the allocation of resources (direct and indirect costs of tax complexity). This section proceeds to consider the macroeconomic, short-term, stabilization impact of tax complexity as a tax.

---

67. Cornelius Müller & Johannes Voget, 'Tax Complexity and Foreign Direct Investment', paper presented at the Oxford University Centre for Business Taxation Annual Symposium, 25–28 June 2012, http://www.sbs.ox.ac.uk/sites/default/files/Business_Taxation/Events/conferences/symposia/2012/voget.pdf.
68. Martina Lawless, *Do Complicated Tax Systems Prevent Foreign Direct Investment?*, 80(317) Economica 1 (2013).

Tax complexity as a tax has different impacts, sometimes in opposite directions, on various building blocks of the macro-economy. On the negative side, tax compliance costs increase the overall tax burden, and decrease aggregate disposable income and thus aggregate consumption. Similarly, the indirect costs of tax complexity reduce aggregate private investment. The combined negative and indirect effects unambiguously depress aggregate demand. On the positive side, tax administrative costs raise overall government expenditure, stimulating aggregate demand.

Using a simple Keynesian model of income determination we can in principle estimate the macroeconomic costs of tax complexity as the effects of tax complexity flow through the economy. Roughly speaking, the macroeconomic costs of tax complexity can be approximated by the equation:

(5) $MCTC = (m_T \times TCC) + (m_I \times \Delta I) - (m_G \times TAC)$

where:

$MCTC$ = Macroeconomic costs of tax complexity;
m_T = Tax multiplier;
m_I = Investment multiplier;
m_G = Government multiplier;
TCC = Tax compliance costs;
TAC = Tax administrative costs; and
ΔI = Reduction in investment due to indirect costs of tax complexity.

In principle, estimates of the various multipliers, tax compliance costs and tax administrative costs can be available. An estimate for ΔI is more difficult to obtain, requiring more sophisticated modelling and special assumptions. Note also that the government multiplier tends to be greater than the tax multiplier, as an increase in government spending affects aggregate demand directly while an increase in taxation influences aggregate demand indirectly via disposable income. However, since tax compliance costs tend to be many times greater than tax administrative costs, it seems plausible to assume that:

(6) $(m_T \times TCC) + (m_I \times \Delta I) - (m_G \times TAC) > (m_T \times TCC) - (m_G \times TAC) > (TCC + TAC)$,

i.e., the macroeconomic costs of tax complexity are likely to be greater than the direct costs of tax complexity.

In short, via the familiar multiplier effects, the direct and indirect costs of tax complexity may be magnified as they flow through the economy.

§5.05   CONCLUSION

This chapter has examined the costs of tax complexity from an economic perspective. This enquiry is motivated by the fact that while the efficiency costs of taxation are

well-established in public finance literature, economists have paid insufficient attention to tax complexity, possibly because of the influence of the optimal theory of
taxation. The overarching aim of the chapter is to present a comprehensive approach
for measuring the costs of tax complexity, which may serve as a theoretical basis for
future empirical studies in this field. The scope of the chapter is confined to costs
associated with tax compliance, ignoring the costs arising from tax non-compliance or
the costs relating to the interaction between tax complexity and equity.

The discussion has covered three related concepts of tax complexity. First, there
are direct costs which measure the value of resources taken away from productive
activities to operate the tax system (see §5.04[B]). Second, there exist indirect costs
which can be defined as the losses in total output resulting from reduced economic
incentives driven by actual or perceived direct costs of complexity (§5.04[C]). Finally,
there are macroeconomic costs of tax complexity (§5.04[C]). As the direct and indirect
costs of tax complexity flow through the economy, their combined impact may be
magnified via the familiar multiplier effect. It is argued that that tax collection costs
alone underestimate the true extent of the adverse effect of tax complexity. While the
magnitude of that underestimation is unclear at this stage, it seems reasonable to
suggest that the underestimation may not be trivial.

There are two broad implications from the chapter. From a theoretical perspective, the principle of tax neutrality should be formally expanded to include the
deadweight losses induced by tax complexity. The challenge is to construct a framework that simultaneously incorporates both direct and indirect costs of tax complexity.
From a policy perspective, the case for tax simplification can be strengthened in view
of the current underestimation of tax complexity costs. More evidence-based studies
are needed to determine how tax complexity costs flow through different parts of the
economy. Finally, while the chapter focuses on taxation, its approach and conclusions
are applicable to government regulation in general.

CHAPTER 6

Paying Taxes: The Global Picture: An Index to Encourage Tax Reform and the Development of Good Tax Systems[*]

Andrew Packman & Neville Howlett

§6.01 INTRODUCTION

'Paying Taxes' is one of eleven indicators used by the World Bank in its annual *Doing Business* project which measures how easy it is to do business in 189 economies. The aim of the *Doing Business* project is to provide an objective basis for understanding and improving the regulatory environment for domestic businesses around the world, promoting reforms that assist businesses, leading to better functioning economies.

[A] *Doing Business* and the Paying Taxes Indicator

First published in 2003, the *Doing Business* project looks at domestic small- to medium-sized companies and objectively measures the strength of laws, business regulations and institutions applying to them throughout their life-cycle.

The report encourages economies to introduce more efficient regulation, offers measurable benchmarks to encourage reform and provides a reference source with details of the business climate of each economy. The eleven areas of regulation covered by *Doing Business 2014* affect everyday business and are broadly grouped into two areas as noted below.[1]

The Paying Taxes indicator is included in the area covering complexity and cost of regulatory processes, along with indicators for starting a business, dealing with construction permits, getting electricity, registering property and trading across borders. The Paying Taxes indicator first appeared in the 2006 report and now covers the years from 2004 to date.[2] The second area, covering strength of legal institutions, includes indicators for getting credit, protecting minority investors, enforcing contracts, resolving insolvency and labour market regulation.

The World Bank gives the economies in the study an overall 'ease of doing business' ranking based on its Distance to Frontier (DTF) measure across ten of these indicators (excluding labour market regulation).

[B]   The *Paying Taxes* Report

The *Paying Taxes* report is prepared by PwC[3] using the paying taxes data that the World Bank has collected for the *Doing Business* project. The report includes additional analysis and commentary by PwC on the results. It focuses on the three key sub-indicators that form part of the Paying Taxes indicator, namely the Total Tax Rate (TTR), 'time to comply' and the 'payments made'. These sub-indicators provide an assessment of not only the tax costs that the case study business faces, but also of the compliance burden that it has to deal with.

The Paying Taxes study has been used by a number of governments and academics in their consideration of tax systems. One of the most recent is in the UK where the Office of Tax Simplification has used the Paying Taxes indicator as one of the starting points for its review of the competitiveness of the UK tax system.[4] Others include a study from the European Commission, 'A review and evaluation of

---

1. See World Bank Group, *Doing Business 2014: Understanding Regulations for Small and Medium-Size Enterprises* (11th ed., 29 October 2013), available at: http://www.doingbusiness.org/reports /global-reports/doing-business-2014.
2. Each report uses the company data for two years prior, so the 2006 report assesses the tax system for the period ended 31 December 2004 and the 2015 report for the period 1 January 2012 to 31 December 2013.
3. PwC refers to the UK member firm, and may sometimes refer to the PwC network. Each member firm is a separate legal entity. Please see www.pwc.com/structure for further details.
4. Office of Tax Simplification (UK), 'Competitiveness review: initial thoughts and call for evidence' (March 2014), https://www.gov.uk/government/uploads/system/uploads/attachment_data/ file/292456/PU1647_OTS_competitiveness_review_call_for_evidence.pdf.

methodologies to calculate tax compliance costs',[5] and an academic study into the Irish Paying Taxes TTR.[6]

§6.02 METHODOLOGY

Doing Business seeks to assess quantitatively and objectively the impact of business regulation and to enable comparisons to be made between different economies. Each of the indicators in *Doing Business* takes into account the cost, the time required and the steps needed for each area of regulation. This structure allows the same information to be collected for each economy and for it to be compared.

The Paying Taxes indicator takes into account the amount of taxes and mandatory contributions that a small to medium-sized company is obliged to pay in a given year, the time it takes for it to comply with the pre-filing tax obligations of the three major taxes (profit tax, labour taxes and mandatory contributions, and consumption tax) and the number of tax payments made (subject to some adjustments which are explained later in this chapter, §6.02[C][2][a]). In doing so, the Paying Taxes indicator provides a measure of how easy it is to pay tax in an economy and an ability to make comparisons with other economies around the world. This includes looking at how complex a tax system is, but it also assesses the help that is given to deal with that complexity in terms of the administration and systems made available. The three sub-indicators are explained in more detail section §6.02[C] below.

[A] The Case Study Company

It is important to have a system of measurement that takes into account multiple elements of a tax system and the interactions between them. Commonly, comparisons of tax systems look only at single taxes such as corporate income tax or personal income tax. Furthermore, they often consider only the headline statutory rate and ignore adjustments that may occur before that rate is applied to a taxable base; a system with a high statutory tax rate may have a much lower effective tax rate once all adjustments and allowances are included. In order to deal with these issues a case study company has been used which enables a comparison of tax systems around the world on a 'like for like' basis. This also uses the PwC Total Tax Contribution Framework[7] to look at all the different taxes to which the company could be subject.

---

5. European Commission, 'A review and evaluation of methodologies to calculate tax compliance costs', Working Paper No. 40 – 2013, FWC TAXUD/2012/CC/116 (25 October 2013), http://ec. europa.eu/taxation_customs/resources/documents/taxation/gen_info/economic_analysis/tax_ papers/taxation_paper_40.pdf.
6. Jim Stewart, 'PwC/World Bank Report "Paying Taxes 2014": An Assessment', Institute for International Integration Studies (University of Dublin) Discussion Paper No. 442 (February 2014), https://www.tcd.ie/iiis/documents/discussion/pdfs/iiisdp442.pdf.
7. See http://www.pwc.co.uk/assets/pdf/ttcframework.pdf.

The *Doing Business* team at the World Bank, together with academic advisers, developed the parameters of the case study company along with the related data collection tool. The key parameters of the case study company are provided below.
TaxpayerCo:

- is a limited liability company operating in a typical manufacturing location in the economy's largest business city. From Paying Taxes 2015,[8] where an economy has a population in excess of 100 million, the second largest business city is also included in the study. This applies to eleven economies, namely Bangladesh, Brazil, China, India, Indonesia, Japan, Mexico, Nigeria, Pakistan, the Russian Federation and the US;
- is 100% domestically-owned by five private individuals;
- performs manufacturing and commercial activities producing ceramic flower-pots and selling them at retail;
- has no exports or imports and no products subject to special tax regimes;
- employs sixty people; four managers, eight assistants and forty-eight workers;
- is treated as being in its second year of operation after making a loss in its first year;
- distributes 50% of net profits as dividends at the end of the second year;
- sells a plot of land at the beginning of the second year for a profit.

All of the company's financial information is calculated as a multiple of gross national income per capita[9] (GNI) for each economy. For example, (*turnover* = *1,050 x GNI*), and (*commercial profits* = *59.4 x GNI*); full details of the company's profit and loss account and balance sheet are also included in the Appendix to this chapter. The salaries of the workers are also calculated by reference to GNI, with workers earning (*1 x GNI*), assistants earning (*1.25 x GNI*) and managers earning (*2.25 x GNI*).

From Paying Taxes 2015, for some economies, where the salaries of the workers in the case study company are below the minimum wage level in those economies, the case study company parameters are based on a multiple of two or three times GNI as required to reach the minimum wage level.

The original Paying Taxes studies used the GNI values as at December 2005. From Paying Taxes 2015, the 2012 GNI values are used. The change has had an impact on the TTR of some economies, but this has been relatively limited as most taxes are based on figures that, for the case study company, are a multiple of GNI and so the ratio of taxes borne to commercial profit stayed the same. There has been some impact where taxes are charged on a fixed basis or where the change in the case study parameters results in the case study company being subject to tax at a different rate from that applied in prior years.

As the parameters show, the case study company is relatively simple and does not reflect all the complexities which may be encountered by companies operating in

---

8. See World Bank Group, *Doing Business 2015: Going beyond Efficiency*, 83 (12th ed., 29 October 2014); World Bank Group & PwC, *Paying Taxes 2015: The Global Picture* (20 November 2014), http://www.doingbusiness.org/reports/thematic-reports/paying-taxes.
9. GNI/capita data sourced from the World Bank database, http://data.worldbank.org/.

the real world. Most notably, it does not consider cross-border transactions, related party transactions or tax issues specific to particular industries; the extra complexities these would introduce would make the study impractical to carry out. In developing the case study parameters it was necessary to develop a robust model that could be used annually to compare 189 economies and to have a company that could potentially exist in all economies.

As the case study company is standardized and the parameters remain the same year-on-year, it becomes relatively straightforward to identify the effects of changes in tax systems in isolation, without adjusting for the effects of economic or other changes.

[B] Some Definitions

Before considering each of the three sub-indicators in detail, it is helpful to define some of the terms used in Paying Taxes.

[1] 'Taxes Borne' and 'Taxes Collected'

The tax payments made by the case study company are divided into 'taxes borne' and 'taxes collected', in line with PwC's Total Tax Contribution Framework.

Taxes borne – all taxes that affect the financial results and are a cost to the company. Typically these include corporate income tax, capital gains tax, employers' social security contributions, and property taxes.

Taxes collected – includes taxes withheld by the company on behalf of others, such as personal income tax and employees' social security contributions withheld from salaries, and value added tax (VAT) collected from customers and paid on to the government. Taxes collected are not included in the TTR as they are not a direct cost to the company, but they do affect the company's administrative burden and so are included in the 'time to comply' and the 'payments' measures.

[2] The Types of Tax

There are different ways of levying tax and sometimes the name of the tax may not reflect the basis on which it is calculated – for example a 'property tax' may be based on headcount. Paying Taxes classifies taxes by the tax base used to calculate the tax and not by the name of the tax.

Profit taxes – all taxes calculated by reference to company profits; mainly corporate income tax, but also any other taxes computed by reference to the taxable income base (e.g., capital gains).

Labour taxes and mandatory contributions – all payments based on salaries of employees; such as payroll tax, unemployment insurance, personal income tax, and social security contributions. This also includes any payments that are required to be paid by law for the benefit of employees even if those payments are made to an individual's private pension or insurance plan rather than to a government or government agency. While such contributions would not meet the OECD's definition of a tax,[10] it is considered necessary to include them in order to facilitate the comparison between those economies where the contributions are paid to the government and those where they are paid to private schemes. This does not include any voluntary contributions that employees may choose to make to pension funds or other savings or insurance plans.

'*Other taxes*' – all taxes that conform to the OECD definition of a tax and are not calculated on the basis of profit or salary. The most significant are VAT and sales taxes, both based on sales, but other consumption taxes, property taxes, turnover taxes and a variety of other payments such as municipal fees and environmental taxes are also included.

[C]   Sub-indicators

As mentioned above, three sub-indicators (TTR, 'time to comply' and 'payments') are calculated for the case study company for each economy. These sub-indicators are explained below.

[1]   Tax Cost: 'Total Tax Rate'

The TTR is the total of all taxes borne as a percentage of commercial profit:

$$TTR = Taxes\ borne/Commercial\ profit^{11}$$

The commercial profit of the company is the profit of the company after all business expenses, but before any tax charges. For each economy the taxes that the company would pay, with the exception of corporate income taxes, are deducted from the commercial profit to give the accounting profit before tax, e.g., employers' social security costs, property taxes, environmental levies. The corporate income tax charge is then deducted to give the profit after tax. The commercial profit is (59.4 x GNI),[12] but the profit before tax (PBT) will vary depending on the taxes (other than corporate income taxes) due in an economy.

The TTR measures the costs of all the taxes a business bears and excludes taxes collected. It is a comprehensive measure of the tax cost as it includes profit taxes, labour taxes and mandatory contributions, and 'other taxes'.

It is worth noting the difference between the profit tax elements of the TTR and the corporate effective tax rate (ETR) which is often used to look at the tax cost to business.

The ETR usually only includes corporate income tax whereas the profit tax element of TTR may include other taxes levied on profits. In addition, the ETR is

---

10. 'The OECD working definition of a tax is a compulsory unrequited payment to the government': OECD, 'Glossary of tax terms', http://www.oecd.org/ctp/glossaryoftaxterms.htm.
11. Commercial profit = PBT + all taxes and contributions above the profit before tax (PBT) line.
12. For economies using (2 or 3 x GNI) as the reference point, due to minimum wages being higher than GNI, the commercial profit will be (118.8 and 178.2 x GNI) respectively.

calculated by reference to profit before corporate income tax, whereas TTR is calculated using the profit before any taxes borne (the commercial profit):

$$ETR = CIT / PBT$$

Consider the following example in Table 6.1 for an economy with a GNI of EUR 32,300:

Table 6.1   Tax Rates Example Calculation

		€ '000
A	Commercial profit	1,916
B	Employer's social security	232
C	Property rates	19
D	Other taxes	6
E	Profit before tax (A-(B+C+D))	1,659
F	Corporate income tax	206
G	Capital gains tax	29
H	Profit after tax (E-(F+G))	1,424

This gives the following ratios:

(a) *TTR = Taxes Borne/Commercial Profit = (B+C+D+F+G)/A = 492/1916 = 25.7%*
(b) *Effective tax rate = (CIT + CGT)/PBT = (F+G)/E = 235/1659 = 14.2%*
(c) *Profit Tax TTR = Profit Taxes Borne/Commercial Profit = (F+G)/A = 235/1916 = 12.3%*
(d) *Labour Tax TTR = Labour Taxes Borne/Commercial Profit = B/A = 232/1916 = 12.1%*
(e) *'Other Taxes' TTR = 'Other Taxes' Borne/Commercial Profit = (C+D) /A = 25/1916 = 1.3%.*

It is of note that the ETR of 14.2% is higher than the profit tax TTR of 12.3%.

[2]   Compliance Sub-indicators: 'Number of Payments' and 'Time to Comply'

With two of the three Paying Taxes sub-indicators relating to compliance, the study is weighted towards measuring the administrative burden of complying with pre-filing tax obligations. The compliance sub-indicators cover the time required to collect the necessary data and to prepare and file tax returns, and also the time required to make payments of tax and the process used for this. While the TTR includes only taxes borne, the compliance sub-indicators also take account of the administrative burden associated with taxes collected.

[a]   'Number of Payments'

This sub-indicator is designed to reflect the total number of taxes and contributions paid, the method of payment, the frequency of filing and the number of agencies involved. It includes payments for taxes borne and collected, including those withheld by the company and employee-borne labour taxes. Although these do not impact the financial statements, they add to the administrative burden of complying with the tax system.

This sub-indicator is a reflection of the complexity that exists in tax systems due to multiple taxes, taxes being levied by multiple levels of government and where there is a need for frequent payments.

At a basic level the sub-indicator merely adds up the number of actual payments made in a twelve month period. However, the sub-indicator will be recorded as only '1' for a tax, if online filing and payment are used by the majority of companies in an economy for that tax, even if the tax is paid several times per year. This approach recognizes the reduction in the compliance burden that electronic systems can afford and was adopted by the World Bank to encourage the use of electronic systems for filing and paying taxes, which increase the traceability of data and reduce the necessity for personal interactions between taxpayers and tax authorities. Also, for payments made through third parties, only one payment is included even if payments are more frequent, again to reflect the low- or non-existent administrative burden. Where taxes are paid jointly, for example where employee and employer taxes are filed and paid together, only one set of payments is recorded in the sub-indicator.

The example of the Colombian payments in Table 6.2 shows how this may look in practice.

Table 6.2   Breakdown of the Payments Sub-indicator for Colombia for 2013

Colombia: Number of Payments			
Tax Type	World Bank Indicator	Actual Payments	Notes
Corporate income tax	1	2	Online filing
Income Tax for Equity - CREE	1	2	Online filing
VAT	1	6	Online filing
Municipal tax	1	6	Online filing
Real estate tax	1	1	
Urban boundary tax	1	1	
Financial transactions tax	1	1	
Social security contributions	1	12	Online filing
Welfare security system	0	12	Paid jointly
Labour risk insurance	0	12	Paid jointly

Colombia: Number of Payments			
Tax Type	World Bank Indicator	Actual Payments	Notes
Payroll tax	0	12	Paid jointly
Vehicle tax	1	1	
Stamp duty	1	1	
Fuel tax	1	1	Embedded in payments to third parties
Total	**10**	**68**	

[b]   *'Time to Comply' (Hours)*

'Time to comply' measures the time in hours per year that it is estimated the case study company needs to prepare, file, and pay its taxes and contributions. Preparation includes all the time spent collecting the necessary information and computing the amount payable. Filing time comprises that required to complete tax returns, any other forms and filing them with the tax authority. Payment time considers the hours needed to make payments online or at the tax authorities' offices.

The 'time to comply' is a reflection of the complexity inherent in tax systems as the time will be increased where complex calculations are required, where detailed analysis or many adjustments are required to convert accounting records into tax calculations, or where multiple returns are required. The 'time to comply' also reflects inefficiencies in the compliance process, such as time required to go in person to tax offices, difficulties in accessing guidance or legislation or the need for manual rather than automatic processing.

It is assumed that the case study company keeps accurate accounting records and follows best practice that a real company with similar characteristics would be expected to apply, and this accounting time is not included in the time to comply. Furthermore, the 'time to comply' measure does not include any hours spent on tax matters after the tax returns have been submitted. It therefore takes no account of the time taken to obtain a refund, to deal with follow up queries from tax authorities or to appeal an assessment from a tax authority. These post-filing obligations are excluded as so far it has not been possible to design an objective method of assessing the time required for these, given the differences between economies in the probability of being audited, and the differences between tax authorities (and even between individual tax inspectors) in pursuing audits.

Unlike the other sub-indicators, which include all profit taxes, labour taxes and mandatory contributions, and 'other taxes', the 'time to comply' measure only covers profit taxes, labour taxes and mandatory contributions and consumption taxes (usually VAT or other sales taxes). This simplification was adopted as data from contributors to the Paying Taxes study indicated that of the 'other taxes' only the consumption taxes imposed a significant time burden.

[D]   Rankings

In previous years the Paying Taxes ranking has been calculated based upon an arithmetic mean of the percentile distributions of the sub-indicator values for each economy. From Paying Taxes 2015 the rankings are prepared using the World Bank's DTF measure. The frontier is defined as the lowest score in each sub-indicator across all economies since inception.[13] The measure shows how far away an economy is from the theoretical best-performing economy which is given a score of 100.

The DTF for the 'time to comply' and the 'number of payments' is computed as:

$$100 * (max\text{-}y)/(max - min),$$

where y is the sub-indicator value for a given economy, max is the maximum score over the ten years of the study, and min is the frontier or the lowest score over the ten years of the study.

The DTF for the TTR is computed as:

$$100 * [(max - y) / (max - min)]^{0.8}$$

for TTR above the 15th percentile. For a TTR value below the 15th percentile, TTR^{DTF} is set at 100. y is the sub-indicator value for a given economy, max is the maximum score over the ten years of the study, and min is the frontier which for the TTR is the rate at the 15th percentile across all years of the study.

The effect of this calculation for the TTR is that an economy that is further away from the TTR frontier will move a greater amount towards the frontier than an economy that is closer to the frontier, for the same reduction in TTR. This provides a greater benefit for reducing TTRs that are higher than average, than for TTRs that are already at a low level.

This DTF measure is taken for each sub-indicator and then aggregated for each economy, and an overall DTF score calculated using a simple mean.

The overall Paying Taxes DTF will then take the form:

$$Paying\ Taxes^{DTF} = 1/3\ [TTR^{DTF} + Time^{DTF} + Payments^{DTF}]$$

The ease of Paying Taxes ranking is then computed by sorting the *Paying Taxes*^{DTF} values such that the highest number is ranked as '1'.

---

13. Frontier for the TTR is the 15th percentile of all TTR values across all economies for all years of the study.

[E]   Data Collection, Contributors and Annual Process

Each year the Paying Taxes process is initiated by a review of the data collection questionnaire by the World Bank and PwC Paying Taxes teams; adjustments to questions are made and this is approved by *Doing Business* management. The questionnaire is sent to at least three contributors in each economy who complete the questionnaire and return it to the World Bank for analysis. (PwC is one of the contributors for 162 economies in the study. Less than half of the respondents are PwC contributors.)

In March and April the contributors complete the questionnaires and raise any queries with the World Bank *Doing Business* team. The World Bank Group then reviews the data from the different contributors in each economy and resolves any differences in the data supplied. Any suggested changes to the sub-indicators are investigated and verified further with third-party contributors. Once the data are finalized, they are entered into the World Bank Group model, the rankings are computed and then signed off by *Doing Business* management at the Bank.

The World Bank Group drafts its Paying Taxes chapter in August for inclusion in the *Doing Business* and *Paying Taxes* reports. PwC undertakes its analysis of the data in August and September and includes a commentary on the year's results in the November publication of *Paying Taxes: The Global Picture.*

§6.03   KEY MESSAGES AND TRENDS: 2004–2013 (PT2006 TO PT2015)[14]

The global averages in the latest study (*Paying Taxes 2015*) are included in Table 6.3 and show that it takes the case study company 264 hours to comply with its taxes, it makes 25.9 payments and has an average Total Tax Rate of 40.9%.

Table 6.3   The Average Global Result for Each Paying Taxes Sub-indicator for 2013

Tax Type	Total Tax Rate %	Time to Comply (Hours)	Number of Payments
Profit taxes	16.3	71	3.1
Labour taxes and contributions	16.2	94	10.2
Other/Consumption taxes	8.4	99	12.6
Total	**40.9**	**264**	**25.9**
Lowest	7.4	12	3.0
Highest	216.5	2,600	71.0

---

14. World Bank Group & PwC, *Paying Taxes 2015*, above n. 8, at 25 (PwC Commentary, 'The global results for the Paying Taxes 2015 study').

The trend has been for all three sub-indicators to fall during the ten years of the study and this has continued in the year to 31 December 2013.[15] This can be seen in Figure 6.1.

Figure 6.1   Trend in the Paying Taxes Sub-indicators, 2004–2013

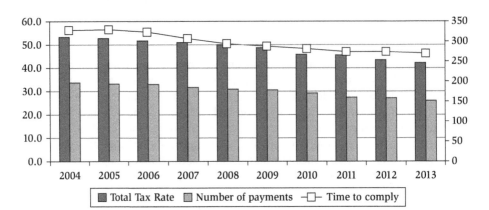

The results for each sub-indicator can also be analysed between the three types of tax as in Table 6.3. This shows that while, on average, profit taxes account for a similar proportion of the Total Tax Rate to labour taxes (almost 40%), they take 25% less time to comply with than labour taxes and almost 30% less time than consumption taxes. 'Other' taxes now account for one-fifth of the Total Tax Rate, but for almost half of the number of payments.

All three of the sub-indicators demonstrate a wide range between the highest and the lowest results. For payments and the time to comply, the minimum and maximum figures have remained the same for the last two years of the study while the range of Total Tax Rates has narrowed with the maximum dropping to 216.5% from 283.2%. In the year to 31 December 2012 (*Paying Taxes 2014*) The Gambia was the economy with the highest Total Tax Rate (283.2%) owing to its cascading sales tax. The replacement of the Gambian sales tax with a value added tax has since left Comoros as the economy with the highest Total Tax Rate (216.5%), again due to its cascading sales tax. The minimum Total Tax Rate also fell between 2012 and 2013, though by less than 1 percentage point from 8.2% to 7.4%. The Former Yugoslavian Republic of Macedonia remains the economy with lowest Total Tax Rate as it only levies corporate income tax on profits once they are distributed as dividends, and its economy is characterized by an absence of labour taxes that are paid by the employer and low levels of 'other' taxes.

Over the ten years of the study, Central Asia & Eastern Europe has been the region that has seen the fastest and most consistent reduction in all three of the sub-indicators. Most recently it has also been interesting to see that, while economies in Africa

---

15. All trend data and figures are on a 'like-for-like' basis and include only the 174 economies and cities for which PwC has a full data set since 2004.

continued to improve in 2013 with reductions in the TTR and the time to comply, on average economies in South America have seen increases in both these sub-indicators from an already high base.

[A]   Total Tax Rate

The global average TTR has fallen in all regions[16] over the ten years of the study. The largest decrease was recorded in Africa (22.5 percentage points) followed by Central Asia and Eastern Europe (20.8 percentage points). The regions showing the smallest reduction in the average TTR were South America (1.4 percentage points) and Central America & the Caribbean (1.5 percentage points). In 2013 the outcome for the TTR was more mixed than in previous years; fifty-one economies implemented measures that reduced their TTR, whilst fifty-eight increased their TTR.

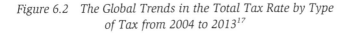

Figure 6.2   The Global Trends in the Total Tax Rate by Type of Tax from 2004 to 2013[17]

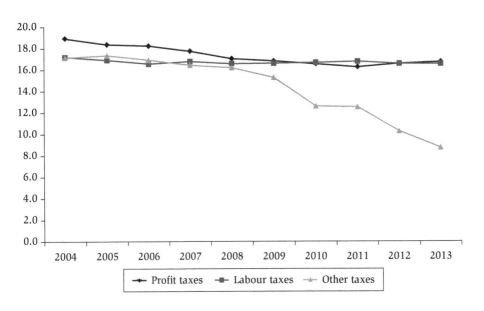

---

16. The regions used are Africa, Asia Pacific, Central America & the Caribbean, Central Asia & Eastern Europe, EU & EFTA, Middle East, North America, South America. See www.pwc.com /payingtaxes for details of which economies are included in each region.
17. All trend data and figures are on a 'like-for-like' basis and include only the 174 economies and cities for which PwC has a full data set since 2004. It should however be noted that an element of the movement on the TTR between 2012 and 2013 arises because of an update to the GNI per capita data used in the case study assumptions to construct the financial statements. For some economies this altered the size of the case study company so that different tax rules applied or the proportion of certain fixed taxes to commercial profits changed.

When analysed into profit taxes, labour taxes and contributions, and 'other taxes' (see Figure 6.2), all three elements of TTR have fallen since 2004; 'other taxes' had the largest fall, at 8.4 percentage points, followed by profit taxes (2.2 percentage points) and then labour taxes (0.7 percentage points).

On a global average basis, labour taxes and profit taxes now make up similar proportions of the TTR, accounting for 39% and 40% respectively. The labour tax proportion however varies by region. The largest proportions are seen in EU & EFTA where they account for 64% of the TTR, 59% in the Middle East and 54% in Central Asia & Eastern Europe. Since 2004, the biggest change for labour taxes has been in Central Asia & Eastern Europe where the proportion has fallen by 7.6 percentage points. A further example of regional variation is that although 'other taxes' are generally the smallest element of the TTR globally, they are the largest element in South America (39%) and are a significant proportion in Africa (30%).

The overall rate of decline in TTR was at its fastest during the crisis of 2008–2010, averaging 1.3 percentage points per year. The average rate for labour taxes and contributions has remained relatively stable with small reductions pre-crisis and slight increases during and after the crisis, but has been flat in 2013. Globally, and in most regions, profit taxes fell consistently from 2004 to 2011 and have then increased slightly in both 2012 and 2013 as a result of economies either increasing their statutory rate or broadening the base of their corporate income taxes. The significant decline in the proportion of 'other taxes' is largely due to the replacement of cascading sales taxes in a number of countries including several African countries and Yemen.

[B]   Time to Comply

Having risen from 2004 to 2005, the global average time to comply then fell year-on-year, and by fifty-nine hours in total. The rate of decline decreased between 2011 and 2012 dropping by only one hour, but then fell by four hours in 2013. In 2013, only South America showed an increase in the time to comply of two hours, North America remained flat and the Middle East, EU & EFTA have shown a much slower rate of decline of one and two hours respectively.

Figure 6.3   *The Global Trends in the Time to Comply Sub-indicator by Type of Tax from 2004 to 2013*[18]

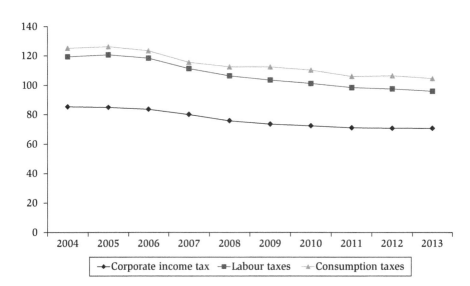

Of the three types of tax, consumption taxes have consistently been the most time consuming, with labour taxes not far behind; corporate income taxes have always taken the least amount of time (see Figure 6.3). This is due in part to the frequency of consumption tax and labour tax filings, which are often monthly, compared to corporate income taxes, which are usually filed annually.

In contrast to TTR, time to comply declined the most just before the crisis for all three types of tax. Since 2004, the greatest simplification has been in labour taxes, at twenty-three hours, demonstrating the impact of introducing electronic filing;[19] consumption taxes have fallen by twenty-one hours and profit taxes by fifteen hours. In the year to 31 December 2013 the reduction in the time to comply was largely driven by the introduction of electronic filing and payment systems or by improvement of existing systems.

The time to comply shows less regional variation than for the TTR with corporate income taxes consistently taking the least time to comply in all regions apart from the Middle East, where consumption taxes are the quickest to deal with, and Asia Pacific and North America where labour taxes are the quickest.

---

18. All trend data and figures are on a 'like-for-like' basis and include only the 174 economies and cities for which PwC has a full data set since 2004.
19. 28% of the Paying Taxes reforms recorded by the World Bank since 2004 relate to the introduction or enhancement of electronic filing. World Bank Group & PwC, *Paying Taxes 2015*, above n. 8, at 2.

[C]   **Number of Payments**

The global average number of payments has fallen each year since the study's inception, and by 7.8 payments in total. The falling trend is exhibited by all regions, due largely to the introduction of electronic filing and payment systems, though the decline slowed in 2012 to a reduction of 0.5 payments but fell again by almost one payment in 2013. The study found in 2013 that 43% of economies around the world had electronic filing and payment systems that are used by the majority of companies in their economy. In Africa and Central America & the Caribbean the trend has recently started to change with small increases in payments due to the introduction of new taxes and more frequent payments in a few economies.

'Other taxes' have consistently accounted for the largest number of payments, with profit taxes requiring by far the fewest (see Figure 6.4); reflecting the fact that corporate income taxes often require one annual payment whilst consumption taxes are often paid monthly. This is generally the case in most regions, apart from the Middle East and Asia Pacific where labour taxes and mandatory contributions have the largest number of payments (62% and 44% respectively). As with the time to comply, the greatest improvement has been for labour taxes at 3.5 payments, followed by 'other taxes' with 3.1 fewer payments, and only 1.2 fewer payments for profit taxes.

Figure 6.4   The Global Trends in the Number of Payments Sub-indicator by Type of Tax from 2004 to 2013

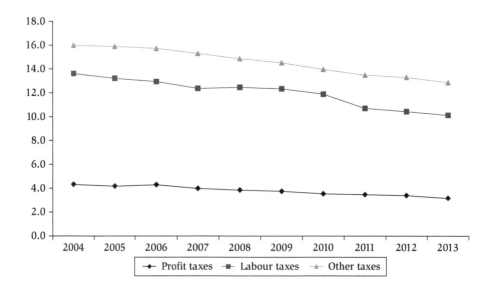

§6.04 ECONOMIC ANALYSIS (TAXATION, ECONOMIC GROWTH AND INVESTMENT)[20]

In addition to the analysis of the Paying Taxes sub-indicators, we have also used the data to look at some of the links between tax and economic factors.

Following the global financial crisis, much attention has been paid to potential methods of demand stimulation and improving the performance of the financial sector. Increasingly, governments have shifted their attention to supply-side measures focusing on businesses; on the understanding that the easier it is to do business, the more start-ups can be expected and the more existing businesses are likely to grow.

Paying Taxes 2013 included a statistical analysis of the relationships between the tax environment and the ability to attract Foreign Direct Investment (FDI)[21] and generate growth – for this purpose 166 economies were assessed[22] using eight years of Paying Taxes data covering 2004 to 2011. The results illustrate the potential benefit to economic growth when economies are actively attempting to reduce the burden of the tax system on business.

[A] How Can a Government Create a More 'Business-Friendly' Tax Environment?

A government can try to reduce the burden of the tax system in several ways. One way would be to reduce tax rates resulting in a reduction in the TTR and easing the direct cost of taxation. However, decreasing the tax revenue a government receives will only be achieved on a sustainable basis if the government reduces its spending to the same extent (in present value terms). A second way of creating a more tax-friendly system would be through tax reforms; for example, shifting taxes that directly impose a burden on income-generating activities towards personal expenditure taxes. The UK's current approach to corporation tax, for example, demonstrates a different method of widening the tax base and lowering the tax rate, and in theory not sacrificing revenue. Another way in which the tax system could help economic growth is by easing the administrative burden placed on businesses through reducing the time that firms spend dealing with tax matters, e.g., by introducing electronic filing and reducing complexity.

[B] Hypotheses

Our analysis considered three hypotheses:

- economies which have higher tax burdens, both in terms of compliance and rates, will experience lower rates of economic growth and of inward investment over the period;

---

20. World Bank Group & PwC, *Paying Taxes 2013: The Global Picture*, 23 (PwC Commentary, 'An economic analysis' – Andrew Sentance, Senior Economic Adviser at PwC UK).
21. Foreign Direct Investment is a cross-border investment by an entity in one economy into an enterprise in another economy, with the objective of attaining a lasting interest.
22. Not all economies were analysed due to incomplete data for the eight years.

- economies that have more complex tax systems will achieve lower growth and lower inward investment over a period of years;
- economies that are actively reducing the burden of their tax system will experience stronger growth.

The analysis has six potential explanatory variables, the average of each of the tax measures and also the change in each of the tax measures. A seventh regressor, (*starting GDP/capita*) is included as a control variable (co-variate), since we would expect developing economies starting from a lower output level to generate a higher growth rate (negative correlation). A tax compliance variable was computed as a weighted average of the change in tax payments (0.96) and time to comply (0.04)[23] – this was used to explain the impacts of the overall reduction in burden of tax administration, and to find a relationship between the simplicity of compliance, and the level of economic growth and inward investment.

Due to the complex nature of the relationship between the tax system and economic growth, caution needs to be exercised when evaluating the results, since there are likely to be other co-variates and variables driving the relationships that are not included; for example, a change in the tax system could be correlated with other policy developments which therefore affect growth.

[C]   Results

[1]   *Economic Growth*

Our analysis supports the view that the tax system creates a drag on economic growth, as the above hypotheses postulate - the 'tax drag' over the period, 2004–2011 is estimated at 1.15% per year, on average. There are three components to the influence that the tax system appears to exert on economic growth: the TTR, the administrative burden (represented by the number of payments) and the reduction in administrative burden (demonstrated by a weighted average of time and payments).

The administrative burden has a drag on growth of approximately 1% across our sample, though this is slightly offset by the boost of 0.24% that, on average, the reduction in the burden of tax administration is having on output. TTR averaged around 50% for 2004–2011 and, according to estimates, a 10 percentage point cut in TTR (relative to business profits) boosts annual economic growth by almost 0.1%, so the total drag created by the tax burden on economic activity is around 0.4%. We therefore observed that changes in the administrative dimension had a larger impact than the tax rate itself; a potential explanation is that tax revenues are recycled within an economy to support government expenditure, which is thus an increase in output

---

23. These weightings are based on the relative size of the time and payments figures, to ensure the variable represents both sub-indicators approximately equally.

(administration and complexity have no such compensating benefit). The difference in tax drag between regions appears to relate more to the number of payments than to the TTR, highlighting the potential benefits in reducing the administrative burden and complexity of the system.

[2]   Foreign Direct Investment

Analysis suggests that the administrative attributes of the tax system do not have a significant impact on the amount of inward investment, whilst the TTR did have a noticeable effect. This could be a reflection of the fact that a complex and time consuming tax system has a greater negative impact on small to medium-sized enterprises which are less involved with flows of international investment; whereas larger companies are more likely to have the management systems to cope with more complex tax systems, but tend to shift their investment to locations where the overall burden (TTR) is lower. Our analysis suggests that a 10 percentage point cut in TTR could boost the growth of inward investment by 0.7% per year, and the average tax drag across all economies in the sample is 3.7%.

§6.05   SUMMARY OF EVIDENCE

The trends over the ten years of the study show that each of the three sub-indicators has fallen. The rates of decline slowed in 2012 but picked up again in 2013.

The trends suggest that the global financial downturn has had a significant impact on tax systems around the world, with governments choosing to implement a range of policies.

While in the first eight years of the study the most common reform was the reduction of profit tax rates, in more recent years the focus has been on introducing electronic systems.

The global average TTR has continued to fall although this has largely been driven by African economies replacing their cascading sales taxes with VAT systems. In the last two years the global average rate for profit taxes has increased while that for labour taxes has been flat. Profit taxes and labour taxes now account for a similar proportion of the overall TTR.

Since 2004, *Doing Business* has reported 379 tax reforms, 105 of which have involved introducing or enhancing electronic filing systems. By the 2013 study, 43% of economies had fully implemented electronic systems for filing and payment.

These developments and others, including merging the filing and payment of taxes levied on the same base into one return and one payment, have simplified the compliance procedures and reduced the time to comply across the three tax types by fifty-nine hours on average and reduced the number of payments by 7.8.

The greatest reduction has been for labour taxes and contributions where, on average, the number of payments has fallen by 3.5 and the time to comply has dropped by twenty-three hours.

Electronic filing and payment has arguably been the greatest simplification to tax systems during the period of the study as it has reduced both the time to comply and the number of payments.

§6.06   WHAT *PAYING TAXES* TELLS US ABOUT COMPLEXITY

Paying Taxes evaluates the cost of the tax system (the TTR) from the point of view of a small to medium-sized case study company and how easy or difficult it is to comply with the tax system, this with the aim of assessing the *ease of paying taxes* across 189 economies globally. It does not assess complexity; a very complex regime with good electronic systems may be evaluated more highly than a simpler tax regime with poorer systems. Since 2004 there have been steady falls in the average TTR, the time to comply and the number of tax payments both globally and across many individual regions. The compliance sub-indicators measure a combination of how a complex system is, and also how effective the systems implemented to deal with that complexity are. With the implementation of electronic filing and payment systems becoming the most common reform in recent studies, this shows that there has been a focus on reforming and improving compliance procedures to make complexity easier to deal with; it does not provide evidence for a reduction in complexity. *Paying Taxes* has however also prompted governments to look more broadly at measures to simplify tax systems, an example being the recent report issued by the Office of Tax Simplification in the UK.[24]

The economic analysis included in *Paying Taxes 2013* focused on the compliance and administrative burden of tax systems along with the number of payments made and the TTR. This analysis suggested that more burdensome tax systems create more 'drag' on GDP growth. Furthermore, the compliance burden of a tax system has a greater influence on the 'tax drag' of GDP than the tax cost. Complexity is one of the factors that contribute to the tax burden and so it seems reasonable to suppose that a reduction in complexity or the implementation of measures to help companies deal with complexity would result in less burdensome tax systems.

While our data suggest that decreases in TTR continue to plateau, further reductions could be expected in the compliance burden. Governments may be reluctant to reduce tax rates significantly as this would reduce the revenues available for public spending, but reductions in the compliance burden of tax systems, either by reducing complexity in the system or by helping companies to deal with complexity, could have a positive effect on GDP by reducing the deadweight of the compliance burden on the economy without affecting government spending.

There may also be an impact on FDI. While our economic analysis showed that FDI seemed to be influenced more by tax rate than by compliance burden, this may be due to the headline rate being more visible than the compliance burden or the complexity of a tax system. It could be argued that a simple and efficient tax system should be of benefit to investors and could afford an economy some competitive advantage.

---

24. See Office of Tax Simplification (UK), above n. 4.

As noted above (§6.03[B] and §6.03[C]), when looking at the role of complexity in the reduction of the compliance indicator it should be noted that the reduction in the compliance indicators is mainly due to the introduction and enhancement of electronic filing and payment systems. Such systems do not reduce the underlying complexity of tax systems, but rather increase the ability to deal with that complexity. As a result, it takes less time for a company to meet its tax compliance obligations and automated systems are likely to reduce the errors resulting from complex and repetitive calculations. It may be possible to use the Paying Taxes data to assess whether or not it reflects changes in complexity, but caution should be observed in forming that view.

The assumptions adopted in the Paying Taxes case study company are relatively simple and so will be relevant to a large number of companies within any tax system. Complexities that are due to particular industries, or to cross-border and intra-group transactions are not considered by the study. It is possible however to use the methodology to look at other such scenarios by choosing parameters for the case study company that take into account specific areas of interest.

It is recognized that the Paying Taxes sub-indicators do not cover all aspects of tax administration and other relevant aspects of the tax rules. Over the years of the study, contributors have been asked a number of supplementary questions to gain added insights on a range of issues including the overall structure of the tax system, simplicity or otherwise of the tax rules and how easy it is to deal with the tax authorities, tax audits and post-filing processes. Some initial analysis of answers to these questions has been included in *Paying Taxes 2015*, and the intention is provide further analysis to enhance the commentary around the results in future editions of the Paying Taxes study.

APPENDIX: FINANCIAL STATEMENT PARAMETERS OF THE CASE STUDY COMPANY

Calculation of Commercial Profit	The Standard Factor to Be Multiplied by per capita GNI (in Each Economy)		Details of the Assumptions
Sales		1050	
Cost of goods sold		875	
Administrative costs		10	
Salaries		67	Total salaries for 4 managers: 9*GNI Total salaries for 8 assistants: 10*GNI Total salaries for 48 workers: 48*GNI
Net profits before depreciation and other expenses	(952)	98	
Depreciation and amortization	*Depreciation Rates (we assume straight-line method of depreciation)*		*Assumptions about the Net Value of the fixed assets. Note that all the below values are net value of fixed assets after accounting for 1st year of depreciation. Therefore; before applying the annual depreciation rate, we need first to calculate the gross book value of the fixed assets and then calculate the deductible annual depreciation expense. Gross Book Value = Net Value/1-Depreciation rate.*
Building	5%	3.1	Building value: 40*GNI (old part of the building) + 18*GNI (new part of building) = 58*GNI. Building is depreciated at 5% annual rate → Annual depreciation = 0.05(40*GNI/0.95) + 0.05(18*GNI) = 3.1*GNI.

Calculation of Commercial Profit		The Standard Factor to Be Multiplied by per capita GNI (in Each Economy)	Details of the Assumptions
Machinery	10%	6.7	Machinery value: 60*GNI Machinery is depreciated at 10% → Annual depreciation = 0.1(60*GNI/0.9) = 6.7*GNI
Computers	33%	2.5	Computers value: 5*GNI Computers are depreciated at 33% → Annual depreciation = 0.33(5*GNI/0.67) = 2.5*GNI
Office equipment	20%	1.3	Office equipment value: 5*GNI Office equipment are depreciated at 20% → Annual depreciation = 0.2(5*GNI/0.8) = 1.3*GNI
Truck	20%	1.3	Truck value: 5*GNI Truck is depreciated at 20% → Annual depreciation = 0.2(5*GNI/0.8) = 1.3*GNI
Business development expenses	10%	1.3	Business development expenses: 12*GNI BDE are amortized at 10% → Annual depreciation = 0.1(12*GNI/0.88) = 1.3*GNI
Total depreciation and amortization expenses		(16.05)	
Other expenses			Assumptions about the value of the other expenses
Start-up expenses		1.00	1*GNI
Advertising expenses		10.50	1% of sales revenue = 1%(1050*GNI) = 10.5*GNI
Leasing expenses		0.50	50% of GNI
Insurance premium - Medical insurance for employees		0.67	1% of total salaries = 1%(67*GNI) = 0.67*GNI
Insurance premium - Building		0.58	1% of building value = 1%(58*GNI) = 0.58*GNI

Business travel expenses	0.10		1% of GNI
Accountancy fees	0.10		1% of GNI
Legal fees	0.10		1% of GNI
Machinery repair expenses	3.00		5% of machinery value = 5%(60*GNI) = 3*GNI
Patent royalties	0.50		50% of GNI
Owners' expenses	0.10		10% of GNI
Total other expenses		(17.5)	
Provisions			*Assumptions*
Bad debt	5.0		10% of accounts receivables (A/R); A/R = 50*GNI → 0.1(50*GNI) = 5*GNI
Pension contributions (for employees)	0.7		1% of salaries = 1%(67*GNI) = 0.7*GNI
Maintenance and repairs	0.6		1% (Net value of building) = 1%(58*GNI) = 0.6*GNI
Total provisions		(6.27)	
Interest expense		(3.65)	Total cash borrowed by the company is charged at 5% interest. Total cash borrowed = value of all fixed assets – Paid-in capital (i.e., any cash that was borrowed on top of the paid-in capital (102*GNI) of shareholders to buy the fixed assets) = 5%((30+58+60+5+5+12)-(102*GNI)) = 3.65*GNI
Other income			*Assumptions*

Calculation of Commercial Profit	*The Standard Factor to Be Multiplied by per capita GNI (in Each Economy)*	*Details of the Assumptions*
Interest income	1.52	We assume that the company has a money-interest bearing account with interest at 4%. Cash in account = $GNI*(20+1/2$ of the proceeds of the sale of the 2nd plot of land)1 = $(20+(30*1.2/2))$ Interest income + 4%$((20+(30*1.2/2))$ = $1.52*GNI$
Capital gains	3.00	2nd plot of land is sold at = $1.2(30*GNI)$ Original cost of land = $30*GNI$ Realtor fees = $1*GNI$ Legal fees = $2*GNI$ Capital gains = $1.2(30*GNI) - (30*GNI) - 1*GNI - 2*GNI$ = $3*GNI$
Total other income	*4.52*	
Total Commercial Profits Factor	*59.4*	

CHAPTER 7

The *Paying Taxes* Report: Will It Guide Tax System Simplification?

Sharon Smulders

§7.01 INTRODUCTION

As explained in Chapter 6 of this volume,[1] the objectives of the World Bank Group & PwC *Paying Taxes* report[2] are to encourage tax reform and to develop a good tax system. *Paying Taxes* aims to achieve this by understanding the regulatory environment in which businesses operate. The study goes further by also providing an assessment of the tax compliance burden on a business and by providing a measure of the tax complexity stemming from the tax system. This is done in such a way as to allow global comparisons to be made. Assessing the help that is given to small businesses to deal with the complexity in terms of administration and systems made available is also considered in the study.

The focus of research in *Paying Taxes* is stated as being on the developing world, and indeed this report has been used by many of these countries' governments to inform them as to where they could potentially modernize and reform their country's tax systems.[3] Interestingly this report is also being extensively used by governments of developed countries. One example of this is the United Kingdom (UK) where the Office

---

1. Andrew Packman & Neville Howlett, Paying Taxes: The Global Picture – *An Index to Encourage Tax Reform and the Development of Good Tax Systems*, this volume, §6.01[A].
2. See most recently World Bank Group, *Doing Business 2015: Going beyond Efficiency*, 83 ('Paying taxes: trends before and after the financial crisis') (29 October 2014); and, separately, World Bank Group & PwC, *Paying Taxes 2015: The Global Picture* (20 November 2014), http://www.doingbusiness.org/reports/thematic-reports/paying-taxes.
3. Erica DeVry, 'PwC Report Finds Global Tax Authorities Modernizing Tax Systems', *Big Four Firms Network* (undated, discussing the 2009 report). http://www.big4.com/news/pwc-report-finds-global-tax-authorities-modernizing-tax-systems/ (accessed on 28 November 2014); 'Paying taxes

of Tax Simplification[4] was requested by the UK government in 2013 to see how the UK can improve its competitiveness (rankings). It is therefore evident, that this report has the attention of governments across the globe and is providing valuable information that can hopefully assist each government to improve its country's tax system. This is a very respectable starting point for any research report and the authors must be highly commended for this.

§7.02   METHODOLOGY USED

The *Paying Taxes* report quantitatively and objectively assesses the impact of tax regulations on a case study company, as described in Chapter 6 of this volume.[5] To provide a measure of how easy it is to pay tax in an economy and an ability to make comparisons with other economies around the world, the study, from 2015 uses the 'distance to frontier' measure (defined as the lowest score in each sub-indicator across all economies since inception) of the following indicators to calculate the overall ranking for a country:

- the total tax rate;
- the number of tax payments made; and
- the time taken to complete tax returns.

The distance to frontier measure is taken for each sub-indicator and then aggregated for each economy, and an overall distance to frontier score is calculated using a simple mean. Using this measure each economy's performance is benchmarked against the regulatory best practice – showing the gap between each economy's performance and the best performance on each indicator. The frontier is set at the lowest number that has occurred in the study for each sub-indicator with exception of the total tax rate, for which a threshold has been established.

Other chapters in this volume consider legislative complexity[6] but the *Paying Taxes* report, by considering the above indicators, evaluates the practical operational complexity that a tax system imposes on taxpayers that are compliant. Operational

---

becomes easier for businesses, Middle East continues to have the least demanding tax frame-work', *GulfNews.com* (24 November 2014), http://gulfnews.com/business/economy/paying-taxes-becomes-easier-for-businesses-1.1417371. See also Mick Moore, 'The Changing Politics of Tax Policy Reform in Developing Countries', *World Bank PREM Notes*, 3 (February 2013, No. 2) (discussing the expansion of global accounting firms into developing countries and noting that '[t]he *Paying Taxes* report produced annually by PwC and the World Bank currently has a global coverage and makes the best of very scarce hard data on tax system performance'), http://siteresources.worldbank.org/PUBLICSECTORANDGOVERNANCE/Resources/285741-13619734 00317/GPSM2_v2.pdf.

4. Office of Tax Simplification (UK), 'Review of the competitiveness of the UK Tax Administration: final report' (October 2014), https://www.gov.uk/government/uploads/system/uploads/attachment_data/file/362302/competitiveness_review_final_report.pdf (accessed on 28 October 2014).

5. Andrew Packman & Neville Howlett, Paying Taxes: The Global Picture – *An Index to Encourage Tax Reform and the Development of Good Tax Systems*, this volume, §6.02[A].

6. See, for example, David Ulph, *Measuring Tax Complexity*, this volume, §4.02; Marco Lugo & François Vaillancourt, *Measuring Tax Complexity: Analytical Framework and Evidence for*

simplicity is just as important as legislative simplicity, as can be seen from, for instance, South Africa, where the value added tax (VAT) registration process has in some instances taken large international companies many months to complete.[7] The interesting point is that the National Treasury was open to amending the law to avoid this happening in future, but after public consultation it was established that it is not the law that is causing these problems, but rather the operational implementation and compliance with the law that was the bottleneck.[8] There is therefore clear merit for the study to consider the operational tax compliance burden that entities are faced with.

§7.03 FINDINGS OF THE STUDY

One of the very interesting findings of the *Paying Taxes* study is that there has been a noticeable simplification in tax systems globally.[9] A further encouraging finding is that it has become easier and less costly to comply with tax regulations, with a slowing in the rates of decline of these indicators in 2012 but increase in these rates again in 2013.[10]

It is evident that the *Paying Taxes* report is being used by policy-makers to improve their tax systems. It is therefore providing very convenient and useful information to many government officials and is described as being a 'thoroughly researched and uniquely informative document'.[11] Notwithstanding this, critics have argued that this report can be improved so as to further assist these officials in simplifying and improving (if necessary) their country's tax systems.[12] These sug-gested improvements will be discussed in the next section of this chapter by consid-ering the criticisms and the limitations of the study. This is then followed (§7.05) by a

---

Individual Income Tax Preferences for Canada, this volume, §9.02; John Whiting, Jeremy Sherwood & Gareth Jones, *The Office of Tax Simplification and its Complexity Index*, this volume, §15.02.

7. KPMG, *SARS [South African Revenue Service] to make it easier for foreign companies* (19 July 2013), http://www.kpmg.com/za/en/issuesandinsights/articlespublications/tax-and-legal-pu blications/pages/sars-foreign-companies-doing-business.aspx (accessed on 28 November 2014).

8. SARS, National Treasury & Recognized controlling bodies, *Meeting with recognized controlling bodies to discuss VAT registration legislative amendments* (attended by author, February 2014). See also Varusha Moodaley, 'The VAT registration amendments: Will these changes streamline the registration process?', *tax ENSight* (23 April 2014) (discussing legislative amendments to the registration under the Taxation Laws Amendment Act No. 31 of 2013, effective 1 April 2014), https://www.ensafrica.com/news/the-VAT-registration-amendments-will-these-changes-strea mline-the-registration?Id = 1406&STitle = tax%20ENSight (accessed on 28 November 2014).

9. Andrew Packman & Neville Howlett, Paying Taxes: The Global Picture – *An Index to Encourage Tax Reform and the Development of Good Tax Systems*, this volume, §6.03[B] and §6.03[C].

10. Andrew Packman & Neville Howlett, Paying Taxes: The Global Picture – *An Index to Encourage Tax Reform and the Development of Good Tax Systems*, this volume, §6.03[B], §6.03[C] and §6.05.

11. Robert Goulder, 'Magnum Opus: "Paying taxes 2015: The Global Picture"', *Forbes.com* (21 November 2014), http://www.forbes.com/sites/taxanalysts/2014/11/21/magnum-opus-payi ng-taxes-2015-the-global-picture/ (accessed on 30 November 2014).

12. Binh Tran-Nam & Chris Evans, *Towards the Development of a Tax System Complexity Index*, 35(3) Fiscal Stud. 341, 356–357 (2014).

discussion of the report's strengths and successes so as to ensure a robust overall evaluation of the report.

§7.04   CRITICISM/LIMITATIONS OF THE STUDY

Although the *Paying Taxes* report has been used by various governments, academics and civil society, the report has also been criticized by various parties both within the World Bank (the Bank) and outside the Bank.[13] The primary criticism is that the *Paying Taxes* study tends to focus the reader's attention on the indicator rankings rather than the underlying data. This is presumably because the press tends to focus on the rankings rather than the evidence and findings that are actually contained on the website and in the Paying Taxes report that is published annually in November. In fact, the report clearly states that a main aim is to provide information to facilitate constructive discussion and to encourage reform rather than to focus purely on a comparison of the rankings of the economies which participate. Indeed the report only refers to the rankings in Appendix 3 after all the insights and commentary of the findings have been discussed in-depth.[14] It has also been argued that the focus of the report on the formal and legal requirements of paying taxes gives a partial or potentially misleading picture of the real situation.[15] Thus, in 2012, World Bank President Jim Yong Kim appointed an Independent Review Panel of experts to review various issues relating to the *Doing Business* report, which includes the *Paying Taxes* report,[16] following an earlier review by the Bank's Independent Evaluation Group in 2008.[17] The rest of this chapter will discuss certain of the findings and recommendations stemming from the report in June 2013 of the Independent Review Panel ('the IRP report') as well as other potential concerns and recommendations that have arisen from the analysis of the IRP report by other parties. Certain of the more controversial indicators and assumptions will be discussed individually.

---

13. See, for example, the independent commentary in Christina Chang, 'The Doing Business review: a test of World Bank leadership', *Bretton Woods Project* (24 June 2013), http://www.brettonwoodsproject.org/2013/06/art-572701/ (accessed on 30 December 2014).
14. European Network on Debt and Development, 'Trade Unions and campaigners slam "strongly flawed" Doing Business report, after World Bank snubs call by two independent panels for root and branch reform', *Press release* (28 October 2014), http://www.eurodad.org/Entries/view/1546281/2014/10/28/Trade-unions-and-campaigners-slam-strongly-flawed-Doing-Business-report-after-World-Bank-snubs-call-by-two-independent-panels-for-root-and-branch-reform (accessed on 30 October 2014).
15. Independent *Doing Business* Report Review Panel (Trevor Manuel, Chairperson), 'Independent Panel Review of the Doing Business report', 39 (June 2013), http://www.dbrpanel.org/sites/dbrpanel/files/doing-business-review-panel-report.pdf (accessed on 27 September 2014).
16. See Independent *Doing Business* Report Review Panel (Trevor Manuel, Chairperson), 'Independent Panel Review of the Doing Business report', above n. 15.
17. World Bank Independent Evaluation Group, *Doing Business: An Independent Evaluation, Taking the Measure of the World Bank-IFC Doing Business Indicators* (1 October 2008), http://ieg.worldbank.org/Data/reports/db_evaluation.pdf.

[A]   Case Study Firm

The case study firm as described in Chapter 6 of this volume is a hypothetical company with defined characteristics – simply explained it is a small to medium-sized (SME) business that is incorporated and operating in the largest city in a particular country (from Paying Taxes 2015,[18] where an economy has a population in excess of 100 million, the second largest business city is also included in the study). Two central assumptions underlie this classification as a SME – that is, that the business has 60 employees and that its annual turnover is 1,050 x the annual *per capita* income of that country. These assumptions in certain instances place this case study entity above many developing countries' definition of a small business.[19] In fact in some countries this might be regarded as a large company. It is for this reason that the *Paying Taxes* report has been criticized for providing information for a specific target market, but yet it excludes, to a large extent, the entities (SMEs) that are its primary focus.[20]

A further assumption made is that the case study company keeps accurate accounting records and follows best practice. This is not generally the case, especially in small businesses in developing countries,[21] but the reasons for making this assumption are understandable.

The relevance and representativeness of the case study firm has thus been highlighted as one of the primary concerns of the study. It is argued in the *Paying Taxes* report that the advantages of using a hypothetical firm are that:

---

18. See World Bank Group, *Doing Business 2015: Going Beyond Efficiency*, above n. 2; World Bank Group & PwC, *Paying Taxes 2015: The Global Picture*, above n. 2.
19. Tom Gibson & H.J. van der Vaart, 'Defining SMEs: A Less Imperfect Way of Defining Small and Medium Enterprises in Developing Countries', Brookings Global Economy and Development paper, 10–17 (September 2008), http://www.brookings.edu/ ~ /media/research/files/papers/ 2008/9/development%20gibson/09_development_gibson.pdf (accessed on 30 November 2014); Dalberg Global Development Advisors (with assistance of the European Investment Bank), *Report on Support to SMEs in Developing Countries Through Financial Intermediaries*, 6 (November 2011), available at: http://www.eib.org/attachments/dalberg_sme-briefing-paper. pdf (accessed on 15 January 2015). For example Egypt defines a large enterprise as having more than fifty employees: Khrystyna Kushnir, Melina Laura Mirmulstein & Rita Ramalho, 'Micro, Small, and Medium Enterprises Around the World: How Many Are There, and What Affects the Count?', World Bank/IFC Indicators MSME Country Indicators, 2–3 (2010), http://www.ifc.org /wps/wcm/connect/9ae1dd80495860d6a482b519583b6d16/MSME-CI-AnalysisNote.pdf?MOD = AJPERES, (accessed on 15 January 2015); Meghana Ayyagari, Thorsten Beck, & Asli Demirgüç -Kunt, 'Small and Medium Enterprises Across the Globe: A New Database', World Bank Policy Research Working Paper 3127, Washington, DC, 5, n. 6 (August 2003), http://papers.ssrn.com /sol3/papers.cfm?abstract_id = 636547 (accessed on 15 January 2015).
20. Tran-Nam & Evans, above n. 12.
21. Stuart McChlery, Alan D. Godfrey & Lesley Meechan, *Barriers and catalysts to sound financial management systems in small sized enterprises*, 7(3) J. Applied Acct. Res. 1, 23–24 (2005). See also Vassili Prokopenko & Paul Holden, 'Financial Development and Poverty Alleviation: Issues and Policy Implications for Developing and Transition Countries', IMF Working Paper, 23 (October 2001), https://books.google.co.za/books?id = 9fvSOaA8dzUC&pg = PA23&lpg = PA23 &dq = accounting + records + developing + countries&source = bl&ots = v_qUl4RwlF&sig = Hu40 nMu-4x1grg8OHp1Fwl8H-Uk&hl = en&sa = X&ei = aeu5VPT8HImU7Aa4voDoCQ&ved = 0CC0Q 6AEwAw#v = onepage&q = accounting%20records%20developing%20countries&f = false (accessed on 15 January 2015); Nelson Maseko & Onias Manyani, *Accounting practices of SMEs in Zimbabwe: An investigative study of record keeping for performance measurement (A case study of Bindura)*, 3(8) J. Acct. & Taxation 171–181 (2011).

- the number of respondents per country can be much smaller (compared to a firm survey);
- the results are more comparable over multiple countries and years.

The Independent *Doing Business* Report Review Panel, chaired by Trevor Manuel, argues that while the methodology allows for international comparisons based on a standard set of assumptions, it is not necessarily representative of the tax compliance cost burden of the majority of actual companies in any particular country.[22] This view is supported by the expert panel that are also of the view that although the hypothetical case study firm's characteristics remain the same, the variations between different countries' (and companies') procedures, practices and general conditions are not taken into account in the report. It is thus evident that using the case study firm presents a single, very detailed, hypothetical case to the respondents, and asks them to answer all the questions about that particular case. It is evident therefore that the study does not consider different types of businesses with circumstances other than those applicable to the case study firm. This limitation is, however, clearly mentioned in the *Paying Taxes* report as one of the limitations.

A further assumption regarding the case study firm is that if the firm qualifies as a 'small' company then it will apply the small company tax rules. Many countries[23] have implemented special tax regimes for this sector and a more in-depth analysis on the use of these by SMEs and their effect on the entities' tax compliance burden could significantly improve the impact of the report.

As mentioned, it is stated that the main aim of the study is to allow policy-makers to make comparisons and thereby to encourage reform, but international investors looking at investing internationally may use this study to inform them on the tax impact of any potential investment in an economy but would do so as one part of a variety of information that they need to consider. As it is generally unlikely that large corporations would be interested in investing in small businesses, the relevance of this report to them is questionable[24] but despite the case study company not reflecting their proposed investment, the report does still provide a basis of comparison particularly on compliance. Furthermore, as mentioned above,[25] generally the case study firm would be classified as a medium to large business, especially in developing countries, so the relevance of this report to them might well be justified. The study has considered the links between tax and economic factors.[26] Regression analyses have been performed in the past to determine the relationship between the *Paying Taxes* findings and the economy's average growth rate over a period as well as the growth of stock of inward investment over the same period. The inclusion of a comparison with foreign direct

---

22. Independent Doing Business Report Review Panel (Trevor Manuel, Chairperson), 'Independent Panel Review of the Doing Business report', above n. 15, at 2, 28, 39, 42.
23. Chris Evans, Ann Hansford, John Hasseldine, Phil Lignier, Sharon Smulders & François Vaillancourt, *Small business and tax compliance costs: A cross-country study of managerial benefits and tax concessions*, 12(2) eJournal of Tax Research 453 (2014).
24. Tran-Nam & Evans, above n. 12, at 356.
25. See text at nn. 19–20, above.
26. Andrew Packman & Neville Howlett, Paying Taxes: The Global Picture – *An Index to Encourage Tax Reform and the Development of Good Tax Systems*, this volume, §6.04.

investment is a welcome addition but the caution expressed in the report on inferring too much from the results of this analysis are duly noted. Suggestions by the expert panel of triangulation of the survey results to the investment/climate survey results are valid and would make the results of the report more robust.[27]

Based on the above limitations of using a case study firm, the panel of experts[28] tasked to review this study suggested, as an alternative to its recommendations for improvement of the existing methodology of the *Paying Taxes* study, that the concept of a single hypothetical case study firm be terminated. Introduction of multiple case study firm scenarios has been suggested by the expert panel but the impact on the cost and time involved in doing this research would need to be justifiable. Considering the impact that the report has already had, this recommendation should not be disregarded but evaluated further.

The three main sub-indicators used in the *Paying Taxes* report will be discussed next.

[B] The Total Tax Rate (TTR)

The total tax rate is the total of all the taxes borne (including, but not limited to, taxes paid) expressed as a percentage of commercial profit and includes taxes that are not generally included in the definition of 'tax' as defined by the International Monetary Fund (IMF) and Organisation for Economic Co-operation and Development (OECD).[29] That is, the TTR includes corporate tax, taxes on property, transfer taxes, employer social security contributions and other payroll taxes, taxes paid on dividends, taxes paid on financial transactions and road taxes, and also compulsory fees payable to non-government entities.[30] The expansion of the definition of the tax is justified as it is indicative of what a business would pay at the central, regional and local levels. A concern has, however, been raised that caution needs to be taken when consolidating these taxes as they are levied on different bases and might have different economic consequences.[31]

Although the World Bank and PwC, in all their presentations, emphasize that the tax system should be expected to reflect the circumstances of the economy, the biggest concern raised by critics with regard to the TTR indicator is that it promotes a 'race to the bottom' in corporate taxation.[32] In an attempt to address this concern a threshold for the total tax rate indicator (26.1% in the 2015 *Paying Taxes* report) was introduced which ensures that any country that has a tax rate below this threshold would not have

---

27. Independent *Doing Business* Report Review Panel (Trevor Manuel, Chairperson), 'Independent Panel Review of the Doing Business report', above n. 15, at 2.
28. Independent *Doing Business* Report Review Panel (Trevor Manuel, Chairperson), 'Independent Panel Review of the Doing Business report', above n. 15, at 40–41.
29. Andrew Packman & Neville Howlett, Paying Taxes: The Global Picture – *An Index to Encourage Tax Reform and the Development of Good Tax Systems*, this volume, §6.02[B].
30. Independent *Doing Business* Report Review Panel (Trevor Manuel, Chairperson), 'Independent Panel Review of the Doing Business report', above n. 15, at 37.
31. Independent *Doing Business* Report Review Panel (Trevor Manuel, Chairperson), 'Independent Panel Review of the Doing Business report', above n. 15, at 38.
32. See European Network on Debt and Development, above n. 14.

their total tax ranking affected. The change in the calculation of the rankings in the 2015 Paying Taxes report makes further adjustments to how the TTR is included in the ranking which restricts further the benefit of reduced TTRs at the lower levels.[33]

A further concern raised is that tax planning has not been factored into the TTR and thus the TTR is an indicator of the tax burden faced by an SME rather than the tax compliance burden it is subjected to.[34] Although this concern is noted, it is submitted that tax planning should not feature in the TTR as the TTR is not aimed at measuring the tax compliance burden but rather the actual tax obligation of the company. Furthermore, it is understood from the assumptions of the case study company that it is a simple company that is tax compliant and hence there is no need for it to spend time on doing any tax planning. Corruption costs are also not taken into account in the calculation of the three sub-indicators. It is very difficult, if not impossible to quantify these costs, but as they are quite prevalent in developing countries[35] and have a real impact on the costs borne by a business, their impact should be mentioned in the report.

Based on the concerns raised above, many critics support removing the TTR indicator.[36] Another reason provided by these critics supporting its removal is that it is not regarded as relevant to the larger report – the *Doing Business* Report – as it does not impact the ease of doing business in a country, which is what the *Doing Business* report is all about. It will be interesting to see if the World Bank decides to adhere to this advice in future publications, as the impact of the TTR on the ease of doing business and the size of the informal sector in instances where the TTR is unfeasibly high (due to, for example, cascading sales tax or turnover tax) deserves some consideration.

[C]   'Number of Payments'

This indicator has been included in the *Paying Taxes* report as it is intended to measure the administrative burden faced by SMEs and indirectly it also provides insight into the impact of the methods of payments used by SMEs including whether those methods are electronic or manual.[37] The number of payments made in respect of various taxes including taxes that are collected on behalf of the government (such as VAT and PAYE) are included in this indicator. By not limiting the number of payments to those made only in respect of the three main taxes (as is done in the 'time to comply' indicator – refer to §7.04[D] below), the calculation improves the report's ability to determine the

---

33. Andrew Packman & Neville Howlett, Paying Taxes: The Global Picture – *An Index to Encourage Tax Reform and the Development of Good Tax Systems*, this volume, §6.02[D].
34. Tran-Nam & Evans, above n. 12, at 356.
35. Benjamin A. Olken & Rohini Pande, *Corruption in Developing Countries*, 4 Ann. Rev. Econ. 479 (2012).
36. Independent *Doing Business* Report Review Panel (Trevor Manuel, Chairperson), 'Independent Panel Review of the Doing Business report', above n. 15, at 38.
37. Andrew Packman & Neville Howlett, Paying Taxes: The Global Picture – *An Index to Encourage Tax Reform and the Development of Good Tax Systems*, this volume, §6.02[C][2][a]; Independent *Doing Business* Report Review Panel (Trevor Manuel, Chairperson), 'Independent Panel Review of the Doing Business report', above n. 15, at 38.

true administrative burden and complexity associated with an SME's tax compliance obligations.

It is of note that with regard to the 'number of payments' indicator, where there is online payment and filing of taxes by the majority of companies in the economy, the indicator is reported as only '1' even if multiple online payments/filings are made. The rationale for this is to reflect the low administrative burden that making online payments/filings has on the business.[38] Although it is acknowledged that making use of online payments/filings is better in some instances than making manual payments/filings, this is not always the case. For instance, in South Africa the South African Revenue Service changed the way in which tax practitioners were able to assist their clients with paying their taxes online. The reason for this change was to curb the fraud that was taking place – payments being withdrawn from incorrect bank accounts.[39] Thus, although the number of payments had remained the same, the time to make these payments had increased substantially in that particular year due to the changes made and in some instances became more time consuming than making manual payments.[40] It is acknowledged that this time should therefore be taken into account in the 'time to comply' indicator, but when it comes to the number of payments indicator, it is evident that reducing this to '1' just because they are online payments/filings does not always hold true and will also not be a valuable indicator if certain economies use online payments/filings.

The expert panel is of the view that only the time and cost of each procedure (and not the number of payments) should be published in the report.[41] This is because the number of payments indicator is not a very good measure of the ease of doing business. It is recommended that the use of online payments should be taken into account in the 'time to comply' indicator rather than treat it as has been explained above.

[D] Time Taken to Complete Tax Returns ('Time to Comply')

This indicator measures the hours it takes an SME to prepare, file and pay three taxes (corporate income tax, consumption taxes (such as VAT and payroll taxes). The first limitation of this indicator is thus that it is only in respect of three taxes – compliance with all other taxes is ignored mainly because no cross-border, related party or complex transactions are assumed to be undertaken by the case study firm and because it was found that these other taxes were not as time consuming as the above three taxes.

---

38. Andrew Packman & Neville Howlett, Paying Taxes: The Global Picture – *An Index to Encourage Tax Reform and the Development of Good Tax Systems*, this volume, §6.02[C][2][a].
39. SARS, 'Discontinuance of debit pull transactions on eFiling', http://www.sars.gov.za/Clie ntSegments/Individuals/How-Pay/Pages/Discontinuation-of-Debit-Pull-Transactions-on-eFiling .aspx (accessed 10 June 2014).
40. Ingé Lamprecht, 'Tax Practitioners up in arms over SARS payments', *Moneyweb* (22 January 2014), http://www.moneyweb.co.za/moneyweb-tax/tax-practitioners-up-in-arms-over-sars-payments (accessed on 23 November 2014).
41. Independent *Doing Business* Report Review Panel (Trevor Manuel, Chairperson), 'Independent Panel Review of the Doing Business report', above n. 15, at 40.

The second limitation is that this indicator does not currently include the time taken to comply after the submission of a tax return. This time would typically include the time taken to check the assessment, object or appeal against the assessment and any litigation proceedings that might be necessary based on the outcome of the previous mentioned steps. Obtaining rulings from the applicable revenue authority to get clarity on the treatment of certain transactions is also not taken into account in this indicator. The procedures involved to obtain and follow up on a VAT refund are also not implicitly included in this measure. A further limitation expressed by the expert panel is that all of these measures are very subjective and dependent on the contributor's experience.[42] The use of more than one contributor in every economy should, however, be noted.[43]

Another issue regarding the time taken to comply is the silence in the report on the time taken by external advisors assisting the case study business with its tax affairs. Although it could be argued that this time is expected to be small for the case study company due to the lack of complex tax issues, research has shown that this time could possibly be costly (if for example different tax regimes are available to small businesses and they need to choose the most appropriate regime) and should be factored into the analysis albeit only for completeness' sake.[44]

Refinement, as briefly discussed above, of the 'time taken to comply' indicator is necessary to obtain a more accurate assessment of the tax compliance burden faced by small to medium enterprises. The expert panel advises that ways in which the tax laws can be simplified and administrative burdens reduced should be incorporated into the report. They also point out that the role of the tax administration in alleviating these burdens should be considered in the research.[45] Using the knowledge obtained in this area by other international organizations could also improve the current data collection methodology.

[E]   Overview of the Above Indicators

It is evident, and acknowledged in the report, that the above indicators do not measure a country's most relevant economic performance policy aspects and the broader measures of the tax law complexity and administrative burden facing SMEs. An alternative recommendation by the expert panel to all of the above suggestions relating to the tax indicators is that perhaps 'a new, more sophisticated set of tax sub-indicators' for SMEs should be developed. They propose that this could entail multiple case studies rather than a single case study (as mentioned above, §7.04[A]), using indicators that measure the complexity of tax legislation, the nature and scale of the administrative

---

42. Independent *Doing Business* Report Review Panel (Trevor Manuel, Chairperson), 'Independent Panel Review of the Doing Business report', above n. 15, at 38–39.
43. See World Bank Group & PwC, *Paying Taxes 2015: The Global Picture* (20 November 2014), http://www.doingbusiness.org/reports/thematic-reports/paying-taxes, above n. 2, at 7, 70.
44. Tran-Nam & Evans, above n. 12, at 356.
45. Independent *Doing Business* Report Review Panel (Trevor Manuel, Chairperson), 'Independent Panel Review of the Doing Business report', above n. 15, at 38–41.

burden and the effectiveness of tax administrations in their interaction with these businesses.[46]

If no restrictions and unlimited resources were available, these recommendations are fully justifiable. Perhaps more information on what resources were/are available and have been/could be allocated to this project would be useful to establish whether there is a real prospect that these recommendations could actually be successfully implemented.

[F] Data and Data Collection

[1] Data Time Periods

The report uses data for the preceding two years; thus the 2015 report assesses the tax system for period ending 31 December 2013.[47] The information, as in most research is not real-time information and readers of the report are made aware of this fact. One suggestion is that perhaps this fact should be made more prominent in the report and especially at media briefings.

[2] Data Collection Procedures

The report provides little information on the data collection procedures used to gather this information – that is, on the way in which the contributors are selected as well as the verification procedures carried out on the responses received to ensure their accuracy and validity, for example.[48] More information on the process should be made available online.

[3] Contributors

Originally, a significant proportion of respondents to the survey were from PwC but over the years more non-PwC contributors were recruited. It had been recommended by the Independent Evaluation Group in its 2008 report that this be improved further by arranging for more firms to contribute.[49] Currently PwC accounts for less than one-third of the respondents and other large accountancy firms, law firms and smaller accounting firms have now been included in the list of respondents.[50] The concern expressed has thus been addressed.

---

46. Independent *Doing Business* Report Review Panel (Trevor Manuel, Chairperson), 'Independent Panel Review of the Doing Business report', above n. 15, at 41.
47. Andrew Packman & Neville Howlett, Paying Taxes: The Global Picture – *An Index to Encourage Tax Reform and the Development of Good Tax Systems*, this volume, §6.01[A].
48. Tran-Nam & Evans, above n. 12, at 357.
49. World Bank Independent Evaluation Group, *Doing Business: An Independent Evaluation, Taking the Measure of the World Bank-IFC Doing Business Indicators*, above n. 17, at 13–14.
50. Independent *Doing Business* Report Review Panel (Trevor Manuel, Chairperson), 'Independent Panel Review of the Doing Business report', above n. 15, at 39.

The poor process of scrutiny of the methods used and internal feedback in the World Bank itself have also been heavily criticized by the expert panel. One of the areas of scrutiny was that the opinions of mainly legal experts (lawyers) who interact with many entities were used to obtain the necessary data for the survey. The concern was raised that this potentially limited the input into the report to the issues that a legal practitioner deals with (that fall within the legal statutes and their enforcement) but these issues might not include aspects of the business environment that are critical for a business when paying its taxes.[51] As stated above, PwC are an important respondent to the survey. Noting the concern raised above, it must be pointed out that PwC is an international firm that employs both accountants and lawyers and assuming that only the lawyers provided input into the research might be unfounded, but clarity on this matter would calm any further fears that the critics might have. Notwithstanding this, PwC's input into the project is still essential and justifiable especially because of the substantial knowledge and expertise that they must have gained over the years of doing the project.

To further dispel any fears of a conflict of interest and lack of transparency because PwC provides their input (as a *pro bono* service),[52] it is recommended that all aspects of this relationship be documented and made publicly available.

To further improve the reliability of the data that is collected for the report, the expert panel has suggested including input from small business task teams (consisting of government, private sector and World Bank representatives). The expert panel also recommended that governments and tax administrations should be more involved in the verification of data.[53] Although this recommendation might make sense, it is uncertain whether some governments and tax administrations (especially those in developing countries) have the capacity and knowledge to perform these functions.[54]

[4]   Data and Adjustments to the Data

It has been argued by some critics that the information and data collected is incapable of capturing the complexities of the legal system.[55] This is true, but it is acknowledged that in order to improve on this shortcoming the costs and complexity of the whole study would increase and this is also a factor that needs to be weighed up against the additional benefits received.

---

51. Independent *Doing Business* Report Review Panel (Trevor Manuel, Chairperson), 'Independent Panel Review of the Doing Business report', above n. 15, at 15.
52. Independent *Doing Business* Report Review Panel (Trevor Manuel, Chairperson), 'Independent Panel Review of the Doing Business report', above n. 15, at 39.
53. Independent *Doing Business* Report Review Panel (Trevor Manuel, Chairperson), 'Independent Panel Review of the Doing Business report', above n. 15, at 41.
54. See, for example, OECD, 'Tax and Development: Draft principles for international engagement in supporting developing counties in revenue matters' (May 2013), http://www.oecd.org/ctp/tax-global/Principles_for_international_engagement_May2013.pdf (accessed on 30 November 2014).
55. Independent *Doing Business* Report Review Panel (Trevor Manuel, Chairperson), 'Independent Panel Review of the Doing Business report', above n. 15, at 42; Tran-Nam & Evans, above n. 12, at 356.

Constant improvements and expansion of the methods used to obtain and evaluate the data in the Paying Taxes report are inevitable. These improvements do, however, result in difficulties in providing comparative information year on year. Losing comparability over time will tend to lock in poor practice and this should be noted and catered for (wherever possible). Another area for improvement that has been identified is that the adjustments made to the current and previous data are not sufficiently transparent.[56] This is an area that is clearly easy to fix and is highly recommended for all future publications.

[G] Aggregate Rankings

The aggregate rankings used in the *Paying Taxes* reports before 2015 provided a consolidated indicator which was a simple average of the rankings obtained for each country for each of the indicators.[57] No weights were used to obtain the aggregated ranking.[58] The use of aggregated rankings was regarded by some critics as a crude measurement that potentially risks being a poor reflection of the formal statutes and how they influence economic performance in a particular country.[59] The arbitrariness of the aggregation method was also of concern to many as it appeared to be based on value judgment rather than robust statistical methods. The three tax indicators are also vastly different and conceptually the aggregation of these different indicators into one overall unweighted tax indicator is problematic.[60] The use of the 'distance to frontier' (DTF) measure from 2015 takes the DTF for each sub-indicator and then aggregates it for each economy, and an overall DTF score is calculated using a simple mean.

It has also been argued that the movements of the rankings over time is not a good reflection of the actual policy change in a country.[61] The DTF measure introduced in 2015 will go some way to addressing this concern. A concern raised by Thomas and Luo[62] is the lack of transparency of how and why the indicators have changed (per country). The expert panel makes the recommendation that aggregation and converted ordinal rankings should no longer be used to rank the countries from 1 to 185. Rather, the forced ranking method that categorizes the countries into categories should be used. Aggregation at topic level is considered by them to be more compelling and

---

56. Independent *Doing Business* Report Review Panel (Trevor Manuel, Chairperson), 'Independent Panel Review of the Doing Business report', above n. 15, at 46.
57. Andrew Packman & Neville Howlett, Paying Taxes: The Global Picture – *An Index to Encourage Tax Reform and the Development of Good Tax Systems*, this volume, §6.02[D].
58. Independent *Doing Business* Report Review Panel (Trevor Manuel, Chairperson), 'Independent Panel Review of the Doing Business report', above n. 15, at 47.
59. Independent *Doing Business* Report Review Panel (Trevor Manuel, Chairperson), 'Independent Panel Review of the Doing Business report', above n. 15, at 42.
60. Independent *Doing Business* Report Review Panel (Trevor Manuel, Chairperson), 'Independent Panel Review of the Doing Business report', above n. 15, at 38–39.
61. Independent *Doing Business* Report Review Panel (Trevor Manuel, Chairperson), 'Independent Panel Review of the Doing Business report', above n. 15, at 42.
62. Vinod Thomas & Xubei Luo, *Multilateral Banks and the Development Process: Vital Links in the Results Chain*, (Transaction Publishers, 2012) cited in Independent *Doing Business* Report Review Panel (Trevor Manuel, Chairperson), 'Independent Panel Review of the Doing Business report', above n. 15, at 20–21.

improved measurement techniques for this need to be explored. The panel also recommends that the raw data and composite index should rather be published in percentage points (cardinal scoring method).

A further concern raised by the expert panel is that the rankings are creating an incentive to manipulate the indicators by altering the proxies that are the focus of the rankings, instead of changing the underlying factors that the proxies are attempting to assess. Critics have also argued that the *Paying Taxes* report does, to a certain extent, promote the presumption that less regulation is better.[63] Improving the communication around the limitations of the study would go some way to alleviating this concern.

The impact of the *benefits* of regulation for the case study company is not taken into account in the *Paying Taxes* report.[64] Although the report does appear to identify these benefits, the measurement of these benefits is not taken into consideration in the methodology employed.[65] As the measurement of the benefits of tax compliance is not an easy task (if not an impossible task),[66] it is certain that many discussions and debates will be held around whether, and if so how, these benefits are to be incorporated into the study.

§7.05   SUCCESSES AND STRENGTHS OF THE STUDY

Despite the limitations discussed in §7.04 above, the *Paying Taxes* report does have many benefits and successful outcomes. The first and most important of these is that this report is being read and used by many governments and other parties to inform future policy/administrative decisions. This is the fundamental purpose of research – that it is used to motivate further changes, improvements and stimulate more thinking on a particular topic or area.

One of the report's greatest benefits (which may, however, also create the report's greatest limitation) is that it uses a very simple and convenient way to perform international comparisons on the tax costs and compliance burden of a business.[67] Performing international comparisons, as most academics are aware, is a process that is renowned for its difficulty and limitations.[68] Notwithstanding this, the report does clearly reflect the limitations inherent in the underlying research. The report also specifically states that it is not intended to capture country nuances and that the results should be interpreted with caution. The report is therefore clearly a good starting point for further work and discussion on this important topic.

---

63. Independent *Doing Business* Report Review Panel (Trevor Manuel, Chairperson), *Global Consultations, March-April 12, 2013, Feedback Summary*, http://www.dbrpanel.org/sites/dbrpanel/files/Doing_Business_Consultations_Feedback_Summary_2013.pdf (accessed on 27 November 2014).
64. Independent *Doing Business* Report Review Panel (Trevor Manuel, Chairperson), *Global Consultations, March-April 12, 2013, Feedback Summary*, above n. 15, at 60.
65. Independent *Doing Business* Report Review Panel (Trevor Manuel, Chairperson), 'Independent Panel Review of the Doing Business report', above n. 15, at 36.
66. Evans, Hansford, Hasseldine, Lignier, Smulders & Vaillancourt, above n. 23, at 455–456, 467.
67. Tran-Nam & Evans, above n. 12, at 356.
68. Evans, Hansford, Hasseldine, Lignier, Smulders & Vaillancourt, above n. 23, at 455–456.

What is also evident is that there is clearly a need for such a study because the report is being used by various governments and researchers to discuss and consider regulatory issues in the tax arena. Examples of countries the governments and academic institutions of which have used the report include the UK,[69] Ireland[70] and South Africa.[71] The European Commission has also relied on the results of the report.[72] It is unmistakable that the report has gained the attention of the world, which is once again the aim of any research project conducted.

Improvements are also constantly being made to various aspects of the report, indicating that the researchers are taking into account the knowledge that they gain from their own experiences and also obtained by various other external parties.[73] An example of the continued improvements being made is the inclusion of the 'Distance to Frontier' measure which now provides the absolute rather than relative improvement of the regulatory environment over time.[74] This measure also highlights the gap between the economies at a single point in time. Another improvement to the report methodology is the use of an updated (more recent) Gross National Income per capita (the last GNI used was for 2005, and the new GNI factor from 2012 will be used). The inclusion of an additional city for the eleven economies with a population of over 100 million is also going to be implemented for future studies.

It is apparent that the authors of the report are making sure that the methodologies used and procedures followed are constantly evolving and remaining relevant to the changing tax landscape.

§7.06   RECOMMENDATIONS

Although the results of the research present a 'snapshot' of a very large and diverse landscape, the results are at least a starting point for further in-depth analyses as it is acknowledged in the *Paying Taxes* report that the results should be interpreted with caution. Perhaps this could be made even clearer and included in the front of the report rather than towards the end. It is therefore suggested that the assumptions underlying

---

69. Office of Tax Simplification (UK), 'Competitiveness review: initial thoughts and call for evidence' (March 2014) cited in Andrew Packman & Neville Howlett, Paying Taxes: The Global Picture – *An Index to Encourage Tax Reform and the Development of Good Tax Systems*, this volume, §6.01[B].
70. See Jim Stewart, 'PwC/World Bank Report "Paying Taxes 2014": An Assessment', Institute for International Integration Studies (University of Dublin) Discussion Paper No. 442 (February 2014), cited in Andrew Packman & Neville Howlett, Paying Taxes: The Global Picture – *An Index to Encourage Tax Reform and the Development of Good Tax Systems*, this volume, §6.01[B].
71. Sharon Smulders, Madeleine Stiglingh, Riel Franzsen & Lizelle Fletcher, *Tax compliance costs for the small business sector in South Africa – establishing a baseline*, 10(2) eJournal of Tax Research 184, 196 (2012).
72. European Commission, 'A review and evaluation of methodologies to calculate tax compliance costs', Working Paper No. 40-2013, FWC TAXUD/2012/CC/116 (25 October 2013), cited in Andrew Packman & Neville Howlett, Paying Taxes: The Global Picture – *An Index to Encourage Tax Reform and the Development of Good Tax Systems*, this volume, §6.01[B].
73. Andrew Packman & Neville Howlett, Paying Taxes: The Global Picture – *An Index to Encourage Tax Reform and the Development of Good Tax Systems*, this volume, §6.01, §6.02, §6.06.
74. Andrew Packman & Neville Howlett, Paying Taxes: The Global Picture – *An Index to Encourage Tax Reform and the Development of Good Tax Systems*, this volume, §6.02[D].

the policies/practices used be made more explicit so that investors/policy-makers can make better informed decisions.

Urging users of the report to remember that any reforms introduced should adhere to and complement the country's broader legal, social and economic systems should be emphasized more in the report as a reminder of this important point. Readers of the report should also be encouraged to use the findings of the research in conjunction with other complementary tools such as the diagnostic tools already developed by the IMF, World Bank, the Forum on Tax Administration and the Inter-American Centre of Tax Administration.[75]

The practicality of making all the above improvements to the study obviously needs to be considered carefully taking into account the cost versus benefit implications of each change. Should it be decided to accept and implement any recommendations made to improve the study, the changes made should be clearly documented – that is, a clear audit trail must be available. Just as important is that when any recommendations are not accepted or adjusted for in the study, the reasons for reaching these decisions be clearly documented. Clear and concise explanations of the rationale behind these decisions should be provided in the report (or in an annexure to the report). Users of the report will all recognize that any changes require trade-offs and inevitably the study cannot cater for all possible situations but at least the best decisions can be taken based on the best information and resources available at the time.

Peer reviewing of the report both internally (within the Bank) and externally has also been suggested[76] and would only improve the quality of the report. Publication of this review and all other information has also been recommended to improve the level of transparency of the report.[77]

§7.07   CONCLUSION

It is known that cross-country and across time comparative studies are by their nature very difficult to do. Notwithstanding all the criticisms received on the *Paying Taxes* report, misinterpretation of the survey findings can be reduced significantly with clear and comprehensive details of the limitations of the study – stated upfront.

Despite all of its challenges, the *Paying Taxes* report succeeds in providing highlights of the various tax reforms instituted by governments across the world. Having insight into these reforms can guide other governments in investigating the applicability of these reforms to the SMEs in their own countries. This information can be used to inform more in-depth research in each country that will determine whether the reform will assist in simplifying the tax compliance burden for their SMEs.

---

75. Independent *Doing Business* Report Review Panel (Trevor Manuel, Chairperson), 'Independent Panel Review of the Doing Business report', above n. 15, at 40.
76. Independent *Doing Business* Report Review Panel (Trevor Manuel, Chairperson), *Global Consultations, March-April 12, 2013, Feedback Summary*, above n. 15, at 41.
77. Independent *Doing Business* Report Review Panel (Trevor Manuel, Chairperson), 'Independent Panel Review of the Doing Business report', above n. 15, at 5, 46.

Collaboration within the Bank and with other public and governmental organizations on developing, collecting, analysing and reporting the data is highly recommended to ensure that the research is robust, transparent and can stand up to any scrutiny.

With no other source providing global information of this magnitude, the information generated by the *Paying Taxes* report is definitely a starting point for future more robust data collection in this arena. The report has brought paying taxes in the global economy to light and has managed to raise debates amongst various governments, academics and organizations across the globe. This research has clearly had an impact on informing policy in many countries and this can only improve as more input into the methodology is received and as more improvements to the research design and implementation processes are made.

The need for this type of information is evident and is going to become more prevalent as the years pass. Having this vital information available will become essential to governments if they want to ensure their tax systems are simple to understand and comply with, but yet robust enough to prevent any potential abuse thereof.

CHAPTER 8

Measuring Tax Compliance Costs: Evidence from Australia

Philip Lignier, Chris Evans & Binh Tran-Nam

§8.01 INTRODUCTION

Tax compliance typically requires taxpayers or third parties to incur recurrent and one-off costs, often not negligible, to fulfil their tax obligations. Estimates of tax compliance costs incurred by taxpayers and others have often been used as broad indicators of, or proxies for, the complexity of tax systems: the higher the compliance costs, the more likely that a tax system is perceived to be, or is, complex or unduly burdensome.

Research into tax compliance costs around the world has developed considerably since the first known empirical study undertaken by Haig in the US, just over three-quarters of a century ago.[1] Once labelled the 'hidden costs of taxation',[2] tax compliance costs have become an established field of international study, owing to the efforts of many tax scholars worldwide, particularly Sandford.[3] There are now many published empirical studies on tax compliance costs using the methodology, and refinements of it, developed by Sandford. Over the past four decades, tax compliance cost studies have spread from 'foundation' countries (the US, Canada, Germany and the UK) to virtually all parts of the globe, including other parts of Western Europe

---

1. Robert Haig, *The Cost to Business Concerns of Compliance with Tax Laws*, 24(11) Mgmt. Rev. 323 (1935).
2. Cedric Sandford, *Hidden Costs of Taxation* (Institute for Fiscal Studies, 1973).
3. See, for example, Sandford, above n. 2; Cedric Sandford, Michael Godwin, Peter Hardwick & Ian Butterworth, *Costs and Benefits of VAT* (Heinemann, 1981); Cedric Sandford, Michael Godwin & Peter Hardwick, *Administrative and Compliance Costs of Taxation* (Fiscal Publications, 1989); Cedric Sandford & John Hasseldine, *The Compliance Costs of Business Taxes in New Zealand* (Institute of Policy Studies, 1992); and Cedric Sandford (ed.), *Tax Compliance Costs: Measurement and Policy* (Fiscal Publications, 1995).

(Ireland, the Netherlands, Spain, Portugal, Sweden and Switzerland), Australasia (Australia and New Zealand), Asia (Singapore, Malaysia, Hong Kong, India, South Korea), Eastern Europe (Croatia and Slovenia), Africa (Tanzania, Ethiopia and South Africa) and South America (Brazil).[4]

International studies of tax compliance costs to date have yielded a number of consistent findings. Evans has identified three major, common features of tax compliance costs around the world: (i) they are not trivial (whether measured in absolute terms or relative to benchmarks such as gross domestic product or tax revenue); (ii) they are regressive in terms of taxpayers' turnover or income; and (iii) they are not decreasing over time.[5]

This chapter reports upon a recent research project into the compliance costs of the Australian tax system, highlighting some of the conceptual issues that underpin compliance costs research generally, as well as methods used in that research and outcomes derived from it.[6] Although the tax systems of countries differ significantly in many respects, the Australian research may be seen as relatively typical, confirming the findings of much of the research into tax compliance costs, and tax system complexity, globally.

A number of empirical studies of taxpayer compliance costs had been carried out in Australia prior to the research study that is the focus of this chapter. For example, in the late 1980s a series of studies led by Pope explored the compliance costs incurred by Australian taxpayers in dealing with federal income tax in 1986–1987,[7] whilst in 1996 the Australian Taxation Office (ATO) commissioned Evans, Ritchie, Tran-Nam and Walpole to undertake a major survey of the compliance costs of Australian personal and business taxpayers in relation to the 1994–1995 fiscal year.[8] The findings of both of these major studies confirmed the trends identified in other countries.

The research project that is the subject of this chapter involved three separate surveys of more than 15,000 taxpayers selected from a national database of taxpayers provided by the ATO, targeted at three broad categories of taxpayers: personal (non-business) taxpayers; small and medium enterprises (SMEs) (annual turnover less than or equal to AUD 250 million); and large businesses (annual turnover exceeding

---

4. For overviews of tax compliance costs research around the world, see, for example, Sebastian Eichfelder & François Vaillancourt, 'Tax compliance costs: A review of cost burdens and cost structures', Arbeitskreis Quantitative Steuerlehre (arqus) Quantitative Research in Taxation Discussion Paper No. 178 (November 2014); and Chris Evans, 'Taxation Compliance and Administrative Costs: An Overview', in Michael Lang, Christine Obermair, Josef Schuch, Claus Staringer & Patrick Weninger (eds), *Tax Compliance Costs for Companies in an Enlarged European Community* 447 (Linde Verlag Wien, Vienna and Kluwer Law International, 2008).
5. Evans, above n. 4, at 457.
6. The research project explored, *inter alia*, the tax compliance burden of Australian personal and business taxpayers in the tax year ended 30 June 2012 (fiscal year 2012). The project was part of an Australian Research Council (ARC) Linkage grant examining tax system complexity, and was conducted by a multi-university research team. The Institute of Chartered Accountants in Australia (ICAA) was an industry partner in the project, and the Australian Taxation Office (ATO) provided support in terms of sample selection and provision of macro-level tax data.
7. Jeff Pope, 'The compliance costs of major taxes in Australia', in Sandford (ed.), *Tax Compliance Costs: Measurement and Policy*, above n. 3, at 101.
8. Chris Evans, Katherine Ritchie, Binh Tran-Nam & Michael Walpole, *A Report into Taxpayer Costs of Compliance* (Australian Government Publishing Service, 1997).

AUD 250 million).[9] The surveys focused on the taxation compliance burden imposed by federal (Commonwealth) and State taxes during the year ended 30 June 2012, and were conducted in Australia between November 2012 and February 2013. The surveys were the first independent large-scale surveys of tax compliance costs conducted in Australia since 1996 and since the introduction of the goods and services tax (GST, Australia's value added tax) in 2000.

The remainder of this chapter is structured as follows. After a discussion of important conceptual issues (§8.02) and a brief description of the implementation of the surveys (§8.03), the results for each of the three categories of taxpayer (personal, SME and large business) are presented in separate sections (§8.04, §8.05 and §8.06 respectively). The chapter concludes (§8.07) by summarizing the outcomes of the study and discussing the implications in the context of the existing research in this area.

§8.02   SOME CONCEPTUAL ISSUES

While the definition and measurement of taxpayer compliance costs are now firmly established in the literature, it is nevertheless helpful to briefly consider a number of conceptual and measurement issues relating to the scope of tax compliance costs, the valuation of time and the estimating methodology.

Sandford, Godwin and Hardwick have defined tax compliance costs as '[t]he costs incurred by taxpayers in meeting the requirements laid on them by the tax law and the revenue authorities [...]'.[10] Most published research adheres to the convention established in the case of that definition and distinguishes between *gross* compliance costs and *net* compliance costs.[11] Net compliance costs are defined as gross compliance costs less tax deductibility and cash flow benefits. Tax deductibility benefits result from the fact that taxpayers are entitled to tax deductions for some of the compliance costs they incur.[12] Cash flow benefits arise because of the difference between the time when the amounts subject to tax (e.g., income or revenue) are collected by the taxpayer and the time when the tax thereon is actually handed over to the tax authorities.[13] In addition, managerial benefits may be derived by the taxpayers, and in particular business taxpayers, where the more stringent record-keeping requirements imposed by tax compliance result in the production of managerial accounting information available for improved decision-making and other business purposes.[14]

---

9. At the time of the surveys, one Australian dollar (AUD) was roughly equivalent to one US dollar (USD).
10. Sandford, Godwin & Hardwick, above n. 3, at 22.
11. Sandford, Godwin & Hardwick, above n. 3, at 13–14.
12. Binh Tran-Nam, Chris Evans, Michael Walpole & Katherine Ritchie, *Tax Compliance Costs: Research Methodology and Empirical Evidence from Australia*, 53(2) Nat'l Tax J. 229, 233 (2000).
13. Tran-Nam, Evans, Walpole & Ritchie, above n. 12, at 232.
14. Sandford, Godwin, Hardwick & Butterworth, above n. 3, at 89, and Philip Lignier, 'A Silver Lining in the Tax Compliance Cloud? A Study of the Managerial Benefits of Tax Compliance in Small Business', in Margaret McKerchar & Michael Walpole (eds), *Further Global Challenges in Tax Administration* 416 (Fiscal Publications, 2006).

Tax compliance costs typically consist of monetary and psychological costs.[15] Monetary costs refer to the value of the resources expended by taxpayers and third parties (e.g., unpaid helpers) to satisfy the requirements of tax law. The conventional approach is to adopt the opportunity cost concept which is broader than the accounting cost concept.[16] Under the opportunity costs approach, both explicit costs (which involve monetary payments to external parties such as tax advisers) and implicit costs (which do not involve monetary payments, e.g., time spent by the taxpayers themselves or unpaid helpers) are included. In the case of business taxpayers, implicit costs also include time spent by internal employees on tax compliance-related tasks as well as non-labour costs (also called incidental costs) corresponding to business overhead costs, such as equipment, stationery, travel and so forth.[17]

The valuation of incidental costs is also problematic and requires an accounting system providing reliable tracking and apportionment of overhead costs; such an accounting system is often not present in small businesses. For this reason, and also because incidental costs are likely to be negligible in small entities, they have often been disregarded in compliance costs studies.[18]

The measurement of explicit costs should be straightforward in theory as they are represented by cash expenditures incurred by the taxpayer. In practice, however, difficulties in measurement may arise, especially in the case of SMEs where tax-related and other types of services such as accounting services are often provided by the same third party and the costs are not easily disentangled. This problem is made even more complex by the fact that it is not always clear in the mind of the taxpayers whether a particular activity (e.g., record-keeping) should be classified as 'accounting' or as 'tax-related'. The present SME taxpayer survey attempted to address this problem by asking respondents to report accounting and tax-related expenditures separately, and also by asking respondents to identify any overlap between the two functions. The same disentanglement issue exists in relation to internal time. In an effort to avoid confusion between accounting and tax-related activities, the SME taxpayer questionnaire asked respondents to report separately the time spent on core accounting functions, such as customer billing and cash monitoring, and time spent on 'pure' tax compliance activities.

A key issue related to implicit costs is how to value internal time. This is a contentious issue which has been abundantly discussed in the literature.[19] For tax compliance activities undertaken by employees of the business, the labour costs can be satisfactorily valued at the prevailing before-tax market rates for different categories of personnel. Valuing time spent on tax activities by personal taxpayers, business proprietors and unpaid helpers is more problematic. One approach is to ask respondents to value their time and the time of unpaid helpers. However, as time valuations made by respondents are typically widely dispersed with some excessive values, it is

---

15. Tran-Nam, Evans, Walpole & Ritchie, above n. 12, at 236.
16. Evans, Ritchie, Tran-Nam & Walpole, above n. 8, at 52.
17. Tran-Nam, Evans, Walpole & Ritchie, above n. 12, at 236.
18. Sandford, Godwin & Hardwick, above n. 3, at 12.
19. Pope, above n. 7, at 101.

important to benchmark them against the prevailing market rates for corresponding functions.[20]

Other aspects of what constitutes tax compliance activities are also contentious. For example, there has been considerable debate about avoidable (voluntary) and unavoidable (involuntary) tax compliance activities where, for example, activities associated with the computation of the tax liability are regarded as 'unavoidable' whilst tax planning activities would be regarded as 'avoidable'. This distinction, first introduced by Johnston,[21] has given rise to an ongoing debate which will never be fully resolved.

In the study that is the subject of this chapter, the view was taken that the costs of all tax-related activities should be included in the measurement of tax compliance costs. A comprehensive inclusion of all tax-related activities is consistent with the broad definition of tax compliance costs (as stated at the beginning of this section). This approach is also useful in that it avoids the need to make a discretionary choice of what is and what is not a component of tax compliance costs. Hence, tax planning is regarded as a legitimate activity of tax compliance. Similarly, tax dispute resolution is also treated as a legitimate tax compliance activity and incorporated into the comprehensive study of tax compliance costs.

A related but different issue is the distinction between preventable and non-preventable costs of tax compliance.[22] Preventable costs refer to those costs incurred by a taxpayer because of poor practice or lack of knowledge in meeting tax legislative requirements (e.g., poor record-keeping or not using 'e-filing'). In contrast, non-preventable costs refer to those arising even when a taxpayer uses best available practice. From a tax policy perspective, the government can only be held responsible for trying to minimize the non-preventable costs of tax compliance. However, in practice, it is not possible to distinguish preventable compliance costs from non-preventable compliance costs. This is a data limitation problem in the sense that primary data collected from taxpayers (typically via questionnaires or interviews) cannot be sufficiently refined to make such a distinction. This study is thus concerned with the observed costs of tax compliance, which will include both preventable and non-preventable costs.

Psychological costs refer to the stress, anxieties and frustrations experienced by taxpayers, especially elderly taxpayers, in having to cope with tax compliance.[23] Psychological costs are problematic because there are no objective and consistent ways to monetize these costs across individuals and over time. It is therefore not possible to add monetary and psychological costs together to arrive at the full costs of tax

---

20. This self-valuation and benchmarking approach was adopted in a recent study of New Zealand business taxpayer compliance costs. Inland Revenue (NZ), *SME Tax Compliance Costs 2009: Evaluation Report 1*, 26 (Wellington, 2010).
21. Kenneth Johnston, 'Corporations' Federal Income Tax Compliance Costs: A Study of Small, Medium-size, and Large Corporations', Bureau of Business Research Monograph No. 110, 67–70 (Ohio State University, 1963).
22. Inland Revenue, *Reducing Compliance Costs: An Evaluation*, 75 (Wellington, 1997).
23. Robin Woellner, Cynthia Coleman, Margaret McKerchar, Michael Walpole & Julie Zetler, *Can simplified legal drafting reduce the psychological costs of tax compliance? An Australian perspective*, [2007] 6 Brit. Tax Rev. 717.

compliance. Thus, the conventional approach is to exclude psychological costs from estimates of the costs of tax compliance, a practice followed in the current study.

§8.03   METHODOLOGY

A variety of techniques are available to estimate the compliance costs incurred by taxpayers in complying with their tax obligations. Traditionally these have included surveys (invariably using questionnaires) conducted through commercial polling organizations, or by post, email and telephone; other interview-based methodologies; diary and case study approaches; and documentary analysis. In more recent years various estimation/simulation techniques, such as the Standard Cost Modelling approach adopted by governments in Denmark, the Netherlands, the UK and elsewhere, have been used in order to identify and measure the tax regulatory burden on business. Often the studies employ a combination of these approaches, and techniques are becoming increasingly sophisticated and detailed.[24]

The current Australian study utilized a traditional survey approach to identify the compliance burden of the three categories of taxpayer that were the focus of the study. However, the survey methodology was customized to take into account the somewhat different characteristics of the large business cohort compared to the other two categories.

The key features of the methodology adopted for the personal taxpayer and SME taxpayer surveys can be summarized as follows:

- collection of primary data via a large-scale survey based on a random sample of taxpayers in each category;
- availability of both paper and electronic questionnaires to survey participants;
- estimation of both sample averages and population averages (by combining sample means and macro-distribution); and
- estimation of both absolute and relative costs of tax compliance.

The survey of the large business taxpayers followed a slightly different approach. The rationale behind this differentiated strategy was based on the particular nature of this category of taxpayers and the internal organization of the ATO. Experience has indicated that targeting the large business sector with traditional survey methodologies (such as paper-based or electronic surveying) results in poor response rates. In addition, the ATO has dedicated market segments within the organization that deal specifically with the large corporate sector.[25]

---

24. Chris Evans, John Hasseldine, Andrew Lymer & Robert Ricketts, *Comparative Taxation* (Fiscal Publications, 2015 forthcoming). See also Andrew Packman & Neville Howlett, Paying Taxes: The Global Picture – *An Index to Encourage Tax Reform and the Development of Good Tax Systems*, this volume, where an alternative approach to the estimation of tax compliance costs is explored.
25. The two units within the ATO that deal with the large corporate sector are the Client Relationship Management (CRM) and Key Client Management (KCM) branches. KCM provides a range of specialized services to large businesses, while CRM provides services related to GST. Australian Taxation Office (ATO), *Large business and tax compliance*, 13 (Canberra, 2011).

Hence the questionnaire for the large corporate taxpayers group was only administered by way of an electronic survey. One week prior to the email broadcast, key employees (usually Group Tax Managers or persons of equivalent status) of potential participants had been contacted in person (usually by phone) by their ATO CRM/KCM counterparts and given a briefing (from a prepared script) about the research project. Roughly one-sixth of those contacted (32 out of 187) indicated that they did not wish to participate in the survey and were therefore removed from the email broadcast list.

A total effective sample of 1,278 useable responses was collected for the three surveys corresponding to an overall response rate of 9.7% (Table 8.1). The response rate for individual surveys varied from 7.5% for the SME survey to 42% for the large business survey. A number of checks were carried out to test for non-response bias and for representativeness of the observed samples compared to the general population. No non-response bias was detected in any of the observed samples. Given that the survey adopted a random but non-proportionate sampling approach, the characteristics of the observed sample sometimes differed markedly from the characteristics of the general population. However, it was considered to be more important that the characteristics of the observed samples should reflect the characteristics of the send-out samples. Analysis of the sample data suggests a reasonable degree of spread in the various demographic and economic variables considered relevant for the purpose of this study: age, education, annual taxable income for personal taxpayers; and business size, activity sector and legal form for business taxpayers.

Table 8.1 Populations, Samples and Response Rates for Each Survey

	Personal Taxpayers	SME Taxpayers	Large Business Taxpayers	Total
Sample frame*	11,986,003	2,177,108	1,850	-
Gross sample	4,003	9,953	187	14,143
Out of frame	143	879	0	1,022
Effective sample	517	682	79	1,278
Response rate†	13.3%	7.5%	42.2%	9.7%

* Some taxpayers were deliberately excluded from the sample frame by the ATO.
† The response rate is calculated as the ratio of the effective sample over the gross sample less out of frame responses.

The results of the surveys for each category of taxpayers are now discussed in detail: personal (non-business) individuals in §8.04; SME taxpayers in §8.05; and large businesses in §8.06.

§8.04   PERSONAL (NON-BUSINESS) TAXPAYERS

Based upon the data provided by over 500 respondents to the survey, the average *gross* tax compliance costs of personal taxpayers were estimated to be about AUD 800.[26] They ranged from an average of AUD 470 for taxpayers in the lowest income group (those earning less than AUD 37,000 per year) through to just under AUD 4,000 for those earning more than AUD 180,000 annually (Table 8.2).

Table 8.2   Estimated Gross Tax Compliance Costs (AUD)
for Personal Taxpayers, 2011–2012[a]

	Taxable Annual Income			
	≤ 37,000	37,001–80,000	80,001–180,000	> 180,000
Tax agent costs	161.30 (34.34%)	229.81 (26.16%)	569.30 (36.58%)	1,787.98 (44.72%)
Incidental costs	70.49 (15.01%)	108.27 (12.33%)	123.71 (7.95%)	147.78 (3.70%)
Own time costs	137.98 (29.38%)	425.38 (48.42%)	762.38 (48.99%)	1,757.22 (43.95%)
Unpaid helpers' time costs	99.95 (21.28%)	114.99 (13.09%)	100.88 (6.48%)	305.05 (7.63%)
Gross tax compliance costs	469.71 (100.00%)	878.44 (100.00%)	1,556.27 (100.00%)	3,998.03 (100.00%)
Gross tax compliance costs (as % of taxable income[b])	2.54%	1.50%	1.20%	-

[a] Percentage of gross tax compliance costs are in parentheses. Totals may not add up due to rounding.
[b] The mid-point of the taxable income range is used for this purpose.

The results indicated that the gross tax compliance costs of personal taxpayers were highly regressive, and especially so for the lowest taxable income group where such costs represented 2.54% of taxable income compared to 1.20% for taxpayers with a taxable income between AUD 80,000 and 180,000. Hence these results confirm the well-observed outcomes of much prior research – that compliance costs are both significant in absolute terms and that they are regressive.

The composition of the gross compliance costs varied significantly between taxable income groups. As a proportion of total costs, external costs (essentially the costs of tax agents) tended to increase as taxable income rose, while incidental costs and unpaid helpers' time cost tended to decrease with income. 'Own time' costs rose

---

26. For full details of the personal (non-business) taxpayer survey, see Binh Tran-Nam, Chris Evans & Philip Lignier, *Personal taxpayer compliance costs: Recent evidence from Australia*, 29(1) Austl. Tax F. 137 (2014).

with income through the first three income groups from about 30% to about 49% of all costs, before declining slightly to about 44% once income rose above AUD 180,000 (Table 8.2).

Net tax compliance costs were calculated on the basis of gross compliance costs adjusted for tax deductibility benefits and cash flow benefits and costs. The estimation of tax deductibility benefits and cash flow benefits/costs required external information to supplement the survey data. This information was obtained from various sources including the Revenue Analysis Branch of the ATO, the Australian Bureau of Statistics and the Reserve Bank of Australia.

The calculation of net tax compliance costs per taxpayer for each taxable income group shows that the regressive nature of these costs was even more salient than for gross compliance costs, varying from 2.55% of taxable income for the lowest income group to 0.75% for the second highest group (Table 8.3).

*Table 8.3   Estimated Net Tax Compliance Costs (AUD)
for Personal Taxpayers, 2011–2012*

	Taxable Annual Income			
	≤ 37,000	37,001–80,000	80,001–180,000	> 180,000
Gross tax compliance costs	469.71	878.44	1,556.27	3,998.03
Tax deductibility benefit	−62.97	−272.32	−591.38	−1,839.09
Cash flow benefits	−2.92	−29.71	−128.93	−1,694.69
Cash flow costs	67.81	93.69	140.73	276.24
Net tax compliance costs	471.64	670.10	976.69	740.49
Net tax compliance costs (as % of taxable income)	2.55%	1.15%	0.75%	-

Comparison of net average compliance costs per taxpayer between the 1995 study by Evans, Ritchie, Tran-Nam and Walpole and this 2012 study reveals that those costs increased from AUD 349 to AUD 605 in constant dollars, an increase of 73% (Table 8.4).[27] A detailed investigation of the components of those costs reveals that, in relative terms, the after-tax tax agent cost is the most dominant contributor to the overall increase in average net tax compliance costs in the seventeen-year period. Also, and perhaps most interestingly, there has been a decline in average cash flow costs to personal taxpayers over the past seventeen years. This has been mainly brought about by the substantial increase in cash flow benefits enjoyed by personal taxpayers in the highest taxable income bracket.

---

27. These are current AUD values as at the June 2012 quarter. Conversions of historical AUD values into current 2012 AUD values are based on the Consumer Price Index (CPI) published by the Australian Bureau of Statistics (ABS) using 2011–2012 as the reference year. See http://www. ato.gov.au/Rates/Consumer-price-index/ (accessed on 30 July 2013). Unless otherwise indicated, all AUD amounts in this chapter are expressed at 2012 current values.

Table 8.4   Increase in Average Net Tax Compliance Costs (AUD) for Personal Taxpayers, 1995–2012

	1994–1995[a]	2011–2012	AUD Increase	% Increase	% of Total Increase
After-tax tax agent costs	70.97	183.98	113.01	159.25%	44.23%
After-tax incidental costs	34.51	68.03	33.52	97.13%	13.12%
After-tax own time costs	188.12	235.49	47.37	25.18%	18.54%
After-tax unpaid helpers' time costs	9.25	82.51	73.25	791.52%	28.67%
After-tax net cash flow costs	46.21	34.53	−11.68	−25.27%	−4.57%
Net tax compliance costs[a]	349.06	604.54	255.48	73.19%	100.00%

Source: Tran-Nam, Evans & Lignier, n. 26 above, Tables 1 and 10; and Evans, Ritchie, Tran-Nam & Walpole, above n. 8, Tables 3.1, 3.2, 3.4, 3.5, 3.6, 3.7, 3.8, 3.10, 3.11 and 3.18.
[a] Amounts may not sum to total due to rounding.

In addition to quantitative data relating to tax compliance costs, the personal taxpayers' survey in 2012 also sought respondents' views about tax system complexity, psychological costs and the impact of technologically driven simplification initiatives. The results are summarized in Table 8.5.

Table 8.5   Personal Taxpayers' Views, 2011–2012

	Disagreed/Strongly Disagreed (%)	Neutral/Don't Know (%)	Agreed/Strongly Agreed (%)
Tax laws have become more complicated since 2007	8.8	33.6	57.6
Tax return is easy to understand	35.6	31.6	32.8
ATO publications are useful	18.0	35.5	46.5
My tax compliance costs are significant	33.7	25.1	41.2
Stress and anxiety level is getting worse	36.2	24.1	39.7
ATO initiatives have reduced my tax compliance costs	21.9	51.0	27.1

Sources: Questions 31 –36, 2012 survey.

A clear majority (almost 58%) of respondents regarded tax laws as having become more complicated since 2007 with only a small minority (less than 9%) disagreeing. This qualitative finding is consistent with the increase in the tax compliance burden over time discussed previously. Respondents were almost evenly divided concerning the comprehensibility of the individual tax return: 33% regarding it as easy to understand while 36% claimed the opposite. There is some good news for the ATO in that 47% of respondents viewed ATO publications as helpful while only 18% disagreed or strongly disagreed with the view that such publications were useful.

Respondents were also somewhat divided about the extent and level of their tax compliance costs: 41% agreed or strongly agreed that their compliance costs were significant as opposed to 34% who disagreed or strongly disagreed. Similarly, there was no clear evidence of any increase in psychological costs, with 40% suggesting that they have experienced higher stress and anxiety in complying with their tax obligations while 36% denied this. A possible way to reconcile this result and the perception of increasing tax complexity over time is that personal taxpayers have outsourced many of their tax obligations to their tax advisers. Concerning technologically driven initiatives such as e-tax or pre-filling, the clear majority of respondents (over 51%) were either neutral or unsure about whether these initiatives have reduced their tax compliance costs. For the remaining respondents, 27% agreed or strongly agreed that their compliance costs have been reduced as a result of these initiatives while almost 22% disagreed or strongly disagreed. It is encouraging that more than a quarter of respondents have found technologically driven initiatives directly beneficial, but this conclusion should be moderated in view of the over-representation of highly educated respondents in the sample and the large number of 'undecided' taxpayers.

Overall, therefore, the study of personal (non-business) taxpayers strongly reinforces the findings of previous research, conducted nearly two decades ago, that the tax compliance costs of Australian personal (non-business) taxpayers are significant in both absolute and relative terms and that they are also highly regressive. It provides robust and reliable estimates of that tax compliance burden. More importantly, the study strongly suggests that the compliance costs burden for personal taxpayers has not reduced over time – indeed it appears to have significantly increased in the last seventeen years. The rise and rise of tax compliance costs of personal taxpayers in Australia is unlikely to be peculiar to Australia itself. Of course some of the increase in real costs can be attributed to the continuing prosperity of the economy (higher personal income implies higher tax compliance costs). But that alone is insufficient to explain the rapid growth in tax compliance costs. The analysis suggests that various simplification initiatives have not been sufficiently effective in combating the rising time trend of tax compliance costs. Whether the rising compliance costs trend for personal taxpayers is an indication of increasing tax complexity, or more tax planning behaviour, or a combination of both, is an important, ongoing topic of consideration for tax researchers, practitioners, administrators and policy-makers alike.

§8.05   SMALL AND MEDIUM ENTERPRISES[28]

The SME taxpayer survey conducted in 2012 was the first independent large-scale survey of business tax compliance costs conducted in Australia since the introduction of the GST in 2000. In view of the fact that the definition of an SME can be a contentious issue, and that many studies have used different criteria to classify businesses,[29] it was decided to break down the sample of respondents into three sub-categories based on annual turnover:

- 'micro-businesses': those SMEs with turnover under the AUD 75,000 turnover threshold for GST registration;
- 'small businesses': those SMEs with turnover in the AUD 75,000–1,999,999 range; and
- 'medium-sized businesses': those SMEs with turnover in the AUD 2 million–100 million range.

For the purpose of this survey, only gross tax compliance costs were analysed, including internal staff time spent on tax compliance and external adviser costs, but excluding incidental costs and psychological costs. There were a number of reasons for the different approach used for measuring the compliance costs of SMEs compared to personal (non-business) taxpayers. First, net compliance costs are far more difficult to determine for business entities than for personal taxpayers, because cash flow benefits can arise from different taxes including GST and payroll tax and tax deductibility benefits will be dependent on the legal form of the business entity, which determines its marginal tax rate. Second, the valuation of incidental costs is also problematic and requires an accounting system providing reliable tracking and apportionment of overhead costs; such an accounting system is often not present in small businesses. For these reasons, and also because incidental costs are likely to be negligible in small entities, such costs have often been disregarded in compliance costs studies.[30]

Based upon the responses from nearly 700 SMEs, the average gross compliance costs per year for all firms (based on population weightings) were found to be AUD 11,004 (Table 8.6). The calculations for each size category resulted in mean gross compliance costs of AUD 3,392 for micro businesses, 12,169 for small businesses and 54,605 for medium-sized enterprises. In all three categories, internal costs were about twice as large as external costs, reflecting a pattern observed in previous research in Australia and overseas.[31] Aggregate gross compliance costs for the SME sector were

---

28. This section is based upon Philip Lignier, Chris Evans & Binh Tran-Nam, *Tangled up in tape: The continuing tax compliance plight of the small and medium enterprise business sector*, 29(2) Austl. Tax F. 217 (2014).
29. For a discussion of this issue, see Philip Lignier & Chris Evans, *The rise and rise of tax compliance costs for the small business sector in Australia*, 27(3) Austl. Tax F. 615 (2012).
30. Sandford, Godwin & Hardwick, above n. 3, at 12.
31. For example, the ratio between internal costs and external costs of tax compliance for Canadian business in 2007 varied from 2.1 for entities with 0-4 employees to 2.7 for entities with more than 500 employees: see François Vaillancourt, Édison Roy-César & Maria Silvia Barros, *The Compliance and Administrative Costs of Taxation in Canada, 2013*, 47 (Fraser Institute, 2013).

estimated at a little over AUD 18 billion, representing 1.2% of GDP and 14% of tax revenue.

Table 8.6   Annual Gross Tax Compliance Costs per SME (AUD), 2011–2012

	All*	Micro	Small	Medium
External costs (adjusted)	3,425	1,049	3,871	16,300
Value of internal time	7,579	2,343	8,298	38,305
Total	**11,004**	**3,392**	**12,169**	**54,605**

* Average calculated on the basis of population weightings for different size categories.

Although *absolute* compliance costs per entity in each category increased with firm size, *relative* costs measured as a proportion of turnover decreased as the firm size grew: average gross compliance cost per AUD 1,000 of turnover were AUD 90.45 for micro businesses, but decreased to 11.72 for small firms and 2.10 for medium-sized entities. Once again this confirmed the regressive nature of compliance costs predicted by theory and already observed for personal taxpayers.

In 1995, Evans, Ritchie, Tran-Nam and Walpole found that gross costs of tax compliance were AUD 5,624 per firm, bearing in mind that the 1995 sample comprised a very small number of large entities (about 1.2%); when large entities were excluded, the average compliance cost per firm was AUD 5,028.[32] The comparison with the findings from the present survey suggest that overall gross compliance costs for Australian SMEs have increased by 118% in constant dollar terms over the period from 1995 to 2012. External tax compliance costs grew much faster between 1995 and 2012 than the internal time spent on compliance activities: 120% compared to 63%. This could indicate that businesses are now outsourcing more of their tax compliance work to external parties. A similar finding was made by two separate and relatively recent investigations of tax compliance activities and tax compliance costs in Australian SMEs.[33]

The major component of SME tax compliance costs – the internal time spent on tax compliance – was analysed in terms of different compliance activities (Table 8.7) and in terms of different tax categories (Table 8.8) and compared with the results from the 1995 survey by Evans, Ritchie, Tran-Nam and Walpole.

---

32. Evans, Ritchie, Tran-Nam & Walpole, above n. 8, at 52.
33. Margaret McKerchar, Helen Hodgson & Michael Walpole, *Final Report: Scoping Study on the Costs of Compliance of Small Business*, Report for the Board of Taxation, Atax, University of New South Wales, 18 (31 August 2006); Lignier & Evans, above n. 29, at 642.

Table 8.7   Mean Annual Compliance Time (Hours)
by Activities: SMEs, 1995 and 2012

Tax Compliance Activity Description	1995* (Hours)	2012 (Hours)
Learning about tax	19.1	17.2
Attending tax seminars	N/A	2.9
Recording information	66.8	129.9
Completing tax returns and paying tax	53.9	55.9
Dealing with ATO etc.	4.8	6.4
Dealing with external tax advisers	23.9	33.8
Other tax compliance activities	6.1	11.6
Total	**174.4**	**256.5†**

* The mean was calculated excluding large businesses.

† Individual times do not sum to totals as some respondents only provided total hours.

Source: Evans, Ritchie, Tran-Nam & Walpole, above n. 8, Table 7.58, at 125 (for 1995 figures) and Lignier, Evans & Tran-Nam, above n. 28, at 235 (for 2012 figures).

Business taxpayers in the SME survey sample in 2012 spent an average of 256 hours per year on their tax compliance activities. The most time consuming activities were recording tax information (130 hours), completing tax returns and paying taxes (fifty-six hours) and dealing with external tax advisers (thirty-four hours). In addition, SME taxpayers spent an average of twenty hours per year learning about tax and attending tax seminars.

The comparison with the 1995 study by Evans, Ritchie, Tran-Nam and Walpole reveals an increase in the annual internal tax compliance time across all types of compliance activity.[34] Annualized compliance time from the 1995 study was 174 hours compared to 256 hours reported by the current study, representing an overall increase from 1995 to 2012 of 63%. A breakdown of internal time by type of compliance activity suggests that the increase in the number of hours was particularly pronounced for recording information (which increased by 94%). By contrast, the time spent on completing and lodging tax returns and on learning about tax (including attending tax seminars) was more or less stable between 1995 and 2012.

Respondents were also invited to report time spent on different taxes by way of a separate question in the survey instrument.[35] The results (Table 8.8) indicate that GST (sixty-nine hours) was the most time consuming tax in 2012, representing almost

---

34. Annual times for the 2012 study are calculated based on sample averages not population weighted averages for all surveys. For comparison purposes, only data from the small and the medium businesses were taken into account to calculate the annual average for the 1995 study by Evans, Ritchie, Tran-Nam & Walpole, above n. 8.

35. Asking respondents to report compliance time in two different questions inevitably led to discrepancy in the totals. This was an issue also noted by Evans, Ritchie, Tran-Nam & Walpole, above n. 8. However, it is generally considered that time reported in relation to specific tax activities is more reliable than time in relation to specific taxes.

38% of total internal costs. Employment related taxation (including withholding tax and superannuation) was the second largest item (fifty-four hours) while income tax was third with thirty-three hours. Remarkably, payroll tax (a State tax only paid by large employers) consumed almost eleven hours of annual SME compliance time.

Table 8.8   Mean Annual Compliance Time (Hours)
on Specific Taxes: SMEs, 1995 and 2012

Taxes	1995* (Hours)	2012 (Hours)
GST	N/A	68.8
Income tax (excluding capital gains tax)	25.6	33.4
Capital gains tax	1.2	4.1
Employee withholding taxes	6.0	35.8
Employee superannuation	3.0	18.6
Fringe benefits tax	0.9	4.2
Other federal taxes	3.4	3.2
Payroll tax	-	10.8
Other State/Territory taxes	-	1.7
Total	40.1*	185.4†

* The mean was calculated excluding large businesses.
† Individual times do not sum to totals as some respondents only provided total hours.
Source: Evans, Ritchie, Tran-Nam & Walpole, above n. 8, Table 7.63, at 129 (for 1995 figures), and Lignier, Evans & Tran-Nam, above n. 28, at 235 (for 2012 figures).

Comparison with the 1995 study by Evans, Ritchie, Tran-Nam and Walpole shows that the total number of hours reported by different taxes increased from forty hours in 1995 to 185 hours in 2012.[36] The GST, which did not exist in 1995, explains a significant proportion (47%) but not all of this increase. It also seems that time spent on employee-related taxes (including superannuation) grew by a significant amount, whilst time spent on other federal taxes such as income tax, capital gains tax and fringe benefits tax also increased over the period. Finally, some of the remainder of the increase may be attributed to the fact that the 1995 survey only considered compliance with federal taxes, excluding, for instance, payroll tax.

The 2012 study sought to examine possible relationships between tax compliance costs and various factors that, based on previous empirical research, were believed to be predictors of tax compliance costs.[37] A multiple regression analysis was performed on the data collected for the 682 usable responses in the sample. The analysis used

---

36. In both studies, the average numbers of hours are based on sample averages, not population weighted averages.
37. Joel Slemrod & Varsha Venkatesh, *The Income Tax Compliance Cost of Large and Mid-Size Businesses*, Report to the Internal Revenue Service LMSB Division, Office of Tax Policy Research, University of Michigan Business School (5 September 2002).

three separate equations, where the dependent variable was total compliance costs, external compliance costs and internal time costs respectively (as natural logarithm in each case). The independent variables in each equation were annual turnover (as natural logarithm), legal form and the number of taxes with which the business had to comply. Each separate legal form was included in the model as a 'dummy' variable. Industry sector, a potential determinant of tax compliance costs, could not be retained as an independent variable because many respondents chose not to identify their activity sector.

As expected, business size measured by annual turnover was a strong predictor of the level of tax compliance costs. The value of the co-efficients (< 1) showed that the increase in compliance costs was less than proportional, confirming regressivity. The number of taxes with which the business had to comply was also a strong predictor of the level of total compliance costs and of internal time costs (though not of external costs). None of the variables representing legal form (dummy variables) were found to be significantly correlated when the model was controlled for business size.

Overall, the results for this study confirm the findings of Slemrod and Venkatesh that the size of the business is a significant predictor of the amount of compliance costs and that the relationship with legal form is not significant.[38] In addition, the 2012 study found that the number of taxes that the entities had to report was a significant predictor of both total compliance costs and internal time costs.

As was also the case in the personal (non-business) taxpayer survey, the SME survey attempted to gauge respondents' perceptions about compliance costs and to seek their views about which factors were driving these costs for their businesses. Respondents were invited to score a number of factors which, on the basis of existing literature, were likely to be drivers of high compliance costs for SMEs. A list of eight factors was included in the question: two factors related to industry sector and commercial circumstances, three factors related to tax legislation design (including complexity and frequency of changes) and three factors related to tax administration requirements. Scoring was applied using a scale from 0 to 10, with 0 meaning no impact and 10 implying an enormous impact. For the overall sample, only two factors, complexity of tax laws and compliance requirements imposed by the ATO, rated above 6 out of 10. Two further factors: frequency of tax changes and the number of taxes the business had to deal with, rated above 5 (Table 8.9).

Table 8.9   SME Perception of Drivers of Tax Compliance Costs (Mean Scores Out of 10), 2012

Drivers of Tax Compliance Costs	Score
Industry sector in which your business is involved	4.68
Complexity of commercial transactions	3.82
Complexity of tax laws	6.22
Frequency of changes in tax rules	5.43

38. Slemrod & Venkatesh, above n. 37.

Drivers of Tax Compliance Costs	Score
Number of different taxes that your business has to deal with	5.03
Frequency of changes in tax administrative practices	4.57
Compliance and regulatory tax requirements imposed by the ATO	6.20
Compliance and regulatory tax requirements imposed by States/Territories	4.27
Other factors	3.55

Overall, the results of the 2012 SME survey confirm the findings of previous research in Australia and elsewhere: tax compliance costs are large, regressive and not declining over time. A further important outcome of this research is the confirmation that business size (measured by annual turnover) is the single most significant determinant of the magnitude of compliance costs at firm level. In addition, the number of taxes the entity has to comply with is also a significant predictor of the magnitude of these costs, even when controlling for size. In contrast, legal form is not found to be significantly correlated with a firm's compliance costs. The results of the study strongly suggest that taxation compliance costs continue to be a significant issue for SMEs, and that policy-shapers and policy-makers need to be very cognizant of the potential impact on that burden whenever changes to legislative and administrative requirements affecting the tax system are contemplated.

§8.06 LARGE BUSINESSES[39]

Although tax compliance costs of large businesses in Australia had been surveyed in previous studies,[40] the 2012 Australian research was the first study that specifically surveyed large corporate groups. The 187 entities included in the gross sample were selected by the ATO, with the characteristics of respondents in the net sample being benchmarked against the population of large businesses in Australia. Business size was broadly consistent with the characteristics of the population; however entities in the sample tended to have a more complex structure with a greater number of operating entities. Also, financial services and mining businesses were over-represented in the sample compared to the reference population, while general manufacturing and other services were under-represented. Notwithstanding these limitations, the data derived from the survey were considered to be sufficiently robust for the purposes of extrapolation to the broader community of large business taxpayers.

---

39. This section is based upon Chris Evans, Philip Lignier & Binh Tran-Nam, 'The tax compliance costs of large corporations: Recent empirical evidence', paper presented at the 106th National Tax Association Conference, Tampa Bay, Florida, November 2013.
40. The survey sample of business taxpayers in the 1995 study by Evans, Ritchie, Tran-Nam & Walpole, above n. 8, included 32 'large' businesses out of a sample of 732 business taxpayers; the tax compliance costs of all Australian corporations were also investigated in Jeff Pope, Richard Fayle & Duncan Chen, *The compliance costs of companies income tax in Australia* (Australian Tax Research Foundation, 1994).

Unlike smaller entities, large corporations generally have sophisticated accounting systems in place. Hence it was anticipated that the internal reporting data would allow respondents (essentially accountants and lawyers) to track and identify external costs related to tax compliance without too much difficulty. For the same reasons, the measurement of internal labour costs and incidental costs relating to tax compliance may not be as problematic as in smaller businesses where accounting and tax record-keeping tasks are often entangled. Furthermore, previous research has indicated that, unlike SMEs where business owners and unpaid helpers often contribute a large proportion of internal time, tax activities in larger entities are almost exclusively undertaken by paid personnel.[41] This means that internal staff time can be easily valued on the basis of salary and on-costs. Hence, for internal labour costs respondents were asked to report dollar values rather than a number of hours.

As was the case with SMEs, only *gross* compliance costs were estimated for this cohort of taxpayers. Managerial benefits, such as the improved quality of the accounting and financial management system and better financial decision-making, or savings on financial reporting costs or reduced likelihood of tax audit, are notoriously difficult to evaluate and in any case have been found to be relatively insignificant in large organizations.[42] They were therefore not taken into account in this study. Cash flow benefits and tax deductibility benefits are difficult to measure when a large number of taxes are taken into consideration, and calculation is problematic and would have required macro-statistics data that were not available to the researchers.

The survey results indicated that the average estimated gross annual compliance costs per firm were highly significant in absolute terms: in excess of AUD 3 million, with internal labour costs on tax compliance comprising just under half of this total (Table 8.10). Relative compliance costs expressed in relation to annual turnover were AUD 0.40 per AUD1,000 of annual turnover, confirming the regressive nature of compliance costs already identified.

Table 8.10   Estimated Gross Compliance Costs of
Large Businesses (AUD), 2011–2012

Cost Category	Average Cost per Firm ('000)	Average Cost per AUD 1,000 of Annual Turnover
External costs	1,030	0.14
Internal staff time costs	1,374	0.18
Incidental costs	603	0.08
Gross compliance costs	**3,008**	**0.40**

Source: Own survey.

---

41. Evans, Ritchie, Tran-Nam & Walpole, above n. 8, at 125.
42. Sandford, Godwin, Hardwick & Butterworth, above n. 3, at 51; Philip Lignier, *Measuring the managerial benefits of tax compliance: a fresh approach*, 24(2) Austl. Tax F. 117 (2009).

The absence of previous comparable research into the tax compliance costs of the large business sector in Australia makes it difficult to evaluate the evolution of those costs over time. However, the comparison with the results from previous research in both the US and Canada tends to support the view that these costs have not diminished over time: a relatively recent study of tax compliance costs of Canadian large businesses estimated the cost of compliance at CAD 2,552,000 (AUD 2,383,000) including CAD 1,366,000 (AUD 1,342,000) for the costs of complying with income tax obligations.[43]

As was the case with SME taxpayers, a multiple regression analysis was performed for the large corporate sector in order to identify the determinants of tax compliance costs. Previous research in the US and Canada has suggested that business size, industry sector and tax profile (number and nature of taxes) potentially contribute to the tax compliance costs encountered by the sector.[44] In addition, the current study also investigated the impact on tax compliance costs of the corporate group's Risk Differentiation Framework (RDF) classification by the ATO: essentially the view taken by the ATO (and shared with the corporate group) as to its exposure to, and appetite for, risk in terms of its tax affairs.

Group turnover and number of entities in the group were found to be strong predictors of gross compliance costs in the 2012 Australian study. The RDF risk classification profile and the number of federal taxes were also found to be significant predictors of both gross compliance costs and one of its principal components – external costs.[45] On the other hand, none of these variables were found to be determinants of internal staff costs expended upon tax compliance. Further analysis of the results indicated a statistically significant relationship between risk classification and tax compliance costs associated with review, audit and litigation, but no significant relationship with the cost of tax planning.[46] It appears that when controlling for size and number of entities in the group, the risk classification of the group had a significant effect on the group's tax compliance costs, and its external costs in particular. It also appears that the influence on the costs related to review, audit and litigation was particularly strong. However, it was not clear whether the risk classification in itself was the driving factor: that is, it may alternatively have been the case that a higher risk classification generated more intense review activity from the ATO and as a result the tax compliance costs incurred by the group increased.

Apart from these statistically measurable determinants, three broad drivers of tax compliance costs were perceived by large business taxpayers: the complexity and uncertainty of tax rules; the administrative compliance requirements imposed by tax authorities; and international exposure.

---

43. Vaillancourt, Roy-César & Barros, above n. 31, at 62.
44. Marsha Blumenthal & Joel Slemrod, *The Income Tax Compliance Costs of Big Business*, 24(4) Pub. Fin. Q. 411 (1996); Slemrod & Venkatesh, above n. 37; Brian Erard, 'The income tax compliance burden on Canadian big business', Department of Economics Working Paper 97-2, Carleton University (April 1997).
45. Level of significance was 5% for the relationship between risk classification and gross compliance costs, number of federal taxes and external costs, and 10% in the other cases.
46. The level of significance was 5%.

The research outcomes for the 2012 large business survey are, therefore, both confirmatory and innovative. They confirm key findings from the literature that tax compliance costs are significant, regressive and not declining over time, but also provide new insights into the compliance costs profile of the large corporate sector.

§8.07   SUMMARY AND CONCLUSIONS

While the three surveys in this research project used slightly different approaches for measuring compliance costs, a broad picture emerges from the results with consistent findings across the different categories of taxpayer.

First, gross tax compliance costs at taxpayer level are significant and (certainly for personal taxpayers and SMEs, and probably for large businesses) have substantially increased in the seventeen years since the previous large-scale survey undertaken in 1995. The increase was relatively lower for personal (non-business) taxpayers (73%) than for SME taxpayers (118%). The different pattern of evolution of compliance costs between the two groups of taxpayers may reasonably be attributed to the introduction of GST in 2000, a tax that only affects the compliance activities of business taxpayers. Much of the increase experienced by the two groups is accounted for by the growth in the external costs of compliance, reflecting perhaps a trend towards the outsourcing of tax activities to professional advisers.

Second, the regressive pattern of tax compliance costs has been confirmed for all three groups. However, the regressivity seems to be more pronounced in the case of business taxpayers than for personal taxpayers.

The level of taxable income appeared to be a driver of the magnitude of tax compliance costs for personal taxpayers. Similarly, size, measured by turnover, was a significant determinant of the gross compliance costs for SMEs and large business taxpayers. However, in the case of business taxpayers, the number of taxes the entity had to comply with was also a significant determinant.

Finally, there was a general consistency of views across all classes of taxpayers regarding the significance of their compliance costs and the increasing complexity of tax laws. However, larger businesses seem to hold more strongly negative views about issues such as the frequency of changes in tax laws and the uncertainty regarding tax administrative practices.

Overall, the main outcome of this research is that tax compliance costs have continued to rise and have risen significantly in the past seventeen years in Australia despite various simplification initiatives such as pre-filled tax returns for personal taxpayers[47] and the 'simplified tax system' legislation for SMEs.[48] Whether this trend is an indication of rising tax complexity, as seems to be the perception of taxpayers, or the result of more tax planning behaviour, or a combination of both, is an important topic that needs to be investigated through further research.

---

47. See, e.g., Chris Evans & Binh Tran-Nam, *Managing tax system complexity: Building bridges through pre-filled tax returns*, 25(2) Austl. Tax F. 245 (2010).
48. For a description of the 'STS' initiative (since unwound from the 2007–2008 year into general small business entity concessions), see, e.g., John Tretola, *The Simplified Tax System – Has It Simplified Tax At All and, If So, Should It Be Extended?*, 17(1) Revenue L.J., Art. 8 (2007).

CHAPTER 9

Measuring Tax Complexity: Analytical Framework and Evidence for Individual Income Tax Preferences for Canada

Marco Lugo & François Vaillancourt[*]

§9.01   INTRODUCTION

The main purpose of this chapter is to make an empirical contribution to the literature on tax complexity by providing estimates of the compliance/complexity cost (CCC) of ten personal income tax preferences for Canada and examining how they are related to the revenue cost and distribution of these preferences. This is of interest not only in the context of the Tax System Complexity conference in September 2014 where this chapter was presented but as a contribution to the evolving literature on both tax complexity and Tax Compliance Costs (TCC). This last literature has evolved since its inception[1] from simple quantification to analysis of determinants of TCC.

The chapter proceeds in the following four sections. Section §9.02 contains a selective review of the literature that links it along the lines of the tax policy process. Section §9.03 presents the tax preferences examined, the survey data used and information on the frequency of the use of tax preferences by survey respondents.

* We thank Joel Slemrod and the participants at the Tax System Complexity Symposium in Prato, Italy, 29–30 September 2014, for their comments on a preliminary version of this chapter. Preliminary work on the compliance costs aspects was carried out for the Fraser Institute, Vancouver, Canada, as reported in Sean Speer, Milagros Palacios, François Vaillancourt & Marco Lugo, *The Cost to Canadians of Complying with Personal Income Taxes* (Fraser Institute, April 2014).
1. For a review of the earlier and most recent literature, see, respectively, François Vaillancourt, *The Compliance Costs of Taxes on Businesses and Individuals: A Review of the Evidence*, 42(3) Public Finance/Finances Publiques 395 (1987); and Sebastian Eichfelder & François Vaillancourt, *Tax Compliance costs: A Review of Cost Burdens and Cost Structures*, 210 (3-2014) Hacienda Pública Española/Review of Public Economics 107.

Section §9.04 examines the determinants of the CCC of tax preferences. Finally, §9.05 links these CCC estimates and other tax policy indicators to indicate what one may take into account to make policy choices that favour simplicity over complexity. Section §9.06 concludes.

§9.02   LITERATURE REVIEW

The literature on tax complexity can be seen as drawing on two streams of writings: the literature on legal complexity in general and the literature on tax compliance costs.

The measurement of legal complexity outside of tax legislation appears to be in its infancy. A recent article by Katz and Bommarito states that '[i]ndeed, outside of tax virtually all dimensions related to law's complexity are still yet to be comprehensively measured'.[2] That said, their article applies a knowledge acquisition protocol to analyse the complexity of the United States Code broken down by Title (bankruptcy, taxation, etc.). The results indicate that the tax section (Internal Revenue Code) is the second most complex (composite rank) title of the Code.[3]

There are general theoretical contributions to the topic of tax complexity. For example, Kopczuk writes that:

> Complexity in the tax code should be thought of as the extent of variation in possible tax treatments of economically related activities. This kind of complexity naturally creates opportunities for tax avoidance, and it also causes difficulties for otherwise honest taxpayers. As a result, it leads to confusion and mistakes that are often hard to distinguish from dishonesty.[4]

Barton has a somewhat more optimistic view, that '[c]omplexity can allow the law to be more closely tailored to very specific cases, and if the area of law is one where it is critical to have very precise calibration, complexity is often necessary, even if not necessarily efficient'.[5]

Turning to empirical work, one finds various contributions that can be ranked by their degree of sophistication in ascertaining what complexity is, what its costs are and how they are linked.

Laffer et al. exemplify those who simply want to argue that the tax code is too complex since it is very costly.[6] They use an extensive definition of costs: *administrative costs + compliance costs + deadweight loss + revenue collected*. Nowhere is there

---

2. Daniel Martin Katz & Michael J. Bommarito II, *Measuring the complexity of the law: the United States Code*, 22(4) Artif. Intell. & L. 337, 345 (2014).
3. Katz & Bommarito, above n. 2, at 368 (Table 12).
4. Wojciech Kopczuk, 'Tax simplification and tax compliance: An economic perspective', Columbia University Research Paper, 19, available at: http://www.columbia.edu/~wk2110/bin/epi.pdf (reproduced in Max Sawicky (ed.), *Bridging the Tax Gap. Addressing the Crisis in Federal Tax Administration* 111 (Economic Policy Institute, 2006)).
5. Benjamin Barton, 'Judges, Lawyers, and a Predictive Theory of Legal Complexity'. University of Tennessee Legal Studies Research Paper No. 31, 8 (June 2008).
6. Arthur B. Laffer, Wayne H. Winegarden & John Childs, *The Economic Burden Caused by Tax Code Complexity* (The Laffer Center for Supply-Side Economics, April 2011).

a definition provided of tax complexity; it is assumed to be directly linked to costs through some unknown functional relationship. Ulph warns against such an approach:

> In thinking about the complexity of the tax system per se it would seem to be really quite important to separately measure tax design complexity from operational complexity, and to measure the costs of tax complexity separately from the measure of tax complexity per se. That way one can tell not just whether tax complexity is high but also whether this is imposing a considerable cost, and whether to direct efforts to reforming the design of the tax system or the guidance/information that is given to taxpayers.[7]

The Tax Foundation, Slemrod and the Progressive Policy Institute each use a different measure of tax complexity. The Tax Foundation uses as its measure of complexity the number of words of the Internal Revenue Code and the IRS regulations, up in total 648% from 1955 to 2005.[8] Slemrod uses as a measure of complexity the number of lines on the income tax form and the number of pages in the instruction booklet, in both cases modified slightly to ensure comparability between states.[9] The Progressive Policy Institute uses the number of tax expenditures by state as an indicator of tax complexity.[10] For the forty-three states for which information is available, this number ranges from 550–600 for Washington to 0–50 for Alaska, with the most common range being 100–150 (eleven states).

Are these three measures good indicators of tax complexity? Both Slemrod and Turnbull-Hall and Thomas note that longer legislation or text in an information booklet may reduce complexity if it allows the use of plain English, for example, or the coverage of various possible types of taxpayers.[11] Also one must be careful to net out non-tax aspects from the documents examined to establish tax complexity, such as income support delivered through the tax system.

The three measures of complexity presented above can be seen as set along a continuum from government policy to taxpayer use. Governments (politicians) choose to favour a specific behaviour by introducing a tax preference in a policy declaration (e.g., Budget speech) that results in a tax expenditure. Said preference must then be transformed into a law or regulations to implement it. Then this legal framework will interface with tax-filers through lines in the tax form and instructions in the tax booklet. The measure most likely to be amenable to measurement is the one used by Slemrod since one can link the number of lines to TCC using an estimation of cost per line. Erard and Vaillancourt do this in simulating the cost of a prospective Ontario autonomous

---

7. David Ulph, 'Measuring Tax Complexity', Office of Tax Simplification (UK), 10 (January 2013), available at: https://www.gov.uk/government/uploads/system/uploads/attachment_data/file/193497/ots_david_ulph_measuring_tax_complexity.pdf.
8. J. Scott Moody, Wendy P. Warcholik & Scott A. Hodge, *The Rising Cost of Complying with the Federal Income Tax*, Tax Foundation Special Report 138, 5 (Tax Foundation, December 2005).
9. Joel Slemrod, *The Etiology of Tax Complexity: Evidence from U.S. State Income Tax Systems*, 33(3) Pub. Fin. Rev. 279 (2005).
10. Paul Weinstein Jr., *The State Tax Complexity Index: A New Tool for Tax Reform and Simplification*, Progressive Policy Institute Policy Memo (April 2014).
11. Slemrod, above n. 9; Caroline Turnbull-Hall & Richard Thomas, 'Length of Tax Legislation as a Measure of Complexity', Office of Tax Simplification (UK) (April 2012).

personal income tax system,[12] while Vaillancourt and Blais use a similar methodology to measure the evolution of TCC over time (1971–1993) for the personal income tax in Canada.[13]

That said, one must be careful as to this link. For example, changes in the composition of real pre-tax income over time with an unchanged tax system may lead to lower (larger share of wage-earners) or higher (larger share of self-employment) TCC. The link between TCC and a specific tax measure can only be established when the impact of other factors has been netted out. More generally, we would argue that one can examine complexity from two perspectives; that of the users (individual, firm, etc.) of the tax system and that of the government. In the case of users, more time spent on tax-related activities may not indicate more complexity but simply a quest for reduced taxes. However, for a given reduction in taxes paid, less complexity reduces TCC. So individuals or firms want to maximize the (tax gain (reduction) / TCC) ratio. In the case of government, a narrowly-focused policy will target tax administration costs (TAC) with the aim of increasing revenues with the lowest TAC possible, so maximize the (tax revenues (increase) / TAC) ratio. A more complete approach will aim at minimizing the sum of TCC and TAC for a given revenue level or change. This is because there is presumed to exist a less complex way of achieving the same outcome in terms of efficiency and fairness as the one reached by the complex policy. However, this may not always be the choice governments have to make; rather one may be faced with a tax complexity-policy outcome trade-off, as shown in Figure 9.1 where we assume decreasing returns to complexity.

Figure 9.1   Tax System Output/Complexity Relationship

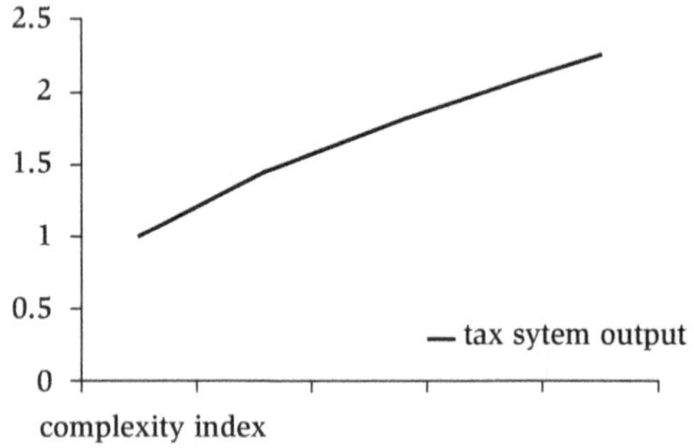

complexity index

Source: Authors.

---

12. Brian Erard & François Vaillancourt, 'The Compliance Costs of a Separate Personal Income Tax System for Ontario : Simulations for 1991', in Allan M. Maslove (ed.), *Taxation in a Subnational Jurisdiction* 137 (University of Toronto Press in co-operation with the Fair Tax Commission of the Government of Ontario, 1993).
13. François Vaillancourt & Étienne Blais, 'The Evolution of Compliance Time of Personal Income Tax-filers in Canada 1971-1993', in Cedric Sandford (ed.), *Tax Compliance Costs Measurement and Policies* 263 (Fiscal Affairs, 1995).

We now turn to literature more closely linked to what we do in this chapter, which is to estimate the TCC of specific provisions of the Canadian personal income tax. We found two papers directly relevant for us. Both focus on the TCC for the US personal income tax (PIT).

Pitt and Slemrod ascertain, using information from a sample of PIT returns, that the cost of using itemization as opposed to the standard deduction was USD 44 in 1982,[14] and thus USD 94 in 2007[15] (or CAD 93[16]). Information for 1987[17] allows us to estimate that this applies to three items on average, thus yielding a cost per item of CAD 31. Pitt and Slemrod note that itemizing will occur when the benefits derived from it exceed the cost of itemizing. Blumenthal and Slemrod on the other hand, using survey data, find no impact of itemizing on TCC.[18]

§9.03 TAX PREFERENCES AND DATA USED

In this second part of the chapter, we first present the tax preferences examined (§9.03[A]), then the survey data used (§9.03[B]) and finally (§9.03[C]) information on the use of tax preferences by survey respondents.

[A] Tax Preferences

The tax preferences examined in this survey are presented in Table 9.1. They are described briefly in column (2) while columns (3)–(7) present information on the complexity of each preference. In the analysis (§9.05), they are used individually as well as regrouped, either all together or into two groups, that is, (a) individual/family-related preferences – made up of the child fitness, education, medical, pension income splitting, and urban transit preferences – and (b) investment-related preferences – made up of foreign tax, investment Labour Sponsored Venture Capital Corporation (LSVCC), natural resources and, stock option, preferences.

14. Mark M. Pitt & Joel Slemrod, *The Compliance Cost of Itemizing Deductions: Evidence from Individual Tax Returns*, 79(5) Am. Econ. Rev. 1224 (1989).
15. Using the US Bureau of Labor Statistics (BLS) calculator: see http://www.bls.gov/data/inflation _calculator.htm.
16. Using the Bank of Canada currency converter as of 31 December 2007: http://www. bankofcanada.ca/rates/exchange/10-year-converter/.
17. Michael Strudler & Emily Ring, 'Individual Income Tax Returns, Preliminary Data, 1988', Internal Revenue Service SOI (Statistics of Income) Bulletin, Spring 1990, Figure 1, http://www .irs.gov/pub/irs-soi/88inintxrpd.pdf.
18. Marsha Blumenthal & Joel Slemrod, *The Compliance Cost of the U.S. Individual Income Tax System: A Second Look after Tax Reform*, 45(2) Nat'l Tax J. 185 (1992).

Table 9.1   Tax Preferences Description and Complexity
(Low = 1; Medium = 2; High = 3)

Tax credit (1)	Description (2)	Lines – Annexes (3)	Comments on Tax Forms (4)	Formal Complexity (5)	Workload Complexity (6)	Total Complexity (7) = (5) + (6)
(a) Individual/Family tax preferences						
Child fitness	Makes it possible to claim a maximum of CAD 500 per child aged less than 16 for the cost of registration or membership for the child in an accepted physical activity, with special treatment of children with disabilities; http://www.cra-arc.gc.ca/fitness/	Line 365 -1	No tax slip provided; receipts must be obtained from service provider	Low 1	Medium 2	3
Education and tuition amount	Makes it possible to claim the amount paid to recognized educational institutions for tuition and for textbooks. http://www.cra-arc.gc.ca/tx/ndvdls/tpcs/ncm-tx/rtrn/cmpltng/ddctns/lns300-350/323/menu-eng.html	Annex with 25 numbered lines	Tax slips provide some information (fees)May require interaction between parents and children (students)	High 3	Medium 2	5

Tax credit (1)	Description (2)	Lines – Annexes (3)	Comments on Tax Forms (4)	Formal Complexity (5)	Workload Complexity (6)	Total Complexity (7) = (5) + (6)
Medical expenses	Makes it possible to claim medical expenses for self, spouse or common-law partner as well as dependent children less than 16 years of age. http://www.cra-arc.gc.ca/tx/ndvdls/tpcs/ncm-tx/rtrn/cmpltng/ddctns/lns300-350/330/menu-eng.html	2x1	No tax slip provided Main source of TCC is establishing list of medically admissible expenses	Low 1	High3	4
Pension income splitting	Makes it possible to split eligible pension income when aged above 60; http://www.cra-arc.gc.ca/pensionsplitting/	2X1	Requires interaction between individual tax returns + optimization with transfer programmes	Medium 2	Low 1	3
Urban transit amount	Makes it possible to claim the amount paid for monthly (or longer) public transit passes for use within Canada http://www.cra-arc.gc.ca/tx/ndvdls/tpcs/ncm-tx/rtrn/cmpltng/ddctns/lns360-390/364/menu-eng.html	Line 364 - 1	No tax slip provided; receipt/ pass should be kept by claimant	Low 1	Medium 2	3

(b) Investment tax preferences

Foreign income tax credit	Makes it possible to claim foreign taxes paid on foreign income if the income is reported in Canada. http://www.cra-arc.gc.ca/tx/ndvdls/tpcs/ncm-tx/rtrn/cmpltng/ddctns/lns409-485/405-eng.html	1 line	Information on tax slips to be added up	Medium 2	Low 1	3
Investment tax preference	Makes it possible to claim a credit for acquiring certain types of property or for research and development expenditures. http://www.cra-arc.gc.ca/tx/ndvdls/tpcs/ncm-tx/rtrn/cmpltng/ddctns/lns409-485/412/menu-eng.html	varies	Various sources	Medium 2	Medium 2	4
Labour Sponsored Venture Capital Corporation (LSVCC) tax credit	Makes it possible to claim a tax advantage for investments made in labour union sponsored funds investing in small and mid-sized firms. http://www.cra-arc.gc.ca/tx/ndvdls/tpcs/ncm-tx/rtrn/cmpltng/ddctns/lns409-485/413-414-eng.html	1	Tax slip provided	Low 1	Low 1	2

Tax credit (1)	Description (2)	Lines – Annexes (3)	Comments on Tax Forms (4)	Formal Complexity (5)	Workload Complexity (6)	Total Complexity (7) = (5) + (6)
Natural resources (including Flow-Through Shares- (FTS)) tax credit	Several tax credits are included here. These credits make it possible to have both a deduction on an investment as well as an additional tax credits on expenses incurred for the investment.http://www.nrcan.gc.ca/mining-materials/taxation/mining-taxation-regime/8892#lnk16	Form T1229	Four different tax slips can be used	High 3	High 3	6
Stock options tax preference	One can claim a tax benefit on option contracts if the securities are bought through the employer at a value lower than the fair-market value. http://www.cra-arc.gc.ca/tx/ndvdls/tpcs/ncm-tx/rtrn/cmpltng/ddctns/lns248-260/249/menu-eng.html	1 deduction		Medium 2	Low 1	3

Source: Authors using tax form information for columns (3)-(4) and informed judgment (second (senior) co-author) for columns (5)-(7).

The complexity information of Table 9.1 will be used in Table 9.5 (§9.05) of the chapter.

[B]   Data

The data used in this chapter were collected between 21 April 2008 and 11 May 2008; these dates bracket the PIT tax-filing deadline of 30 April 2008 for 2007 returns. A total of 2,000 federal PIT tax-filers for the year 2007 were surveyed. The sample includes individual tax-filers from all ten Canadian provinces but excludes tax-filers from the three (northern) territories and those living abroad; they account for less than 1% of tax-filers.

In the analysis (§9.05) we exclude observations missing values for our variables of interest as well as outliers (defined as observations belonging to the highest 1% and those with the lowest 1% of TCC) in order to avoid extreme values. The resulting sample contains 1,196 observations.

Calculating total TCC requires both ascertaining direct expenditures on compliance activities as well as the value of time used in compliance activities. Evidence indicates that the most important source of TCC is the time spent on such tasks.[19] This time is the sum of time gathering and preparing documents, time preparing returns, time interacting with tax preparers if the task is delegated to someone else (for both paid and unpaid help) as well as the time of the unpaid tax preparer.

In this chapter, following Vaillancourt et al.,[20] the value of time is ascertained in one of three ways:

(1) When reported by the survey respondent, the gross (before tax) hourly wage is used.[21]

(2) For workers who did not report a wage rate, a wage is estimated using the characteristics of the individual (sex, age, education, marital status and region of residence) and a wage regression estimated for those respondents with a positive wage.

(3) Those retired are assumed to have a value for each hour spent on tax compliance work of CAD 10.

Finally, the value of time of unpaid tax preparers is set as follows. First, given that not-for-profit tax preparing organizations are usually run by volunteers, the attributed hourly value is again CAD 10. The value assigned when the unpaid tax preparer happens to be a family member or a friend is the tax-filer's own wage rate (observed,

---

19. François Vaillancourt, Édison Roy-César & Maria Silvia Barros, *The Compliance and Administrative Costs of Taxation in Canada* (Fraser Institute, 2013).
20. Vaillancourt, Roy-César & Barros, above n. 19.
21. Strictly speaking, we collected wage information in interval form and use the following values in our analysis:
    (8.0 if $w \in [0,10)$);(12.5 if $w \in [10,15)$); (17.5 if $w \in [15,20)$); (22.5 if $w \in [20,25)$); (27.5 if $w \in [25,30)$@;(32.5 if $w \in [30,35)$); (37.5 if $w \in [35,40)$); (42.5 if $w \in [40,45)$); (47.5 if $w \in [45,50)$); (60.0 if $w \in [50,\infty)$).

estimated or CAD 10). This rule of attribution is reasonable since usually it is the more experienced family member who helps others with the filing process.

The remainder of direct compliance costs are the sum of expenses incurred for tax-related activities. This broad definition includes the cost of paying a tax preparer, the cost of preparing documents, making photocopies, mailing documents and buying software or other online services in order to file the return.

[C] Use of Tax Preferences

Table 9.2 presents information on the use of tax provisions for individuals using at least one tax preference, in general or by type. Examining it, one finds for example that the presence of a child (or being married) is associated with a 12 (17) percentage point increase in the use of family tax preferences while the use of such preferences shows a U-shaped relationship with age, due to the use of the education preference when young and the pension splitting preference when old. Use of investment preferences jumps sharply when income is above CAD 150,000 (18 percentage points higher when compared with the next-lower income group).

Table 9.2 *Percentage of Individuals Using at Least One of Ten, or Aggregated, Tax Preferences, by Socio-Demographic Characteristics, Canada, PIT, 2007*

Characteristics	Tax-Filers Using at Least One Tax Preference (%)	Tax-Filers Using an Individual / Family Tax Preference (%)	Tax-Filers Using an Investment Tax Preference (%)
(a) Sex			
Men	61.77	58.35	15.49
Women	58.08	55.36	11.73
All tax-filers	59.62	56.61	13.29
(b) Minors in the household			
None	55.95	53.39	12.88
At least one	67.45	65.62	14.17
(c) Age			
18–24	68.42	65.79	10.53
25–34	57.89	55.56	9.36
35–44	62.07	59.61	14.29
45–54	55.64	51.75	13.62
55–64	52.90	50.58	8.88
65 +	67.91	64.18	19.40
(d) Employment situation			
Employed full-time	56.07	52.27	13.27
Employed part-time	57.93	57.92	10.38

Characteristics	Tax-Filers Using at Least One Tax Preference (%)	Tax-Filers Using an Individual / Family Tax Preference (%)	Tax-Filers Using an Investment Tax Preference (%)
Unemployed	60.71	60.71	6.25
Homemaker	53.13	52.63	10.53
Retired	66.77	64.05	15.71
Other	65.00	65.00	12.50
(e) Education			
Less than high school	46.20	44.14	8.28
High school completed	50.00	45.87	11.57
Post-secondary technical school or college degree	57.94	54.91	13.55
Completed undergraduate degree	71.07	67.77	13.64
Post-graduate degree	75.53	74.10	20.14
(f) Marital status			
Married	65.11	62.58	14.66
Single	50.00	45.83	11.98
Other	47.89	44.13	9.39
(g) Language skills			
Poor knowledge of English or French	54.58	51.28	13.55
Good knowledge of English or French	61.11	58.78	13.22
(h) Region			
Atlantic	61.90	60.71	14.29
Quebec	61.39	59.44	8.88
Ontario	56.86	53.26	15.51
Prairies	61.26	56.54	17.80
British Columbia	60.34	57.76	10.34
(i) Income level (CAD)			
Less than CAD 10,000	50.57	48.85	8.05
CAD 10,000–CAD 29,999	53.45	51.44	10.34
CAD 30,000–CAD 49,999	60.93	57.95	12.25
CAD 50,000–CAD 69,999	67.51	64.97	14.72
CAD 70,000–CAD 99,999	70.97	64.96	22.22
CAD 100,000–CAD 149,999	69.44	61.11	22.22
CAD 150,000 and greater	63.64	54.55	40.91

Source: Calculations by the authors using survey data.

Finally we present in Figure 9.2 the total compliance costs incurred by users of one or another tax preference. These are not the marginal impact on TCC of using these tax preferences but are of interest for illustrative purposes.

Figure 9.2   Mean TCC, CAD, Canada, PIT, 2007, Users of Specific and Aggregated Tax Preferences

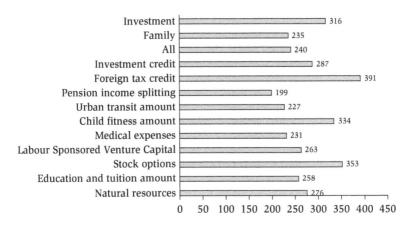

Source: Authors using survey data.

§9.04   DETERMINANTS OF THE TCC OF TAX PREFERENCES

In this part of the chapter we first present the variables used in the multivariate analyses (§9.04[A]) then the results (TCC estimations, §9.04[B]).

[A]   Variables

The dependent variable is TCC in CAD with Ordinary Least Squares (OLS) estimations used. The independent variables are discussed in Table 9.3.

Table 9.3   Variables Determining TCC, PIT, Canada, 2007: Description and Expected Impact

Variable	Description	Expected Impact
Experience with the tax system	Numbers of years for which a return has been filed (four categories: first year, two to four years, five to nine years, ten years or more)	The impact of experience with taxes on the TCC is not certain; it may make users more efficient thus reducing TCC or more knowledgeable about how to use little-used provisions of the tax code thus increasing TCC.

Variable	Description	Expected Impact
Income types	Sources of income in 2007 (thirteen categories).	The receipt of some types of income is expected, given the evidence in the literature, to generate higher TCC than others. Interest or pension income should have lower TCC than self-employment or stock-related investment income.
Language skills	Level of knowledge of the two official languages of the federal government (two categories)	A lower level of knowledge should increase TCC as it makes it more difficult to understand the rules or tools commonly used.
Preparation mode	Possible ways of preparing a tax return (six categories).	This can influence TCC but may also be linked to tax complexity; for example filers facing more complexity may choose different modes (tax software or paid expert) than those facing less complexity (paper or family/ friend).
Income level	Seven income ranges.	TCC should increase with income as the value of tax avoidance activities increases with income when the PIT is progressive as is the case in Canada.
Region	Five regions within Canada.	This captures unmeasured differences between regions. Uncertain impact on TCC.
Marital status	Four marital statuses	Couples can be expected to have more opportunities for income splitting, deduction shifting and other choices that increase TCC than single individuals (there is no joint filing in Canada).
Education	Highest degree achieved (five categories).	Higher education may increase the knowledge of the tax system and thus the use of various aspects of it increasing TCC. It also increases the wage of the tax-filer and thus the value of time included in TCC.
Age	Six age categories.	Age as a proxy for work experience should have an inverted U-shaped impact on wages and thus on the value of time included in TCC. Older individuals have access to tax preferences specific to their age group; this could increase their TCC.

Variable	Description	Expected Impact
Employment status	Six categories.	TCC will vary with the type of employment. Self-employment is linked in the literature to higher TCC; in this chapter this is captured by self-employment income.
Children in the household	A categorical variable for whether a child lives in the household or not.	The presence of a child creates opportunities to use specific aspects of the tax code or to participate in tax-delivered income transfer programmes and thus may increase TCC.
Gender	A categorical variable.	This captures the effect of gender on wages and thus time TCC.
Tax provisions	*Ten variables each accounting for the use or not of a specific tax code provision along with three grouped variables are used.*	*TCC should vary by type of tax code /expenditure used.*

Source: Authors.

[B]   TCC Estimations

Before turning to the empirical results, one should recall that eligibility to use a specific provision of the tax code does not make its use mandatory. Therefore, we only observe tax-filers who decided to make use or not of the said tax provision. The survey data makes it impossible to know which individuals were eligible but decided not to take advantage of the fiscal measure, or perhaps were even unaware of their own eligibility or even of the tax expenditure itself. The lack of information is not uncommon; using survey data, Fisher et al. found that about 35% of Canadian parents with children under the age of 18 had not even heard about the Child Fitness Tax Credit.[22]

If we suppose that only those who are eligible and judge *ex ante* their compliance costs of claiming a tax preference to be lower than the potential tax benefit reaped will choose to use the tax preference, a selection bias may be present in our data. In other words, if only those who believe that there is a net positive benefit to claiming the tax credit do claim it, those with higher costs will self-select out of the sample. Unobserved eligibility makes it impossible to use a two-stage method to correct for this problem.

The non-exhaustiveness of the tax credit list observed in the survey also introduces a potential problem. If the use of unobserved but claimed tax credits is

---

22. Koren L. Fisher, Amin Mawani, Barbara von Tigerstrom, Tamara Larre, Christine Cameron, Karen E. Chad, Bruce Reeder & Mark. S. Tremblay, *Awareness and Use of Canada's Children's Fitness Tax Credit*, 61(3) Can. Tax J. 599 (2013).

correlated with the use of the ten for which we have information, then the cost coefficients may be biased upwards.

Table 9.4   *Multivariate Analysis of the TCC, PIT Filers, Canada, 2007*

(Dependent variable, TCC)			
	(1)	(2)	(3)
Tax Preferences:	Grouped in 1	Grouped in 2	Ten Separate
(a) Sex (women as a reference)			
Men	17.28	17.55	15.77
	(14.30)	(14.34)	(14.44)
(b) Minors in the household (none as reference)			
At least one	47.88**	48.58**	37.54
	(22.63)	(22.73)	(23.58)
(c) Employment situation (employed full-time as reference)			
Employed part-time	-32.92	-30.85	-32.78
	(22.22)	(22.44)	(21.83)
Unemployed	-50.73*	-46.64*	-51.24*
	(26.57)	(26.50)	(27.83)
Homemaker	-21.29	-17.01	-23.05
	(62.14)	(62.83)	(59.61)
Retired	-125.5***	-120.7***	-131.3***
	(30.02)	(31.03)	(29.60)
Other	-50.65	-48.59	-52.96
	(32.79)	(32.58)	(33.50)
(d) Age (18-24 as reference)			
25–34	-11.53	-11.86	-22.40
	(33.24)	(33.31)	(33.76)
35–44	34.70	33.96	16.81
	(40.47)	(40.38)	(42.25)
45–54	-14.82	-14.27	-29.82
	(40.27)	(40.30)	(42.31)
55–64	28.01	28.53	16.42
	(42.13)	(42.11)	(46.39)
65 +	37.63	33.98	31.30
	(44.46)	(44.28)	(48.50)
(e) Education (some high school or less as reference)			
High school completed	0.783	1.496	5.122

(Dependent variable, TCC)

Tax Preferences:	(1) Grouped in 1	(2) Grouped in 2	(3) Ten Separate
	(20.04)	(20.15)	(20.29)
Post-secondary technical school or college degree	-15.41	-15.46	-13.54
	(19.67)	(19.71)	(19.96)
Completed undergraduate degree	41.93*	45.05*	45.63*
	(24.62)	(24.64)	(25.08)
Post-graduate degree	46.67	47.94	46.05
	(31.03)	(31.49)	(30.96)
(f) Marital status (married or living in common-law as reference)			
Single	-26.45*	-26.66*	-30.79*
	(15.93)	(15.67)	(15.74)
Other	7.373	8.485	2.247
	(15.10)	(15.12)	(15.46)
(g) Region (Atlantic as reference)			
Quebec	-41.16*	-38.45	-35.51
	(23.77)	(23.67)	(24.09)
Ontario	-27.55	-26.92	-26.74
	(24.48)	(24.41)	(24.76)
Prairies	-3.720	-4.032	-0.657
	(27.31)	(27.21)	(27.17)
British Columbia	0.376	3.435	2.874
	(29.76)	(29.64)	(30.08)
(h) Income, CAD (less than CAD 10,000 as reference)			
CAD 10,000–CAD 29,999	-10.98	-9.945	-9.593
	(15.91)	(15.82)	(16.03)
CAD 30,000–CAD 49,999	15.76	18.69	21.79
	(22.25)	(22.16)	(21.56)
CAD 50,000–CAD 69,999	8.225	10.58	12.49
	(24.13)	(23.92)	(24.05)
CAD 70,000–CAD 99,999	43.15	46.13	53.59*
	(28.96)	(28.64)	(29.53)
CAD 100,000–CAD 149,999	67.65	73.93	70.60
	(46.50)	(46.79)	(45.54)
CAD 150,000 and greater	189.9**	185.6**	180.3**
	(80.56)	(81.61)	(83.01)

(Dependent variable, TCC)

Tax Preferences:	(1) Grouped in 1	(2) Grouped in 2	(3) Ten Separate
(i) Experience with the tax system (first year as reference)			
Two to four years	49.04	43.95	43.04
	(38.81)	(37.02)	(36.87)
Five to nine years	74.33	68.62	71.79*
	(45.75)	(43.59)	(41.52)
Ten years or more	51.26	42.98	44.97
	(39.49)	(37.81)	(35.77)
(j) Official language skills (none as reference)			
Yes	5.667	6.303	5.415
	(15.99)	(15.99)	(15.89)
(k) Type of income (not received as reference for each type of income)			
Wages and salary	-25.56	-27.46	-30.18
	(22.38)	(22.41)	(22.16)
Self-employment income	109.0***	108.3***	108.8***
	(24.85)	(24.77)	(24.86)
Child tax benefit	6.479	6.248	2.024
	(26.10)	(25.93)	(26.12)
Government transfer payment	8.982	9.170	14.48
	(15.25)	(15.29)	(15.01)
Private pension	-0.446	-1.762	0.336
	(15.39)	(15.22)	(15.61)
Interest income	21.88	24.42	23.85
	(16.09)	(15.97)	(15.87)
Dividend income	17.52	11.59	14.19
	(20.04)	(20.21)	(20.55)
Rental income	51.33*	42.59	46.44
	(28.65)	(28.59)	(29.42)
Capital gains	50.83*	48.44*	44.19*
	(26.13)	(26.15)	(26.38)
Other investment income, Canadian	3.667	-6.112	-1.503
	(24.36)	(24.45)	(24.98)
Investment income, non-Canadian	31.49	17.01	-18.70
	(47.18)	(50.85)	(65.71)
Labour income, non-Canadian	86.53	85.17	106.7

(Dependent variable, TCC)			
	(1)	*(2)*	*(3)*
Tax Preferences:	*Grouped in 1*	*Grouped in 2*	*Ten Separate*
	(114.9)	(109.5)	(101.1)
Pension income, non-Canadian	-47.85	-53.18	-53.78
	(37.47)	(36.97)	(37.35)
(l) Preparation mode (self, using paper form as reference)			
Self, using software	43.16*	44.06*	43.05*
	(23.89)	(23.87)	(23.15)
Self, using online software	4.854	5.210	5.183
	(23.67)	(23.65)	(24.57)
Not-for-profit	10.72	9.754	10.79
	(26.96)	(25.86)	(24.79)
Friend or family	15.43	14.78	14.33
	(18.70)	(18.70)	(18.83)
Paid tax preparer	102.7***	101.8***	101.8***
	(16.74)	(16.74)	(16.86)
(m) Use of tax expenditure provision (none as reference for each provision)	**One**	**Two**	**Ten**
Natural resources (various including FTSs)	–	–	4.688
			(59.34)
Education and tuition amount for self or transferred	–	–	20.53
			(23.76)
Stock options	–	–	69.12
			(45.75)
Labour Sponsored Venture Capital Corporation	–	–	-30.61
			(57.70)
Medical expenses	–	–	34.02**
			(15.87)
Child fitness amount	–	–	51.08
			(33.81)
Urban transit amount	–	–	-8.649
			(31.13)
Pension income splitting	–	–	-25.30
			(21.36)
Foreign tax credit	–	–	141.2*
			(83.16)

(Dependent variable, TCC)			
	(1)	(2)	(3)
Tax Preferences:	Grouped in 1	Grouped in 2	Ten Separate
Investment credit	–	–	4.162
			(29.36)
Investment tax preference	–	58.22**	–
		(28.82)	
Individual/family tax preference	–	34.32**	–
		(13.40)	
Any tax preference	49.83***	–	–
	(12.28)		
Constant	44.15	53.66	73.68
	(56.20)	(54.52)	(55.95)
Observations:	1,196	1,196	1,196
Adjusted R-squared:	0.212	0.213	0.216

Robust standard errors in parentheses
*** p < 0.01, ** p < 0.05, * p < 0.1

For the first model (1), all ten tax credits are represented by a single dichotomous variable. For the second model (2), the tax credits are grouped in two dichotomous variables accounting for five tax credits each as discussed above (§9.03[C]). Finally, the third model uses ten dichotomous variables, one per tax credit.

The results of model (1) suggest that the act of claiming tax preferences has a non-negligible cost that can ultimately reduce the net benefit obtained by the tax-filer. On average, tax-filers who benefited from one or more of the ten tax preferences studied claimed 1.6 tax preferences and saw their direct compliance costs rise by CAD 49.8 after controlling for several other factors likely to affect direct compliance costs. Thus one can compute a per-tax-preference cost of CAD 31. The second model (i.e., splitting tax credits into sub-groups of individual/family and investment) yields an estimated cost of using an investment tax preference of CAD 58.2; given there is an average of 1.3 investment tax preferences claimed by these tax-filers, this implies a unit cost of CAD 45. The estimate for the individual/family tax preferences is CAD 34.3; given there is an average of 1.4 individual/family tax preferences claimed by these tax-filers, this implies a unit cost of CAD 24. This difference in unit cost may be due in part to the fact that, on average, those who claim investment tax preferences have higher wages than those who claim individual/family[23] tax preferences; they also use the services of a paid tax preparer more often. The third model yields only two statistically significant results that are not discussed further here.

---

23. Calculation by the authors using survey data. Those claiming 'investment choice' tax credits have an average hourly wage of CAD 22.07 while those claiming 'family or individual choice' tax credits have an average hourly wage of CAD 20.82.

§9.05 TCC, TAX COMPLEXITY AND PUBLIC POLICY

We now have gross and net estimates of TCC associated with the use of ten personal income tax preferences for Canada in 2007. One possible use of this information is to link it to the tax complexity associated with these ten tax preferences. Figure 9.3 links the tax complexity information of Table 9.1 to the gross (Figure 9.2) and net (Table 9.4) TCC of these ten tax preferences. Examining Figure 9.3, one can only conclude that the relationship is tenuous at best. This may indicate that the complexity index is incorrectly computed. It may also be linked to the inappropriateness of using gross TCC and to the lack of significant estimates of net TCC for the ten tax preferences. But even using net TCC for preferences grouped under two headings yields no obvious relationship.

Figure 9.3 TCC Gross and Net for Ten PIT Tax Preferences Ordered by Increasing Complexity Indicator, Canada, 2007

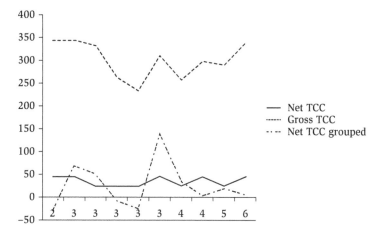

Source: Authors.
Note: Gross TCC Figure 9.2; Net TCC Table 9.4. We neglect significativity when drawing the net TCC line. Credits are ordered according to complexity index of Table 9.1 as follows: LSVCC; Stock options; Child fitness amount; Urban transit amount; Pension income splitting; Foreign tax credit; Medical expenses; Investment credit; Education/ tuition; Natural resources.

How do the ten tax preferences interact more generally with tax policy in Canada? Table 9.5 presents some information when available on this:

- Column (2) shows that the tax preferences examined vary in importance as measured by the associated reduction in tax revenues by a factor of 12 to 1 (CAD 1,155 million to CAD 90 million).
- Column (3) shows, for the subset of tax preferences for which we have the required information, that the most commonly used tax preference is the

medical expenditure preference, followed closely by the education preference, while the least commonly used is the LSVCF.

- Column (4) presents the value of the tax credits /deductions claimed to generate the tax expenditures amount. They again vary substantially between tax preferences.
- Columns (6) and (7) are perhaps those of greater relevance for policy-makers. Column (6), obtained by combining columns (2) and (5), presents the ratio of (TCC / tax expenditures); it varies by a factor of 10, being higher for two family-oriented measures. One may wonder if a tax expenditure that requires spending 40%–50% of its value to taxpayers in TCC to claim it is an efficient tax policy choice.
- Column (7) presents the share of users of a tax preference that report a taxable income above CAD 100,000. This is a rough distribution indicator; it would be preferable to have the distribution of the tax expenditure as such, either as a percentage above a cut-off or computed using a Gini-type index. We again see variations between tax preferences, with the investment ones for which we have the information more concentrated in the upper income group than the family ones.

Table 9.5 Tax Expenditures, Tax Credits/Deductions and % Use, TCC, Use by Income Groups, PIT Tax Preferences, Canada, 2007

Tax Credit	Value Tax Expenditure (CAD Million) (2)	Users as % of Taxpayers (3)	Tax Credit/Deduction CAD '000 (4)	Compliance Costs Associated with Tax Measure CAD '000 (5)	% Compliance Cost/Tax Expenditure (6) = (5)/(2)	% users Income > CAD 100,000 (7)
(a) Family tax preferences						
Child fitness	90	5.2	643,208 (C)	43,594	48.4%	18%
Education and tuition amount	980	11.1	10,055,214 (C)	92,709	9.5%	5%
Medical expenses	915	14.6	7,996,602 (D)	121,753	13.3%	4%
Pension income splitting	840	3.5	8,840,354 (D)	29,330	3.5%	10%
Urban transit amount	110	5.2	843,333 (C)	43,411	39.5%	6%
(b) Investment tax preferences						
Foreign income tax credit	780	4.1	793,995 (C)	58,587	7.5%	28%
Investment tax preference	20	n.a.	n.a.	n.a.	n.a.	n.a.
Labour Sponsored Venture Capital Corporation (LSVCC) tax credit	120	1.6	253,450 (C)	22,762	19.0%	20%
Natural resources (including Flow-Through Shares) tax credit	150	n.a.	n.a.	n.a.	n.a.	n.a.
Stock options tax preference	1,155	n.a.	n.a.	n.a.	n.a.	n.a.

Sources:

Column (2): Canada, Department of Finance, *Tax Expenditures and Evaluations 2012* (2013);

Columns (3), (4) and (7): Canada Revenue Agency, *Income Statistics 2009–2007 tax year, Basic Table 2, All returns by total income class*. Note that the total number of tax returns filed for 2007 is 24,600,590. For column (7), % for LSVCF is ½ of 50,000 + 100 + amount in F. Vaillancourt, 'Labour Sponsored Venture Capital Funds in Canada: Institutional Aspects Tax Expenditures and Employment Creation', in P. Halpern (ed.), *Financing Growth in Canada* 571, 580, Table 6 (University of Calgary Press, 1997);

Column (5): we multiply the number of users of a given tax preference by either CAD 24 for family ones or CAD 45 for investment ones. In column (1), 'Education' is the sum of Education tax credit, Textbook tax credit, Tuition tax credit and Transfer of Education, Textbook and Tuition tax credit. 'Natural resource' is almost only flow through shares. Note that the Foreign tax credit is a memorandum item;

In column (3) the number for the foreign tax credit is from Canada Revenue Agency, *Income Statistics 2009–2007 tax year Basic Table 10 Selected Items by Total Income Class*;

Also the number for Labour Sponsored Venture Capital Corporation is computed as follows:

Number of users in Québec in 2007, that is 259,410 x (1 / (Number for Québec 1993 / number for Canada as a whole)), that is, (1 / (92,540 / 140,110) = 0.661), thus 392,450. The numbers for Québec 2007 are from Ministère des Finances du Québec, *Statistiques fiscales des particuliers 2007*, Tableau 2, line item 81, p. 47. Numbers for 1993 are from Vaillancourt, 'Labour Sponsored Venture Capital Funds in Canada: Institutional Aspects Tax Expenditures and Employment Creation', as above, 580, Table 6.

§9.06 CONCLUSION

The main conclusions of this chapter are that:

- The measurement of tax complexity has yet to settle on the best practice in this field. We argue that various indicators used in the literature can be ordered along a continuum from government policy (tax expenditures) to tax law (number of pages / lines in the tax laws) to requirements on taxpayers (number of lines / items in tax forms and guidebooks) to tax compliance costs. Each indicator adds to our understanding of tax complexity.
- It is net TCC, obtained from multivariate analysis, and not mean (gross) TCC that should be used in policy work. Estimating net TCC will require survey data that may not be robust to detailed analysis, as our work shows. Attempts to link our TCC estimates to simple complexity measures were not successful; more robust analysis is required.
- TCC can be linked to one indicator of tax complexity, tax expenditures, to ascertain the net value for taxpayers of a given tax preference. This can be seen as one aspect of the efficiency of tax preferences, but not the sole one. We also provide some information on the distributional aspect of tax preferences.

The methodology used in this chapter can be used in other countries where both survey information on TCC of specific tax preferences and general information on tax preferences is available. Such work would provide information on the usefulness of this methodology in countries other than Canada.

CHAPTER 10

Administering Tax Complexity versus Simplicity

Kristin E. Hickman

§10.01 INTRODUCTION

Chapters in this volume, and the broader literature to which they contribute, are replete with discussions of types, sources, and measures of tax complexity. However, one chooses to define or measure tax complexity, the US tax system has plenty of it.

My goal with this chapter is to address the relationship between tax complexity and tax administration in the US, both in terms of the challenges that the Internal Revenue Service (IRS) faces in administering the Internal Revenue Code (IRC) and the implications for judicial review of IRS actions. To that end, I will elaborate two main points.

First, the tax complexity in the US has transformed the IRC from a statute designed to raise revenue to one aimed at accomplishing a substantially broader menu of regulatory and social welfare goals that are in tension with the revenue-raising function. As a result, tax administration is increasingly indistinguishable from the administration of regulatory and social welfare programmes by other government agencies.

Second, tax administrative practices in the US are out of step with general administrative law doctrines and norms that govern the actions of other federal agencies as they administer regulatory and social welfare programmes. The courts are in the process of bringing tax administration back into line with those general administrative law doctrines and norms. That jurisprudential trend cannot be traced directly to tax complexity; at least, no court has made that connection. Nevertheless, I suggest that tax administrative practices have been shaped by a set of premises that assume a relatively simple, or at least internally coherent, tax system oriented primarily toward the revenue-raising function. Those premises are not so consistent with the US tax system's present multi-functional complexity.

Many tax lawyers and tax administrators in the US dislike the courts' rejection of tax exceptionalism from general administrative law doctrines and norms.[1] To some extent, the 'horse has left the barn', and putting it back would be difficult. Nevertheless, supporters of tax exceptionalism from general administrative law doctrines and norms ought to recognize that tax complexity undermines their case. Also, proponents of tax simplification may wish to highlight the administrative implications of integrating regulatory and social welfare programmes into the tax system.

§10.02   THE NATURE AND SCOPE OF US TAX SYSTEM COMPLEXITY[2]

At one level, the primary purpose of any tax system is to raise revenue. Or, at least, taxes are the principal, if not the sole, source of the revenue that governments need to fund their operations and programmes. The tax system includes the laws that impose those taxes and the government agencies that administer those laws.

The scholarly literature on tax complexity recognizes, nevertheless, both that tax systems pursue regulatory and social welfare goals beyond mere revenue-raising and also that the provisions designed to accomplish those other goals are a source of complexity.[3] The progressivity of the individual income tax – sometimes recognized as a contributor to income tax complexity[4] – is frequently justified at least partly as a remedy for societal inequality.[5] Historical evidence suggests that Congress enacted the corporate income tax not only to raise revenue but also to provide a mechanism by which the government could regulate corporate activity and constrain corporate political power.[6]

What may be under-appreciated in the literature is the extent to which regulatory and social welfare programmes have invaded the US tax system, to the point that they rival revenue-raising as the principal focus of tax administration efforts. Tax expenditures represent a key part of this trend. The biennial compendium of tax expenditures prepared by the Congressional Research Service in 2012 lists 250 such items totalling

---

1. See, e.g., Steve R. Johnson, *Preserving Fairness in Tax Administration in the* Mayo *Era*, 32(2) Va. Tax Rev. 269, 272 (2012) (documenting and responding to concerns).
2. This part of this chapter draws substantially from Kristin E. Hickman, *Administering the Tax System We Have*, 63(8) Duke L.J. 1717 (2014).
3. See, e.g., Samuel A. Donaldson, *The Easy Case Against Tax Simplification*, 22(4) Va. Tax Rev. 645, 654–659 (2003).
4. See, e.g., Edward J. McCaffery, *The Holy Grail of Tax Simplification*, [1990] 5 Wis. L. Rev. 1267, 1274, 1282–1283.
5. Henry C. Simons, *Personal Income Taxation: The Definition of Income as a Problem in Fiscal Policy*, 15–19 (University of Chicago Press, 1938); Meredith R. Conway, *Money, It's a Crime. Share It Fairly, but Don't Take a Slice of My Pie!: The Legislative Case for the Progressive Income Tax*, 39(2) J. Legis. 119, 130–132 (2013).
6. Steven A. Bank, *From Sword to Shield: The Transformation of the Corporate Income Tax, 1861 to Present*, 43–44 (Oxford University Press, 2010); Reuven S. Avi-Yonah, *Corporations, Society, and the State: A Defense of the Corporate Tax*, 90(5) Va. L. Rev. 1193, 1217–1220 (2004); Marjorie E. Kornhauser, *Corporate Regulation and the Origins of the Corporate Income Tax*, 66(1) Ind. L.J. 53 (1990).

well over USD 1 trillion, and even that extensive list does not purport to be comprehensive.[7] Many tax expenditures are small and, sometimes, short-lived, like recent credits for first-time homebuyers and purchasers of electric vehicles.[8] Some are larger, long-standing, and complicated – like accelerated depreciation deductions for equipment, exclusions for employer contributions for employee health coverage and retirement plans, or the deduction for home mortgage interest.[9]

Tax expenditures require tax administrators to orient their efforts toward programmes, purposes, and functions that have little to do with revenue-raising and, indeed, more closely resemble the regulatory and social welfare programmes of other, non-tax government agencies. As former Assistant Secretary of the Treasury for Tax Policy Pamela Olson has acknowledged:

> The continual enactment of targeted tax provisions leaves the IRS with responsibility for the administration of policies aimed at the environment, conservation, green energy, manufacturing, innovation, education, saving, retirement, health care, child care, welfare, corporate governance, export promotion, charitable giving, governance of tax exempt organizations, and economic development, to name a few.[10]

For example, Congress increasingly utilizes refundable tax credits rather than direct subsidies to alleviate poverty and support working families.[11] Amounts expended by the government on the earned income tax credit (EITC) and the child tax credit each surpassed those for Temporary Assistance for Needy Families and its

---

7. Congressional Research Service, *Tax Expenditures: Compendium of Background Material on Individual Provisions*, 1, 11 (US Government Printing Office, 2012) [hereinafter *2012 CRS Tax Expenditures Compendium*]. The compendium draws its data from tax expenditure estimates compiled by the Joint Committee on Taxation (JCT): *2012 CRS Tax Expenditures Compendium*, at 1. The JCT, in turn, acknowledges that it does not include *de minimis* items that fall below USD 50 million or items for which quantification is unavailable. Staff of J. Comm. on Taxation, 112th Cong., *Estimates of Federal Tax Expenditures for Fiscal Years 2011–2015*, 27–30 (US Government Printing Office, 2012).
8. The tax expenditure estimates compiled by the JCT in 2012 documented more than thirty items valued at less than USD 50 million each. See Staff of J. Comm. on Taxation, above n. 7, at 27–28. The same report included seventy-six tax expenditure items that expired in 2010 and 2011, including, for example, the IRC s. 36 first-time homebuyer credit (which was available for homes purchased between 9 April 2008 and 1 May 2010) and the IRC s. 30 credit for purchasing a plug-in electric vehicle (which was available for vehicles purchased between 18 February 2009 and 31 December 2011). Staff of J. Comm. on Taxation, above n. 7, at 28.
9. According to the Congressional Research Service, the amounts attributable to these four tax expenditure items in 2011 were, respectively, USD 52.3 billion, USD 109.3 billion, USD 105.3 billion, and USD 77.6 billion. *2012 CRS Tax Expenditures Compendium*, above n. 7, at 5–6.
10. Pamela F. Olson, *And Then Cnut Told Reagan . . . Lessons from the Tax Reform Act of 1986* (Laurence Neal Woodworth Memorial Lecture, 6 May 2010), 38(1) Ohio N.U. L. Rev. 1, 12–13 (2011).
11. See, e.g., Francine J. Lipman, *Access to Tax InJustice*, 40 Pepp. L. Rev. 1173, 1180–1184 (2013); David A. Weisbach & Jacob Nussim, *The Integration of Tax and Spending Programs*, 113(5) Yale L.J. 955 (2004); Lawrence Zelenak, *Tax or Welfare? The Administration of the Earned Income Tax Credit*, 52(6) UCLA L. Rev. 1867 (2005); see also IRS, *EITC & Other Refundable Credits*, http://www.eitc.irs.gov (accessed on 21 March 2014) (highlighting and facilitating claims to the EITC and other refundable tax credits).

predecessor, Aid to Families with Dependent Children, years ago.[12] In other words, the IRS is now one of the government's principal welfare agencies, on par with the Department of Health and Human Services (HHS) and the Social Security Administration.[13]

Treasury and the IRS also play a leading role in regulating private sector pension and health care benefits under the Employee Retirement Income Security Act of 1974 (ERISA).[14] Congress enacted ERISA to protect participants in employee pension and welfare plans, including health coverage plans, by imposing various participation, vesting, funding, reporting, and disclosure requirements on the private sector employers and labour unions that sponsor them.[15] The role of Treasury and the IRS in administering the pension aspects of ERISA largely corresponds to provisions in the IRC that exclude qualifying pension contributions and earnings from taxable income.[16] (By contrast, Treasury and IRS responsibilities for administering ERISA health coverage requirements relate most closely to a financial penalty, styled as an excise tax, imposed by the IRC on non-conforming group health plans.[17] From what I understand, the excise tax is rarely paid because the parties providing the health coverage in question avoid the tax by conforming with IRC requirements.) In administering ERISA, Treasury and the IRS tax personnel have worked with the Department of Health and Human Services and the Department of Labor to adopt regulations that, among other things, govern the length of hospital stays for new mothers and their newborn infants[18] and ensure that the mental health and substance abuse disorder benefits provided by group health plans enjoy parity with those plans' medical and surgical benefits.[19]

Treasury and the IRS also play a key role in regulating the activities of the exempt organization sector. Defining which organizations are eligible for tax-exempt status

---

12. Nat'l Taxpayer Advocate, *2009 Annual Report to Congress: Volume Two: Research and Related Studies* 78 (2009), available at http://www.irs.gov/pub/tas/09_tas_arc_vol_2.pdf.
13. Lipman, above n. 11, at 1173.
14. Employee Retirement Income Security Act of 1974, Pub. L. No. 93-406, 88 Stat. 829.
15. Steven J. Sacher, James I. Singer & Teresa M. Connerton, *Employee Benefits Law*, 22–35 (2nd ed., Bureau of National Affairs, 2000); Anne Tucker, *Retirement Revolution: Unmitigated Risks in the Defined Contribution Society*, 51(1) Hous. L. Rev. 153, 163–66 (2013). Although historical accounts of ERISA focus primarily on pension reform, Congress drafted ERISA to cover a broader array of employee welfare plans, including employer-sponsored health insurance plans. Sacher et al., at 28.
16. For example IRC ss 401–407, 410–418E, 457 (2012). Many of these provisions have parallel provisions in ERISA, and Treasury claims interpretive jurisdiction over both. See Colleen E. Medill, *Introduction to Employee Benefits Law*, 95–96 (3rd ed., West Academic Publishing, 2011).
17. Specifically, for any group health plan that fails to meet the requirements of IRC chapter 100, IRC s. 4980D imposes an excise tax upon a sponsoring employer of one hundred dollars per day, per individual affected. Chapter 100, in turn, imposes an array of portability, access, and renewability requirements, as well as benefit requirements for mothers and newborns and for mental health, among other things. IRC ss 9801–9802, 9811–9812 (imposing group health plan requirements); see also Medill, above n. 16, at 354–355 (discussing the 'excise tax penalty' adopted to enforce group health plan requirements).
18. T.D. 9427, Final Rules for Group Health Plans and Health Insurance Issuers Under the Newborns' and Mothers' Health Protection Act, 73 Fed. Reg. 62,410 (20 October 2008).
19. T.D. 9479, Interim Final Rules Under the Paul Wellstone and Pete Domenici Mental Health Parity and Addiction Equity Act of 2008, 75 Fed. Reg. 5410 (2 February 2010).

and, separately, which may receive tax deductible contributions is complicated.[20] Current Treasury and IRS administration efforts in this one area now involve an entire IRS division (out of only four) monitoring more than 1.6 million tax-exempt organizations[21] across a few dozen separate statutory classifications.[22] Evaluating applications for exempt status and monitoring existing organizations for continued compliance with eligibility requirements are even more difficult. Tax administrators in this sector routinely make decisions implicating issues as varied as free speech, politics, and religion;[23] election law and campaign finance;[24] and, again, health policy and hospital governance.[25] Assessing and monitoring the exempt status of such a broad array of organizations is tremendously challenging. For a prime example of the difficulties Treasury and the IRS face in accomplishing this task, one need look no further than recent regulations, proposed in the wake of the IRS 'Tea Party' scandal, attempting to identify for IRC section 501(c)(4) social welfare organizations exactly which activities are candidate-related political activities.[26] The IRS received more than 150,000 comments – many critical – from a broad array of interested parties and members of the public, prompting the IRS to delay the implementation of those regulations.[27]

---

20. Only some exempt organizations can receive tax deductible contributions. Compare IRC s. § 501 (listing types of exempt organizations) with IRC s. 170(c) (listing organizations eligible to receive deductible contributions).
21. See IRS, *At-a-Glance: IRS Divisions and Principal Offices*, http://www.irs.gov/uac/At-a-Glance: -IRS-Divisions-and-Principal-Offices (accessed on 21 March 2014) (listing four primary IRS divisions: Wage and Investment; Large Business and International; Small Business/Self-Employed; and Tax-Exempt and Government Entities); IRS, *Tax Exempt & Government Entities Division at a Glance*, http://www.irs.gov/Government-Entities/Tax-Exempt-&-Government-Entities-Division-At-a-Glance (describing the work of the TE/GE division).
22. IRC ss 501(c)(1)–(29), (d)–(f); Charles A. Borek, *Decoupling Tax Exemption for Charitable Organizations*, 31(1) Wm. Mitchell L. Rev. 183, 201–207 (2004); James J. Fishman, *The Nonprofit Sector: Myths and Realities*, 9(2) N.Y. City L. Rev. 303, 303–305 (2006).
23. See, e.g., Johnny Rex Buckles, *Does the Constitutional Norm of Separation of Church and State Justify the Denial of Tax Exemption to Churches that Engage in Partisan Political Speech?*, 84(2) Ind. L.J. 447 (2009); Richard W. Garnett, *A Quiet Faith? Taxes, Politics, and the Privatization of Religion*, 42(4) B.C. L. Rev. 771 (2001); Steffen N. Johnson, *Of Politics and Pulpits: A First Amendment Analysis of IRS Restrictions on the Political Activities of Religious Organizations*, 42(4) B.C. L. Rev. 875 (2001).
24. In 2011, the *Election Law Journal* published an entire volume on this topic. For just a few of the contributions to that volume, see Richard Briffault, *Nonprofits and Disclosure in the Wake of Citizens United*, 10(4) Election L.J. 337 (2011); Lloyd Hitoshi Mayer, *Charities and Lobbying: Institutional Rights in the Wake of Citizens United*, 10(4) Election L.J. 407 (2011); Donald B. Tobin, *Campaign Disclosure and Tax-Exempt Entities: A Quick Repair to the Regulatory Plumbing*, 10(4) Election L.J. 427 (2011).
25. See, e.g., Jessica Berg, *Putting the Community Back into the 'Community Benefit' Standard*, 44(2) Ga. L. Rev. 375, 377 (2010) (discussing IRS-developed 'community benefit' criteria that non-profit hospitals must satisfy to maintain exempt status).
26. Notice of Proposed Rulemaking, Guidance for Tax-Exempt Social Welfare Organizations on Candidate-Related Political Activities, 78 Fed. Reg. 71,535 (29 November 2013). For comprehensive coverage of the IRS 'Tea Party' scandal through 5 April 2014, including but not limited to reaction to the proposed regulations, see Paul Caron, *The IRS Scandal, Day 547*, TaxProf Blog (7 November 2014), http://taxprof.typepad.com/taxprof_blog/2014/11/the–2.html.
27. For example *IRS Update on the Proposed New Regulation on 501(c)(4) Organizations*, http:// www.irs.gov/uac/Newsroom/IRS-Update-on-the-Proposed-New-Regulation-on-501%28c%29 %284%29-Organizations (22 May 2014); *IRS to rewrite nonprofit rules amid criticism*, http:// www.politico.com/story/2014/05/irs-rewrite-nonprofit-rules-amid-criticism-107015.html.

Anecdotally, Treasury and IRS officials bemoan the amount of time they spend implementing the Patient Protection and Affordable Care Act (ACA). Enacted in 2010,[28] the ACA is a complicated and massive piece of legislation that endeavours to expand health insurance coverage and control health care costs through various mandates, regulations, and subsidies administered by a combination of federal and state agencies.[29] The ACA's connection with the IRC is not primarily tax expenditure-based. Rather, the ACA raises revenue through a variety of provisions, including a 'shared responsibility payment' (i.e., the penalty for failing to acquire health insurance),[30] an expanded Medicare tax on self-employment income,[31] and a new net investment income tax[32] – all of which are assessed via individual income tax returns – as well as new excise taxes on indoor tanning services[33] and medical devices[34] and a new insurance policy 'fee'.[35] Notwithstanding these revenue items, however, the legislation's core aims are health care access and cost control rather than revenue-raising, and the roles that Treasury and IRS officials play in ACA implementation extend far beyond taxation.[36] Since the ACA's enactment, Treasury and the IRS have worked with HHS and the Department of Labor (Labor) to draft regulations that, among other things, accommodate religious organizations that object to mandatory contraceptive coverage;[37] elaborate the extent to which group health plans are precluded from denying coverage to individuals with pre-existing health conditions;[38] and identify ways in which health insurance providers may or may not offer incentives for participating in wellness programmes.[39]

Despite their prevalence, many, and perhaps even most, tax expenditures and excise taxes are relatively straightforward, particularly when compared to more complicated income tax issues like transfer pricing, consolidation of affiliated groups, and Subpart F, or the never-ending 'whack-a-mole' of tax shelters and the statutes and regulations adopted to combat them. Consequently, scholars focusing on types, causes, and measures of tax complexity may underestimate the relative administrative burden

---

28. Patient Protection and Affordable Care Act, Pub. L. No. 111-148, 124 Stat. 119 (2010).
29. See *National Federation of Independent Businesses v. Sebelius*, 132 S. Ct. 2566, 2580 (2012) (noting the ACA's goals and size).
30. IRC s. 5000A; see also *National Federation of Independent Businesses v. Sebelius*, 132 S. Ct. 2566, 2582–2584, 2600 (2012) (holding that the shared responsibility payment is a penalty not a tax for statutory purposes, even though it is a tax for constitutional purposes).
31. IRC s. 1401(b).
32. IRC s. 1411.
33. IRC s. 5000B.
34. IRC s. 4191.
35. IRC s. 4375.
36. For a list of ACA tax provisions and discussion of Treasury and IRS responsibilities with respect to the ACA, see IRS, *Affordable Care Act Tax Provisions*, http://www.irs.gov/uac/Affordable-Care-Act-Tax-Provisions (accessed on 15 November 2014).
37. T.D. 9578, Group Health Plans and Insurance Issuers Relating to Coverage of Preventive Services Under the Patient Protection and Affordable Care Act, 77 Fed. Reg. 8725 (15 February 2012).
38. T.D. 9491, Patient Protection and Affordable Care Act: Preexisting Condition Exclusions, Lifetime and Annual Limits, Rescissions, and Patient Protections, 75 Fed. Reg. 37,188 (28 June 2010).
39. Notice of Proposed Rulemaking, Incentives for Nondiscriminatory Wellness Programs in Group Health Plans, 77 Fed. Reg. 70,620 (26 November 2012).

of the seemingly tangential elements of the tax laws. Yet from the perspective of tax administrators, a small tax expenditure item or excise tax may represent the tip of a much larger administrative iceberg. And collectively, the non-revenue-raising aspects of the tax laws take up a tremendous proportion of tax administration efforts and resources.

In other work, I evaluated Treasury and IRS regulatory efforts for their focus on tax expenditures and other social welfare and regulatory programmes as opposed to revenue-raising.[40] According to that study, from 2008 through 2012, Treasury and the IRS spent almost as much time and effort drafting regulations addressing tax expenditures and other social welfare and regulatory matters like the ACA, ERISA, and exempt organizations as they did drafting regulations addressing individual and corporate income tax matters.[41] Specifically, Treasury and the IRS published 154 major rulemaking documents totalling 1,364 pages of proposed, temporary, and final regulations and explanations thereof in connection with eighty-six regulation projects that addressed tax expenditures, the ACA, exempt organizations, ERISA, and campaign finance, and excise tax issues.[42] By comparison, Treasury and the IRS published 171 major rulemaking documents totalling 1,117 pages in connection with 104 regulation projects that concerned individual and corporate income tax matters as well as partnerships and other pass-through entities.[43] In 2012, roughly 86% of IRS revenue collections came from the individual income tax and payroll taxes, with the corporate income tax providing another 11%.[44] Yet across several measures, tax administrators spent only about 20% of their regulation drafting efforts on the revenue-raising aspects of the individual income tax and payroll taxes, and another 20% on the corporate income tax, while dedicating between 33% and 40% to tax expenditures and other regulatory and social welfare programmes.[45]

§10.03 IMPLICATIONS FOR TAX ADMINISTRATION AND JUDICIAL REVIEW

The trend of using the tax system increasingly to serve regulatory and social welfare goals carries significant implications for tax administration. For some decades, tax administrative practices have reflected a sense of tax exceptionalism from the requirements, doctrines, and norms that govern other areas of government regulation.[46] Courts have been complicit, emphasizing the tax system's unique revenue-raising

---

40. Hickman, *Administering the Tax System We Have*, above n. 2.
41. Hickman, *Administering the Tax System We Have*, above n. 2, at 1746–1753.
42. Hickman, *Administering the Tax System We Have*, above n. 2, at 1746–1753.
43. Hickman, *Administering the Tax System We Have*, above n. 2, at 1746–1753.
44. Internal Revenue Service, *Internal Revenue Service Databook, 2012*, 3 (2013), available at http://www.irs.gov/pub/irs-soi/12databk.pdf.
45. Hickman, *Administering the Tax System We Have*, above n. 2, at 1746–1753.
46. See, e.g., Paul L. Caron, *Tax Myopia, or Mamas Don't Let Your Babies Grow Up to Be Tax Lawyers*, 13(3) Va. Tax Rev. 517, 518 (1994); Kristin E. Hickman, *A Problem of Remedy: Responding to Treasury's (Lack of) Compliance With Administrative Procedure Act Rulemaking Requirements*, 76(5) Geo. Wash. L. Rev. 1153, 1155–1156 (2008); Steve R. Johnson, Intermountain *and the Importance of Administrative Law in Tax Law*, 128 Tax Notes 837, 838 (2010).

function. For example, in *Bull v. United States*, the Supreme Court justified special limitations on a taxpayer's ability to challenge tax assessments and collections on the ground that 'taxes are the life-blood of government, and their prompt and certain availability an imperious need'.[47] In *Bob Jones University v. Simon*, the Court similarly explained statutory limitations on judicial review in tax cases as 'protect[ing] the Government's need to assess and collect taxes as expeditiously as possible with a minimum of pre-enforcement judicial interference'.[48]

More recently, a few high-profile cases have rejected claims of tax exceptionalism in favour of treating administration of the tax system like that of other government programmes. In *Mayo Foundation for Medical Education and Research v. United States*, the Supreme Court admonished, '[W]e are not inclined to carve out an approach to administrative review good for tax law only'.[49] A few months later, the D.C. Circuit Court of Appeals, sitting *en banc* in *Cohen v. United States*, reinforced this policy of administrative law uniformity. In allowing a suit challenging IRS guidance for failing to comply with general administrative law requirements, the court said, 'The IRS is not special in this regard; no exception exists shielding it – unlike the rest of the Federal government – from suits under the [Administrative Procedure Act]'.[50] In *Dominion Resources, Inc. v. United States*, the Federal Circuit Court of Appeals became the first court to reject a Treasury regulation not for its inconsistency with statutory meaning but for the IRS's failure to explain contemporaneously its reasons for choosing one interpretation rather than another – a long-time expectation in other areas of government regulation that courts had not previously imposed on tax administrators.[51]

Tax complexity has not played an obvious role in this trend in the courts. The key cases do not discuss tax complexity outright, and the substantive issues that they raise are mundane. *Mayo Foundation* addressed whether stipends paid to medical residents were subject to certain payroll taxes.[52] *Cohen* concerned the adequacy of a refund procedure for excess collections of a telephone service excise tax.[53] *Dominion Resources* involved whether certain interest payments could be deducted or had to be capitalized for federal income tax purposes.[54] Even a relatively simple tax system will face definitional questions and procedural issues, and whether business expenditures may be deducted or must be capitalized is a classic income tax problem.

Nevertheless, if the revenue-raising function justifies tax exceptionalism from general administrative law norms, then the migration of the tax laws away from the revenue-raising mission and toward a greater emphasis on social welfare and regulatory programmes and functions undercuts that justification. Meanwhile, a judicially

---

47. *Bull v. United States*, 295 U.S. 247, 259–260 (1935).
48. *Bob Jones University v. Sion*, 416 U.S. 725, 736 (1974).
49. *Mayo Foundation for Medical Education and Research v. United States*, 131 S. Ct. 704, 713 (2011).
50. *Cohen v. United States*, 650 F.3d 717, 723 (D.C. Cir. 2011) (en banc).
51. *Dominion Resources, Inc. v. United States*, 681 F.3d 1313 (Fed. Cir. 2012).
52. *Mayo Foundation for Education and Research v. United States*, 131 S. Ct. 704, 704 (2011).
53. *Cohen v. United States*, 650 F.3d 717, 720-21 (D.C. Cir. 2011) (en banc).
54. *Dominion Resources, Inc. v. United States*, 681 F.3d 1313, 1314 (Fed. Cir. 2012).

driven shift in tax administrative practices toward greater uniformity with general administrative law presents its own challenges for tax administrators.

[A] General Administrative Law Premises

Contemporary US administrative law revolves around a few key premises. The first is that Congress cannot possibly be expected to anticipate and address all of the operational aspects of any government programme.[55] Instead, when Congress enacts a statute and designates one agency or another to implement and administer its provisions, Congress typically leaves a fair amount of programmatic detail unresolved and relies on the administering agency to fill in the gaps.[56]

Another, related premise is that ambiguities in statutory meaning represent delegations of policy-making discretion to the administering agency.[57] Lawyers can be clever manipulators of statutory language, and not every colourable dispute over a statute's meaning falls into this category.[58] Sometimes, courts and administrators alike can rely on statutory text, history, and purpose to discern congressional intent about statutory meaning, leading them to recognize a single 'right' answer to an interpretive question.[59] Often, however, Congress clearly intends to give agencies latitude in deciding among different approaches to achieving statutory goals – or, at least, courts construe congressional intent thusly – and courts are expected to defer to agency interpretations and choices so long as they are reasonable.[60]

---

55. See, e.g., *Mistretta v. United States*, 488 U.S. 361, 372 (1989) ('[O]ur jurisprudence has been driven by a practical understanding that in our increasingly complex society, replete with ever changing and more technical problems, Congress simply cannot do its job absent an ability to delegate power under broad general directives').

56. See, e.g., McNollgast, *The Political Origins of the Administrative Procedure Act*, 15(1) J. L. Econ. & Org. 180, 184 (1999) (suggesting that delegation allows elected officials 'to write simpler statutes, allows the details of policy to adjust to new knowledge and changed circumstances, and creates an expert body that can provide useful information about the needs for changes in either legislation or appropriations'); Mathew McCubbins, *The Legislative Design of Regulatory Structure*, 29(4) Am. J. Pol. Sci. 721, 722 (1985) ('[T]he delegation of legislative authority to regulatory agencies has come to be regarded as the "natural" method of intervening in the economy or society').

57. See, e.g., *Chevron USA Inc., v. Natural Resources Defense Council, Inc.*, 467 U.S. 837, 843–844; Abbe R. Gluck & Lisa Schultz Bressman, *Statutory Interpretation from the Inside - An Empirical Study of Congressional Drafting, Delegation, and the Canons: Part I*, 65(5) Stan. L. Rev. 901, 996–998 (2013) (documenting attitudes of statute drafters regarding statutory ambiguity and the role of agencies in filling statutory gaps).

58. See, e.g., *United States v. Home Concrete & Supply, LLC*, 132 S. Ct. 1836, 1844 (2012) (recognizing that not every linguistic ambiguity in a statute represents a congressional delegation of gap-filling authority to an agency); *American Bar Association v. Federal Trade Commission*, 430 F.3d 457, 469 (D.C. Cir. 2005) ('Mere ambiguity in a statute is not evidence of congressional delegation of authority').

59. See *Chevron U.S.A. Inc. v. Natural Resources Defense Council, Inc.*, 467 U.S. 837, 843, n. 9 (1984) (calling on courts to 'employ[] traditional tools of statutory construction' to determine whether Congress intended the statute to carry a single construction or authorize agency gap-filling).

60. See *Chevron*, 467 U.S. at 844 (instructing courts, in cases of congressional delegation, that they 'may not substitute [their] own construction of a statutory provision for a reasonable interpretation made by the administrator of an agency'); Antonin Scalia, *Judicial Deference to Administrative Interpretations of Law*, [1989] 3 Duke L.J. 511, 516 (stating that, when 'Congress had no

These two assumptions, working together, mean that the federal agencies that administer government regulatory and social welfare programmes enjoy a tremendous amount of policy-making discretion. To counter concerns about the political legitimacy of what is essentially law-making by unelected bureaucrats, US administrative law places a high value on public participation in an open and transparent agency deliberative process, policed through judicial review, as the best way to protect the rights and interests of parties affected by agency action.[61]

Specifically, Congress and the courts have imposed a variety of procedure and process burdens on administrative agencies exercising delegated power to make law. For agency rules that determine private party rights and obligations,[62] the Administrative Procedure Act requires the promulgating agency to publish a written notice of proposed rulemaking, offer interested parties the opportunity to submit written comments in response, and then publish a 'statement of basis and purpose' or preamble in conjunction with the final rules.[63] Over time, the courts have interpreted these requirements expansively. For example, courts have required an agency's notice to include sufficient information about the data and assumptions upon which the agency relied in developing its proposed rules, so that the public may have an opportunity to address and potentially contradict that data.[64] Courts have demanded that an agency issue an additional notice if it changes its mind about a critical element of the proposal, so that the public has a meaningful opportunity to consider and comment upon the change.[65] Courts have insisted further that the preamble to final rules contain the agency's response to all significant comments received.[66] Courts also require an agency to justify its choices contemporaneously by outlining the available alternatives and explaining the data, factors, or other considerations that prompted the agency to pursue one and reject the others.[67] Complying with Administrative Procedure Act requirements provides the agency with 'the facts and information relevant to a particular administrative problem, as well as suggestions for alternative solutions',[68] 'reintroduce[s] public participation and fairness to affected parties after governmental

---

particular intent on the subject but meant to leave its resolution to the agency', then 'the only question of law presented to the courts is whether the agency has acted within the scope of its discretion – i.e., whether its resolution of the ambiguity is reasonable').

61. See, e.g., Jim Rossi, *Participation Run Amok: The Costs of Mass Participation for Deliberative Agency Decisionmaking*, 92(1) Nw. U. L. Rev. 173, 174–176 (1997) (documenting and criticizing the centrality of deliberative process and public participation agency decision-making).

62. *Chrysler Corp. v. Brown*, 441 U.S. 281, 301–302 (1979); *American Mining Congress v. Mine Safety and Health Administration*, 995 F.2d 1106, 1109 (D.C. Cir. 1993).

63. 5 U.S.C. § 553(b)-(c) (2006).

64. For example *American Radio Relay League, Inc. v. F.C.C.*, 524 F.3d 227, 236–240 (D.C. Cir. 2008).

65. For example *Shell Oil Co. v. E.P.A.*, 950 F.2d 741, 750–752 (D.C. Cir. 1991).

66. For example *United States v. Nova Scotia Food Products Corp.*, 568 F.2d 240, 253 (2d Cir. 1977).

67. For example *Motor Vehicle Manufacturers Association v. State Farm Mutual Automobile Insurance Co.*, 463 U.S. 29, 43–44 (1983).

68. *American Hospital Association v. Bowen*, 834 F.2d 1037, 1044 (D.C. Cir. 1987) (quoting *Guardian Federal Savings and Loan Association v. Federal Savings and Loan Insurance Corp.*, 589 F.2d 658, 662 (D.C. Cir. 1978)).

authority has been delegated to unrepresentative agencies',[69] and facilitates transparency and accountability by developing a written record to support judicial review of agency action.

Lastly, US administrative law places courts in a key role of ensuring that agencies pursue the deliberative process seriously and in good faith, or at least demonstrate the appearance thereof. Since the Supreme Court's decision in *Abbott Laboratories v. Gardner* in 1967,[70] the courts have interpreted the Administrative Procedure Act as establishing a presumption in favour of pre-enforcement judicial review of agency rulemaking efforts. In other words, regulated parties may challenge the validity of legally binding agency rules in court as soon as the agency finalizes them, before the rules become too entrenched. Regulated parties are not left with a choice between incurring the costs to organize their primary behaviour to conform with arguably invalid rules or suffering the uncertainty and potential penalties of non-compliance.

[B]   Tax Administrative Practice Premises

Like other administering agencies, Treasury and the IRS possess tremendous policy-making authority. The Code contains several hundred individual provisions that specifically instruct Treasury to adopt implementing regulations[71] and also authorizes Treasury to 'prescribe all needful rules and regulations for the enforcement of' its provisions.[72] Nevertheless, contemporary tax administrative practices reflect a different set of premises than the general administrative law assumptions described above.

For one, ambiguities in the tax laws are not necessarily viewed as opportunities for Treasury and the IRS to exercise policy discretion after consulting with interested stakeholders. Instead, at least anecdotally, my sense is that both tax administrators and the transaction planners who populate the elite tax bar believe that most tax provisions support only one objectively correct interpretation. The IRS and taxpayers may disagree over what that objectively correct interpretation is in a given case, but resolving such disputes is simply a function of carefully analysing statutory text, history, and purpose – not choosing among competing policy alternatives. Deductions and credits derive from legislative grace so should be narrowly construed, irrespective of whether doing so would accomplish other congressional goals.[73] When in doubt, Treasury and the IRS are expected to err in favour of protecting the fisc.[74] The IRS is cast as an adversary, a tax collector, with a bias toward revenue collection over

---

69. *American Hospital Association v. Bowen*, 834 F.2d 1037, 1044 (D.C. Cir. 1987) (quoting *Batterton v. Marshall*, 648 F.2d 694, 703 (D.C. Cir. 1980)).
70. 387 U.S. 136 (1967).
71. New York State Bar Association Tax Section, *Report on Legislative Grants of Rulemaking Authority*, 2 (3 November 2006), available at: http://old.nysba.org/Content/ContentFolders20/TaxLawSection/TaxReports/1121Report.pdf (claiming more than 550 such grants).
72. IRC s. 7805(a).
73. *INDOPCO v. Comm'r*, 503 U.S. 79, 84 (1992); *Bingler v. Johnson*, 394 U.S. 721 (1969).
74. For example Irving Salem, Ellen P. Aprill & Linda Galler, *ABA Section of Taxation Report of the Task Force on Judicial Deference*, 57(3) Tax Lawyer 717, 722–725 (2004).

accuracy in interpretation.[75] The role of the IRS is to maximize revenue collection, not evaluate and weigh the competing viewpoints of interested stakeholders. Courts are just as capable as Treasury and the IRS of evaluating statutory text, history, and purpose to discern congressional intent, so broad judicial deference to Treasury and IRS interpretations of the tax laws is unnecessary if not downright inappropriate, 'depriv[ing] taxpayers of an opportunity to convince a neutral arbiter that the government's position is wrong'.[76]

Consistent with this perception of the IRS's role, for some decades at least, tax administrative practices have prioritized certainty and speed over the public participation and deliberative process concerns that animate general administrative law doctrines and norms. The IRS professes to want, and clearly values, public participation in determining agency priorities and developing regulations and other guidance.[77] Tax professionals and taxpayers likewise want their views to be heard. But particularly for the transaction planners who dominate the tax bar elite, and the large corporate taxpayers and wealthy individuals they represent, binding the IRS to a single interpretation of the Code generally seems more important than the procedures and deliberative process through which that end is achieved. Even a disadvantageous interpretation can be sidestepped, so long as it is clear.

Treasury and IRS practices reflect this preference for certainty and speed over public participation and deliberative process. Treasury's compliance with Administrative Procedure Act rulemaking requirements is irregular. For example, a substantial percentage of Treasury regulations are adopted in temporary, binding form without the benefit of formal public participation.[78] In such instances, the opportunity for public comment comes later, usually.[79] Although Treasury does not typically justify this delay,[80] when it does, Treasury ordinarily invokes taxpayer demands for immediate guidance.[81] In fact, the Internal Revenue Manual specifically states that 'IRS/Treasury temporary regulations are generally issued when there is a need to provide taxpayers

---

75. Salem, Aprill & Galler, above n. 74, at 724–725.
76. Salem, Aprill & Galler, above n. 74, at 725.
77. Internal Revenue Manual §32.1.2.3(3) (claiming that most Treasury regulations are exempt from APA notice-and-comment rulemaking procedures but noting that 'the IRS usually publishes its [notices of proposed rulemaking] in the Federal Register and solicits public comments' in any event); Internal Revenue Manual s. 32.1.5.4.7.5.1 (making similar statements).
78. Kristin E. Hickman, *Coloring Outside the Lines: Examining Treasury's (Lack of) Compliance with Administrative Procedure Act Rulemaking Requirements*, 82(5) Notre Dame L. Rev. 1728, 1748–1749 (2007) (documenting 84 of 232 regulation projects, or 36.2%, over a three-year period as including temporary regulations).
79. Since 1996, IRC § 7805(e) has required the IRS to finalize all temporary regulations through notice-and-comment rulemaking within three years, but many older temporary regulations remain outstanding, meaning that taxpayers remain bound by regulations promulgated without their input.
80. Hickman, *Coloring Outside the Lines: Examining Treasury's (Lack of) Compliance with Administrative Procedure Act Rulemaking Requirements*, above n. 78, at 1749–1751.
81. For example T.D. 9685 (claiming need 'to provide corporations with immediate guidance' as the reason for issuing temporary regulations regarding NOL carry-forward limitations); T.D. 9478 (claiming need 'to provide tax return preparers and taxpayers with immediate guidance' regarding when tax return preparers may disclose or use client information without the taxpayer's consent).

with immediate guidance' and instructs regulation drafters to include language to that effect in the preambles to all temporary regulations.[82]

Correspondingly, Treasury and the IRS do not feel compelled formally to justify their interpretive choices in the preambles to their regulations.[83] Treasury and IRS preambles describe how the adopted regulations operate, but they typically do not explain why Treasury and the IRS chose one approach over other available alternatives. Again, until very recently, the Internal Revenue Manual prompted this approach, instructing IRS regulation drafters that 'it is not necessary to justify the rules that are being proposed or adopted or alternatives that were considered'.[84] Moreover, while Treasury and IRS preambles discuss comments received from the public in response to proposed regulations, they frequently do so only succinctly – for example, acknowledging a suggested change and noting its rejection, again without explaining why – this time notwithstanding an Internal Revenue Manual instruction that '[t]he drafting team should explain why the agency found some comments persuasive, and others not, in issuing the final regulations'.[85]

Lastly, IRS revenue rulings, revenue procedures, and notices that carry significant legal consequences for taxpayers typically are not put through any sort of public deliberative process at all.[86] The IRS relies particularly heavily on notices as a mechanism for providing quick guidance, sometimes in the face of actual emergencies, but in other instances simply to discourage transactions and return positions of which it does not approve.[87] Taxpayers can be penalized for failing to comply with these pronouncements, notwithstanding the lack of public participation and deliberation in their promulgation.[88]

[C] The Consequences of Tax Complexity

Prioritizing certainty and speed over public participation and deliberative process is arguably compatible with a relatively simple, or at least internally coherent, tax system oriented primarily toward revenue-raising. If interpretations of ambiguous tax provisions can be labelled as right or wrong based on common law reasoning, then public participation in the Treasury and IRS decision-making process becomes less important.

---

82. Internal Revenue Manual s. 32.1.5.4.7.5.1 (7)–(9).
83. Patrick J. Smith, *The APA's Arbitrary and Capricious Standard and IRS Regulations*, 136 Tax Notes 271 (2012).
84. Smith, *The APA's Arbitrary and Capricious Standard and IRS Regulations*, above n. 83, at 274 (quoting the prior language). This language was removed as of 20 October 2014, although the new language merely calls upon IRS drafting personnel to 'describe the substantive provisions of the regulations' and says nothing about justifying or explaining their interpretive choices. Internal Revenue Manual s. 32.1.5.4.7.3(1).
85. Internal Revenue Manual, s. 32.1.5.4.7.3(2).
86. See, e.g., Kristin E. Hickman, *IRB Guidance: The No Man's Land of Tax Code Interpretation*, [2009] 1 Mich. St. L. Rev. 239; Leslie Book, *A New Paradigm for IRS Guidance: Ensuring Input and Enhancing Participation*, 12(7) Fla. Tax Rev. 517, 550–551 (2012).
87. See Hickman, *IRB Guidance: The No Man's Land of Tax Code Interpretation*, above n. 86, at 249–252; Book, above n. 86, at 550.
88. See Hickman, *IRB Guidance: The No Man's Land of Tax Code Interpretation*, above n. 86, at 265–269.

Public participation in Treasury and IRS deliberative processes offers taxpayers the opportunity to persuade Treasury and the IRS that their interpretations of the tax laws are mistaken but carries no greater legitimizing weight. If the government adopts the 'wrong' answer, then if and when the IRS tries to assert a deficiency or deny a refund, disadvantaged taxpayers can resolve the difficulty either by negotiating a compromise with the IRS or by persuading the courts that Treasury and the IRS erred. If only one interpretation of the tax laws can be objectively correct upon consideration of statutory text, history, and revenue-raising purpose, then explaining the 'why' of Treasury and IRS interpretive choices is substantially less significant as well. A reviewing court's role is not to ensure that the IRS properly considered all relevant viewpoints but, rather, is to correct Treasury and IRS interpretive errors.

For regulatory and social welfare programmes integrated into the tax laws as tax expenditures or otherwise, however, the premises on which contemporary tax administrative practices are based make much less sense. Maximizing revenue collection, for example by construing deductions and credits narrowly, may actually undermine the goals that prompted Congress to adopt those deductions and credits in the first place. Stakeholders in those regulatory and social welfare programmes do not fall so neatly into the old 'IRS versus taxpayer' narrative; their concerns and needs are not so readily satisfied by negotiating with the IRS or seeking judicial review when the IRS assesses deficiencies against them or denies their refunds. The premises that allowed tax administrators to prioritize certainty and speed over public participation and deliberative process (and get away with it) may still hold true for large corporate taxpayers and transaction planners at elite law firms, but they do not carry to many other matters with which Treasury and the IRS must now grapple.

§10.04   CONCLUSION

As noted, the courts are already pushing tax administrators away from their own past habits and toward compliance with general administrative law norms and requirements. With that push will come a greater emphasis on public participation and deliberative process, whether or not tax administrators want it or transaction planners care about it. Again, the courts are not necessarily responding to tax complexity in making this move. Nevertheless, the administrative environment created by integrating regulatory and social welfare programmes into the tax laws makes arguments for tax exceptionalism from general administrative law norms and doctrines more difficult. Meanwhile, the desire to maintain said tax exceptionalism arguably offers another justification for pursuing tax simplification.

Chapter 11

Tax Complexity: A Necessary Evil?

Michael Walpole

§11.01 INTRODUCTION

This chapter considers some of the reasons why complexity in the tax system, although unwelcome, may be necessary. It notes as a topical example recent commentary on tax minimization by Multinational Entities (MNEs) and the anti-avoidance responses to these activities. The community does not actually want, nor can it afford, a tax system that is too simple. This is because a simple tax system cannot withstand all efforts to reduce the tax burden of taxpayers that are inclined to test the law. This observation is somewhat ironic in the face of complaints that an overly complex tax system may create opportunities for avoidance. Thus, it may be that complexity of a specific type to reduce avoidance (through reporting requirements and general anti-avoidance rules (GAARs)) is what is required. Later in the chapter, the argument is also made that there can be a case for complex tax provisions in situations where this complexity leads to greater operational or administrative simplicity or if the result aligns with the community's expectations of equity.

§11.02 TAX COMPLEXITY: ITS MEANING AND CONSEQUENCES

The forms of tax complexity considered in this chapter are those often encountered by practitioners, especially lawyers, when advising clients on their tax affairs. They include:

- Complexity of language, especially the use of ordinary terms to mean, in the context of a statute, something that is very different to the ordinary meaning.

Complexity of language also refers to the use of awkward, constructed terms whose meaning is difficult to divine.[1]

- Difficult concepts that are counter-intuitive to an educated reader (an example of this is the creation in the Australian goods and services tax (GST) law[2] of the concept of 'an acquisition supply' which arises in the context of financial supplies, as the definition of a financial supply includes the borrowing of money – thus an acquisition of loan funds is in fact a supply for the purposes of GST[3]).
- Large volumes of rules in statute, regulations and administrative advice.
- Multiple inter-connected and inter-related provisions requiring lengthy side excursions away from principal rules to ascertain the application of peripheral provisions.

The consequences of such complexity where it occurs are many. Complexity of this sort leads to:

- high costs of compliance with the tax rules through the investment of effort and professionals' time in learning, researching and ultimately advising on the law;[4]
- non-compliance with the tax rules through misunderstanding them;[5]
- non-compliance with the tax rules through exploitation of complexities (sometimes termed 'creative compliance');[6] and
- possible inadequate administration of the tax system because the administrator lacks the resources to properly monitor the application of the rules.[7]

Thus an examination of tax complexity, its sources and consequences, is justified. In the process, an argument will be made that some level of complexity is nevertheless justified.

---

1. Take as an example the concepts of 'disaggregated attributable decrease' and 'disaggregated attributable increase' in ss 727–775 and ss 727–805 of the *Income Tax Assessment Act 1997* (Cth.), which set out rules pertaining to the taxation of variations of value of interests in equities and loans.
2. *A New Tax System (Goods and Services Tax) Act 1999* (Cth.).
3. This occurs by operation of the definition of 'financial supply' achieved through the operation of Reg. 40-5.09 of the *A New Tax System (Goods and Services Tax) Regulations 1999*.
4. See Binh Tran-Nam, Chris Evans & Philip Lignier, *Personal Taxpayer Compliance Costs: Recent Evidence from Australia*, 29(1) Austl. Tax F. 137, 142–143 (2014).
5. See Margaret McKerchar, *Complexity, Fairness and Compliance: A Study of Personal Taxpayers in Australia*, 197 (Australian Tax Research Foundation, 2003).
6. See a theoretical model for this: Tracy Oliver & Scott Bartley, *Tax system complexity and compliance costs – some theoretical considerations*, Economic Roundup, Fig. 5 (Winter 2005), available at: http://archive.treasury.gov.au/documents/1009/HTML/docshell.asp?URL=05_Tax_Complexity_and_Compliance.htm. The term 'creative compliance' is used by Doreen McBarnet & Christopher Whelan in *The Elusive Spirit of the Law: Formalism and the Struggle for Legal Control*, 54(6) Mod. L. Rev. 848.
7. For a discussion of this risk, see Matthijs Alink & Viktor van Kommer, *Handbook on Tax Administration*, 74ff. (IBFD Publications, 2011).

§11.03   TAX MINIMIZATION: THE RECENT 'BROUHAHA'

Recent publicity surrounding tax minimization, particularly by large multinational corporations, has brought the challenge of tax avoidance to the front of the public mind. There is little need in this chapter to describe every headline-hitting tax scheme that has been publicized, but for illustrative purposes, it is worth identifying the most striking features of some of the more prominent of these because those features are pertinent to the argument in this chapter.

[A]   The Starbucks Corporation Arrangement

One of the earliest reports[8] about tax minimization by the Seattle-based company Starbucks Inc. stated that it had operated on a grand scale in the UK since 1998 in which time it made sales worth over GBP 3 billion. It was alleged that in the relevant period, it had, however, paid only GBP 8.6 million in income tax (after disallowance of certain deductions). In the three years preceding the report the company had, apparently, disclosed no taxable profit. Its tax payments were much lower than those of comparable global food chains.[9]

According to the report, the company's Chief Financial Officer (CFO) attributed the contradiction between profitability for shareholders and poor tax profits to payments of royalties on intellectual property (like brands and business processes) and intra-group payments. Royalties were set at 6% of total sales and were paid to a Dutch company, Starbucks Coffee EMEA B.V. The CFO also explained that it was required to allocate UK-generated funds to other companies in its supply chain. Some of these were for coffee beans:

> Starbucks buys coffee beans for the UK through a Lausanne, Switzerland-based firm, Starbucks Coffee Trading Co. Before the beans reach the UK they are roasted at a subsidiary which is based in Amsterdam but separate from the European HQ.[10]

The CFO said that the allocation of some profits to the Netherlands and Switzerland was a requirement of the tax authorities in those jurisdictions. The report explained that the Netherlands company tax rate was 25%, whereas the Swiss company tax rate was potentially as low as 5% for '...profits tied to international trade in commodities like coffee...'.[11]

The report went on to suggest that Starbucks also used debt as a way of reducing its tax liabilities in the UK;[12] that this is a common tactic used to reduce taxable income; and that Starbucks charged a much higher interest rate on the loans to the UK entity when compared to the McDonalds group and the Kentucky Fried Chicken chain.

---

8. See Tom Bergin, 'Special Report: How Starbucks avoids UK taxes', *Reuters* (15 October 2012), http://uk.reuters.com/article/2012/10/15/us-britain-starbucks-tax-idUKBRE89E0EX20121015 (accessed on 1 August 2014).
9. Bergin, above n. 8.
10. Bergin, above n. 8.
11. Bergin, above n. 8.
12. Bergin, above n. 8.

The Starbucks arrangements illustrate two key features typical of the tax mini-mization practices of companies in similar situations to that of Starbucks. The first of these is that the devices used to achieve a lower taxable income than that borne by comparable companies are standard transfer pricing and loan financing techniques. And secondly, the tax arrangements were not illegal and had not been successfully challenged by HM Revenue & Customs (HMRC).

[B]   The Google Arrangement

Another high-profile tax minimization participant attacked in the media was the California-based multinational company Google Inc. In December 2012 this company was reported[13] to have transferred USD 9.8 billion to a shell company in Bermuda, thus avoiding USD 2 billion in 'worldwide taxes'. The report explained that the company had used a tax structure known as a 'Double Irish and Dutch Sandwich' in order to send royalties paid by subsidiaries in Ireland and the Netherlands to '...a Bermuda unit headquartered in a local law firm'.[14] It was alleged that, although the UK was responsible for USD 4.1 billion of Google's earnings in 2011, the company paid only USD 9.6 million in income tax in the UK. The report explained that the manner in which the tax saving was achieved was for an Irish subsidiary to collect the revenues from advertisements sold by Google in countries such as the UK and France. It then paid royalties to another subsidiary in the EU – thus avoiding the requirement to pay a royalty withholding tax that would have been incurred had the royalties been paid to a non-EU-resident entity.[15] From Ireland, payments were then channelled via a Netherlands subsidiary to a Bermuda entity taking advantage of concessions available under Double Tax Agreements. The Netherlands entity explains the 'Dutch sandwich' part of the structure and the involvement of Irish entities explains the 'Double Irish' part of the name for this structure.

Signal features of this arrangement are (once again) that the structures and transactions involve no illegality; and that they rely on standard techniques of royalty payments. In this case the arrangements involve astute positioning of entities and structuring of transactions so as to benefit from Double Tax Agreement provisions that would alleviate the impact of tax on the revenue passing from entity to entity. Although the report suggested that the Google structures had attracted the attention of tax authorities in the UK, France and Italy,[16] there was no indication that these agencies were able to effect any significant change in the tax recovered as a result.

---

13. Jesse Drucker, 'Google Revenues Sheltered in No-Tax Bermuda Soar to $10 Billion', *Bloomberg News* (10 December 2012), available at: http://www.bloomberg.com/news/2012-12-10/google-revenues-sheltered-in-no-tax-bermuda-soar-to-10-billion.html (accessed on 1 August 2014).
14. Drucker, above n. 13.
15. The precise residence of the other subsidiary is differently reported – in Drucker's report at above n. 13 it was Ireland. In another report also by Drucker ('The Tax Haven That's Saving Google Billions', *Bloomberg Business Week* (21 October 2010)), the subsidiary was said to be in the Netherlands and the Bermuda-based entity was registered in Ireland but managed and controlled in Bermuda.
16. Drucker, above n. 13.

[C]   The Apple Arrangement

The multinational technology company Apple Inc. has also been prominent amongst those accused of engaging in tax avoidance. A lengthy *New York Times* article in April 2012[17] even suggested that it was Apple that pioneered some of the techniques described above:

> Apple was a pioneer of an accounting technique known as the 'Double Irish With a Dutch Sandwich', which reduces taxes by routing profits through Irish subsidiaries and the Netherlands and then to the Caribbean. Today, that tactic is used by hundreds of other corporations – some of which directly imitated Apple's methods....[18]

The 'sandwich' according to the journalists was not Apple's only contribution to the menu of tax minimization techniques:

> Apple, ... was among the first tech companies to designate overseas salespeople in high-tax countries in a manner that allowed them to sell on behalf of low-tax subsidiaries on other continents, sidestepping income taxes....[19]

Apple's international tax arrangements have been described and analysed with clarity by Ting[20] and, notwithstanding Duhigg's reference to the 'Double Irish Dutch Sandwich', according to Ting, Apple's international structure did not actually make use of that device. Its structure simply took advantage of the way the company residence rules operated in Ireland and the US at the time. As a result, it was resident for tax purposes neither in the US (where the place of incorporation rule operates) nor in Ireland (where the test was the location of central management and control).[21] Ting has noted that the corporate residence rules in Ireland have since been amended to '...address the issue of "stateless" companies...'.[22]

In other ways the Apple structure shares features with the Google and Starbucks arrangements already described. They are legal;[23] and they take advantage of well-established opportunities to split income and activities.

---

17. Charles Duhigg & David Kocieniewski, 'How Apple Sidesteps Billions in Taxes', *New York Times* (28 April 2012).
18. Duhigg & Kocieniewski, above n. 17.
19. Duhigg & Kocieniewski, above n. 17.
20. Antony Ting, *iTax – Apple's International Tax Structure and the Double Non-Taxation Issue*, [2014] 1 Brit. Tax Rev. 40.
21. Ting, above n. 20.
22. Antony Ting, *Old wine in a new bottle: Ireland's revised definition of corporate residence and the war on BEPS*, [2014] 3 Brit. Tax Rev. 237.
23. Referring to Homeland Security and Governmental Affairs Subcommittee on Investigations, *Offshore Profit Shifting and the US Tax Code – Part 2 (Apple Inc.)* (2013), Ting explains that '[i]n the US hearing there is no dispute that Apple's tax planning structure is in full compliance with the tax laws of the countries involved': *iTax – Apple's International Tax Structure and the Double Non-Taxation Issue*, above n. 20, at 45.

§11.04   THE EFFECT OF TAX AVOIDANCE ON COMPLEXITY

The opportunities for tax minimization referred to above are fundamentally simple, and these opportunities are deliberately created by governments competing for the 'foreign direct investment dollar'. Colloquially one might say 'this is not rocket science'[24] – indeed the techniques used are reminiscent less of advanced aerospace engineering than of a game of chess where the desired result is obtained by means of planning well ahead and carefully positioning the individual parts of one economic entity so as to achieve a certain strategic outcome within a set number of moves.

Despite the public and official outrage that has accompanied these and other revelations of tax minimization by corporations, one despairs of an effective solution being found that removes the incentive to engage in such structures and transactions. Two factors undermine the likelihood of removing these incentives. One is the apparent determination of states to compete for economic activity and investment through tax breaks and competitive tax rates. Ironically, the US, which has steadfastly retained its corporation tax rate at 35% for over 25 years, is itself one of the jurisdictions engaging in these 'beggar thy neighbour' tactics through its ineffective Controlled Foreign Company (CFC) rules.[25]

The other is the obvious appetite on the part of large corporations to take advantage of the competition by the governments of various countries for their economic involvement in that jurisdiction, no matter how modest the involvement might be.

The solution, it is submitted, is greater complexity in the legislation to anticipate and counter the opportunities that will be taken by taxpayers. Although anti-avoidance legislation is not the ideal remedy for fundamental defects in the rules,[26] the complexity involved in anti-avoidance rules is necessary to limit the more outrageous forms of abusive structure that might be used to minimize tax liability. Thus, it is argued that avoidance of tax can be controlled by complicating the tax law with anti-avoidance rules. As the avoidance is achieved by legal means and subtle use of officially sanctioned opportunities, the anti-avoidance measures must themselves be subtle and nuanced to target unacceptable avoidance whilst not stifling commerce. The Australian experience suggests that an effective anti-avoidance provision must be relatively lengthy and comprehensive if it is to withstand any tendency to limit its terms through literal interpretation.

Other remedies to deal with the types of tax minimization described here might include statutory source rules to ensure income earned in a jurisdiction can be taxed

---

24. A suggested origin of this term meaning 'it is simple' may be found at http://www.phrases.org .uk/meanings/its-not-rocket-science.html.
25. The US CFC rules are rendered ineffective – as explained by Ting – by the way the US 'check-the-box' rules undermine the CFC rules and by the way they exclude from the CFC regime payments of passive income between CFCs. See Ting, *iTax – Apple's International Tax Structure and the Double Non-Taxation Issue*, above n. 20, at 53.
26. A point made by Freedman who writes: 'GAARs are not the correct tools for fundamental tax reform but a moderate general anti-abuse rule should be part of any modern tax system...'. See Judith Freedman, *Designing a General Anti-Abuse Rule: Striking a Balance*, 20(3) Asia-Pac. Tax Bull. 167, 173 (2014).

there, limits on royalty and interest deductibility, or changes to the permanent establishment rules. All would lead to greater complexity.

§11.05 NECESSARY COMPLEXITY

Sometimes the complexity to be found in our legislation is the direct result of lobbying and requests by taxpayers and their representatives. There are many examples of this. A few will be discussed here.

During the consultation period that preceded the introduction of the GST in Australia in 1998–1999, the Australian Taxation Office (ATO) and Treasury received many submissions and requests. Evidence of some of these is to be found in the legislation. One such example is the odd inclusion in the definition of the term 'supply'[27] (which generally means any form of supply) of the following:

> (3A) For the avoidance of doubt, the delivery of:
> (a) livestock for slaughtering or processing into *food; or
> (b) game for processing into *food;
> under an arrangement under which the entity making the delivery only relinquishes title after food has been produced, is the supply of the livestock or game (regardless of when the entity relinquishes title). The supply does not take place on or after the subsequent relinquishment of title.

The refinement to the meaning of a simple word is a necessary addition which seems complex to read but which is effective in reducing complexity. Its effect, in context, is to ensure that farmers sell livestock subject to GST[28] and to avoid a messy and long-winded process where (e.g.,) a grazier might be required to deliver a live animal to an abattoir, be charged for its slaughter and preparation as a service by the abattoir and then make a GST-free supply to the butcher or other purchaser of the individual cuts of meat and other products derived from processing the carcass. The apparent complexity of the drafting leads in fact to simplicity in the system and sets the point in the food chain at which supplies become GST-free supplies of food for final consumption. The provision is actually an example of simplicity in disguise.

Other examples of complexity in rules but leading to simplicity in process are to be found in the GST grouping provisions and their income tax equivalent (discussed further below) – the consolidation rules. The GST grouping rules are designed to simplify the operation of group companies and eliminate from the GST system a churn of internal taxable supplies and input tax credits that produce a limited yield in revenue. Under these provisions, companies that are members of a 90%-owned group may form a GST group (which may include certain other qualifying entities like not-for-profit entities) and arrange that one member of the group deal with all the GST liabilities and entitlements relating to the group. In particular, transactions between

---

27. See *A New Tax System (Goods and Services Tax) Act 1999*, ss 9–10.
28. See Hon. Peter Costello (Treasurer), 'Amendments to the Goods and Services Tax Act and Related Legislation', *Media Release No. 037* (3 May 2000); and Explanatory Memorandum to the Indirect Tax Legislation Amendment Bill (No. 92) 2000.

group members are excluded. The simplicity of outcome is obvious. The rules however add twenty lengthy sections and some twenty pages of law to the Act.[29]

Perhaps the most extreme form of 'complex simplification' is the Australian income tax consolidation provisions in Part 3-90 of the *Income Tax Assessment Act 1997* (ITAA 1997). These rules are intended to simplify tax treatment of transactions within a group of entities under common ownership to obviate the need to treat transactions within a single economic entity as taxable. The simplification reduces compliance costs and compliance activity by ignoring transactions between members of the wholly-owned group; pooling tax losses and dividend franking credits as well as credits for foreign tax paid. It also replaces multiple single entity income tax returns with a single income tax return and single pay-as-you-go (PAYG) instalments for the group as a whole.[30] As the ATO says, '[c]onsolidation also reduces opportunities for tax avoidance through loss creation and value shifting'.[31]

On any measure, this would seem to be a good thing. The loss of simplicity, however, is very striking as the volume of legislation in Part 3-90 amounts to (in one commercial publication of the Act) in excess of 300 pages of provisions from sections 700-1 to 721-40.[32] Lehmann has referred to the Australian system as the most advanced consolidation regime in the world.[33] Expertise in the consolidations legislation is extremely useful, highly sought after and, no doubt, expensive to obtain. The issue that needs to be considered is whether it is desirable, or not, to have a consolidations regime because of the other benefits, especially the benefit of encouraging foreign direct investment and of improving integrity of the tax system while reducing compliance costs.[34]

Finally, the link between equity and simplicity should not be overlooked. Many complex aspects of the tax law arise from the need to quarantine their impact and to shelter taxpayers or groups of taxpayers from adverse impacts. There are few more obvious examples of this than the rules in Australia concerning the taxation of superannuation. These rules are well-known for their 'grand-parenting' elements which perpetuate the operation of tax rules for the benefit of persons who would be adversely affected by a change in rules that has taken place after they have settled into a tax and financial position with an expectation of certain outcomes. Just one example from many is the difference in tax treatment of a superannuation stream that commenced prior to 1 July 2007, at which date the manner of taxing such streams changed.

---

29. See *A New Tax System (Goods and Services Tax) Act 1999*, ss 48-1 to 48-115. Pages counted from CCH Australia, *Australian GST Legislation with Overview* (2014).
30. See ATO, *Consolidation reference manual: Taxing wholly-owned corporate groups as single entities*, B0-1 ('Consolidation – key points and pathway'), 1 (15 July 2011).
31. ATO, above n. 30, at 1.
32. These numbers are inflated as the published version of the Act used is the CCH *Australian Income Tax Legislation* which includes details of amendments and withdrawn sections (arguably necessarily for full understanding), and the sections of the Act under the form of drafting used in the ITAA 1997 are not numbered consecutively but have gaps to accommodate future insertions.
33. Geoffrey Lehmann, 'Consolidations – some tips and traps', paper presented at the Manoeuvring the Maze forum, Taxation Institute of Australia New South Wales, 24 May 2007, 1.
34. See ATO, 'Consolidation: overview', https://www.ato.gov.au/Business/Consolidation/In-detail/Overview/Consolidation--overview/.

The 'old' way of taxing such streams persists for existing recipients until such time as they either turn 60 years of age (when even more favourable taxation commences); or they commute the superannuation income entitlement; thus triggering a different form of tax treatment.[35]

§11.06   COMPLEXITY AS A CAUSE OF MINIMIZATION

Some of the academic literature on the topic suggests that a part of the problem of tax minimization and non-compliance is attributable to the difficulty of the tax laws themselves. McKerchar makes the following observation:

> Taxation is generally used to provide for the collective needs of society rather than those of the individual. The consequence naturally must be that the benefit accruing to the individual taxpayer is not always obvious and is therefore difficult to quantify. This questioning of the value of the contribution to taxation can lead to disenchantment for the individual. Constantly changing or incomprehensible tax laws and systems may further nurture this disenchantment, as may the waning of commitment to government or society. This disenchantment, or lack of commitment, may result in individuals opting out of the tax system, in whole or in part, either intentionally or unintentionally. As more fail to comply, a tax gap results as government fails to raise the intended level of revenue.[36]

Thus, there is a suggestion that frequent changes to complex laws and complex laws that are unworkable or hard to comply with undermine morale and willing compliance.

In addition, laws that, when combined, provide the well-advised taxpayer with gaps and choices may result in complicated responses that not only lead to tax minimization by exploitation of the gaps but also lead to unnecessarily complex business structures. They are thus distortionary in the extreme. The descriptions of tax minimization structures by multinationals referred to above (§11.03[A]–[C]) illustrate this point. The question that needs to be asked because of this, however, is whether mere simplification is enough. That question is addressed further in the following section.

§11.07   SIMPLICITY AS A CAUSE OF MINIMIZATION

As discussed above, in the face of tax complexity eroding morale and the compliance culture a possible response would be to make the tax laws much simpler. The tax system in Hong Kong is often cited as an example of tax simplicity. Littlewood is an advocate of simplicity in several of his descriptions of the Hong Kong tax system. Hong Kong's simplicity partly relies on the absence of many of the facets that together comprise the tax burden in other jurisdictions. For example, it has no capital gains tax,

---

35. See the formula basis in *Income Tax Assessment Act 1936* (Cth.), s. 27H. For income streams
   commencing after 1 July 2007, the formula in ITAA 1997, s. 307-125(6) applies.
36. McKerchar, above n. 5, at 197.

'...no general sales tax, no VAT and no goods and services tax',[37] although GST was apparently recently proposed.[38]

The problem with such simplicity is that it results in a lack of revenue. As Littlewood concedes, the Hong Kong government is heavily reliant on other sources of revenue such as stamp duty,[39] licence fees,[40] land sales,[41] and fees for services.[42] There is also a very low level of public spending in Hong Kong, as there is not the revenue to sustain a high level.[43]

The income tax in Hong Kong is also very simple, and applies at a low rate that is 'flat'– yet in it Littlewood sees signs of desirable progressivity.[44]

Littlewood describes the simplicity of the Hong Kong tax system as follows:

> The Inland Revenue Ordinance is only about 200 pages in total, and it contains not only the substantive law relating to the taxation of income but also the machinery for its administration…. Moreover, the ordinance, together with the cases bearing on its interpretation (themselves relatively few in number), constitutes virtually the whole of the law; …Tax practitioners from other jurisdictions, encountering Hong Kong tax law for the first time, typically have difficulty in accepting that so simple a system can function satisfactorily, or even at all. Rules that elsewhere are widely assumed to be obvious necessities are simply not there.[45]

However, according to Littlewood, the tax system does not suffer as badly because of its rudimentary nature. In his words, '...the system works better than most'.[46]

A problem with such simplicity and the lack of detailed rules is that it throws a greater burden on the courts to work out how the rules apply to specific situations.[47] Littlewood approves of this, whereas others might regard this as a drawback. The over-reliance on judge-made law is liable to contribute to uncertainty in cases where it is not known in advance what tax outcome will result from an action or transaction. This can also contribute to compliance costs by leaving the taxpayer to pay for clarification through the courts when the government might alleviate the taxpayer of that burden by clarification in the legislation. This lack of clarification might also, it is argued, leave the government 'hostage to fortune' in having to live with the decisions of the courts, which will not always be sympathetic to the revenue-raising ambitions of the government. Littlewood sees no evidence of this in Hong Kong and he explains that the judges have filled the vacuum well:

---

37. Michael Littlewood, *Tax System Design and the Instructive Case of Hong Kong*, 63(3) Tax Notes Int'l 193, 198 (2011).
38. Littlewood, above n. 37, at 198.
39. Littlewood, above n. 37, at 198–199.
40. Littlewood, above n. 37, at 198–199.
41. Littlewood, above n. 37, at 198–199.
42. Littlewood, above n. 37, at 198–199.
43. Littlewood, above n. 37, at 199–200.
44. Littlewood, above n. 37, at 194, 200–201.
45. Littlewood, above n. 37, at 202.
46. Littlewood, above n. 37, at 202.
47. Littlewood, above n. 37, at 202.

Hong Kong's judges, however, have succeeded in producing entirely workable interpretations of the territory's relatively skeletal statute. They have produced interpretations that are principled, economically sound, respectful of taxpayers' rights, and protective of the government's revenues.[48]

One should be reluctant to throw one's weight behind calls for an income tax system such as Hong Kong's, which seems to fall short of revenue needs to the extent that other indirect taxes are required to shore it up. Similarly an income tax that relies heavily on the courts to explain what the tax rules are in given circumstances is expensive and unclear to operate and falls short of the certainty and clarity which are expected of modern tax systems.

There are many other examples of simple laws having an effect that is undesirable because they are just too simple. One example that springs to mind can be found in an early iteration of the general income tax anti-avoidance provision in the South African statute. It is a term of section 103 of the Income Tax Assessment Act 58 of 1962 (South Africa) that, should it be proved that the (tax avoidance) activity in question '…would result in the avoidance or the postponement of liability for payment of any tax, duty or levy imposed by this Act or any previous Income Tax Act or any other law administered by the Commissioner, or in the reduction of the amount thereof', the taxpayer bears the burden of showing that the activity was not entered into for a tax avoidance purpose.[49]

The words previously referred only to a tax, duty or levy 'imposed by this Act or any previous Income Tax Act'. Thus, a taxpayer[50] was able to demonstrate that they lacked a tax avoidance purpose under the income tax law because they had entered into a structure that had the effect of reducing estate duty. As this charge was levied under another statute, the assumption of an income tax avoidance purpose could be shrugged off. Anyone who has provided private income tax and financial planning advice in a jurisdiction that imposes estate duty and donations tax will appreciate that a trust structure for high-wealth clients will usually limit exposure to these taxes as well as providing income-splitting opportunities. It was necessary, of course, to amend the section to add the avoidance of taxes etc. imposed by '…any other law administered by the Commissioner'. The addition of these corrective words did not overly complicate the Act but it did extend it and add words. It thus did complicate the sense of the sub-section and add incrementally to complexity. It would be surprising, indeed, if this additional complexity were to be criticized. It is simply a necessary integrity measure that had to be included.

§11.08   COMPLEXITY CAN BE DESIRABLE AND NECESSARY

In light of the points that have been made in this chapter, it is argued that in many instances complexity of tax laws is necessary on a number of grounds. These grounds include the need to:

---

48. Littlewood, above n. 37, at 202.
49. Income Tax Assessment Act 58 of 1962 (South Africa), s. 103(4).
50. *Secretary for Inland Revenue v. Gallagher* 1978 (2) S.A. 463 (A).

  – ensure that a tax law is as comprehensive as possible in terms of what it taxes and in what circumstances;
  – ensure a statute cannot be easily avoided because the integrity measures in the statute are overly simple and inadequate to safeguard proper compliance;
  – respond to the requests of particular groups for the purposes of including special interest concerns in the manner in which the tax system operates;
  – respond to the needs of equity in the manner in which the tax system impacts on taxpayers;
  – provide taxpayers with certainty as to the consequences of their transactions and other activities; and
  – (linked to the preceding point above) avoid shifting the burden of clarification of the law onto either or both of the revenue administration and the courts.

Some complexity, it is argued, is unavoidable and might best be described as a necessary evil.

CHAPTER 12

Exploring Individual Taxpayers' Perceptions of Tax Complexity: A Pilot Study

Kudakwashe M.M. Muli & Theuns Steyn[*]

§12.01 INTRODUCTION

Tax systems globally are designed with the aim of raising revenue by governments to finance the provision of public goods and services to their citizens. These systems are generally set out in statutes that prescribe the manner in which taxes are established and administered. Legislatures are faced with the challenge of drafting legislation that ensures adequate revenue is raised while at the same time adhering to the four maxims of taxation, of equity, certainty, economic efficiency and administrative efficiency.[1] However, certainty is often overlooked as legislatures attempt to ensure that the tax system is equitable.[2] Aggressive tax planning as a result of lack of certainty in tax legislation often leads to the constant changing of tax legislative provisions which in turn adds more detail and complexity to existing tax legislation.

Tax legislation amendments affect those who abuse tax laws, those who do not comply with tax laws and those who comply with the spirit of the law. Among non-compliant taxpayers are those who are intentionally non-compliant as they have

---

* This chapter is based on the study by Kudakwashe M.M. Muli, *Exploring Individual Taxpayers' Perceptions of Tax Complexity*, unpublished Masters dissertation, University of Pretoria (2014).
1. Adam Smith, *An Inquiry into the Nature and Causes of the Wealth of Nations*, 676–677 ([1776], Jim Manis ed., Pennsylvania State University, 2005).
2. Kate Krause, *Tax Complexity: Problem or Opportunity?*, 28(5) Pub. Fin. Rev. 395, 412 (2000); Victor Thuronyi, *Comparative Tax Law*, 19 (Kluwer Law International, 2003).

the means to evade their tax liabilities, and those who are unintentionally non-compliant as they lack the necessary skills to administer their own tax affairs.[3] Tax legislation often imposes an obligation on the taxpayer to be knowledgeable about all legislation in relation to their tax affairs.[4]

In South Africa, from the 2009–2010 to 2013–2014 financial years of assessments, there has been a decline in the revenue contributions through corporate income tax. During the 2013–2014 year of assessment and the five preceding years, personal income tax has made the highest contribution to the total tax revenue.[5] Mechanisms such as 'eFiling', presenting taxpayer workshops, preparing taxpayer guides and brochures and other compliance programmes have been introduced by the South African Revenue Service (SARS) to relieve the compliance burden faced by taxpayers as well as to encourage voluntary tax compliance.[6] Taxpayers other than natural persons are usually in the position of having the necessary resources to employ or appoint a person to administer their tax affairs. This comes with the advantage that the payment for these services can be written off as a deductible tax expense. The question is then posed as to whether individual taxpayers who administer their own tax affairs are aware of and are able to utilize the simplification mechanisms within the current tax system. Failure to capitalize on these simplification mechanisms results in taxpayers bearing an avoidable tax burden through either penalties being imposed on them due to unintentional non-compliance or increased compliance costs.

Thus, the main purpose of the study described in this chapter was to investigate, from a qualitative approach, how individual taxpayers perceive tax complexity. As revenue authorities acknowledge the willingness to comply by most taxpayers, the study aimed to investigate whether taxpayers were cognizant of any of the tax simplification mechanisms available to them. The study also investigated whether tax complexity influenced these taxpayers' tax burden, and analysed suggestions by respondents on how the tax system could be simplified for individual taxpayers.

The chapter proceeds as follows. As the theoretical aspects of tax complexity are discussed in greater depth elsewhere in this volume, §12.02 provides a brief review of existing literature on tax complexity and its influence in shaping taxpayer perceptions. This is followed (§12.03) by a description of the methodology followed in designing and gathering empirical data. An analysis of the empirical data is presented (§12.04) and a conclusion is drawn (§12.05) from these results.

---

3. Gregory A. Carnes & Andrew D. Cuccia, *An Analysis of the Effect of Tax Complexity and its Perceived Justification on Equity Judgments*, 18(2) J. Am. Tax'n Ass'n 40, 42 (1996).
4. In South Africa, the Tax Administration Act, No. 28 of 2011, ss 22–33, imposes a duty on the taxpayer to register for tax and submit all necessary returns and settle any tax liabilities with the South African Revenue Service (SARS). The taxpayer referred to in the Act includes those that are registered as taxpayers and those that are required to be registered for tax in terms of a tax Act. However, for compliance with a tax Act to occur, a person first needs to be aware of the existence of the tax Act and be able to understand its contents.
5. South African Revenue Service, *2014 Tax Statistics*, 8 (19 January 2015).
6. South African Revenue Service, *SARS Compliance Programme 2012/13-2016/17*.

§12.02   REVIEW OF RELATED LITERATURE

[A]   Perspective of Complexity

As with beauty, complexity lies in the eyes of the perceiver. Therefore, in order to discuss tax complexity in context,[7] the following need to be defined:[8]

(1) from whose perspective is tax complexity being discussed? This is due to the fact that different users of the tax system experience it differently as user needs and experiences are diverse;

(2) in what sense is tax complexity being experienced? This can be through the difficulties encountered in interpreting tax legislation and the time and effort expended in countering these difficulties ('technical' or 'rule complexity'). This can also be through a failure to appreciate the consequences of economic transactions as well as a lack of confidence in planning one's tax affairs ('structural complexity'). This can also be experienced through all the activities that the taxpayer needs to complete in order to meet the taxpayer's tax obligations ('compliance complexity');

(3) to what extent is tax complexity being experienced? Complexity can be experienced throughout a tax Act or at section level or when tax Act provisions need to interact with other legislation. Complexity is often perpetuated when piecemeal amendments are made to tax provisions while overlooking how the amendments impact on the rest of the tax Act or with other legislation.

For the purpose of this study, tax complexity is analysed from the perspective of the individual taxpayer. The extent and the sense in which tax complexity is experienced by the individual taxpayers is to be explored based on their responses to the questions of how they perceive the tax system, and how tax complexity affects their tax burden.

[B]   Taxpayer Perceptions

Perception is the 'awareness of complex environmental situations as well as single objects'.[9] The awareness is affected by the following factors:[10]

---

7. See Joel Slemrod, *Old George Orwell Got It Backward: Some Thoughts on Behavioral Tax Economics*, 66(1) Pub. Fin. Analysis 15, 16 (2010); David Ulph, 'Measuring Tax Complexity', Office of Tax Simplification (UK), 2 (January 2013).
8. Edward J. McCaffery, *The Holy Grail of Tax Simplification*, [1990] 5 Wis. L. Rev. 1267, 1270–1273.
9. Floyd H. Allport, *Theories of Perception and the Concept of Structure: A Review and Critical Analysis with an Introduction to a Dynamic-Structural Theory of Behavior*, 14 (John Wiley, 1955).
10. Gay Lumsden, Donald L. Lumsden & Carolyn Wiethoff, *Communicating in Groups and Teams: Sharing Leadership*, 92 (5th ed., Cengage Learning, 2010).

- motives, needs, drives, wants and experiences play a significant role in terms of selecting what one chooses to see or ignore;
- background, culture, language, gender and experience shapes how one views and reflects on situations;
- how one perceives others, and how one thinks that others perceive them, are different. This can only be proved or disproved through actual interactions with others.

An individual's thoughts and actions are guided by perceptions.[11] As perceptions influence human behaviour, investigating taxpayer perceptions may provide insight into what shapes taxpayer attitudes.[12] Tax complexity has been found to have a negative impact on taxpayer perceptions of making tax contributions.[13] Tax complexity has also been cited as a contributing factor to both intentional and unintentional non-compliance.[14] Tax complexity has been said to also be the cause for high compliance costs and consequently increasing the tax burden borne by taxpayers.[15] This is contrary to the desired goals of an ideal tax system of raising as much tax revenue as possible with as little distortion to the economy as possible.[16] Such a tax system should be assessed over time and be simplified when the benefits of having a complex tax system become insignificant.[17]

From the above, it can be concluded that perceived tax complexity may have an influence on the perceived tax burden of individual taxpayers. Complexity in tax legislation and taxpayer compliance activities may be instrumental in shaping how taxpayers perceive the complexity of the tax system. Due to the different ways in which taxpayers experience and interact with the tax system, it is not yet clear as to how taxpayers' cognitive abilities and the complexity of the tax system interact.

---

11. Casey O'Callaghan, 'Perception', in Keith Frankish & William M. Ramsey (eds), *The Cambridge Handbook of Cognitive Science* 73 (Cambridge University Press, 2012).
12. Ruanda Oberholzer & E.M. Stack, *Perceptions of Taxation: A Comparative Study of Different Population Groups in South Africa*, 40(2) Pub. Rel. Rev. 226, 238 (2014).
13. Ruanda Oberholzer, *Perceptions of Taxation: A Comparative Study of Different Population Groups in South Africa*, unpublished Doctoral thesis, University of Pretoria, 175 (2007) (available at: http://upetd.up.ac.za/thesis/available/etd-05192008-170854/ (accessed on 30 April 2013)); Richard K. Gordon & Victor Thuronyi, 'Tax Legislative Process', in Victor Thuronyi (ed.), *Tax Law Design and Drafting*, Vol. 1, 2 (International Monetary Fund, 1996).
14. Compliance efforts by taxpayers may not be adequate to ensure total compliance. Which is why those taxpayers who can afford it incur additional costs to comply to the letter with tax laws. Those who cannot afford the extra cost may find themselves in a situation where they are unintentionally non-compliant. This is also influenced, to a large extent, by the complexity of the tax as there is a direct relationship between complexity and compliance costs. See Margaret McKerchar, *The Impact of Complexity Upon Unintentional Non-compliance for Australian Personal Income Taxpayers*, published Doctoral thesis, University of New South Wales, 289–290 (2002).
15. Additional compliance costs incurred due to the complexity of taxes are seen as an additional tax which increases a taxpayer's perceived tax burden. See Theunis L. Steyn, *A Conceptual Framework for Evaluating the Tax Burden of Individual Taxpayers in South Africa*, unpublished Doctoral thesis, University of Pretoria, 350–354 (2012). Available at: http://upetd.up.ac.za/thesis/available/etd-01252013-123649/unrestricted/00front.pdf (accessed 30 April 2013).
16. Brian Galle, *Hidden Taxes*, 87(1) Wash. U. L. Rev. 59, 61 (2009).
17. Joel Slemrod & Jon Bakija, *Taxing Ourselves: A Citizen's Guide to the Great Debate Over Tax Reform*, 135 (Massachusetts Institute of Technology, 1996).

§12.03 METHODOLOGY

A qualitative study[18] was conducted in order to examine and try to understand the phenomenon of tax complexity from the perspective of a sample of individual taxpayers in South Africa. As this was an exploratory study, it was not necessary to obtain a representative sample of the whole taxpaying population. Data was collected through an online survey using Qualtrics Survey Software. Three core open-ended questions were posed to the respondents in order to explore their perceptions of tax complexity. These were:

(1) if they thought the South African tax system was complex, and provide a reason for their response;
(2) for those who said that the South African tax system was complex, whether tax complexity affected their tax burden and, if it did, how;
(3) how the South African tax system may be simplified for individuals.

An online survey was thought to be appropriate in order to minimize researcher bias, as in this way respondents could put forward their views on the questions asked anonymously and without any influence from the researcher. A purposive sampling approach was taken in order to identify prospective respondents. This sample set comprised persons who had indicated that they would like to take part in the study beforehand. 'Snowball' sampling was also utilized, where an anonymous survey link was sent to these prospective respondents who were encouraged to forward the survey link to any other person whom they thought might also be interested in taking part in the survey.

A generic approach to qualitative data analysis was taken.[19] This comprised:

– reviewing the data and creating codes that were to be used to identify the data;
– assigning the codes to the data;
– generating themes that described the general focus within the coded data;
– developing theories that attempted to answer the research question based on the themes generated; and
– drawing and reaffirming conclusions based on the collected data, themes generated and theories developed.

§12.04 RESULTS AND DISCUSSION

There were eighty responses to the structured question that asked the respondent if the South African tax system was complex. The respondents were from both the private and public sector, approximately 70% of whom earned employment income only, while 21% earned both employment and other income. The remaining 9% of the

---

18. See Paul D. Leedy, & Jeanne E. Ormrod, *Practical Research: Planning and Design*, 139 (10th ed., Pearson Education, 2013) on the characteristics of qualitative research.
19. See Mark Saunders, Phillip Lewis & Adrian Thornhill, *Research Methods for Business Students*, 557–562 (6th ed., Pearson Education, 2012).

respondents either earned business or other income only. The results as to whether the South African tax system is complex are presented in Figure 12.1.

Figure 12.1   Is the South African Tax System Complex?

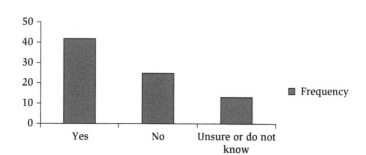

Of these eighty respondents, only fifty-one provided reasons as to why the South African tax system was or was not complex. This consisted of thirty-five respondents who said that the South African tax system was complex, twelve respondents who did not think that the South African tax system was complex and four respondents who were unsure or did not know whether the South African tax system was complex or not.

Four themes were used to summarize the respondents' perceptions of the complexity of the South African tax system, namely:

– tax legislation - referring to any aspect of tax legislation including the number of tax statutes, specific legislative provisions;
– tax compliance – referring to any activities conducted by the respondent in order to comply with tax legislation as well as reference to any costs, both monetary and non-monetary, incurred while conducting compliance activities;
– knowledge – referring to the knowledge the respondent perceived they had or one needed to have in order to comply with tax legislation;
– perception of others – referring to how a respondent would assume other taxpayers may perceive the tax system.

[A]   Is the South African Tax System Complex? 'Yes'

Tax legislation and tax compliance were cited as the main contributing factors as to why respondents perceived the tax system to be complex.

[1]   Tax Legislation

In terms of tax legislation, the structure was said to be dated and frequently subjected to too many changes. These changes include additions of sections on an ad-hoc basis which leads to either complexity in the whole legislation and or complexity to specific sections in the legislation. The South African tax system is said to be characterized by too many tax types, too many taxes being applicable to a single transaction and by taxes that are imposed on too many events and transactions. Tax laws are also said to be too integrated with different rules and rates applicable to different individuals. Thus, the application of tax legislation is deemed to be complex.

[2]   Tax Compliance

Respondents noted that the complexities in the tax system were due to the fact that the reporting requirements are burdensome for people who earn more than one income, as some of the taxpayers are obliged to submit a tax return even when they are below the tax threshold. Another issue related to this was the fact that a pension is considered to be a separate income which needs to be accounted for by the taxpayer. Most of the taxes imposed are based on the individual's earnings. This then raises the challenge of how to account for these transactions. The respondents indicated that some taxpayers are not aware of how to accurately calculate their tax liability. This is due to the fact that tax legislation is perceived to have too many parts, provisions and rules on what can be deducted and allowances available to the taxpayer. These make it difficult to understand and apply tax laws. The resultant effect is that taxpayers pay too much for their taxes due to the payment for the number of taxes imposed and the failure to claim deductions and allowances available to them. Thus, some of the respondents employ the services of a tax practitioner in order to avoid incorrectly reporting their taxes.

However, though some of the respondents point out that 'eFiling' assists in reducing the compliance burden, there are challenges in interpreting the various codes when filing tax returns, and those who have faced difficulties with 'eFiling' resorted to using tax practitioners to do their taxes. The system was also said to be not user-friendly. The requirements imposed on taxpayers, in terms of the information the taxpayer is supposed to know and keep, make it difficult to understand the tax system when changes are made frequently to existing legislation. The inefficiency in the use of tax revenues and improper prioritization of projects was cited as one of the reasons that led to the complexity of the tax system.

[3]   Knowledge

The lack of knowledge about the tax system was also cited as one of the reasons leading taxpayers to perceive that the South African tax system is complex. Some of the respondents indicated that one needs some level of experience and education in order to understand and apply the tax system. This lack of knowledge is said to create a challenge for those who do not have the necessary technical skills in dealing with tax issues. These issues include the inability to correctly calculate taxable income, claim benefits and allowances and complete tax returns. The resultant effect, even for those who are well-educated, is said to be a lack of understanding of the tax system. Some respondents indicated that they used tax practitioners to handle their affairs as they lacked the necessary understanding of the tax system to competently handle their own tax affairs.

[4]   Perception of Others

Respondents also indicated that the tax system may be complex for other people. These other people were described as being those who are not good with mathematics, who do not know accounting or tax, the 'person on the street' and those who have more than one source of income. This category of taxpayers was assumed to lack the capabilities to accurately calculate and report their tax liabilities.

[B]   Is the South African Tax System Complex? 'No'

[1]   Tax Compliance

Tax compliance was cited as the largest contributing factor to why respondents were of the opinion that the South African tax system is not complex. This was mainly attributed to the ease with which one can register for tax and submit tax returns which has been made easier by the introduction of 'eFiling'. Some of the respondents noted that it is the responsibility of the taxpayer to utilize the various tools available in the public domain in order to educate themselves on how the tax system works. The resources mentioned to be available and accessible to all include tax legislation and SARS guides and training.

[2]   Tax Legislation

It was noted that the tax system:

- – is regulated by an Act that is accessible to all;
- – is clearly defined in terms of what is taxable and how it is taxed;
- – there is certainty of the calculation and amount to be taxed.

However, one of the respondents noted that it may be appropriate for SARS to look into providing free information sessions for owners and prospective owners of small businesses on the statutory requirements and basics of taxation.

[3]   Knowledge

One of the respondents found taxes to be quite easy as that respondent had completed an honours degree in tax. A couple of the respondents noted that it is the taxpayer's responsibility to educate him or herself. The rationale given for this statement is that, with education, the complex become 'ordinary everyday things'.

[4]   Perception of Others

One respondent noted that tax for individuals is simple, though 'the more complex your transactions, the more complex the taxes thereon become'.

[C]   Is the South African Tax System Complex? 'Not Sure' or 'Do Not Know'

[1]   Tax Compliance

Only one of the respondents indicated that tax compliance was an issue. The respondent noted that the basics were fine. The respondent also noted that this was dependent on what a taxpayer needed from the underlying laws of the tax system.

[2]   Knowledge

The remaining three respondents stated that they were not knowledgeable about the tax system. One of the respondents stated that the reason that they were not knowledgeable was because they were still newly acquainted with the system.

[D]   Does the Complexity of the Tax System Affect the Tax Burden?

The respondents who indicated that the complexity of taxes affected their tax burden were asked to provide reasons why and how they held this perception. Only twenty-five of the twenty-nine respondents provided reasons why they thought that the complexity of taxes affected their tax burden. The responses were analysed and the themes of compliance cost, number of taxes and fairness were identified to best group these responses.

[1]   Compliance Cost

Compliance cost was cited as the main reason why the respondents believed that tax complexity influenced their tax burden. Monetary costs mentioned included paying too much for taxes, as well as the additional costs incurred from the need to employ the services of tax practitioners and tax lawyers to assist taxpayers with their tax compliance activities. Some respondents noted that they were not sure if they accurately calculated their tax liability. Other respondents noted that this calculation was compounded by uncertainty over what, how and how much one could deduct when determining one's tax liability or submitting a tax return.

As one respondent noted, one is not certain whether they are paying too much or not enough. This, along with the paperwork needed to complete tax returns, was said to cause respondents to spend a lot of time and effort administering and managing their tax affairs. In addition, respondents noted that they were afraid of misinterpreting tax legislation as the cost of submitting inaccurate tax returns in the form of tax audits, penalties and interest is quite high. One respondent noted that complexity causes procrastination which eventually leads to non-submission of tax returns, late submissions of tax returns or the employment of a tax practitioner. To quote one of the respondents, tax complexity is said to add 'extra stress to the already financially tense atmosphere'.

[2]   Number of Taxes

A respondent said that his tax burden was too high because there are too many taxes imposed and that as one's income increases, so does the tax burden. From the respondent's perspective, taxes are said to be imposed on every purchase transaction.

[3]   Fairness

The tax system is said to be unfair as not all people pay taxes. Examples given of these persons are taxi drivers and entrepreneurs that work on a cash basis. This is said to increase the tax burden of salaried employees. The taxable amount of each individual is said to be different due to the various tax relief measures awarded to various entities as well as the different rates and tax calculation methods for these entities. This is said to cause complexities in the tax system which in turn affect the tax burden. Respondents noted that taxes should be imposed on earnings only and not on both earnings and consumption. One respondent noted that they did not receive a direct benefit from most of the activities the taxes are spent on. The same respondent also noted that government mismanages tax revenues while another respondent noted that they were not sure where their money was going to.

[E]   How Can the South African Tax System Be Simplified?

All respondents were asked to provide comments on how the tax system could be simplified for individual taxpayers. However, only twenty-four respondents completed this question. Four themes were identified from the responses collected, which are: tax reform, education, administrative support, and efficiency and transparency in revenue use.

Respondents who perceive the tax system as being complex stated all four measures, tax reform, education, administrative support, and efficiency and transparency in revenue use, as means of addressing complexity for individual taxpayers. Respondents who perceive the tax system as not being complex suggest tax reform, education and administrative support as possible means to make the tax system simpler for individuals. Respondents who were uncertain if the tax system is complex suggested education as a means to make the tax system simpler for individual taxpayers.

[1]   *Tax Reform*

Most of the responses given suggest that there is a need for reform of the current system. One respondent pointed out that they do not believe that the tax system can be simplified beyond its current state. Other suggestions for tax reform included:

- re-writing of current legislation;
- reducing the volume of tax legislation;
- bringing structure into the Income Tax Act;
- learning from simplification initiatives in other countries;
- reducing the number of taxes individual taxpayers need to comply with;
- introduction of one tax or a flat tax;
- abolition of taxes;
- simplification of Value Added Tax registration provisions for new businesses; and
- simplifying tax compliance for people without tax qualifications.

[2]   *Education*

Tax education was also suggested as a means by which the tax system could be made simpler for individual taxpayers. Suggestions included:

- the introduction of a compulsory tax introductory course in high school;
- the use of videos;
- university and employment workshops;
- advising new employees on how the tax system works;
- publicizing the possibility of getting a tax refund to encourage taxpayers to take the initiative to learn more about taxes;
- enlightening uneducated people about the tax system and their tax burden;
- teaching the general public in a simple way about all aspects of the tax system including why they have to pay taxes, how to minimize their tax liability and what the taxes are used for;
- the use of newspaper articles.

[3]   *Administrative Support*

The administrative provision that sets a minimum income threshold for the submission of tax returns was cited as one of the means being used to assist low income earners. The appointment of tax advisors by SARS to complete tax returns for free for taxpayers below a certain income bracket was suggested. One of the respondents suggested that SARS branch employees should be available to assist taxpayers with tax matters or alternatively, be able to refer taxpayers to external tax advisors. Another respondent also emphasized the need to 'encourage and provide more one-on-one agents support'.

With regard to 'eFiling', one respondent suggested that it could be made easier and simpler. Another respondent gave the suggestion that this could be achieved by introducing a step-by-step guide that explains and demonstrates the filing process.

Another suggestion was made to have tax clearance certificates, once approved, available on 'eFiling'.

[4]   Efficiency and Transparency in Revenue Use

One respondent noted that complexity is a result of government's need to increase revenue collections and to 'make the effects of the recession neutral'. The respondent then suggested that government increases its efficiency in the use of tax revenues in order to reduce the tax burden. Another respondent noted that there is need for accountability by government in terms of use of tax revenues.

§12.05   CONCLUSION

The findings are that not all respondent taxpayers perceive the tax system in South Africa to be complex. These respondents mainly acknowledge the various means available, such as 'eFiling', to counter the effects of tax complexity introduced by the South African Revenue Service. However, a greater number of people believe that the tax system is complex. The complexity is mainly attributed to the challenges taxpayers face in attempting to comply with tax legislation. These challenges include difficulties in keeping up to date with constant changes to legislation, the fear of filing an inaccurate tax return and the general lack of adequate knowledge to confidently handle one's tax affairs.

From the empirical results, it can be said that, though taxpayers acknowledge the innovations introduced to make the tax system easier for taxpayers to comply with, such as the introduction of 'eFiling', the quality of service experience is not perceived in the same way by all taxpayers. As innovation is a continuous process, there is a need for revenue authorities to continuously assess and improve the functionality of 'eFiling', the call centre and other customer support mechanisms they have in place.

Despite the consensus in tax literature that tax systems are complex, this is subjective as users of the tax system, taxpayers, hold different perceptions about tax complexity. These perceptions seem to be influenced by the legislation, user needs and user abilities. Those taxpayers who have managed to grasp the different mechanisms available to ease the compliance burden tend to disagree with the statement that the tax system is complex. However, this is not the case for everyone else. Thus, a significant investment in taxpayer education and awareness may need to be considered to ensure that interactions with the tax system are not deemed to be either overwhelming or burdensome.

A major limitation of the study was that the survey only utilized few respondents who are natural persons and had internet access. Coupled with the fact that the sample size was not representative of the whole population, it is not possible to generalize the results of the survey to the rest of the South African population. These limitations could be addressed in future studies. Future studies may also specifically assess the tax literacy levels and needs of the greater South African population. These studies may also investigate taxpayers' awareness of their rights and obligations under tax laws.

CHAPTER 13

Six Degrees of Graduation: Law and Economics of Variable Sanctions

*Alex Raskolnikov**

§13.01 INTRODUCTION

If one believes that people respond to incentives, legal sanctions are just as important as legal rules. Get one wrong and the legal regime fails no matter how well the other one is designed. Yet with few exceptions, the economic analysis of law has paid little attention to sanctions. This lack of interest would be understandable if sanctions could only be designed in a limited number of ways, or if the actual sanctions were simple and uniform. Neither is true, however. Sanctions can and do vary a great deal along a number of dimensions. Do these variations make sense? Are they consistent with plausible assumptions about individual decision-making? Are they likely to improve efficiency or facilitate compliance? Strange as it may sound, the economic analysis of law is not close to answering these questions.

This chapter highlights the complexity of sanctioning regimes and our limited understanding of the resulting incentives, using tax penalties as a primary example. Several reasons make tax law a good case study. The actual tax penalties are complex. They are endlessly debated by practitioners and frequently adjusted by rule-makers. And they have been scrutinized by legal academics and economists more extensively than penalties for many other regulatory violations. In tax, enforcement is always a 'hot topic'. So it is particularly useful to consider how the real-life tax enforcement machinery reflects – or fails to reflect – theoretical insights.

* I am grateful to workshop participants at Columbia University and Harvard University law schools, the 2014 Tax System Complexity Symposium, the Tax Club, the Tax Forum, and the 2013 annual meeting of the National Tax Association for valuable comments and suggestions. Financial support from the Gerber Program is gratefully acknowledged. All mistakes are solely my own.

The chapter has a simple structure. Section §13.02 explains what I mean by sanctions complexity and identifies six dimensions (or axes) along which penalties may vary. These are the six degrees of sanctions graduation. While I use US tax penalties as an example, the analysis is neither US- nor tax-specific. Any enforcement regime may exhibit each of the six degrees of graduation, and many actually contain more than one graduation axis. Section §13.03 summarizes and evaluates the economic rationales for varying sanctions along each axis of graduation. Again, these rationales are not limited to any regulatory area. Although tax enforcement literature is relatively rich in its analysis of various enforcement factors, studies that are not tax-specific offer valuable insights as well. I conclude that the three graduation axes of great practical significance – aggressiveness, culpability, and offence history – are the least developed theoretically. Two other dimensions – the likelihood of detection and the effort to comply with the law – are more conceptually advanced. Even there, however, the theory is fairly removed from the realities of tax enforcement. In contrast, economic analysis reveals a good grasp of the magnitude axis and a clear path to modelling the real-life features that have remained overlooked thus far. By highlighting the complexity of sanctioning regimes and emphasizing the related theoretical successes and shortcomings, this chapter identifies fruitful areas of future research, some of which I pursue in related work.

§13.02   SIX DEGREES OF SANCTIONS GRADUATION

There are many ways to define complexity.[1] For the purposes of this inquiry, sanctions are more complex if they vary along a greater number of legally relevant dimensions – if they have more degrees of graduation. For instance, a sanction that depends on the magnitude of lost profits is less complex than a sanction that depends on that magnitude and also on the putative offender's state of mind. That latter sanction, in turn, is less complex than the one that depends on the same two factors and also on the offender's effort to conceal the violation. Saying that sanctions determined only by the size of lost profits are not complex does not mean that calculating lost profits is a trivial matter. But making this determination plus the other two clearly places higher demands on decision-makers and complicates the incentives of potential offenders.

Most discussions of legal sanctions recognize that sanctions often vary along a certain dimension. Commentators frequently state that acts that are more aggressive, egregious, reprehensible, and the like are subject to a greater punishment. These terms, however, have no accepted meanings. The term 'egregious', for instance, has been used to refer to acts that are particularly harmful,[2] especially culpable,[3] artfully

---

1. David Bradford, for instance, spoke of rule complexity, compliance complexity, and transactional complexity. See David F. Bradford, *Untangling the Income Tax*, 266–267 (Harvard University Press, 1999).
2. See *TXO Prod. Corp. v. Alliance Res. Corp.*, 509 U.S. 443, 459–466 (1993).
3. See *BMW of N. Am., Inc. v. Gore*, 517 U.S. 559, 582 (1996).

concealed,[4] or reveal a great departure from community norms.[5] Needless to say, one cannot analyse a graduated penalty regime without a precise understanding of a particular axis of graduation. Many different axes may and do exist, and tax sanctions vary along all of them.

To a legal analyst, the most important dimension is what lawyers call *aggressiveness* of a particular act or position.[6] Aggressiveness is the extent to which one's behaviour deviates from legally permissible conduct. Thus, if a speed limit is 55 mph, driving at 60 mph is a less aggressive speeding violation than driving at 90 mph. If the standard is reasonable care, negligent behaviour is less aggressive than a grossly negligent action, which itself is less aggressive than a reckless action. And if the statute outlaws 'restraints of trade',[7] an exchange of pricing information among competitors is a less aggressive action than a general discussion of a possible cooperation in setting prices, which, in turn, is less aggressive than a written agreement establishing a secret cartel.[8] The last two examples highlight the relationship between aggressiveness and legal uncertainty. What care is 'reasonable'? What actions 'restrain' trade?[9] Law is full of similarly vague terms, and tax law is no exception. When the meaning of the law is

---

4. See A. Mitchell Polinsky & Steven Shavell, *Punitive Damages: An Economic Analysis*, 111(4) Harv. L. Rev. 869, 874 (1998).
5. See Robert D. Cooter, *Economic Analysis of Punitive Damages*, 56(1) S. Cal. L. Rev. 79 (1982).
6. This use of the term 'aggressiveness' is well-established in tax law scholarship. See Joseph Bankman, *The Economic Substance Doctrine*, 74(1) S. Cal. L. Rev. 5, 5 (2000); Mark P. Gergen, *The Logic of Deterrence: Corporate Tax Shelters*, 55(2) Tax L. Rev. 255, 275 (2002); Kyle D. Logue, *Optimal Tax Compliance and Penalties When the Law Is Uncertain*, 27(2) Va. Tax Rev. 241, 251 (2007); Leigh Osofsky, *Some Realism About Responsive Tax Administration*, 66(1) Tax L. Rev. 121, 144–145 (2012); Alex Raskolnikov, *Relational Tax Planning Under Risk-Based Rules*, 156(5) U. Pa. L. Rev. 1181, 1181 (2008); David M. Schizer, *Sticks and Snakes: Derivatives and Curtailing Aggressive Tax Planning*, 73(6) S. Cal. L. Rev. 1339, 1339 (2000); Daniel Shaviro, 'Disclosure and Civil Penalty Rules in the U.S. Legal Response to Corporate Tax Shelters', in Wolfgang Schön (ed.), *Tax and Corporate Governance* 229, 230–231 (Springer, 2008); David A. Weisbach, *An Economic Analysis of Anti-Tax-Avoidance Doctrines*, 4(1) Am. L. & Econ. Rev. 88, 107 (2002). The accountancy literature often uses the term aggressiveness in a similar manner. See Paul J. Beck & Woon-Oh Jung, *Taxpayers' Reporting Decisions and Auditing Under Information Asymmetry*, 64(3) Acct. Rev. 468, 474 (1989); Michelle Hanlon & Shane M. Heitzman, *A Review of Tax Research*, 50(2-3) J. Acct. & Econ. 127, 137 (2010); Peggy A. Hite & Gary A. McGill, *An Examination of Taxpayer Preference for Aggressive Tax Advice*, 45(4) Nat'l Tax J. 389, 389 n. 3 (1992); Petro Lisowsky, Leslie Robinson & Andrew Schmidt, *Do Publicly Disclosed Tax Reserves Tell Us About Privately Disclosed Tax Shelter Activity?*, 51(3) J. Acct. Res. 583, 590 (2013). Economists occasionally refer to 'aggressiveness' to convey the same or similar concept. See Kate Krause, *Tax Complexity: Problem or Opportunity?*, 28(5) Pub. Fin. Rev. 395, 396 (2000). I use the term 'aggressiveness' rather than degree of 'fault' – the term typically used in the general optimal deterrence analysis, see, e.g., A. Mitchell Polinsky & Steven Shavell, 'The Theory of Public Enforcement of Law', in A. Mitchell Polinsky & Steven Shavell (eds), *Handbook of Law and Economics*, vol. 1, 403, 407 (North-Holland, 2007). I do so both to reflect the customary use in the tax literature and to avoid moral connotations of the latter term.
7. 15 USCA § 1.
8. The legality of price information exchanges has long been a subject of debate. See Richard A. Posner, *Information and Antitrust: Reflections on the* Gypsum *and* Engineers *Decisions*, 67(5) Geo. L.J. 1187 (1979).
9. The Supreme Court has long held that not only must there be a 'restraint' of trade (itself an unclear term) to produce an antitrust violation, but that the restraint must be 'unreasonable' as well. See *Nat'l Collegiate Athletic Ass'n v. Bd. of Regents of Univ. of Okla.*, 468 U.S. 85, 98 (1984).

207

uncertain, more aggressive acts have a higher likelihood of being found to violate the law. Aggressiveness, therefore, is closely related to the probability of legal punishment.

Because more aggressive acts are more likely to be sanctioned, even a fixed statutory fine yields higher expected penalties for more aggressive violations. Sometimes, however, statutory fines themselves vary with aggressiveness. Speeding fines are the most familiar example. Greater speeds in excess of the speed limit lead to higher fines.[10] The same is true of particularly serious violations of environmental regulations.[11] But no regulatory regime that I am aware of comes close to tax in the degree of refinement of the aggressiveness-based penalty graduation.

Instead of presenting this feature of tax sanctions in all its splendour,[12] the following summary gives only a glimpse of the nuance and complexity involved. If a judge in a US tax case decides that a taxpayer underpaid taxes, the judge then needs to address the penalty issue. Whether the penalties are due, and how high they ought to be, depends on the judge's *ex post* evaluation of the *ex ante* strength of the taxpayer's position. 'Strength' is yet another term that lawyers often use in reference to the likelihood of success on the merits, with stronger (less aggressive) positions being more likely to succeed than weaker (more aggressive) ones. Civil tax penalties vary from zero to 75% of the tax underpayment (with the intermediate values of 20%, 30%, and 40%) depending on whether the position is 'more likely than not' to be correct, or is supported by a 'substantial authority', or at least has a 'reasonable basis', or, worse yet, is just a 'colorable claim', is merely not 'frivolous', or not 'patently improper'.[13] Much ink has been spilled debating whether this or that tax position satisfies one of these thresholds, and whether this or that fine percentage should correspond to a particular level of aggressiveness. Thus, aggressiveness (or strength) of a legal position is an important axis of penalty graduation, especially in tax.

The review of aggressiveness-based tax penalties reveals the second axis of graduation. All penalties just described are calculated as a percentage of a tax underpayment rather than a fixed dollar amount. The higher the underpayment, the higher the penalty. So tax sanctions depend on the magnitude of the underpayment. Thus, *magnitude* is another axis of graduation present in tax and many other regulatory regimes. Tax, however, reveals a rather complex magnitude-based graduation scheme. Some tax sanctions increase *disproportionately* with the size of the underpayment. For instance, a penalty for a 'substantial valuation misstatement' is 20% of the misstated amount.[14] This means, of course, that greater misstatements lead to higher penalties. If, however, a misstatement is particularly large ('gross' rather than 'substantial'), the

---

10. See Massachusetts General Laws Annotated (MGLA) 90 § 20 (West, 2010) (imposing increasing fines for greater speeds in excess of the speed limit).
11. See US Environmental Protection Agency, *Resource Conservation and Recovery Act (RCRA) Civil Penalty Policy* (June 2003), available at http://www2.epa.gov/enforcement/resource-conser vation-and-recovery-act-rcra-civil-penalty-policy.
12. For thorough reviews, see Michael Doran, *Tax Penalties and Tax Compliance*, 46(1) Harv. J. on Legis. 111, 118–119 (2009); Sarah B. Lawsky, *Probably? Understanding Tax Law's Uncertainty*, 157(4) U. Pa. L. Rev. 1017, 1050 (2009); Logue, above n. 6, at 256.
13. IRC §§ 6662, 6664; Treas. Reg. § 1.6662-3(b)(3).
14. See IRC § 6662(a), (b).

penalty rises to 40% of the misstated amount.[15] This disproportionate increase in sanctions for particularly large misstatements produces additional magnitude-based graduation of penalties.[16] Punitive damages (when conceived as either applicable or appropriate for particularly great external harms) are the most well-known example of this additional magnitude-based graduation. There are others.[17]

As soon as we recognize two different axes of graduation, it is important to emphasize that they may be independent. A taxpayer may engage in outright evasion of a USD 10 tax liability (high aggressiveness; small magnitude) or take an uncertain but rather conservative position saving USD 1 million in taxes (low aggressiveness; high magnitude). Of course, one may evade USD 1 million in tax (high aggressiveness, high magnitude) or take a conservative USD 10 deduction (low aggressiveness, small magnitude). The potential independence of behavioural variation along the two axes underscores an important point: it is essential to be clear about which particular axis of graduation one investigates. If a given term such as 'egregious' is used to describe both aggressiveness and magnitude – as it sometimes is – confusion is inevitable. Thus, recognizing just two degrees of graduation highlights the importance of conceptual precision.

Culpability, or the offender's mental state, is the third degree of graduation. This axis is most relevant in criminal law, where punishment often depends on whether the defendant acted with reckless disregard, knowledge, intent, or specific intent (which itself has multiple levels). Purpose, wilfulness, *scienter*, and similar concepts all reflect various points on the culpability axis. Conceptually, culpability is just a subset of aggressiveness-based graduation where the relevant legal threshold is the actor's state of mind. One may think of culpability as mental aggressiveness. Nonetheless, graduation along this axis deserves a separate treatment because changes in aggressiveness and culpability are often independent of each other.

Tax penalties offer many examples of culpability-based graduation. Numerous tax provisions deny tax benefits (and raise the spectre of sanctions) if a taxpayer acts with 'a principal purpose',[18] 'the principal purpose',[19] 'a significant purpose',[20] or just 'a purpose'[21] of tax avoidance or evasion. All of the quoted terms refer to mental states, and each means a different degree of intentionality.[22] For losing tax positions, sanctions vary depending on whether the underpayment is 'willful',[23] and whether a

---

15. See IRC § 6662(h)(1).
16. The same magnitude-based graduation applies to overstatements of pension liabilities and estate or gift tax valuation understatements. See IRC § 6662(a), (b), (h)(2)(B)-(C). Moreover, the 'valuation misstatement' penalty results in another disproportionate magnitude-based increase as the size of an understatement changes from insubstantial (and not subject to that penalty) to 'substantial' (and penalized at 20% of the understatement).
17. See Securities Exchange Act of 1934 § 21(d)(3)(B)(iii), 15 USC § 78u(d)(3)(B)(iii), establishing increased 'third-tier' sanctions for violations that 'result[] in substantial losses'.
18. IRC § 382(l).
19. IRC § 269(b).
20. IRC § 6662(d).
21. IRC § 357(b).
22. For a seminal discussion, see Walter J. Blum, *Motive, Intent, and Purpose in Federal Income Taxation*, 34(3) U. Chi. L. Rev. 485 (1967).
23. See Michael I. Saltzman & Leslie Book, *IRS Practice and Procedure* ¶ 7B.02 (WG&L, 2013).

taxpayer acted with 'willful neglect'.[24] The economic substance doctrine conditions tax benefits on the taxpayer's state of mind as well.[25] This is particularly important because the penalty increases from 20% to 40% for underpayments that result from transactions lacking economic substance.[26] Thus, culpability is an important factor in determining sanctions for tax law violations.

It is well-known that an act (more precisely, an act of a given aggressiveness) may be subject to civil or criminal sanctions, or no sanctions at all, depending on the offender's state of mind.[27] Less understood, perhaps, is the fact that a more aggressive conduct can be less culpable and vice versa. Tax law provides ready examples. A losing tax position taken intentionally and with full knowledge that it is more likely to be illegal than legal is not subject to any sanctions as long as it is not too aggressive (has 'substantial authority') (high culpability, moderate aggressiveness).[28] Another position taken with no knowledge or intent to evade the law that happens to be more aggressive (has only a 'reasonable basis') is subject to fines if not disclosed (low culpability, high aggressiveness).[29] Of course, aggressiveness and culpability may vary in tandem as well. One may intentionally evade (high culpability, high aggressiveness), or comply while intending to do so (low culpability, low aggressiveness). And it is equally apparent that culpability and magnitude may vary independently in almost every legal regime. Thus, we have now identified three separate axes of penalty graduation, all potentially independent, and all present in the tax setting.

The fourth axis is the degree of care taken by a putative offender to comply with the law. Tax penalties, for example, depend on whether taxpayer's actions reveal 'negligence or disregard of rules or regulations', where 'the term "negligence" includes any failure to make a reasonable attempt to comply with the provisions of this title and the term "disregard" includes any careless, reckless, or intentional disregard'.[30] Notably, these provisions do not focus on aggressiveness (or, at least, not only on aggressiveness). Rather, they depend on taxpayer's 'effort to assess the taxpayer's proper tax liability',[31] such as by ascertaining the rules, making inquiries, and the like.[32] Perhaps the most important decision in that regard is whether to obtain expert

---

24. IRC § 6651(a).
25. Specifically, the courts must inquire into whether the taxpayer had a 'non-tax business purpose'. See Martin J. McMahon, Jr., Ira B. Shepard & Daniel L. Simmons, *Recent Developments in Federal Income Taxation: The Year 2011*, 12(5) Fla. Tax Rev. 235, 364 (2012).
26. See IRC § 6662(i).
27. For a detailed analysis of a wide range of such acts, see Alex Raskolnikov, *Irredeemably Inefficient Acts: A Threat to Markets, Firms, and the Fisc*, 102(4) Geo. L.J. 1133 (2014).
28. A position is generally believed to have 'substantial authority' if it has at least a 40% chance of success on review. No penalties apply to such positions even if the taxpayer was convinced that the likelihood of success was less than 50–50. For a discussion and critique of this feature see Doran, above n. 12.
29. See IRC § 6662(d)(2)(B). 'Reasonable basis' is generally viewed as about a 25% chance of success on review. For a discussion, see Logue, above n. 6.
30. IRC § 6662(b), (c).
31. Treas. Reg. § 1.6664-4(b)(1).
32. Similarly, sanctions for violating the Securities Exchange Act increase if the offender exhibits a 'deliberate or reckless disregard of a regulatory requirement'. 15 USC § 78u(d)(3)(ii).

advice. The importance is due both to cost considerations and to the legal consequences of the decision.[33] I will refer to this axis of penalty graduation as *effort*.

While it is probably obvious that effort is distinct from magnitude, it may be less
clear that effort is different from aggressiveness and culpability. Yet it is. Starting with
aggressiveness, it may seem intuitive that if one ignores the law one will end up
breaking some rules. Low effort, one may think, leads to high aggressiveness (and high
effort to low aggressiveness). Perhaps sometimes it does; but other times it does not.
One may just happen to take a conservative tax position while making no effort to
understand the relevant rules (low effort, low aggressiveness). One may also take an
aggressive 'reasonable basis' position after engaging expert advisors and while retaining all the relevant records (high effort, high aggressiveness). Effort and culpability
may diverge as well. One taxpayer may learn the law and then deliberately break it
anyway (high effort, high culpability). Another taxpayer may fail to comply with an
obscure rule that the taxpayer made no effort to understand because the taxpayer was
unaware of the rule's existence (low effort, low culpability). A third taxpayer may work
hard to understand a legal command, but make an innocent mistake (high effort, low
culpability). More scenarios may be readily imagined.

Without claiming to identify all possible axes of penalty graduation, I will
highlight two more. The likelihood of detection is a well-known variable in the
deterrence literature. Not surprisingly, sanctions may vary along this dimension, and
tax sanctions do vary in that manner. For instance, losing positions supported by a
'reasonable basis' are penalty-free if they are disclosed, but not otherwise.[34] Transactions lacking economic substance are subject to a 20% or 40% penalty depending on
whether a taxpayer discloses them on a return (with a higher penalty applying to
non-disclosed transactions).[35] And efforts to conceal a tax underpayment make an
imposition of a fraud penalty more likely.[36] At the risk of stating the obvious, I will note
that the *detection* axis is potentially independent from aggressiveness, culpability,
magnitude, or effort. As the number of axes increases, it becomes burdensome to give
examples showing all possible combinations. But just to raise a few possibilities, one
taxpayer taking a somewhat aggressive position may try to hide it while another may
not. In each case, the amount of underpayment may be large or small, and the same is
true of a taxpayer's effort to ascertain what the law requires.

Finally, sanctions may and do vary based on the offender's history of prior
violations. This *history* axis is very familiar in criminal law. Criminal tax penalties
increase with the number of prior offences, just like most other criminal sanctions do
under the US Sentencing Guidelines.[37] At the same time, lack of prior criminal history
is a mitigating factor in tax evasion sentencing.[38] Offence history is important for civil

---

33. In many cases, reliance on professional advice immunizes the taxpayer from penalties. In some
    cases it does not. There has been much litigation on this issue, including recently. See Saltzman
    & Book, above n. 23, at ¶ 7B.03.
34. See IRC § 6662(d)(2).
35. See IRC § 6662(i).
36. See Saltzman & Book, above n. 23, at ¶ 7B.02[4][a].
37. See US Sentencing Guidelines Ch. 4, 5.
38. See *United States v. Moore*, 344 Fed. Appx. 767, 769 (3rd Cir. 2007).

penalties as well. For example, a penalty for failure to disclose a reportable transaction may be rescinded if a 'taxpayer has established history of properly disclosing other reportable transactions and complying with other tax laws'.[39] Similarly, a penalty for failure to file certain returns is increased if the taxpayer's offence 'is part of a pattern of conduct ... of repeatedly failing to file timely or repeatedly failing to include correct information' on the return.[40] As is probably obvious, the offence history may be independent from any of the other five graduation axes.

I have repeatedly qualified the point about the independent variation along each of the six axes with terms like 'potentially' and 'often' for a reason. While sanctions may vary independently along each axis, policy-makers may make the variations interdependent as well. Again, tax provides some stark examples. A tax understatement is subject to sanctions if it is 'substantial' but not otherwise.[41] 'Substantiality' is determined by the size of the understatement, revealing magnitude-based graduation.[42] However, a taxpayer who discloses the relevant information on the return is not viewed as understating any tax.[43] Thus, the rule intertwines magnitude-based and detection-based graduation. But this is not the end of the story. A disclosed position does not count as being disclosed if it is not supported by a 'reasonable basis' (aggressiveness-based threshold), or is not properly substantiated (effort-based threshold), or is attributable to a tax shelter.[44] The last clause introduces a culpability-based threshold because a 'tax shelter' is defined by reference to a taxpayer's purpose for entering into the transaction.[45] In sum, the substantial understatement penalty – a rule that takes less than a quarter of a page in the Code of Federal Regulations – blends together thresholds reflecting five (!) different axes of graduation, leaving only the offence history out of the picture. Is it any wonder that tax lawyers make a nice living explaining tax law to the uninitiated?

Why are tax sanctions so complicated? Does it make sense to vary penalties along so many different dimensions? What assumptions about people's behaviour support any of these variations? Which graduated penalty structures are likely to improve efficiency or facilitate compliance? The next section searches for answers to these questions in the legal, economics, and accounting literature on tax compliance and optimal deterrence more generally. The inquiry is limited to economic analysis and it follows the order in which the degrees of graduation appeared above: aggressiveness, magnitude, culpability, effort, detection, and history. I do not claim that these are the only possible axes, but I believe that they are the most important ones as a practical matter. Thus I limit the discussion to these six.

---

39. Treas. Reg. § 301.6707A-1(d)(3)(B)(iii).
40. Treas. Reg. § 301.6721-1(f)(3).
41. See Treas. Reg. § 1.6662-4(a).
42. Specifically, 'substantial' means in excess of the greater of 10% of the correct amount of tax or USD 5,000, with some further complications. See Treas. Reg. § 1.6662-4(b).
43. See Treas. Reg. § 1.6662-4(e).
44. Treas. Reg. § 1.6662-4(e).
45. A tax shelter is 'a partnership or other entity, any investment plan or arrangement, or any other plan or arrangement, if a significant purpose ... is the avoidance or evasion of Federal income tax'. IRC § 6662(d)(2)(C)(ii).

§13.03   EVALUATING GRADUATED SANCTIONS

Multiple axes of penalty graduation do not necessarily make penalty calculations difficult. As one can glean from the US Sentencing Guidelines, these calculations may be quite mechanistic. 'For each dollar of tax underpayment, add ten cents', the rules may say, 'for each prior offence, multiply by 1.3; for lack of disclosure, raise to a square', and so on. In reality, however, simple schemes like this are rarely possible. Aggressiveness, culpability, and effort are vague concepts that may not be defined precisely or applied easily most of the time. Moreover, the history of the Sentencing Guidelines suggests that even the sanctioning characteristics that do lend themselves to a precise definition and predictable application violate our sense of justice, or at least that of the US Supreme Court.[46] These difficulties, however, are only a small part of the problem with complex sanctions. From a theoretical perspective, each degree of penalty graduation requires an independent investigation and justification. The more degrees there are, the more analysis is needed to evaluate a penalty regime. The following discussion turns to this analysis.

[A]   Aggressiveness: Critical in Law; Overlooked in Economics

Law is often uncertain and people respond to this uncertainty in different ways. Some stay on the safe side, others come close to the blurry line separating legal and illegal conduct, and there are those who completely disregard the law's commands. These variations are important in any legal regime, but they are particularly important in tax and other settings where statutory fines depend on the actor's choice of aggressiveness. Needless to say, one cannot evaluate this penalty structure without having a model of actors responding to legal uncertainty by taking positions of varying legal strength.

Yet the literature has little to offer in modelling legal uncertainty. Although this uncertainty has received more attention in tax than in many other contexts, most economic analysis of tax enforcement ignores legal uncertainty altogether. There is not even a term describing uncertain tax positions. The standard approach in the economic analysis of tax enforcement allows only two choices: evasion and compliance (called 'avoidance' by most economists).[47] While decision-making under uncertainty is at the core of this approach, the uncertainty relates to detection, not the strength of a legal position.[48]

---

46. See *United States v. Booker*, 543 U.S. 220 (2005) (holding that mandatory Sentencing Guidelines violate the Sixth Amendment of the US Constitution).
47. See Joel Slemrod & Shlomo Yitzhaki, 'Tax Avoidance, Evasion, and Administration', in Alan J. Auerbach & Martin Feldstein (eds), *Handbook of Public Economics*, vol. 3, 1423, 1428 (North-Holland, 2002).
48. The foundational model by Allingham and Sandmo incorporated only detection uncertainty, and the literature mostly followed this approach. See Michael G. Allingham & Agnar Sandmo, *Income Tax Evasion: A Theoretical Analysis*, 1(3–4) J. Pub. Econ. 323 (1972). Curiously, even though Allingham and Sandmo acknowledged that other forms of uncertainty exist and briefly discussed these other forms (at 324–325), they said nothing about legal uncertainty in that discussion.

Some work in economics and accounting does incorporate legal uncertainty into tax compliance models. However, most of this work does not interpret legal uncertainty in the way I do here. Several authors conceptualize uncertainty as a random variation of taxable income around the mean.[49] Their analyses do not incorporate the concept of aggressiveness, do not consider aggressiveness-dependent penalties, and do not investigate any specific rules. Moreover, their models operationalize an increase in uncertainty as an increase in a mean-preserving spread.[50] In contrast, a change in aggressiveness changes the mean as well as the variance. Another approach views uncertainty as a taxpayer's lack of knowledge of the tax consequences. This ignorance may be reduced or eliminated by learning the rules or acquiring tax advice.[51] In contrast, legal uncertainty is often irreducible. In fact, acquiring tax advice may increase it.[52] Other economic models of uncertainty are even further removed from this chapter's conceptualization of this term.[53]

A few investigations by economists and accountants do consider variations in aggressiveness. David Ulph offers a model that includes taxpayers who face uncertain rules and purchase tax schemes of various degrees of aggressiveness.[54] However, one of his model's main drivers – the risk of retroactive legislation – is not a serious concern for US taxpayers.[55] Other features of the model lead to further difficulties in applying it

---

49. See Paul J. Beck & Woon-Oh Jung, *Taxpayer Compliance Under Uncertainty*, 8(1) J. Acct. Pub. Pol'y 1, 10 (1989); Woon-Oh Jung, *Tax Reporting Game Under Uncertain Tax Laws and Asymmetric Information*, 37(3) Econ. Let. 323, 323–324 (1991); Louis Kaplow, *Accuracy, Complexity, and the Income Tax*, 14(1) J.L. Econ.& Org. 61, 72 (1998); Suzanne Scotchmer & Joel Slemrod, *Randomness in Tax Enforcement*, 38(1) J. Pub. Econ. 17, 19 (1989).

50. See James Alm, *Uncertain Tax Policies, Individual Behavior, and Welfare*, 78(1) Am. Econ. Rev. 237, 238 (1988); Beck & Jung, *Taxpayer Compliance Under Uncertainty*, above n. 49, at 10–11; Kaplow, *Accuracy, Complexity, and the Income Tax*, above n. 49, at 75; Scotchmer & Slemrod, above n. 49, at 19.

51. See Beck & Jung, *Taxpayer Compliance Under Uncertainty*, above n. 49, at 13–14; Kaplow, *Accuracy, Complexity, and the Income Tax*, above n. 49, at 74–75, 78; Krause, above n. 6, at 399; Suzanne Scotchmer, *Who Profits from Taxpayer Confusion?*, 29(1) Econ. Let. 49, 49–50 (1989). Some of the contributions expressly set aside the investigation of 'arguability' (i.e., aggressiveness) of legal positions (Scotchmer, *Who Profits from Taxpayer Confusion?*, at 51). Note that uncertainty as lack of knowledge and uncertainty as a random variation around the mean are not mutually exclusive. One can model uncertainty as a random variation with taxpayers capable of reducing the distribution's variance by acquiring information.

52. For instance, a taxpayer may be aware of a 'home office' deduction and may think that a 'home office' means something like 'a room in the house where the taxpayer works when he or she works at home'. Asking an expert about this deduction would complicate things quite a bit. To start with, it would introduce the taxpayer to a detailed regulatory scheme in section 280A. While the tax advisor may be an expert in interpreting this section (so that the taxpayer need not master it), the advisor will also explain that some key statutory terms are ambiguous and the guidance from the courts has been far from clear. See Boris I. Bittker & Lawrence Lokken, *Federal Taxation of Income, Estates, and Gifts*, ¶ 22.6.3 (WG&L, 2005) (discussing the controversy regarding the 'principal place of business' term).

53. James Alm, for example, investigates uncertainty that arises due to possible future legislative changes. See Alm, above n. 50, at 237, 241. Under the current law, this possibility affects neither the aggressiveness of a particular tax position nor the possible penalties.

54. Ulph uses the term 'legal effectiveness' rather than aggressiveness; see David Ulph, *Avoidance Policies – A New Conceptual Framework*, Oxford Univ., Ctr. for Bus. Taxation, Working Paper No. 09/22, at 1, 7 (2009).

55. See Ulph, above n. 54, at 8-20 (variables p_u and ϕ). Another key driver is the variation in reputational costs (Ulph, above n. 54, at 10). Yet we know very little about the magnitude of

to real-life tax planning.[56] Paul Beck, Jon Davis and Woon-Oh Jung investigate legal uncertainty and variation in tax reporting aggressiveness in a series of articles.[57] Kate Krause models a parameter that may be interpreted as the level of aggressiveness as well.[58] Lillian Mills, Leslie Robinson and Richard Sansing present a model where taxpayers of varying aggressiveness face uncertain tax rules.[59] And Michael Graetz, Jennifer Reinganum and Louis Wilde investigate the effect of tax advice on decisions of taxpayers facing differing probability that their deductions would be disallowed (which the authors call 'exposure').[60] None of these models, however, investigates aggressiveness as an endogenous variable. Beck and co-authors introduce it as a *'prior probability'*[61] and operationalize it in experimental settings by assigning a number reflecting this probability to the subjects.[62] Mills and co-authors equate the strength of a position with the taxpayer type, which the taxpayer 'observes' as a 'realization of a random variable'.[63] Graetz and co-authors do not allow taxpayers to change their exposure

---

these costs and their variation among taxpayers.

56. For instance, the model assumes that 'the probability that the tax authority successfully challenges the scheme' does not vary among schemes or taxpayers. Ulph, above n. 54, at 9–10. Not only is this assumption unrealistic, the variation of probability in question is a key factor accounting for variation in aggressiveness of real-life tax positions.

57. See Paul J. Beck, Jon S. Davis & Woon-Oh Jung, *Taxpayer Disclosure and Penalty Laws*, 2(2) J. Pub. Econ. Theory 243 (2000) [hereinafter Beck, Davis & Jung, *Taxpayer Disclosure*]; Paul J. Beck, Jon S. Davis & Woon-Oh Jung, *Tax Advice and Reporting under Uncertainty: Theory and Experimental Evidence*, 13(1) Contemp. Acct. Res. 49 (1996) [hereinafter Beck, Davis & Jung, *Tax Advice*]; Paul J. Beck, Jon S. Davis & Woon-Oh Jung, *Experimental Evidence on an Economic Model of Taxpayer Aggression under Strategic and Nonstrategic Audits*, 9(1) Contemp. Acct. Res. 86 (1992) [hereinafter Beck, Davis & Jung, *Strategic Audits*]; Paul J. Beck, Jon S. Davis & Woon-Oh Jung, *Experimental Evidence of Taxpayers Reporting under Uncertainty*, 66(3) Acct. Rev. 535 (1991) [hereinafter Beck, Davis & Jung, *Reporting under Uncertainty*]; Beck and Jung, *Taxpayer Compliance Under Uncertainty*, above n. 49.

58. See Krause, above n. 6, at 400.

59. See Lillian F. Mills, Leslie A. Robinson & Richard C. Sansing, *FIN 48 and Tax Compliance*, 85(5) Acct. Rev. 1721, 1726–1727 (2010) (introducing x as the expected tax benefit from the transaction, also referring to it as the 'strength' of a taxpayer's position, and interpreting $x > 0.5$ as a position 'for which the taxpayer is more likely than not to prevail').

60. See Michael J. Graetz, Jennifer Reinganum & Louis Wilde, *Expert Opinions and Taxpayer Compliance: A Strategic Analysis*, Cal. Inst. Tech. Soc. Sci. Working Paper 710 (1989).

61. See Beck, Davis & Jung, *Taxpayer Disclosure*, above n. 57, at 247 (emphasis added).

62. See Beck, Davis & Jung, *Strategic Audits*, above n. 57, at 98. For another experimental operationalization of exogenous aggressiveness, see Beck, Davis & Jung, *Reporting under Uncertainty*, above n. 57, at 538 (introducing experimental subjects to income uncertainty as a bingo case with sequentially numbered balls representing particular taxable incomes and varying the number of balls in the bingo cage). Beck, Davis and Jung model the strength of a legal position as the probability that the taxpayer's income is high (because, for example, a tax deduction may not be properly taken). See Beck, Davis & Jung, *Strategic Audits*, above n. 57, at 89. Because their model does not allow that strength (probability) to vary, the authors vary uncertainty by manipulating the gap between high and low incomes – something they themselves tend to refer to as the 'amount at risk' rather than the degree of aggressiveness. See Beck, Davis & Jung, *Strategic Audits*, above n. 57, at 89; see also Beck, Davis & Jung, *Tax Advice*, above n. 57, at 49.

63. Mills, Robinson & Sansing, above n. 59, at 1727, 1729.

levels.[64] Krause imposes the same restriction on the levels of a tax position's ambiguity.[65]

Yet from a lawyer's perspective, the most important feature of aggressiveness is that it is endogenous. Taxpayers may vary the strength of their positions from certain legality to certain illegality by adjusting their actions. For instance, it is unclear what a 'substantial'[66] decline in risk is, but it is abundantly clear that a 99% decline is substantial and a 1% decline is not. Taxpayers may often choose any degree of risk diminution between 100% and zero in designing their tax reduction strategies. Likewise, even if a taxpayer is unsure how much time must pass for the Internal Revenue Service (IRS) to conclude that a later event has followed the earlier one 'immediately',[67] there is no doubt that a minute-long gap between the two satisfies the test and a year-long gap does not. Again, taxpayers may often choose the length of time separating the two events. Thus, the legal uncertainty surrounding many tax positions, and their aggressiveness, are endogenous – they are the products of taxpayer's choice. No work in economics or accounting that I am aware of reflects this feature of aggressiveness.[68] That is, no model incorporates the case where a change in the taxpayer's behaviour affects the strength of that person's tax position.[69]

Legal scholars fully appreciate the role of legal uncertainty in taxation and taxpayers' ability to vary the strength of their positions. Their analysis of tax penalties is highly illuminating, but it has significant limitations. Sarah Lawsky suggests that

---

64. See Graetz, Reinganum & Wilde, above n. 60, at 7 (listing a number of strategies available to taxpayers, but not considering a strategy of changing the exposure, π).
65. See Krause, above n. 6, at 401 (considering three potential taxpayer responses to uncertainty, but not considering changing e_1 as a possible additional strategy). Rather, Krause considers how exogenous changes in tax position's ambiguity affect taxpayer incentives, see Krause, above n. 6, at 404–405.
66. IRC § 1092(c).
67. IRC § 351(a).
68. Note that the models interpreting income uncertainty as a random variation around the mean do incorporate endogeneity by allowing taxpayers to reduce uncertainty by purchasing tax advice. See, e.g., Beck & Jung, *Taxpayer Compliance Under Uncertainty*, above n. 49, at 13–16. However, a change in uncertainty in these models amounts to a change in the mean-preserving variance of an income distribution (Beck & Jung, *Taxpayer Compliance Under Uncertainty*, above n. 49, at 14), not a change in the mean of that distribution that reflects positions of different aggressiveness.
69. James Alm and Mark Cronshaw offer a model that includes a parameter (α) defined as 'the probability that a high-income taxpayer reports low (i.e., the probability of noncompliance or cheating)'. James Alm & Mark B. Cronshaw, *Tax Compliance with Two-Sided Uncertainty*, 23(2) Pub. Fin. Q. 139, 144 (1995). Importantly, the taxpayer in the model is free to choose the value of α, making it endogenous. It is unclear, however, what this probability corresponds to in real life, that is, *how* a taxpayer may choose this probability.
    Aside from an inquiry into legal uncertainty, the tax enforcement literature does address endogenous probabilities. For instance, Yitzhaki considers probability of detection that depends on the amount of evaded income which is chosen by the taxpayer. See Shlomo Yitzhaki, *On the Excess Burden of Tax Evasion*, 15(2) Pub. Fin. Q. 123, 127 (1987). Kaplow investigates the variation in the probability of detection due to the taxpayers' expenditures on concealing their evasion. See Louis Kaplow, *Optimal Taxation with Costly Enforcement and Evasion*, 43(2) J. Pub. Econ. 221, 230 (1990). These investigations, however, do not link the uncertainty to the aggressiveness of a tax position. Therefore, they cannot shed light on the aggressiveness-based penalty graduation.

aggressiveness-based graduation of tax sanctions may be appropriate, but her arguments suffer from several problems.[70] First, her model is a narrower version of Louis Kaplow's model that, in Kaplow's own view, does not yield any specific prescription for sanctions design.[71] Second, Kaplow's model is inapplicable in the tax setting because it is built on a foundational assumption that '[i]f and only if an act is harmful is it illegal ....'.[72] This assumption is implausible in the tax field.[73] Third, Lawsky replaces Kaplow's 'probability of harm' with 'lawmakers' perceived probability of harm (i.e., lawmakers' estimation of the probability that the transaction would be struck down by a court if reviewed)'.[74] It is unclear how lawmakers may estimate the likely outcomes of future legal decisions regarding yet-unknown tax positions.

Kyle Logue does not investigate a continuous aggressiveness-based variation of sanctions, but he does consider whether penalties should apply to all tax underpayments or only those that cross a particular aggressiveness threshold.[75] Following the general deterrence literature, Logue refers to penalties that have this feature as 'fault-based'. I find this term unfortunate both because it introduces a moralistic overtone into a purely technical analysis and (relatedly) because its use may lead to a confusion between aggressiveness and culpability. In any case, Logue does not reach clear conclusions regarding the desirability of fault-based sanctions.[76] Mark Gergen also finds fault-based penalties plausible, but only if cross-cutting psychological biases and diverging subjective evaluations of legal uncertainty affect the outcomes in a particular way.[77] Furthermore, Gergen's normative framework is unique and emphasizes the value of moderation.[78]

Daniel Shaviro generally advocates against fault-based penalties (and, necessarily, against aggressiveness-based graduation).[79] His analysis, however, only explains why a penalty multiplier needed to offset uncertain detection should apply regardless of the degree of aggressiveness.[80] He mentions that it may be desirable to vary penalties

---

70. See Lawsky, above n. 12.
71. See Louis Kaplow, *Optimal Deterrence, Uninformed Individuals, and Acquiring Information about Whether Acts Are Subject to Sanctions*, 6(1) J.L. Econ. & Org. 93, 111–113 (1990).
72. Kaplow, *Optimal Deterrence, Uninformed Individuals, and Acquiring Information about Whether Acts Are Subject to Sanctions*, above n. 71, at 96.
73. Endless harmful tax-motivated acts are perfectly legal. A worker who reduces his or her work hours to avoid extra taxes, an investor who retains an unwanted appreciated asset to avoid the tax on the gain, an elderly taxpayer who engages in extra consumption in order to avoid the looming estate tax all engage in socially harmful yet perfectly legal activities.
74. Lawsky, above n. 12, at 1054.
75. See Logue, above n. 6, at 257–264.
76. Moreover, Logue's analysis relies on a problematic concept of 'transaction'. Problems with placing a heavy emphasis on this concept are clear from David P. Hariton, *The Frame Game: How Defining the 'Transaction' Decides the Case*, 31(2) Va. Tax Rev. 221 (2011). Logue is not the only one relying on a transaction-by-transaction evaluation of aggressive tax positions. See, e.g., Mills, Robinson & Sansing, above n. 59, at 1726 (basing the model on 'the value of transaction in the absence of the tax benefit').
77. See Gergen, above n. 6, at 484.
78. See Gergen, above n. 6, at 456.
79. See Shaviro, above n. 6, at 239–241.
80. Shaviro's further claim that a multiplier reflecting detection uncertainty leads to optimal penalties (Shaviro, above n. 6, at 240) cannot be sustained in the welfarist framework for the reasons discussed in Alex Raskolnikov, *Accepting the Limits of Tax Law and Economics*, 98(3)

based on 'whether the transaction, even if potentially legally defensible, has a significant tax avoidance aspect'.[81] However, he does not elaborate, and a plausible interpretation of 'significant tax avoidance aspect' as a reference to aggressiveness appears to contradict his earlier conclusion.[82] In any case, Shaviro does not investigate why taxpayers take uncertain positions in the first place, let alone positions of varying aggressiveness.

The most illuminating work on legal uncertainty outside of tax was done by Richard Craswell and John Calfee thirty years ago.[83] Not much progress has occurred since then. Craswell and Calfee focused on whether legal uncertainty leads to over- or under-deterrence in the presence of an optimal legal rule. Their conclusions are indeterminate, with over-deterrence resulting from some assumptions and under-deterrence from others. Given these findings, and recognizing that socially optimal rules may not be plausibly assumed in tax and many other settings, it should be clear why Craswell and Calfee's research has not led to many conceptual advances, including in the tax enforcement literature.[84]

In sum, people often face uncertain rules. Legal uncertainty is not random. It may not be eliminated by learning the law or soliciting expert advice. Instead, actors may choose the degree of this uncertainty – and vary the aggressiveness of their positions – by adjusting their actions. The analysis of legal uncertainty and the incentives it creates is central to thinking about aggressiveness-based penalty graduation. The explicit link between statutory tax fines and the tax position's aggressiveness makes this analysis even more important in the tax setting. Yet the literature has had a very limited success in modelling legal uncertainty and analysing aggressiveness-based sanctions. I model this uncertainty and make some progress toward understanding rational decision-making under uncertain, non-optimal legal rules in related work.[85] Yet clearly, much more needs to be done in thinking about aggressiveness-based penalty graduation.

[B]   Magnitude: Clear Insights, Attainable Improvements

In contrast with aggressiveness, magnitude-based variation of sanctions follows easily from the basic model of tax enforcement and, more generally, from the theory of complete (or absolute) deterrence. Using tax as a convenient example, the basic

---

Cornell L. Rev. 523 (2013). This claim is also questionable in the complete deterrence framework because Shaviro does not address the variation of taxpayer's private costs for positions of various degrees of aggressiveness.

81. See Shaviro, above n. 6, at 244.
82. Note that 'significant tax avoidance aspect' may equally plausibly refer to culpability (the taxpayer's purpose for entering into a transaction or taking a return position) rather than aggressiveness.
83. See John E. Calfee & Richard Craswell, *Some Effects of Uncertainty on Compliance with Legal Standards*, 70(5) Va. L. Rev. 965 (1984); Richard Craswell & John E. Calfee, *Deterrence and Uncertain Legal Standards*, 2(2) J.L. Econ. & Org. 279 (1986).
84. The tax-specific inquiries by Gergen, Lawsky, Logue, and Shaviro just discussed post-date Craswell and Calfee's work but find no way to build on their analysis.
85. See Alex Raskolnikov, *Legal Uncertainty and Rational Compliance*, working paper on file with the author.

argument is simple and intuitive. Taxpayer's incentives in choosing the magnitude of an underpayment are obvious: the greater the magnitude, the greater the taxpayer's gain. In a world without legal uncertainty (the world that we may properly assume for the purposes of investigating graduation based on magnitude alone), every tax underpayment is illegal. If we posit that all illegal acts are undesirable (a big assumption that generally underlies the tax enforcement and complete deterrence literatures and that I do not question here), we would want to eliminate all of them.[86] Denying all gains from tax evasion eliminates the incentive to evade, so a sanction equal to the private gain (the tax saved) assures compliance. The same logic applies to theft, fraud, and any other offence analysed in the complete deterrence framework with its gain-based sanctions.[87] The greater the gain, the greater the sanction – this is magnitude-based graduation.

All of this is well-known, uncontroversial, and consistent with the actual sanctions calculated as a percentage of the tax due. But it does not explain a further graduation where this percentage increases with the magnitude of the underpayment. To my knowledge, this extra degree of graduation has been neither analysed nor justified.

This shortcoming may be remedied. One only needs to replace the standard model's fixed penalty coefficient with a variable coefficient that is a function of the tax underpayment or income understatement. This change will lead to a somewhat more complicated math. But most results currently available in the literature can probably be restated and reinterpreted taking this additional complication into account. In fact, a recent article has already started down this path.[88] I by no means suggest that no interesting insights will emerge.[89] After all, tax scholars know well that a seemingly slight change in the penalty calculation may lead to an important change in the model's prediction.[90] But there is little doubt that the magnitude-based graduation of a kind found in the Internal Revenue Code can be readily incorporated into the existing models. Whether the revised models will support the specific magnitude-dependent sanctions found in the tax code and some other enforcement regimes is another matter.

[C]   Culpability: A Long-Standing Challenge

The picture is less bright when we turn to the next axis of graduation – culpability. Here, tax enforcement scholars are in large company. The entire law and economics literature has struggled to explain why so many legal rules incorporate the mental state

---

86. Of course, this conclusion changes once the costs of eliminating taxpayers gains are considered.
87. See Keith N. Hylton, *Punitive Damages and the Economic Theory of Penalties*, 87(2) Geo. L.J. 421 (1998); Jeffrey S. Parker, *Criminal Sentencing Policy for Organizations: The Unifying Approach of Optimal Penalties*, 26(3) Am. Crim. L. Rev. 513, 552 (1989).
88. See Mark D. Phillips, *Deterrence v. Gamesmanship: Taxpayer Response to Targeted Audits and Endogenous Penalties*, 100 J. Econ. Behav. & Org. 81, 85 (2014).
89. Mark Phillips' article introduces a model that is dramatically more complicated than the standard model of tax evasion, so it is difficult to isolate the effects of making the penalty rate a function of the evaded amount.
90. I refer, of course, to Shlomo Yitzhaki's adjustment to the seminal Allingham-Sandmo model. For a summary, see Slemrod & Yitzhaki, above n. 47, at 1430.

of a putative offender, be it the *mens rea* requirement of the criminal law, the 'willful breach' doctrine of the contract law, or the references to knowledge, purpose, and good faith in a variety of regulatory regimes from environmental to securities regulation, corporate governance, and taxation. It is revealing that the chapter on public enforcement of law in the *Handbook of Law and Economics* makes no mention of the offender's mental states despite inquiring into such subjects as social norms and fairness considerations.[91]

In a certain sense, the economic importance of a taxpayer's mental state is obvious to any public finance economist. The fundamental cost of taxation – its excess burden – depends on that mental state. If a taxpayer decides to work an hour less without taking taxes into account, no excess burden arises; otherwise it does.[92] But this basic insight does not come close to justifying the culpability-based penalty graduation. All sorts of tax-motivated acts are perfectly legal.[93] In some cases, such as a tax-motivated reduction in the work effort, outlawing tax-motivated behaviour is simply impossible.[94] In other instances, such as corporate inversions, making tax-driven transactions illegal is possible. Yet it is often not done in practice, and it is unclear whether it should be done in many cases.[95] Moreover, the basic argument about excess burden is not very relevant if the tax system under consideration is not close to the optimal one. Pretty much every real tax system fits this description.[96] In sum, the economic analysis of tax enforcement sheds little light on the culpability-based penalty graduation, at least at present.

[D]   Effort: Some Findings, Few Clear Results

Tax penalties also vary based on a taxpayer's effort to understand the law, including by obtaining legal advice. A taxpayer who 'fails to make a reasonable attempt to ascertain the correctness of a deduction' that seems too good to be true is subject to a negligence penalty.[97] A taxpayer who 'does not exercise reasonable diligence to determine the correctness of a return position' is penalized for disregard of rules and regulations.[98] On the other hand, if a taxpayer obtains advice of a qualified professional, that taxpayer is often viewed as having 'good cause' to underpay taxes, no matter how aggressive the offending tax position happens to be.[99] In other words, lack of effort leads to penalties,

---

91. See Polinsky & Shavell, above n. 6. For an argument that intent plays a key role in the economic analysis of a particular category of socially undesirable acts, see Raskolnikov, *Irredeemably Inefficient Acts: A Threat to Markets, Firms, and the Fisc*, above n. 27.
92. Here I address taxes enacted to raise revenue rather than to regulate conduct (i.e., Pigouvian taxes).
93. See above n. 73.
94. I have called this the 'undeterrability problem'. See Raskolnikov, *Accepting the Limits of Tax Law and Economics*, above n. 80, at 543.
95. Corporate inversions, for instance, may be reducing an inefficient corporate income tax.
96. For an expanded discussion, see Raskolnikov, *Accepting the Limits of Tax Law and Economics*, above n. 80, at 566–589.
97. Treas. Reg. § 1.6662-3(b)(2).
98. Treas. Reg. § 1.6662-3(b)(3).
99. See Saltzman & Book, above n. 23, at ¶ 7B.03.

and evidence of effort protects from penalties, especially if that effort manifests itself through obtaining expert advice. That, at least, is the basic scheme.

But there are complications. First, taxpayers may use reliance on expert advice as a defence against sanctions only if the reliance is reasonable.[100] If a taxpayer knows enough about tax to realize that the advice is 'too good to be true', the penalty protection is off. Ignorance is, indeed, bliss in this case. Second, tax advisors are subject to their own sanctions. A recent trend has been to regulate tax advisors more and to make some forms of advice more expensive.[101] Assuming the advisors pass some of their costs to the clients, these developments create a disincentive to obtain advice. Third, a taxpayer is not liable for criminal (and perhaps even civil) tax fraud unless that taxpayer violates a 'known legal duty'.[102] A good faith subjective belief that no such duty (to pay tax) exists – no matter how unreasonable – is a complete defence.[103] The resulting incentive to *not* know the law is obvious. In sum, the US tax system provides a set of complicated and inconsistent incentives to understand the law. But there is no doubt that sanctions depend on this effort.

Does economic theory support such effort-based penalty graduation? The good news is that, unlike for aggressiveness- and culpability-based graduation, models of resolving legal uncertainty through learning do exist. The bad news, however, is that the models' implications are inconclusive.

Paul Beck and Woon-Oh Jung find that taxpayer incentives to purchase advisory services increase with tax rate, penalty rate, and audit probability (for realistic audit rates).[104] These findings do not tell us whether compliance or welfare is likely to increase with the purchase of legal advice. Suzanne Scotchmer concludes that if the government can base its audit policies on taxpayer's receipt of advice, it may (or may not) be optimal for taxpayers to resolve some – but never all – uncertainty.[105] In a related paper, Scotchmer finds that if penalties and audit probabilities do not depend on whether tax advice is sought, the government revenue may (or may not) go down when taxpayers seek advice, but social welfare is likely to go up because taxpayers will bear less risk.[106] Given the significant problems with evaluating welfare gains from adjusting the actual tax rules and sanctions,[107] even the latter finding is uncertain.

Several articles investigate the role of tax preparers in a game theoretic setting. Beck, Davis and Jung describe a signalling model in which a taxpayer's decision to

---

100. See Treas. Reg. § 1.6664-4(b), (c).
101. See Brian Gale & David A. Weisbach, *The Regulation of Tax Advisors*, 139 Tax Notes 1279–1302 (2011).
102. *Cheek v. United States*, 498 U.S. 192, 203 (1991).
103. See Bittker & Lokken, above n. 52, ¶ 114.6 (civil fraud), ¶ 114.9 (criminal fraud).
104. Beck & Jung, *Taxpayer Compliance under Uncertainty*, above n. 49, at 15–16.
105. See Scotchmer, *Who Profits from Taxpayer Confusion?*, above n. 51, at 53–54.
106. See Suzanne Scotchmer, 'The Effect of Tax Advisors on Tax Compliance', in Jeffrey A. Roth & John T. Scholz (eds), *Taxpayer Compliance: Social Science Perspectives*, vol. 2, 182, 184 (University of Pennsylvania Press, 1989). The conclusion is subject to many caveats, and is reached while assuming that advice is costless (at 186–189).
107. See Raskolnikov, *Accepting the Limits of Tax Law and Economics*, above n. 80, at 582–585; see also above n. 52.

obtain legal advice conveys unique information to the IRS.[108] The relationship between advice-seeking and government revenue is ambiguous, however, and the assumptions used to identify this relationship are strong.[109] Graetz, Reinganum and Wilde study a game involving taxpayers who may take uncertain positions, tax advisors who may not only resolve the legal uncertainty but protect taxpayers from penalties by issuing tax opinions, and a revenue-maximizing tax agency.[110] They reach interesting results with very limited practical significance.[111] They also discuss inconclusive findings of related research by Jennifer Reinganum and Louis Wilde.[112] Nahum Melumad, Mark Wolfson and Amir Ziv investigate the deductibility of fees paid for tax advice, and conclude that 'in spite of the simplicity of the setting considered, the efficiency implication of allowing the [deduction] is rather ambiguous'.[113]

In a more recent work, Kate Krause investigates the problem facing a taxpayer deciding whether to take a tax credit while being unsure about eligibility and aware of potential IRS errors.[114] She concludes that the IRS may (or may not) maximize its revenue by incentivizing some taxpayers to become informed.[115] As is the case with Scotchmer's analysis, several assumptions weaken this already equivocal conclusion.[116] Kaplow considers whether incentives to acquire information and resolve uncertainty about true taxable income are likely to be socially excessive, in a sense of exceeding the incentives of uninformed taxpayers.[117] He finds that they are if the penalty exceeds a fine based on the well-known multiplier (something that almost never happens in practice).[118] Otherwise, the incentives may be excessive or

---

108. Paul J. Beck, Jon S. Davis & Woon O. Jung, *The Role of Tax Practitioners in Tax Reporting: A Signalling Game*, Working Paper No. 89-1578, available at https://www.ideals.illinois.edu/bitstream/handle/2142/30116/roleoftaxpractit1578beck.pdf?sequence=2.

109. The authors assume that both the tax agency and tax advisors know the true tax liability, that taxpayers who hire advisors never conceal evasion from them and never choose to file their own returns inconsistently with the tax advice received. All these assumptions strengthen the information content of the signal provided to the government by the presence of an advisor – a key feature of the model.

110. See Graetz, Reinganum & Wilde, above n. 60.

111. For instance, one of their results obtains if the tax agency audits all returns with risky positions; another if taxpayers are evenly distributed with respect to the likelihood that the deduction would be allowed on audit; and yet another depends on conditioning audits on the presence of a tax opinion (something the IRS cannot do because these opinions are almost never disclosed on the return and are often protected by attorney-client privilege). Graetz, Reinganum & Wilde, above n. 60, at 3.

112. Graetz, Reinganum & Wilde, above n. 60, at 1–2.

113. Nahum D. Melumad, Mark A. Wolfson & Amir Ziv, *Should Taxpayers Be Subsidized to Hire Third-Party Preparers? A Game-Theoretic Analysis*, 11(1-II) Cont. Acct. Res. 553, 555 (1994).

114. See Krause, above n. 6.

115. Krause, above n. 6, at 408, 410–411.

116. These include the assumption that the IRS is indifferent between revenue collected from ineligible taxpayers and eligible taxpayers taxed due to an IRS mistake (see Krause, above n. 6, at 406), and the assumption that taxpayers always follow the law despite imperfect detection (once they learn what the law requires, that is); see Krause, above n. 6, at 398.

117. See Kaplow, *Accuracy, Complexity, and the Income Tax*, above n. 49.

118. Given probability of detection p, that multiplier in the tax setting is equal to $(1-p)/p$. For the analysis, see Kaplow, *Accuracy, Complexity, and the Income Tax*, above n. 49, at 75.

not.[119] Empirical research suggests that involving an accountant or a tax attorney in return preparation increases tax underpayments significantly.[120] None of this suggests that we should penalize taxpayers for failing to learn the tax law and for declining to hire advisors.

Finally, an effort to understand the law affects future tax compliance: once a taxpayer understands a rule in a given tax year, the taxpayer knows that rule for all future years. Are effort-based penalties justified by these benefits of greater knowledge? To answer this question, we need to decide whether knowledge of the law is socially desirable. Here, tax is different from most other regulatory regimes.[121] These other regimes aim to induce actors to respond to the incentives the regimes create. If a given regulatory regime is socially desirable, so is the knowledge of this regime by its subjects. Tax law also creates incentives, but these are distortions that efficiency-minded policy-makers should try to minimize.[122] Thus it is not obvious that we should incentivize taxpayers to understand the tax law.

David Weisbach and Kaplow each elaborate on this intuition.[123] Weisbach's analysis proceeds at a high level of generality. He considers uniform commodity taxes, non-linear labour income taxes, and tax shelters in a stylized form. Even at that level, he finds it difficult to reach clear conclusions, especially if taxes are not assumed to be optimal. Kaplow's results are similarly indeterminate.[124] Whether knowledge of the actual federal income tax is socially desirable remains an open question. So incentives to acquire this knowledge do not appear to support penalties based on the effort to understand the law.

What can we conclude about the effort-based penalty graduation? Taxpayers' knowledge of the law presents the government with a conundrum. Greater knowledge may be desirable if it leads to greater compliance, though even in this case the costs may outweigh the benefits. Greater knowledge is probably undesirable if it helps taxpayers to reduce their taxes by taking more aggressive positions or finding opportunities to 'game' the rules, though even here some ambiguity remains.[125] Some of the complexity of the real-life knowledge-related rules may well be due to this conundrum. But economic research has not approached the level of detail where this conundrum is relevant. For now, economic models provide little support for effort-based graduation of sanctions.

---

119. See Kaplow, *Accuracy, Complexity, and the Income Tax*, above n. 49.
120. See Brian Erard, *Taxation with Representation: An Analysis of the Role of Tax Practitioners in Tax Compliance*, 52(2) J. Pub. Econ. 163, 164–168, 191 (1993).
121. Again, I am not discussing Pigouvian taxes here.
122. See Raskolnikov, *Accepting the Limits of Tax Law and Economics*, above n. 80, at 543; David A. Weisbach, *Is Knowledge of the Tax Law Socially Desirable*, 15(1) Am. L. Econ. Rev. 187, 187 (2013).
123. See Weisbach, above n. 122; Kaplow, *Accuracy, Complexity, and the Income Tax*, above n. 49.
124. See Kaplow, *Accuracy, Complexity, and the Income Tax*, above n. 49, at 72–73.
125. Gaming clearly inefficient taxes may be welfare-increasing after all.

[E]   Detection: A Continuing Inquiry

Detection uncertainty is at the centre of the economic analysis of deterrence. It features prominently in Gary Becker's seminal analysis of crime[126] and in Michael Allingham and AgnarSandmo's foundational model of tax evasion.[127] The penalty adjustment needed to account for detection uncertainty is well-known: the so-called damages multiplier.[128] It is also well-known that the standard multiplier has a fundamental flaw. The probability of detection often increases with the aggressiveness of the violation, making any fixed multiplier non-optimal.[129] For instance, it is both intuitive and highly likely that egregious speeding is more likely to be detected than a slight speed limit violation. For that reason, the optimal deterrence analysis suggests that fines for the former should be lower than for the latter – the exact opposite of what actually occurs. This is a persisting puzzle in the law and economics literature.

Here, however, tax analysts get a rare break. In contrast with speeding and many other offences, aggressiveness and ease of detection are not related in tax. Very aggressive tax positions (such as under-reporting of tips as income) may be almost undetectable while less aggressive positions (such as deductions from known tax shelters) may be relatively easy for the government to find. Thus, the main optimal deterrence complication with accounting for detection uncertainty does not arise in the tax setting. Plenty of other complications exist, however.

Probability of detection varies dramatically from one tax return item to another. Income understatements are certain to be identified if income is subject to information reporting but are much more difficult to detect otherwise. Undeclared income not subject to information reporting is less detectable than many deduction overstatements, which themselves vary in detectability. For a given deduction, the size of the overstatement affects the ease of detection. Items subject to mandatory disclosure have a different probability of detection than items that are not required to be disclosed. The detection probability varies among the disclosed items as well, depending on whether the required disclosure is on a case-by-case or the aggregate basis.[130]

These nuances have received some attention in the literature, but progress has been slow. Over two decades ago, Steven Klepper and Daniel Nagin offered a model of taxpayer decision-making based on the assumption that the perceived probability of

---

126. See Gary S. Becker, *Crime and Punishment: An Economic Approach*, 76(2) J. Pol. Econ. 169 (1968).
127. See Allingham & Sandmo, above n. 48.
128. In the general optimal deterrence literature where the optimal sanction equals the external harm, the multiplier is the inverse of the probability of detection, p. See Richard Craswell, *Deterrence and Damages: The Multiplier Principle and Its Alternatives*, 97(7) Mich. L. Rev. 2185, 2186 (1999). In tax evasion models, the payment (including tax) reflecting the detection uncertainty is the tax multiplied by $(1-p)/p$. See Slemrod & Yitzhaki, above n. 47, at 1430; Shlomo Yitzhaki, *A Note on Income Tax Evasion: A Theoretical Analysis*, 3(2) J. Pub. Econ. 201, 201 (1974).
129. See Craswell, above n. 128, at 2193–2194.
130. The case-by-case disclosures are required for the so-called listed and reportable transactions. See Treas. Reg. § 1.6011-4; the aggregate disclosure is required for uncertain tax items reportable on Schedule UTP. See J. Richard Harvey, Jr., *Schedule UTP–Why So Few Disclosures?*, 139 Tax Notes 69 (2014).

detection varies across different lines of a tax return.[131] They found that actual taxpayers strongly respond to these variations.[132] This line of research is promising, but it has seen only a limited development thus far.[133] Similarly limited is the analysis of the relationship between the detection likelihood and the size of the tax understatement – whether absolute[134] or relative.[135] Recent articles introduce a detection probability that varies with income into the basic tax evasion model,[136] and study the effects of mandatory[137] and voluntary disclosure of uncertain tax positions.[138] There is some empirical evidence supporting the recent models.[139]

Overall, there is a solid economic foundation for incorporating the detection variations into the analysis of sanctions. Actual tax penalties reflect the basic theoretical point that difficult-to-detect violations should be subject to higher penalties. More research is needed to make the models more realistic and to produce more nuanced empirical estimates. But no conceptually insurmountable problems appear to exist, and the continuing scholarly interest in the subject is encouraging.

[F] History: A Persistent Puzzle

Finally, most sanctions increase with the number of previous offences. From the so-called three strikes laws adopted by many US states[140] to the special chapter of the US Sentencing Guidelines dedicated to the subject,[141] history-based graduation of sanctions is perhaps the most widespread and widely known feature of punishment regimes. Equally well-known in the law and economics literature is the fact that history-based graduation is very difficult to explain. In the words of Winand Emons who has studied this issue for some time, '[a]t the very best the literature … has shown that under rather special circumstances escalating penalty schemes may be optimal'.[142] At the same time, plausible arguments suggest that optimal sanctions should decline

---

131. Steven Klepper & Daniel Nagin, *The Anatomy of Tax Evasion*, 5(1) J. L. Econ. & Org. 1, 2 (1989).
132. Klepper & Nagin, above n. 131, at 22.
133. One of a few more recent papers is Jorge Martinez-Vazquez & Mark Rider, *Multiple Modes of Tax Evasion: Theory and Evidence*, 58(1) Nat'l Tax J. 51 (2005).
134. See Yitzhaki, *On the Excess Burden of Tax Evasion*, above n. 69.
135. See Alex Raskolnikov, *Crime and Punishment in Taxation: Deceit, Deterrence, and the Self-Adjusting Penalty*, 106(3) Colum. L. Rev. 569 (2006).
136. See Henrik Jacobsen Kleven, Martin B. Knudsen, Claus Thustrup Kreiner, Søren Pedersen & Emmanuel Saez, *Unwilling or Unable to Cheat? Evidence from a Tax Audit Experiment in Denmark*, 79(3) Econometrica 651 (2011).
137. See Mills, Robinson & Sansing, above n. 59.
138. See Beck, Davis & Jung, *Taxpayer Disclosure*, above n. 57; Lisa De Simone, Richard C. Sansing & Jeri K. Seidman, *When Are Enhanced Relationship Tax Compliance Programs Mutually Beneficial?*, 88(6) Acct. Rev. 1971 (2013).
139. See Paul J. Beck & Petro Lisowsky, *Tax Uncertainty and Voluntary Real-Time Tax Audits*, 89(3) Acct. Rev. 867 (2014).
140. See Thomas B. Marvell & Carlisle E. Moody, *The Lethal Effects of Three-Strikes Laws*, 30(1) J. Legal Stud. 89, 89 (2001).
141. See United States Sentencing Commission, *Guidelines Manual*, §4 (1 November 2014).
142. Winand Emons, *A Note on the Optimal Punishment for Repeat Offenders*, 23 Int'l Rev. L. & Econ. 253, 254 (2003).

with an increase in the number of previous offences, especially for regulatory offences such as tax law violations.[143] Most likely, explanations for the history-based graduation lie outside the economic analysis of law.

§13.04   CONCLUSION

What follows from identifying six degrees of sanction graduation and reviewing their economic rationales? Sanctions can be highly complex. Many real-life sanctions *are* quite complex. This complexity is under-appreciated in legal discourse and under-conceptualized in economic theory. If one thinks that sanctions create real-world incentives, there is much to examine and explain.

It may be tempting to suggest that behavioural law and economics is the most promising area of future research. I am somewhat sceptical. Once we start incorporating the nuances of human psychology into the rational actor model, it becomes implausible to analyse sanctions at large. For example, both speeding fines and prison sentences depend on the aggressiveness of a violation. But it is quite obvious that people think about these two sanctioning regimes in very different terms. So it is both understandable and appropriate that the most recent comprehensive volume on behavioural law and economics does not have a chapter on the general behavioural analysis of sanctions.[144] In contrast, insights from the standard economic theory are more likely to apply across many different legal regimes. Thus, the payoffs from developing further insights using the basic rational actor model are significant.

One of the payoffs is to identify areas where sanctions complexity may be unnecessary, or at least excessive. Overly complicated sanctions are socially costly just as overly complicated rules are. In fact, sanctions are particularly costly because they apply to violations of many different legal rules. So we should pay special attention to sanctions complexity. Does it make sense to have a penalty that varies along five different dimensions at the same time? Why have fines that give rise to incentives that we do not clearly understand, let alone intend? Recognizing six degrees of sanctions graduation – both in theory and in practice – illuminates our thinking about these and many other questions of legal punishment.

---

143. See David A. Dana, *Rethinking the Puzzle of Escalating Penalties for Repeat Offenders*, 110(5) Yale L.J. 733, 737–739 (2001).
144. See Eyal Zamir & Doron Teichman (eds), *The Oxford Handbook of Behavioral Economics and the Law* (Oxford University Press, 2014). In contrast, this volume has chapters dedicated to ten different substantive legal regimes as well as to regulation (at large), judicial decision-making and plea bargaining.

CHAPTER 14

Some Cautions Regarding Tax Simplification

J. Clifton Fleming Jr

§14.01 INTRODUCTION

Tax simplification enjoys the attractiveness of being the opposite of tax complexity, which is usually viewed askance because of its possible negative effects. For example, tax complexity might have a detrimental impact on taxpayer behaviour because taxpayers might find the complexity so overwhelming that they do not comply completely or at all.[1] Moreover, average taxpayers might believe that they are justified in cheating because wealthy individuals and companies that can afford superior professional advice have an unfair advantage over ordinary people.[2] Finally, the revenue administration might not be able to effectively police compliance because revenue officers might not be able to master the complex rules or because the intricate audits that result might be so time consuming that their number falls below an optimal enforcement level.[3]

In addition, complexity might have a negative effect on the tax base because complexity often creates planning opportunities. To the extent of those opportunities, taxation is effectively elective and taxpayers always elect contrary to the interests of the

---

1. See Joint Committee on Taxation, *Study of the Overall State of the Federal Tax System and Recommendations for Simplification, Pursuant to Section 8022(3)(B) of the Internal Revenue Code of 1986, Volume 1: Study of the Overall State of the Federal Tax System*, JCS-3-01, 101–111 (April 2001).
2. Joint Committee on Taxation, *Study of the Overall State of the Federal Tax System*, above n. 1, at 101–111.
3. Joint Committee on Taxation, *Study of the Overall State of the Federal Tax System*, above n. 1, at 101–111.

fisc.[4] This point has implications for the distribution of the tax burden because high income taxpayers usually have access to the professional advice and capital required to exploit electivity while middle and lower income taxpayers often do not.

Because of these and other factors, tax simplification invites uncritical approval and implementation for no other reason than that it is the converse of tax complexity. This tendency should be resisted by tax policy-makers because it is a dangerously facile approach that can lead to untoward results.

§14.02   SIMPLIFICATION IS NOT ALWAYS GOOD

For example, a capitation tax is the essence of simplicity. The government's revenue goal is divided by the number of taxpayers and *voila!* – the amount to be paid by each taxpayer is known without the complexities of deductions, capital cost allowances, separation of income into various classes, tax accounting rules, etc.[5] However, if a capitation tax were used as a major part of a country's revenue system, it would either impose crushing, regressive burdens on lower and middle income taxpayers or it would raise inadequate revenue, or it might do both.[6]

A second example to consider is an international income tax regime that: (1) avoids the complexities of consolidated accounting for corporate groups by employing separate accounting for all entities, (2) avoids the complexity of the controlled foreign corporation (CFC) rules by having none,[7] and (3) avoids the complexity of transfer pricing rules by accepting all intra-group transaction prices at face value.[8] This would be a marvellously simple system but it would allow massive base erosion through profit shifting that would have a negative effect on the revenue available for government functions. Moreover, by encouraging domestic taxpayers to make their new investments and expansions in low-tax countries, it would lead to inefficient choices regarding business location.

As a final example, when I taught at the University of Nairobi more than thirty-five years ago, I discovered that the Kenyan income tax Act of the day dealt with

---

4. See, generally, J. Clifton Fleming, Jr., Robert J. Peroni & Stephen E. Shay, *Worse Than Exemption*, 59 Emory L.J. 79 (2009) (explaining tax planning opportunities under the highly complex US international income tax system).
5. See Joseph J. Cordes, 'Head Tax', in Joseph J. Cordes, Robert D. Ebel & Jane G. Gravelle (eds), *The Encyclopedia of Taxation and Tax Policy* 175 (Urban Institute Press, 2005).
6. See Joseph M. Dodge, J. Clifton Fleming, Jr. & Robert J. Peroni, *Federal Income Tax: Doctrine, Structure & Policy*, 74 (4th ed., Lexis Nexis, 2012). For an effort to defend the capitation tax approach, see Jeffrey A. Schoenblum, *Tax Fairness or Unfairness? A Consideration of the Philosophical Bases for Unequal Taxation of Individuals*, 12 Am. J. Tax Pol'y 221 (1995).
7. See Deloitte, *Guide to Controlled Foreign Company Regimes*, 71 (2014), available at: www 2.deloitte.com/content/dam/Deloitte/global/Documents/Tax/dttl-tax-guide-to-cfc-regimes-2102 14.pdf (accessed on 21 October 2014) (listing countries, including Belgium, India, Ireland, and Switzerland, that have no CFC regime).
8. See Matthew Karnitschnig & Robin van Daalen, *Business-Friendly Bureaucrat Helped Build Tax Haven in Luxembourg*, Wall Street Journal, A1 (22 October 2014) (describing how Luxembourg operated without established transfer pricing rules until 2013); KPMG Ireland, *Irish Transfer Pricing FAQ*, www.kpmg.com/ie/en/issuesandinsights/articlespublications/pages/transfer-pricing-faq.aspx (accessed 21 October 2014) (explaining that Ireland did not have a comprehensive transfer pricing regime before 2010).

the consequences of corporate mergers by providing that such a transaction was not a taxable event if the Finance Minister found that the merger was in the public interest. On its face, this was a major simplification measure but it embraced all the evils of non-transparent law including the danger of corruption.

As these examples show, simplification is not always good and complexity is not always bad. Thus, a reflexive embrace of simplification proposals does not represent good policy-making. In practice, choices between greater and lesser simplification must be weighed with great care against other important values such as preservation of the tax base, distributional considerations, efficiency considerations, administrability, and governmental integrity. The following comments based on US experience may be helpful in determining how to perform this balancing process.

§14.03 COMMENTS ON THE BALANCING PROCESS

First, large US multinationals complain vigorously about complexity only when it involves compliance with provisions that prevent them from eroding the tax base. They are perfectly willing to deal with the complex tax provisions that reduce their tax liabilities.[9] Not surprisingly, they have the resources to deal with both kinds of complexity.[10] The need for simplification is an overblown concern with respect to large US corporations and that is surely the case in other countries as well.

At the other extreme, most wage earners satisfy their tax liabilities through withholding and have few deductions. For them, tax complexity is not a problem. To the extent they have complexity problems, it is mostly because governments have chosen to use the tax system to deliver various subsidies that have intricate qualification and limitation rules. That, however, is not tax law complexity; it is welfare law complexity, that must be evaluated and addressed in light of welfare system design criteria as well as its impact on the operation of the tax system.[11]

Thus, speaking broadly, the taxpayers who are the most burdened by tax law complexity are small business taxpayers who lack the resources of large corporations to deal with complexity but who nevertheless face many of the tax accounting, capital cost recovery and other intricacies faced by large corporations.[12] On this point, the

---

9. For example, US multinationals have effectively and quietly coped with the complex distinction between manufacturing and non-manufacturing income required by IRC §199, with various intricate look-through rules in the US foreign tax credit and Subpart F provisions, and with the challenging details of the IRC §902 deemed paid credit for foreign taxes.
10. One study found that, when measured as a percentage of revenues collected by the US federal government, compliance costs of large US corporations were lower than the compliance costs of individuals. See Marsha Blumenthal & Joel B. Slemrod, *The Compliance Cost of Taxing Foreign-Source Income: Its Magnitude, Determinants, and Policy Implications*, 2(1) Int'l Tax & Pub. Fin. 37, 39 (1995).
11. See Joint Committee on Taxation, *Study of the Overall State of the Federal Tax System*, above n. 1, at 68–72; Joel Slemrod & Jon Bakija, *Taxing Ourselves: A Citizen's Guide to the Debate over Taxes*, 169–170 (4th ed., MIT Press, 2009).
12. See President's Economic Recovery Advisory Board, *The Report on Tax Reform Options: Simplification, Compliance, and Corporate Taxation*, 46 (2010) ('[C]ompliance costs fall disproportionately on smaller businesses, as smaller firms bear a larger compliance burden relative to the size of their business than do larger firms'); President's Advisory Panel on Federal Tax

challenge for tax system reformers is to develop simpler rules that ease small business burdens without creating holes that large corporations can drive a truck through.

A second observation from US experience is that tax policy debate participants who have a 'small government' agenda can use tax expenditure analysis (TEA) to argue that subsidies delivered through the tax system to individuals in need are bad per se because they add complexity to the tax statute.[13] This is a misuse of TEA. TEA cannot be fairly understood as a weapon to advance an agenda of limiting humanitarian subsidies that are delivered through the tax system. TEA simply demands that those subsidies be subjected to the same holistic cost/benefit scrutiny that would hopefully be applied to direct cash spending by the government for any end.[14]

Because TEA involves much more than a consideration of complexity, it has only a minor role to play in the complexity discussion. It is not an automatic disqualifier of subsidies delivered through the tax system.[15]

But it would also be a mistake to go to the other extreme and argue that humanitarian tax subsidies should be exempted from TEA precisely because they are motivated by humanitarian purposes. Two US examples will illustrate this point.

Owners of their own residences are permitted an income tax deduction for interest paid on debt incurred to purchase their residence. This deduction is not an element of a normative income tax. It is typically justified as subsidy assistance to lower and middle income taxpayers to help them achieve the 'American dream' of owning their own homes.

But excellent economic studies suggest that a substantial part of the subsidy may be captured by real estate brokers and the financial industry, that what remains for the homeowners disproportionately benefits upper income taxpayers rather than the middle and lower income earners, and that the overall effect is to make residences more expensive than would otherwise be the case.[16]

If such a regime were proposed as a cash subsidy to help lower and middle income earners achieve the American dream, it would be firmly rejected. Tax expenditure analysis would prevent these flaws from being hidden by dressing the subsidy as

---

Reform, *Simple, Fair, and Pro-Growth: Proposals to Fix America's Tax System*, 3 (2005) ('Studies have found that the smaller the business, the higher the cost of complying with the tax code per dollar of revenue').

13. See Joint Committee on Taxation, *Study of the Overall State of the Federal Tax System*, above n. 1, at 70–72 (explaining how tax expenditures increase the complexity of the US federal income tax); William M. McBride, *A Brief History of Tax Expenditures*, Tax Foundation Fiscal Fact No. 391, 8 (2013), available at: http://taxfoundation.org/sites/taxfoundation.org/files/docs/ff391. pdf (accessed on 23 October 2014).

14. See Slemrod & Bakija, above n. 11, at 169–170.

15. See J. Clifton Fleming, Jr. & Robert J. Peroni, *Reinvigorating Tax Expenditure Analysis and Its International Dimension*, 27(3) Va. Tax Rev. 437, 487–489 (2008).

16. See President's Advisory Panel on Federal Tax Reform, *Simple, Fair, and Pro-Growth: Proposals to Fix America's Tax System*, above n. 12, at 70–72; Joint Committee on Taxation, *Present Law, Data, and Analysis Relating to Tax Incentives for Homeownership*, JCX-50-11, 27–28 (2011); Joint Committee on Taxation, *Present Law, Data, and Analysis Relating to Tax Incentives for Residential Real Estate*, JCX-10-13, 36–37 (2013); Adam J. Cole, Geoffrey Gee & Nicholas Turner, *The Distributional and Revenue Consequences of Reforming the Mortgage Interest Deduction*, 64(4) Nat'l Tax J. 977 (2011).

a tax provision. This tax provision ought not be sheltered from TEA because it is said to have a humanitarian objective.

A second example is that US income tax law provides two different tax credits for the costs of tertiary education. This is justified as helping America compete in a globalized world and as helping low and middle income Americans achieve the dream of higher education. There is evidence that tertiary institutions, many of which are non-governmental and some of which are operated for profit, capture most of these subsidies by the simple expedient of raising their tuition charges.[17] If a cash subsidy programme were proposed that effectively transferred money from the public treasury to tertiary institutions without significantly reducing student costs or without buying any research product for the government, the proposal would surely fail. TEA prevents these flaws from being hidden under tax camouflage, and the education credits ought not be shielded from TEA by the fact that they are said to be motivated by public interest and humanitarian objectives.

Having said all this, I recognize the frustrating reality that in the present political situation in some countries, including my own, it is often impossible to enact direct expenditure provisions for the benefit of those who truly need special treatment. Often the only way to deliver benefits to those individuals is through tax subsidies that cut against the goal of a simpler tax system. In that case, the choice is not between a direct expenditure programme and a tax provision; it is usually a choice between a complex addition to the tax system and doing nothing at all.[18]

The most trenchant US example is the significantly complex wage supplement provided to workers through a provision called the Earned Income Tax Credit. Because of the wage structure at the bottom of the US labour market, it is quite possible for a person to have a full-time job and a secondary job and still be on the margin of poverty. In current American politics, direct cash transfers to those individuals are impossible to enact into law. Thus, the choice is to either deliver a wage supplement through the tax system or do nothing. Here the role of TEA is to force a decision as to whether the tax system subsidy is so expensive, so difficult to confine to the desired population, so prone to fraud, and so loaded with perverse incentives that doing nothing is indeed the better alternative, or whether these enumerated problems either do not exist or are small enough to be tolerable when the alternative is nothing. That kind of analysis should not be forgone simply because the subsidy has a humanitarian objective.

But to return to the main point, although eliminating subsidies from the tax law has a simplifying effect, that is a minor theme in TEA. TEA is an important tax policy

---

17. See Stephanie Riegg Cellini & Claudia Goldin, *Does Federal Student Aid Raise Tuition? New Evidence on For-Profit Colleges*, NBER Working Paper No. 17827 (2012); see also Marie Sapirie, *Tax Incentives for Education: Not Making the Grade*, 137(4) Tax Notes 335, 337–338 (2012).
18. See Jasper L. Cummings, Jr. & Alan J.J. Swirski, *Interview with Congressman Ben Cardin (D. Md.)*, 21(3) ABA Section of Taxation Newsletter 17, 19 (Spring 2002) ('It is better if you can do things directly rather than using the tax Code, but when we are talking about trying to help people, empower people – whether employers to provide jobs for people coming off of welfare or finding jobs for people who need training – sometimes it is a lot easier for us to get those policies done through the tax Code and pay the price in the complexity of the tax Code, than to do nothing and to have people who can't find employment in our community').

analysis tool because it illuminates hard choices. It does not, however, have a significant role to play in the tax simplification conversation.

Another observation that is relevant to the tax simplification conversation is that tax policy is a struggle between self-interested parties. As the American tax policy commentator, Louis Eisenstein, put it, '[o]ur taxes reflect a continuing struggle among contending interests for the privilege of paying the least'.[19] Thus, the contending parties will employ rhetorical devices, including paeans to simplification, to dress up their self-interested pleading as something else. Good tax policy analysis, including the pursuit of simplification, requires us to deflect those rhetorical devices and get to the core of the matter.

Finally, policy-makers must realize that real world tax systems are inherently complex and that if nations try to deny that reality by enacting laws in generalities or as statements of principles, the complexity will merely re-emerge in other places. Perhaps it will appear in administrative law issued by the revenue authority[20] or perhaps in judicial decisions.[21] And if matters migrate to the courts, those institutions will be sorely tempted to create anti-avoidance rules which may be simple to state but which can introduce great uncertainty as well as complexity into the tax system.[22]

§14.04   CONCLUSION

Once we recognize that the extreme examples of simple taxes with which I began my analysis are 'non-starters', then we must accept that our complex national and world economies demand correspondingly complex tax regimes, and that the complexity will inevitably reside somewhere in the legal system where it will have to be endured.[23] We most certainly should pursue the goal of tax system simplification but in doing so, we must thoughtfully balance simplification objectives against tax base preservation, tax burden distribution concerns, efficiency concerns, administrability, and political realities. The creation of institutional structures that ensure that simplification always receives appropriate consideration in this process would clearly constitute an important contribution. Compromise will, however, be the inevitable result. Consequently, we should not have unrealistic expectations regarding the amount of simplification that can be achieved. As a former US Treasury official has observed:

---

19. Louis Eisenstein, *The Ideologies of Taxation*, 3–4 (Ronald Press, 1961).
20. See Joint Committee on Taxation, *Study of the Overall State of the Federal Tax System*, above n. 1, at 64–65.
21. See Joint Committee on Taxation, *Study of the Overall State of the Federal Tax System*, above n. 1, at 65–66.
22. See Tracy A. Kaye, *The Regulation of Corporate Tax Shelters in the United States*, 58(Supp.) Am. J. Comp. L. 585 (2010) (including a discussion of the uncertainty and complexity introduced into the US federal income tax system by the judicially created economic substance doctrine); Martin J. McMahon, Jr., *Living With the Codified Economic Substance Doctrine*, 128(7) Tax Notes 731 (2010) (same).
23. See Joint Committee on Taxation, *Study of the Overall State of the Federal Tax System*, above n. 1, at 58–100 (listing and describing the sources of complexity in the US federal tax system, most of which are unavoidable).

The problem with simplification ... is not that there's any disagreement that simplification is needed. The problem is that it's not really a priority. It's on everyone's list of important tax policy objectives, but it's just never close enough to the top that it generates serious momentum.[24]

---

24. Jasper L. Cummings, Jr. & Alan J.J. Swirski, *Interview with Robert P. Hanson*, 22(2) ABA Section of Taxation News Quarterly 20, 22 (Winter 2003). Mr Hanson served as Tax Legislative Counsel in the US Treasury Department during the George W. Bush Administration.

CHAPTER 15

The Office of Tax Simplification and Its Complexity Index

*John Whiting, Jeremy Sherwood & Gareth Jones**

§15.01   INTRODUCTION: THE OFFICE OF TAX SIMPLIFICATION

The Office of Tax Simplification (OTS) in the UK was established in July 2010 as a result of the Coalition (Conservative and Liberal Democrat parties) agreement consequent on the formation of the new government after the May 2010 election.[1] It came about in response to a growing body of views that the complexity of the UK's tax system was increasing unreasonably and was becoming a problem.[2]

The OTS was established as an independent agency of HM Treasury (HMT). Funding is provided by HMT; there is no formal statutory constitution or Parliamentary oversight. The OTS is overseen by a Board which comprises its Chairman and Tax Director, together with a very senior official from each of HM Revenue & Customs

---

* The authors would like to place on record the considerable input received from Caroline Turnbull-Hall of PricewaterhouseCoopers and Phillip Rice of the Knowledge, Analysis & Intelligence (KAI) team of HM Revenue & Customs to the development of the index and on drafts of this chapter and preceding papers. We are also grateful for the comments received from a wide range of other commentators in response to previous versions of the index, all of which have helped shape this final version. Any views expressed in this chapter are those of the authors and are not to be taken as an indication of the view of HM Treasury.
1. Documents relating to the OTS's formation and running and all its reports and papers are published on our website at: www.gov.uk/government/organisations/office-of-tax-simplification.
2. See, in particular, the Conservative Working Party report *Making Taxes Simpler: the final report of a Working Party chaired by Lord Howe of Aberavon* (July 2008), available at: http://conservativehome.blogs.com/torydiary/files/making_taxes_simpler.pdf (accessed on 18 December 2014).

(HMRC)[3] and HMT plus two independent members. Reports are addressed to the Chancellor of the Exchequer and Treasury Ministers and are all published.

The OTS's Chairman is the Rt. Hon. Michael Jack, a former MP and Treasury Minister and its Tax Director is John Whiting, one of the co-authors of this chapter and formerly a partner with PricewaterhouseCoopers. Both are part-time appointments; day-to-day running of the OTS rests with Jeremy Sherwood, also a co-author and the Head of Office. Staffing of the OTS is a mix of civil servants drawn from HMRC and HMT, who normally work with the OTS for twelve to fifteen months, and part-time secondees from the private sector. The latter are typically with the OTS for six months or so for two days a week: some are seconded to the Office by their firms; some are hired directly. The total staffing of the OTS is a maximum of six full-time equivalent staff members.

[A]   What Does the OTS Do?

The OTS takes on projects to study areas of the tax system with a view to developing recommendations for simplification. We aim to develop ideas for:

- technical simplification – so trimming or revising the tax code; and
- administrative simplification – making it easier to deal with the tax.

When the OTS was first set up, the thinking was that it would aim to trim the length of the tax code, and so would focus on the first category. However, it quickly became apparent that we could make simplification gains at least as much through the second category – indeed arguably this is more important as it is in effect the real 'user interface'. Our focus is simplification: we do not make tax rate or tax policy recommendations, but inevitably at times it is difficult to develop simplification ideas without touching on policy matters. Our test is whether something will deliver simplification; we will acknowledge and identify policy matters and will also have regard to revenue implications. In principle we should be revenue neutral in our reports but it is difficult to avoid revenue impacts (and 'winners and losers'): again our approach is to identify clearly where we think a revenue change is 'worth it' to generate a simplification dividend. At the end of the day it will be for Ministers to decide which of our recommendations to take forward and revenue implications will no doubt be a factor in their decision.

To develop our recommendations, we have made a virtue out of the necessity forced upon us by our small size. We have a policy of meeting with as wide a range of interested parties as possible during our projects: taxpayers (business and individual), tax advisers, representative bodies, academics and HMRC front line staff.[4] We work closely with HMRC and HMT at all times and receive particularly useful input from

---

3. The UK tax authority, formed in 2005 from the combination of the Inland Revenue and HM Customs & Excise.
4. To give an example, for our Partnerships report we held around fifty meetings and in doing so spoke to around one thousand people. See Office of Tax Simplification, 'Review of partnerships: update and call for evidence' (July 2014).

HMRC's Knowledge Analysis and Intelligence (KAI) team of economists and analysts. But our reports remain our own and independent: the key is that the recommendations are evidence-based and carefully tested out in our meetings and researches.

The OTS cannot change the law: we can only make recommendations. It is up to Ministers, with input from HMT and HMRC, to decide which ideas to take forward. Some smaller points, particularly administrative ones, can be taken forward by HMRC quickly but changes of any significance are normally taken forward by formal consultation.

[B]   What Have We Looked At So Far?

We have carried out projects on:

- tax reliefs;
- small business taxation (in various phases and some five reports);
- pensioners;
- share schemes (separately on 'approved' and 'unapproved' arrangements);
- employee benefits and expenses (three reports); and
- partnerships (two reports so far).

We are currently finalizing a major study on improving the competitiveness of the UK tax administration and an initial study of penalties. We are about to start a project on employment status.

We have also been carrying out a long-running underpinning project on complexity. This has led to papers on aspects including:

- length of legislation;
- thresholds;
- definitions in tax law; and
- complexity index (the subject of the main body of this chapter).

It is continuing into a study of the possible link between avoidance and complexity.

[C]   What Have We Learned So Far?

This chapter is not in any sense an evaluation of or report on the OTS. That will be the subject of a separate paper which will evaluate the work of the OTS, given that it formally comes to an end with the general election in the UK in May 2015.

We have at various times looked for lessons on what makes complexity – with a view to developing guidelines for avoiding unnecessary complexity. In our first small business report,[5] we reported that our researches had established the following as the

---

5. Office of Tax Simplification, *Small business tax review* (Interim Report), 5–6 (March 2011).

top causes of complexity (the top three are in order; the order of the other three is less certain):

(1) change (frequency and volume);
(2) PAYE/National Insurance Contribution issues (i.e., the differing rules for taxing income and subjecting it to national insurance (social security) contributions);
(3) HMRC administration and interactions;
(4) the employed/self-employed dividing line;
(5) allowances for capital expenditure: *capital allowances v. depreciation*;
(6) value added tax (VAT) boundary issues.

The guidelines that we have developed for avoiding complexity are:

- *stop changing things*: is your change really needed? (common feedback has been that once businesses 'get the hang of' something, it changes);
- *consult*: the people who will be affected ... consider their *ability* to understand;
- *resist pleas* by *special interest groups* for (unnecessary?) exceptions;
- *boundaries and fault lines* – aim for low substitution elasticity (avoid distortions), align with *commonsense* boundaries;
- *anti-avoidance*: detailed rules can create more loopholes, leading to layers of legislation ... consider broad principles;
- use existing *categories and definitions*; align with common sense;
- *vagueness* can be an advantage of the law (e.g., VAT deliberately 'sketched out' for case law to decide ... but double edged?);
- consider *administration* from the start; and
- *keep rules up to date* with the changing environment (sunset clauses or set reviews could help).

An overriding point, that is probably obvious but cannot be stated often enough, is that *fairness and simplicity pull against each other*.

We have had a fair measure of success in terms of volume of recommendations taken forward, with our 'score' running at well over 50%. This is a very crude measure and we are considering ways of arriving at a better method of evaluation of the impact of the OTS. At the same time, the man or woman in the street will have seen little impact of our work and undoubtedly still thinks the tax system is too complex.

In many ways the OTS has been an experiment to see if simplification is possible and practical. We think we have proved successful and undoubtedly provide value for money (but then again, we would say that). Partly that is due to our working methods: (a) we look at discrete areas of the tax code and do so relatively quickly; (b) we develop practical, evidence-based recommendations to make the case for change based on wide-scale gathering of input from all parties; and (c) we test our ideas with relevant parties, including especially HMRC so that, although in the end we will say what we think is right, we can have some confidence that most points are seen as at least possible by the tax authorities.

The remainder of this chapter will discuss the OTS's Complexity Index. A version of this chapter is published on the OTS's website.

§15.02   THE OTS COMPLEXITY PROJECT AND THE COMPLEXITY INDEX

Soon after the Office of Tax Simplification (OTS) was established, we were inevitably challenged on the question 'what is simplification'. The answer to that question was couched in terms of making the tax system easier to deal with for all concerned – taxpayers, agents and HMRC – with the important connotation that it encompassed both technical (i.e., legislative) simplification and administrative improvements. Indeed, the latter has become the more productive area for simplification in many ways.

However, discussion of the definition of simplification in turn raised the question of 'what is complexity'. Our first small business project spent time ascertaining small businesses' views on what, to them, were the main causes of complexity.[6] With these results, and the general experience of our first year's work, we took on a general project on complexity, with the broad aim of answering that question and trying to develop some lessons on how to avoid adding to complexity. This would be part of our legacy to those who come after us.

Our complexity project has a number of strands but the main component is the subject of this chapter: the development of a complexity index.

[A]   The Purpose of the Index

The index was originally designed to give a single 'star rating' for each area of tax. This could be used to prioritize future OTS projects - as it would be possible to identify, on a relative basis, which areas of tax are most complex.[7]

It is important that the index be able to indicate not only which areas of tax are most complex, but also why. This informs the structure of the index: the requirement for the index to be a diagnostic tool has not changed over time, although other uses of the index are also possible and are discussed below (§15.02[B]).

This chapter sets out a final version of the OTS's methodology for assessing the relative complexity of a tax measure. By 'tax measure', for these purposes we mean a 'chunk' of legislation (normally primary, but also including secondary legislation where relevant) describing and setting out the rules for a part of the tax code. Following on from further comments (including at a presentation delivered at the International Tax Analysis Conference of the Economic and Social Research Council in January

---

6. Office of Tax Simplification, *Small business tax review* (Interim Report), above n. 5 at 5–6; as can be seen, the top three causes of complexity were established as: (1) volume of change, (2) PAYE/NIC boundary issues, and (3) HMRC administration.
7. The index is naturally focused on the tax system but we have been aware from the outset that the principles and structure used could make it usable in other areas of legislation. With this in mind, the OTS has shown the Index to people involved in other areas of the law and informal feedback has been positive. Inevitably some different indicators would have to be developed: for example, avoidance risk would not be relevant in many areas but assessment of guidance probably would be.

2014[8]), the index has been modified to measure relative tax complexity more accurately. This has included simplifying the weightings system substantially to remove the need for a potentially confusing aggregation formula, as well as some changes to the indicators used.[9]

The constitution of what is, and is not, complex changes with the cultural, socio-economic and technological climate. As the tax system evolves, the assumptions on which the index is based could change; as an example, if annual changes were no longer made in a single Finance Bill, a change would be required to the 'number of Finance Bills' section of the index.[10] The index will require monitoring to ensure the indicators are kept up to date. Thus work on complexity is not complete, and indeed probably never will be!

The index is still best used as a diagnostic tool rather than as a rigorous academic analysis of complexity. The index is valuable in identifying what areas of tax are most complex and why, but the measuring factors it uses are indicators (i.e., symptoms) of complexity rather than the direct causes. And it is important to remember that it is a relative measure, not an absolute measure of complexity.

As a diagnostic tool, it succeeds, which gives it a good variety of uses and applications. However, as a precise measure of complexity, it may not, as there may not be 1:1 mapping between complexity and the indicators: there could be complex interactions between indicators. This is compounded by difficulties in establishing an objective definition of complexity.

Figure 15.1   Potential Models of Complexity

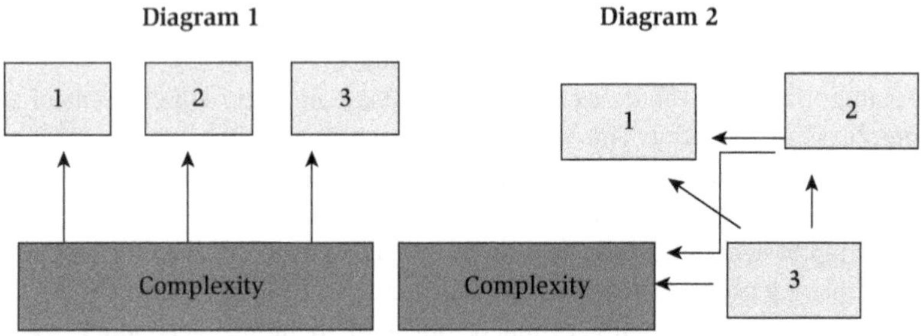

Note: An arrow indicates a sufficient relationship between two concepts; so in diagram 1, if a tax is complex, this results in indicator 1 occurring.

---

8. See www.esrc.ac.uk/hmrc/conference.
9. For example, avoidance risk was changed significantly.
10. For those unfamiliar with the UK tax system, it is important to appreciate that the UK has an annual process of change to the tax system. This starts with the annual Budget speech, usually involves consultation on the main measures and culminates in the legislation necessary to effect the changes being included in the annual Finance Bill. The point is that there will always be a Finance Bill in a calendar year (occasionally there are two) which will include almost all of the changes to the primary tax legislation for the year. Changes to secondary legislation – statutory instruments – can be made at any time.

In Figure 15.1, the model in Diagram 1 is the assumption the index is based on, in which complexity causes particular 'symptoms' of the tax system, which are measured as indicators. It would be naïve, however, to assume that the indicators have a sufficient or necessary relationship with complexity.[11] In reality (e.g., Diagram 2) the truth could be much more complex; complexity may only give rise to a few (or no) indicators, and there may be other factors which are not measured here, or one of the indicators could be a cause of complexity rather than an effect.

[B]   How Would the Index Be Used in Practice?

We envisage that the index could be used in two ways:

- to prioritize and target efforts to simplify the tax system (i.e., to assess the existing system); and
- to give policy-makers a tool to track the relative complexity of their policy changes (i.e., to monitor changes to the system).

The first of these could be valuable for both the OTS and policy professionals in HMRC. As there are a large number of tax measures and sections in the index, a regular review using the index could be done to identify which areas of the tax system are displaying relatively high levels of complexity. The index can then be used to diagnose why the tax system is complex in these areas, and may also indicate what could be done to simplify it.

For instance, a policy-maker could look at the index and see that the rules around plant and machinery are particularly complex. They could then look at the indicators and see that this is because of the complex guidance and the large number of pages of legislation. This may then inform a project to review the plant and machinery rules in detail, with a priority of removing obsolete information and making guidance clearer and more available.

The second way in which the index could be used would be to give policy-makers the chance to track changes in relative complexity to their parts of the tax system over time. A new policy can result in changes to the tax system, such as changes in the number of reliefs or pages of legislation. These changes would be included in the index rankings, which would result in a change to the headline figure for the relevant tax measure. This would allow the impact of new policies on complexity to be assessed.[12]

---

11. A sufficient relationship is one such that A → B, where if A is true then B is also true. A necessary relationship is one where A ← B, so for A to be true, B must be true.
12. Whether such 'ratings' would be published is an interesting question. In discussions with French officials about tax complexity, the OTS was told about the French system which experimentally gives a 'star rating' of 1 (= simple) to 5 (= complex) to new legislation being introduced to Parliament.

Some complexity in the tax system is inevitable: life, business and tax are all complex. The OTS has previously distinguished between 'necessary' and 'unnecessary' complexity[13] as follows:

- necessary complexity is the minimum complexity necessary to achieve the policy aim to a sufficient extent: as noted, there will always be some complexity in a measure, though the key point is that this should be minimized as far as possible;
- unnecessary complexity is anything in addition to necessary complexity, such as duplicate processes, overly complex legislation, over-cautious anti-avoidance legislation or involved forms and procedures around compliance. A measure of unnecessary complexity (discussed below, §15.02[G]) will also need to be developed alongside this, to ensure that simplification can be feasibly achieved.

The two methods of using the index referred to above could ideally be done in parallel: this could integrate simplification of the tax system into the policy process, and would encourage policy-makers to identify simplification improvements to the tax system on a regular basis. In turn, this would help to ensure that simplification plays a part in keeping the tax system modernized and up to date with the current economic environment, as obsolete or burdensome tax measures could be removed on a timely basis (more timely at least than might otherwise be the case) if policy-makers were able to consider the complexity of their tax areas actively.

[C]   A Definition of Complexity for the Index

Before attempting to actually measure complexity, it is important that we are clear about complexity. The original intention of the index was to have a single 'star rating', but this seemed to us very simplistic and we wanted to develop a more sensitive tool. In particular we wanted to assess the intrinsic complexity in a tax and the impact of that complexity. The index was later developed to include two figures:

- *the underlying complexity*: a measurement of the structural complexity of a tax measure, based on the policy, legislative and administrative complexity;
- *the impact of complexity*: a measure of the costs of complexity in the tax system, to both the taxpayer and HMRC.

The separate consideration of these two figures is very important - the distinction between complexity and its impact is very clear when an example is considered.

---

13. The OTS is indebted to Professor David Ulph of St Andrews University (and author of Chapter 4 of this volume) who introduced us to the idea of necessary and unnecessary complexity during our early work on complexity. The definitions and discussion of the terms are the OTS's.

To give such an example: the Annual Investment Allowance (AIA) is a tax measure[14] which adds complexity to the tax system, as it provides another option to taxpayers to choose from, increases the amount of legislation, etc. However, it reduces the impact of the complexity of the tax system, as it effectively removes 99% of businesses from the administration burden of capital allowances.

This points to two important features of the complexity scores, both of which are important but neither of which is surprising:

- there is no established relationship between the underlying complexity and the impact of complexity;[15] and
- in some cases reducing the impact of complexity upon taxpayers may require additional underlying complexity.

The factors which affect the impact of complexity are the ones which need to be dealt with to produce much of the benefit to taxpayers.

Underlying complexity can be loosely defined as a measure of the complexity of the 'maze' a taxpayer would be required to go through to comply with their tax responsibilities and to understand their tax obligations (and the result of those obligations) with no prior knowledge. Navigability of the tax system is absolutely vital for a taxpayer new to a particular area or the tax system as a whole. The ability to easily know the tax outcome of an investment could present an advantage to, for example, multinationals hoping to invest in the UK.[16] The underlying complexity of the tax system is as important as the impact of complexity, but for very different reasons.[17]

The index cannot in its current state indicate what complexity an individual taxpayer may experience while navigating the tax system, as this is not what it has been designed to do. This data is better found through using alternate tools such as 'total cost to serve' to identify what steps an individual customer has to take.

---

14. The AIA allows a business that invests in plant and machinery – as defined – to claim 100% of the cost of the investment against its taxable profits for the year in which the spending takes place. Thus the business can write off the investment completely for tax purposes, irrespective of the amount of depreciation charged in the accounts. The AIA replaces depreciation, which is not tax deductible. One issue with the AIA is that the amount allowed to be 'expensed' has changed regularly; it is currently GBP 500,000 but is due to be reduced to GBP 25,000 from 1 January 2016.
15. Though a regression analysis could be done to review whether there is a relationship between the two.
16. Although many of those companies would no doubt have financial advisers, this simply displaces the point - it is valuable to a financial adviser to painlessly know the outcome of an investment in advance.
17. An analogy the OTS often uses is that of the computer: we suspect everyone reading this chapter, and almost all the people we talk to, use a computer regularly. Most will find the interface and carrying out the tasks they do day-to-day easy. But few will have any idea of what really goes on inside the machine to make those tasks work. In other words, the underlying complexity is considerable; but its impact is well-managed to produce a simple, usable system. That said, the underlying complexity is far from eliminated and continues to have an impact: who has not been frustrated at their inability to get the computer to do something, or been surprised when a colleague shows with a few clicks how something can be done?

[D]   Indicators

As already mentioned, the complexity index is composed of indicators. Indicators are then aggregated to obtain figures for the underlying complexity and impact of complexity.

Before explaining the composition of the index, it is important to consider how tax complexity arises within the policy implementation process. Figure 15.2 provides a diagram which shows the different stages at which complexity can arise in the tax system: the policy, legislative and implementation stages.

Figure 15.2   Tax System Complexity Process Diagram

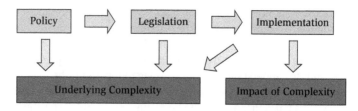

Figure 15.2 indicates that complexity in one part of the system will often (but not always) lead to complexity in subsequent parts,[18] as a complex policy invariably requires complex legislation, which may need to be interpreted into a complex administrative process.[19]

One point that Figure 15.2 illustrates is that while the underlying complexity is determined by complexity inherent in the entire process, the impact of complexity is determined largely by the implementation, i.e., the administrative process. This is for two reasons:

- as demonstrated above, additional complexity in a policy can actually reduce the impact of complexity; and
- good administrative processes will reduce the impact of what is otherwise a complex policy.

However, although the arrows in Figure 15.2 illustrate the main 'flows', it is clearly possible for arrows to flow in additional directions – complex policy and legislation can mean complex impact. But the point is that complex impact can be mitigated by care over implementation.

---

18. One example of an exception to this rule might be PAYE, the system of deduction of income tax from an employee's pay. The policy (income tax) might be thought of as fairly complex, the legislation is quite complex, but the implementation is very simple for at least one set of users. Essentially employees – who actually are due to pay the tax concerned – get the calculation, deduction and payment done for them. It is of course complex for HMRC and (especially) employers, so it does not solve all of the issues.
19. Though not necessarily, in terms of the *impact* of complexity, as the various factors on the index try to test.

[1]   Underlying Complexity

To develop the index we chose indicators based on the three areas of the policy implementation process and to use two measures of complexity for each (see below, paragraphs (1)–(6)). Using two for each area is both pragmatic and reflects findings from our work. The first iteration of the index used the majority of the indicators that are in the final version but two more were added (and two dropped) to give a better balance and an improved link to the theory discussed above.

[a]   Policy Complexity

(1) *Number of exemptions plus the number of reliefs* – much of the structural complexity within a tax system stems from the existence of reliefs and special cases. Increasing the number of exemptions also increases the complexity, as it increases the complexity in deciding whether or not a taxpayer is exempt from tax. It helps to think of the process for identifying eligibility for a tax exemption/relief as a flow chart: the more items which have to be sorted through to determine taxpayer treatment, the more complex the flow chart.

(2) *The number of Finance Acts with changes (since 2000[20])* – change is a significant contributor to complexity: during OTS consultations change has repeatedly been identified as the single largest cause of complexity. In particular, change makes it difficult to plan for the future, which has an effect on the future treatment of a transaction or course of action.

It has been suggested that this indicator does not measure change, as it does not measure the *magnitude* of each change. A possible method for changing this would be to, for example, grade each year based on the number of new reliefs, exemptions and information obligations a tax measure requires of the taxpayer, and then give an average of the measured period to indicate the magnitude of change over time (possibly scaling the weighting of each year so that more recent years have more weight, as recent change provides more complexity). This has not been attempted here because there is an overriding need to keep the Index simple, but we note it as a possible future refinement.

[b]   Legislative Complexity

(3) *The Gunning-fog readability index[21]* – this gives a comparative indication of how easy the legislation is to read. Other measures are available, but

---

20. Using the year 2000 as a base is entirely subjective – we could go back to the introduction of the first UK income tax in 1799 or start more recently. But our aim was to get a measure over a reasonable period of how much change there had been, given that volume of change has consistently been cited as the leading cause of complexity by businesses. A base year of 2000 gives a reasonable time span.
21. See the calculator provided at http://gunning-fog-index.com.

generally involve similar calculations, and for these purposes the main requirement is consistent appraisal across legislation.

One potential flaw is that the 'readability' test does not make any reference to definitions in legislation. The previous OTS project on definitions[22] identified several ways in which definitions contributed towards complexity. At its simplest, a multiplicity of definitions of the same term adds complexity.[23] We note in passing that section 301 of the Finance Act 2014 (which allows a definition included in any Act to be amended by secondary legislation and was influenced by the OTS paper) will lead to some improvements.

(4) *Number of pages of legislation*[24] – this measure gives a simple objective indication of complexity in terms of how long the legislation is. A complex policy can be expressed in simple, short legislation, and a simple policy in longer legislation. As is discussed in previous OTS publications, length of legislation is an indicator of complexity.

However, in using this indicator we readily acknowledge that there is a counter argument: that longer legislation can allow a measure to be better explained. Short legislation can appear almost as code. What has convinced us to continue using this indicator is, first, that the Gunning-Fog measure will balance this issue; but secondly (and importantly) that most people we talk to (and popular opinion) see length of legislation as an indication of complexity.

[c]   Operational Complexity

(5) *Complexity of HMRC guidance* – this is often the first, and sometimes only, place taxpayers will look when trying to meet their obligations. Therefore how easy it is to use is crucial. Complexity includes the availability of the guidance - sometimes guidance may not be in a single consolidated location and so will be more difficult to find. Here 'guidance' covers not only the HMRC manuals but also help-sheets and guides to completing HMRC forms. 'Guidance' could also be extended to cover the readability and accessibility of case law and extra-statutory concessions. These fall under the term 'guidance' in that they help with interpreting legislation. The effect of these on underlying complexity is not covered elsewhere in the index.

(6) *Complexity of information requirement to make a return* – this criterion was added to include the difficulty for a taxpayer of gathering the information to meet their obligations. It is typically easier for a taxpayer to understand their

---

22. See Office of Tax Simplification, 'Review of definitions in tax legislation' (3 October 2013), published on the OTS website and at www.gov.uk/government/publications/definitions-in-tax-legislation-and-their-contribution-to-complexity.

23. To give two of the examples in our definitions paper (above n. 22), the corporation tax legislation includes 45 definitions of 'group' and 37 of 'company'.

24. Ideally number of words should be used, as pages can be set out differently, different font sizes may be used or large footnotes can distort the true number of pages. However, it may be impractical to count the number of words unless a computer is involved.

tax obligations when less information is required to be collected and submitted to HMRC to make their return.

In the previous iteration of the index this factor was graded on a scale of 1 to 5. This approach had advantages, though a more objective approach may work better, such as by measuring the number of information obligations a taxpayer is required to provide to meet their obligation to HMRC.

[2]   *Impact of Complexity*

Impact of complexity is currently measured using four separate indicators:

(1) *Number of taxpayers* – it is uncontroversial to suggest that there is a direct relationship between the number of taxpayers a tax affects and the impact of its complexity: a tax measure's impact is doubled if it affects two taxpayers rather than one.

(2) *Aggregated compliance burden for a taxpayer and HMRC* – compliance burden measures the total cost to a taxpayer to fulfil their tax obligation. Costs to HMRC are also included, so that shifts between the two are captured, e.g., if HMRC creates new processes which remove obligations from HMRC but cost taxpayers or their agents more.

(3) *Average ability of taxpayers* – Again, it seems evident that the lower the taxpayer's ability, the greater the impact a complex tax area will have on them, as this affects their ability to deal with the tax.

This impact may already be reflected in the aggregated compliance burden. Irrespective of this, the information this indicator gives is important. We have therefore retained this figure in the index.

This differs substantially from the other indicators in that it is not an indicator of complexity, as the 'ability' of a taxpayer *determines* the impact of complexity rather than being a symptom of it.

(4) *Revenue at risk due to error, failure to take reasonable care (FTRC) and avoidance* – the final impact of a complex tax system is that the tax paid is not always correct: in 2012–2013, HMRC identified that they failed to collect GBP 34 billion worth of tax.[25] Of this, GBP 10.2 billion was due to either error, failure to take reasonable care, or avoidance. Each of these is a consequence of complexity inherent in the tax system. Loss of revenue affects the government's ability to maintain public finances and invest in new developmental projects.

Previously this measure only took account of the amount of tax at risk from avoidance. This has been extended to reflect the fact that complexity has an

---

25. See HMRC, *Measuring tax gaps 2014 edition*, 4 (16 October 2014), available at: https://www. gov.uk/government/publications/measuring-tax-gaps.

impact upon the error rate. Additionally, complexity can provide opportunities for avoidance: the OTS is starting work on this to see if it is possible to identify a more concrete link.

HMRC's current tax gap figures are not sufficient for this indicator – they fail to take into account errors in HMRC's favour, such as failure to adequately record all due expenses. HMRC do not currently record or publish figures for this amount.

[E]   Aggregating the Indicators

It will be noted that we have ten indicators – an obvious round number, but not a requisite. The first version of the index aggregated the complexity factors into two figures through a formula which required weighting each individual indicator of complexity. This created a number of problems, including:

- it created a loss of clarity when presenting the index, and was difficult to explain;
- the formula could produce scores above ten, which meant that truncation had to be applied to the final complexity scores; and
- to take account of changes to the tax system, the weightings would have to be adjusted every year to keep each of the indicators in equal value in relation to each other.

For these reasons, this iteration uses a standardization formula, which scales each of the indicators into a number between 0 and 1. The formula is:

$$Y^1 = (Y - Y^{min}) / (Y^{max} - Y^{min})$$

'Y' is the value of the indicator for a tax measure. 'Y^{min}' represents an indicator's lowest value across all tax measures, while 'Y^{max}' indicates the highest. This formula will always produce a number between 0 and 1. This removes the need for truncation entirely, gives a much smoother presentation, and removes the need to adjust the weightings every year.[26]

The aggregation formula is much simpler. A multiplication factor is also included to stretch the index to give scores between 1 and 10:[27]

$$((Y^1 + Z^1 + ... n^1) / 6) * 10$$

Here n^1 represents a normalized indicator. A score of 10 indicates the most complex tax, and a score of 0 the least complex.

The Appendix to this chapter contains an illustrative summary example of the index.

---

26. Changes to Y^{max} and Y^{min} will still need to be made, though these will be very easy to identify.
27. Though it could just as easily give scores between 1 and 6 and remove the need to divide by 6 and multiply by 10. The 'impact of complexity' formula differs slightly, as it divides by 4 and multiplies by 10.

[F]   Necessary and Unnecessary Complexity

When the underlying complexity and impact of complexity have been calculated, it is possible to assess whether a tax is relatively complex or not, and why. However, although this will inform the OTS's work, it cannot be the sole determinant, as often complexity in a tax measure is a consequence of real-world commercial complexity, which cannot be simplified.

Some taxes may in fact be necessarily complex. This could be because they seek to tax complex financial transactions or commercial structures. This means that simplification of the tax is not possible without either:

- changing the policy objective;[28]
- finding a way to simplify the business situation or transaction;[29] or
- creating avoidance or non-compliance where additional complexity could have prevented it.

Since the key objective of the index is to provide policy-makers with a measure to identify areas of tax which are appropriate for simplification, the ability to capture which taxes are necessarily complex and which are not is helpful.

Professor Ulph has suggested to us that this could be done through a comparison of underlying complexity and impact of complexity in relation to the measure of the complexity of the policy objectives involved. This has not been analysed in depth here as it would require an entirely different index to measure policy objective complexity, which is outside the remit of this chapter. Using the index to its fullest effect in practice will require a measure of unnecessary complexity, to ensure that simplification is only achieved where it does not create damage to the overall tax system.

[G]   Structure of the Tax Index

We will in due course be publishing a further paper with 'scores' for a large part of the tax system. The tax system has been broken down into 107 areas, divided by function. Some taxes are presented as a single whole, such as the aggregates levy, while others have been divided up by function, such as corporation tax.

The way the tax system has been broken down can result in some changes to the figures: this is most notable when comparing whole taxes such as inheritance tax against smaller tax areas, such as a major relief.[30] This is one approach to structuring the index; it is wholly arbitrary and dependent on the requirements users of the index have. The framework can be further changed and divided however desired. For instance, if the index was used in a policy context it could be modified so that each area aligned with an area that a policy professional was responsible for.

---

28. As an example, the OTS did suggest an alternative way of taxing the smallest business, perhaps taxing on the basis of a percentage of turnover, as a route to a simpler system that might be worth exploring.
29. Changes in accounting rules may well mean that the tax treatment can follow more simply.
30. Research and development relief would be a good example.

The only concern with modifying the structure of the index would be the effect this has on the scorings of each individual figure of the measures used to calculate Y^{max} and Y^{min} figures for an indicator. For example, inheritance tax currently has 89 reliefs, the most of any tax area.[31] This means it is used as Y^{max} for the standardization formula. If this was split into more than one tax measure, then Y^{max} may decrease, which would result in a lower $(Y^{max} - Y^{min})$ figure. This would impact the complexity of every other tax in the index.

This sounds problematic but is not. It needs to be kept in mind that the index is a relative measure of tax complexity, not an objective one. Changes in the composition of the index result in a change to what a tax measure is being measured relative to in the first place. Changes to the scores in the index following a change in the composition of the index are to be expected. This is not a problem if the index retains a constant structure over time. If greater transparency over this is sought, any use of the complexity figures could be published alongside the tax areas which are being used to benchmark Y^{max} and Y^{min}.

§15.03   CONCLUSION

The OTS believes that it has developed the index sufficiently in line with the aims of the project. We believe that it includes indicators and tax measures relevant to the current economic climate. The evolving tax system may create requirements or an opportunity for more tax measures or indicators, so the index is by no means a fixed, final work. We have already noted some possible further refinements.

We have discussed how the index may be used in practice to track the relative complexity of measures in the tax system, and to prioritize simplification reviews of the tax system. The index could potentially be a useful tool for the UK government if it was used to track the complexity of the tax system over time, identify where that complexity is creating difficulty for taxpayers, and to simplify the tax system. As we noted, we think the index could readily be adapted for use in areas other than taxation.

One area the index does not cover is a measure of necessary or unnecessary complexity. Some areas of the tax system will be necessarily complex, and for these areas substantial simplification is not possible. To properly take advantage of the opportunities afforded by the index, a measure of necessary complexity needs to be established and measured alongside the index.

Finally, it has been suggested that the index could be aggregated into a single measure of the complexity of the UK's tax system. This has obvious potential attractions: a rolling measure of complexity would allow an assessment of the impact of each Finance Act. Did it increase or reduce the complexity of the system?

---

31. See Office of Tax Simplification, *Review of tax reliefs: final report* (March 2011), https://www. gov.uk/government/uploads/system/uploads/attachment_data/file/198570/ots_review_tax_ reliefs_final_report.pdf.

It would then potentially be possible – at least in theory – to compare countries' tax systems. It would be an interesting indication of the attractiveness of Country A's tax system if it had a rating of 4.5 compared with Country B's rating of 7.2. But we must caution against any assumption that such extension of our work would be easy. We also have to reiterate the aims of the index: primarily to inform the OTS's future work. But extending the index in these directions would undoubtedly be interesting!

APPENDIX: ILLUSTRATIVE EXAMPLE OF COMPLEXITY INDEX

Area of Tax	Y^{max}	Y^{min}	Air Passenger Duty	Inheritance Tax	Landfill Tax
Number of exemptions + number of reliefs	89	0	10/0.11	89/1	9/0.1
Number of Finance Acts with Changes	13	0	8/0.6	13/1	7/0.54
Readability Index	33.35	9.3	11.67/0.1	11.72/0.1	13.49/0.17
Number of Pages of legislation	198.75	2	62*/0.3	198.75*/1	47.25*/0.23
Guidance Complexity	5	1	2/0.25	5/1	3/0.5
Complexity of information required	5	1	3/0.5	4/0.75	2/0.25
Total Underlying Complexity	(total out of 10)		3.1	8.1	3.0

* The Finance Act 2014 includes provisions for all these taxes, albeit small ones. The 'number of pages' indicator is therefore slightly out of date, as the Tolleys books used to measure it have not been released.

Area of Tax*	Air Passenger Duty	Inheritance Tax	Landfill Tax
Net average cost to taxpayers and HMRC	1/0	5/1	1/0
Number of taxpayers affected	1/0	2/0.25	1/0
Average ability of taxpayers	2/0.25	4/0.75	3/0.5
Avoidance Risk	1/0	5/1	1/0
Total Impact of Complexity	0.6	7.5	1.3

* Y limits have been omitted for the sake of space; $(Y^{max} - Y^{min})$ is 4 in every instance.

CHAPTER 16

Managing Tax Complexity: The Institutional Framework for Tax Policy-Making and Oversight

*Judith Freedman**

§16.01 INTRODUCTION: THE INEVITABILITY OF COMPLEXITY

The title of this volume is *Tax Simplification*. There is a widespread view that tax systems are too complex and that simplification would be a desirable outcome. The length of legislation is often cited in support of this observation, as is the method of drafting. Compliance costs are another factor; uncertainty in genuine commercial or personal situations coupled with the ease with which taxpayers can exploit 'loopholes' is a further characteristic often related to complexity.[1] There may also be a more fundamental objection to complexity: that people should understand the financial rules that govern their lives and upon which they are required to act and take decisions and also upon which, in a democratic society, they need to make decisions about voting for

---

* Some parts of this chapter build on an editorial by the author published in the *British Tax Review*: *Creating new UK institutions for tax governance and policy making: progress or confusion?*, [2013] 4 Brit. Tax Rev. 373.
1. These factors are discussed in a systematic way in the chapter by David Ulph, *Measuring Tax Complexity*, this volume, §4.02. See also Chris Evans, 'Taxation in the UK – Commentary', in Stuart Adam, Tim Besley, Richard Blundell, Steve Bond, Robert Chote, Malcolm Gammie, Paul Johnson, Gareth Myles & James Poterba (eds) for the Institute for Fiscal Studies, *Dimensions of Tax Design: The Mirrlees Review* 78 (Oxford University Press, 2010) (hereinafter *Mirrlees Review* (2010)).

a political party. There is a point at which complexity becomes so great and unmanageable that it begins to undermine the rule of law, because it does not enable individuals to regulate their affairs properly.[2]

This chapter will not take issue with the view that complexity described in these terms is undesirable, but accepts that it is, to some extent, inevitable. The trade-off for a very simple tax system would be loss of equity and the inability to use the tax system for purposes such as redistribution and the provision of incentives, which many believe to be important functions. This author has argued elsewhere for more care in the use of tax incentives and reliefs and her view has not changed.[3] However, this chapter will focus rather more on administrative techniques and institutions for the management of some inevitable complexity on the basis that there is a need to enable taxpayers to manage their affairs in advance and, if that can be done then, despite the complications, the basic requirements of the rule of law may be satisfied. Thus, the thesis here is that complexity should be reduced wherever possible, but where that cannot be achieved consistently with other objectives, there should be mechanisms to help taxpayers and revenue authorities to navigate through the remaining intricacies. Improved institutions could assist in providing ways of managing uncertainty and increasing understanding, as well as leading to improvements in the tax system. In the UK, however, lack of clear thought about the operation of our relevant institutions means that they do not play the part they should do in improving tax law. Whilst this chapter focuses on the UK and its institutions, many of the problems encountered will be seen to be similar to those in other jurisdictions.[4] In some cases, the institutions utilized to deal with the problems encountered in providing oversight, policy input and planning in the tax system in the UK have emerged and apparently shaped themselves, rather than being designed. It may well be time for a 'root and branch' review of how we manage these matters.[5]

This chapter will deal (in §16.02) with the question of simplicity as a driver for reform in the UK and the political background to this debate. It will then turn (§16.03) to the value of an institutional approach to this problem. Section §16.04 will examine recent approaches in the UK. There is a proliferation of institutional approaches and, in

---

2. As defined by Joseph Raz and others, the rule of law requires that the law should be clear enough to allow individuals to regulate their affairs in advance: see Joseph Raz, *The Authority of Law: Essays on Law and Morality*, Ch. 11 ('The Rule of Law and Its Virtue') (2nd ed., Oxford University Press, 2009).
3. See, e.g., Claire Crawford & Judith Freedman, 'Small Business Taxation', in *Mirrlees Review* 1028 (2010).
4. For a comparative survey see Christopher John Wales & Christopher Peter Wales, *Structures, processes and governance in tax policy-making: an initial report*, Oxford University Centre for Business Taxation (December 2012), available at: http://www.sbs.ox.ac.uk/sites/default/files/Business_Taxation/Docs/Publications/Reports/structures-and-processes-in-tax-policy-making.pdf.
5. The Labour party in the UK has announced its intention to set up a review of certain aspects of HMRC should it be elected in the General Election in 2015. This will be a review focusing on treatment of avoidance and evasion and not a root and branch review as is needed. It will also take only three months, which casts doubt over its thoroughness. See UK Labour Party, 'Miliband promises to shine a light into Britain's tax system', *Press Release* (14 February 2015), available at: http://press.labour.org.uk/post/110986640489/miliband-promises-to-shine-a-light-into-britains.

particular, the Office of Tax Simplification (OTS) was created specifically to tackle the issue of complexity, but new institutions need to tackle the problems at root and it is not clear that the OTS or any of the other new institutions created over recent years have been able to do that. Section §16.05 concludes that there remains a need for institutional reform.

§16.02   SIMPLIFICATION OF TAX SYSTEMS

[A]   Simplification Cannot Be the Only, or Even the Main, Driver of Reform

Modern taxation systems in most jurisdictions are complex and this complexity is not confined to large business dealings or the very wealthy taxpayer. Even those of modest means and with relatively straightforward financial affairs can experience confusion and obscure provisions in everyday life: what expenses are deductible from their salaries, how are pensions taxed, is VAT/GST payable on a certain type of confectionery or not?

It is elementary that a fundamental cause of tax complexity lies in flawed underlying policy. The ideal starting point for removing complexity would be to simplify tax philosophy and legislate in accordance with clear, coherent tax principles. However, given the intensely political nature of taxation and the complexity of the law that governs property, contract and commercial law, corporate law and other relationships that underlie taxation, it is unrealistic to expect that any jurisdiction will manage to set up completely coherent tax policies and tax legislation. The tensions between the characteristics of a good tax system mean that the search for an optimal tax system will always be an imperfect balancing act.[6] The technical requirements of good tax system design and political pressures that increase complexity are all too evident in everyday discussion of taxation. The immediate reaction of politicians to a problem is often to create a tax relief. It is only subsequently that they realize that they have also created an opportunity for tax minimization, which then requires further legislation to prevent it from creating too much leakage of revenue.

Against this background, simplification can be one driver of reform efforts, but it will always be a mistake to make it a sole or overriding objective. To show the dangers of promoting simplicity above all else, consider what might theoretically appear to be the simplest kind of tax – a flat tax levied per head (or 'poll' tax). Conceptually this is a straightforward idea that can be easily embodied in legislation, but a problem arises due to the lack of any relationship to ability to pay. The reaction to this fundamental problem, the lack of fairness that will be perceived by many observers of such a tax, will lead to pressure for exemptions and modifications. The resultant attempts to make

---

6. James Mirrlees, Stuart Adam, Tim Besley, Richard Blundell, Steve Bond, Robert Chote, Malcolm Gammie, Paul Johnson, Gareth Myles & James Poterba, *Tax by Design: The Mirrlees Review*, 39–45 (Oxford University Press, 2011).

an unfair tax fairer will introduce complexity.[7] So, an attempt to create a conceptually simple tax will either be defeated due to the failure to consider other factors necessary for a good tax, or will become complex due to attempts to incorporate those other characteristics. This does not mean that simplification should not be considered, but it should only ever be one factor amongst many.

[B]   Attempts at Simplification May Create Complexity

Well-meaning attempts to simplify the law can create complexity: a phenomenon that has been called alternatively 'complification',[8] 'complex simplification' and 'attractive complexity'.[9] Steven Dean shows how relying on taxpayer preferences to guide simplification efforts may produce forms of deregulation that are not simplifications at all. For example, the US check-the-box entity regime resulted from taxpayer pressure and has been a popular means of reducing tax burdens, but, in addition to simplification for some, it has produced opportunities for arbitrage for others, and created tax avoidance opportunities at a domestic as well as an international level. Other types of small business relief can also be seen to have introduced a host of new rules, thresholds and requirements, the simplification benefits of which can be questioned.[10]

The fact that simplification attempts can result in increased complexity underlines the need to consider the essence of simplification. For example, tax legislation rewrite processes have frequently been criticized for increasing the length of legislation, despite (perhaps) using better and clearer drafting techniques. More fundamentally, it has been strongly and convincingly argued that unless the underlying law can be improved, a tax law rewrite is of limited value.[11] Others, however, maintain that improvements in drafting can be of value, even without conceptual simplification. It is this debate about the indicators of simplification that has led the UK OTS to produce an index of complexity against which to benchmark the existing legislation and to help prioritize its activities. It might also be used as a measure of the success of the OTS itself. John Whiting, Jeremy Sherwood and Gareth Jones give further details of this

---

7. Thus the UK's poll tax, the 'community charge' of 1989–1993, was not only a failure in political terms but also very complex. See David Butler, Andrew Adonis & Tony Travers, *Failure in British Government: The Politics of the Poll Tax*, 102 (Oxford University Press, 1994): '[d]rafting the Bill in Scotland turned out to be "something of a nightmare". The more they got into complexities the more concerned became the Scottish Office at the problems of implementation'.
8. A word that has been used by various tax authors; see, e.g., Mike Thexton, 'Complification', *Taxation* 14 (19 June 2013), available at: http://www.taxation.co.uk/taxation/Articles/2013/0 6/19/309331/complification (accessed on 1 October 2013).
9. Judith Freedman, *Why Taxing the Micro-business is Not Simple - A Cautionary Tale from the 'Old World'*, 2(1) J. Australasian Tax Teachers Ass'n 58 (2006); Steven A. Dean, *Attractive Complexity: Tax Deregulation, the Check-the-Box Election and the Future of Tax Simplification*, 34(2) Hofstra L. Rev. 405 (2005).
10. Freedman, *Why Taxing the Micro-business is Not Simple - A Cautionary Tale from the 'Old World'*, above n. 9.
11. Adrian Sawyer, *Moving on from the Tax Legislation Rewrite Projects: A Comparison of the New Zealand Tax Working Group/Generic Tax Policy Process and the United Kingdom Office of Tax Simplification*, [2013] 3 Brit. Tax Rev. 321.

index in their chapter in this volume.[12] The range of complexity indicators discussed there shows that simplicity is not a simple idea and that a single driver of 'simplicity' does not tell us very much about the appropriate tax reform.

[C]   Managing the Tax System

If we accept the inevitability of a certain degree of complexity in the tax system, our thoughts must turn to the way in which it is best to decide on the balance between the different characteristics that might be sought, such as efficient revenue-raising, redistribution, provision of incentives and fiscal management. It will be important to consider each tax in the context of the system as a whole and to look not only at its design and objectives but also at its implementation, impact and efficiency and the way in which it operates in relation to other systems, such as the social security system, pension provisions, financial regulation, the labour market and so on. The management of these taxes and their practical impact will also need to be scrutinized. These are heavy demands that require joined-up and well thought through institutional solutions. In the UK we do have a number of institutions designed to assist with these tasks, but they have sometimes been created as knee-jerk reactions to particular problems or have emerged rather than being designed. There have been many calls for improvement but we have experienced 'institution creep' rather than complete overhaul.[13]

§16.03   INSTITUTIONAL APPROACHES

[A]   Variety of Institutions Needed

Complex tax systems need a variety of institutions to ensure good management. This cannot negate complexity but it may help to reduce it or alternatively to provide a framework in which the impact of the complexity on administrations and taxpayers is reduced. These institutions need to provide scrutiny and oversight on the one hand and input into tax policy on the other; functions that are different and require diverse skills and approaches. In addition, there need to be institutions or procedures that facilitate communication with taxpayers about the tax system. This can be done by consultation, which may work well in the case of interaction with the professions and with large

---

12. See John Whiting, Jeremy Sherwood & Gareth Jones, *The Office of Tax Simplification and its Complexity Index*, this volume; see also David Ulph, *Measuring Tax Complexity*, this volume, §4.05.
13. For some significant calls for institutional reform around UK tax policy-making, see Lord Howe of Aberavon, *Simplicity and Stability: The Politics of Tax Policy*, [2001] 2 Brit. Tax Rev. 113; Tax Law Review Committee (Sir Alan Budd, chair), *Making Tax Law: Report of a Working Party on the Institutional Processes for the Parliamentary Scrutiny of Tax Proposals and for the Enactment of Tax Legislation*, Institute for Fiscal Studies TLRC Discussion Paper No. 3 (March 2003), available at http://www.ifs.org.uk/comms/budd03.pdf; Tracey Bowler, *Tax Policymaking in the UK*, Institute for Fiscal Studies TLRC Discussion Paper No. 8 (June 2010), http://www.ifs.org.uk/comms/dp8.pdf.

business and the trade unions, but when it comes to the ordinary taxpayer it is much more difficult to create the environment for these conversations. What is more, consultation will not necessarily lead to simplicity: the more views that are taken into account, the more a policy will need to be qualified, which may lead to more complex legislation.

It is important that these institutions have clear functions that do not overlap and that they do not become rivals, which will itself increase complexity. They also need to be given time to do the work allotted. There is a need for organizations that can react rapidly but also for those that can be deliberative, take evidence and consider issues in a joined-up manner.

[B]   Tax Policy-Making

In a parliamentary democracy such as the UK, in theory the controls over tax policy and the making and drafting of tax law will come from the legislature, but the more complex the system the less likely policy input is to be possible at this stage and scrutiny may not be fully effective. Add into this the political dynamic, and it will be seen that enabling parliamentarians to review tax legislation in a thorough manner is problematic. In their review of tax policy-making around the world, Wales and Wales found that there is room for improvement in the way in which scrutiny of taxation issues is handled in most if not all parliaments.[14] They suggest more qualified support for parliamentary committees involved with taxation issues to help overcome the asymmetry of expertise and information that currently and overwhelmingly favours the executive against the legislature. This is not a new observation, but remains an important one.[15] They go on, however, to recognize that 'debate in parliament is often highly partisan and the value of scrutiny is significantly diminished by the constraints of political allegiance'.[16] It must be doubtful whether this last observed fact would be entirely counteracted by expert support. In any event, expertise is contested. The idea that there is a pure truth available from experts can be overplayed. Even analysis of data is based on assumptions and, in the end, decisions may need to be based on political judgments. As Peter Riddell has noted, in a comment on the Mirrlees Review:

> There is certainly a case for greater transparency, auditing and accountability but tax decisions cannot be taken out of politics. They are the stuff of the party battle.[17]

But data analysis is important nonetheless and can at least prevent the worst mistakes and encourage deliberation. In the UK at least, politicians seem to spend little time thinking about the implications of tax decisions beyond the immediate headlines. As King and Crew have pointed out:

---

14. Wales & Wales, above n. 4.
15. See Lord Howe, above n. 13; Tax Law Review Committee (Sir Alan Budd, chair), above n. 13; Bowler, above n. 13.
16. Wales & Wales, above n. 4, at 8.
17. Peter Riddell, 'The Political Economy of Tax Policy - Commentary', in *Mirrlees Review* 1280 (2010).

'Deliberation' is not a word one hears very often in connection with British politics – for the good reason that very little deliberation actually takes place. British politicians meet, discuss, debate, manoeuvre, read submissions, read the newspapers, make speeches, answer questions, visit their constituencies, chair meetings and frequently give interviews, but they seldom deliberate.[18]

All too often, decisions are rushed and made under political pressure to react to criticism or produce a novel idea. Much of the 'debate' takes place in the media at a fairly superficial level. Social media has exacerbated this tendency. This leads to tinkering, badly thought through and ultimately often counter-productive changes, the need for frequent amendment and, of course, complexity. Politicians must make the final decisions, but they need to be better informed and they should think more deeply about the implications of their decisions. Far too often promises are made based on little or no evidence of their likely impact. In the UK this is exacerbated by the annual Budget, which has become a media event and is seen to require exciting announcements. This skews the entire tax policy-making timetable. More evidence-based policy-making and the availability of expert analysis would be of value, so that at the very least potential pitfalls could be pointed out.

For the reasons given above, we should abandon the idea (if anyone ever seriously entertained it) that tax policy can be completely turned over to a technical committee. Experts are not guaranteed to get everything right - indeed sometimes there is no 'right' or 'wrong' because no solution is perfect and trade-offs are needed. In the end the decisions must reflect the views of the population. The best way we have so far found to do this in a representative democracy is through our politicians. What could and should be done, however, is to integrate expertise into the policy-making process using better processes than those currently employed.

This problem of integrating expertise with political views and the practical advice of civil servants is one that needs to be tackled through the creation of the right institutions and modes of consultation and proper use of expert civil servants. Bacon and Hope have argued that:

> The last thing we need is government by technicians. It is of the first importance to have politically neutral professional administrative civil servants of the highest calibre...[19]

The system of government needs to ensure that the 'expertise of the expert' in the area of taxation is absorbed in a way that can be rationalized and understood - and that its proper relationship to policy can be analysed successfully.[20] Expertise must be harnessed but subjected to scrutiny itself. No one source of expertise should be taken to be infallible. Consultation must not be permitted to turn into a lobbying exercise or to add unnecessary complexities because consultees are asking for special protections or exemptions that are not really required, just to be on the safe side. To allow this is

---

18. Anthony King & Ivor Crewe, *The Blunders of our Governments*, 386 (Oneworld Publications, 2013).
19. Richard Bacon & Christopher Hope, *Conundrum: Why Every Government Gets Things Wrong – And What We Can Do About It*, 304–312 (Biteback Publishing, 2013).
20. Bacon & Hope, above n. 19, at 304–312.

to permit consultation to increase complexity, rather than to reduce it. To ensure this is achieved, it is important that the civil servants and others engaged in the absorption and relaying of this information to the politicians are well-versed in these issues and able to ask the right questions from an independent stance.

It is also vital to nurture different sources of information and expertise, both internal and independent, which can feed into these processes. Different standpoints need to be considered but evidence must be subject to scrutiny, even where those making the points purport to have analysed the data. All too often we see a number or a 'fact' take hold in the press, following which the 'fact' becomes widely accepted and it becomes hard to argue against it. There is a temptation to over-simplify to make a point:

> The public, impatient for solutions to its pressing concerns, rewards those who offer simple analyses leading to unequivocal policy recommendations. These incentives make it tempting for researchers to maintain assumptions far stronger than they can persuasively defend, in order to draw strong conclusions.[21]

Being able to ask the right questions of those experts presenting data is an important skill.[22]

Finally it is important that a way is found for fully informed scrutiny to be undertaken by politicians in such a way that it does not become bogged down in party politics and point scoring and is not subject to the political pressures of a fixed timetable for action. If there is a need for urgent action this should arise from real necessity and not be manufactured by the media, non-governmental organizations, business, lobby groups or other politicians. Given the nature of politics and politicians, this also requires an institutional approach.

[C]   Scrutiny of Implementation and Administration

Policy-making institutions need to be separated from, but retain links to, those tasked with scrutiny of implementation and administration. The policy may be excellent in theory but the implementation could be poor and could create complexities and inequities. In one sense, oversight of administration is beyond the scope of this chapter, yet it cannot be ignored, since reviews of implementation must be fed back into the policy-making process and lessons need to be learned when policy does not work as well as the experts and law-makers thought it would.

Once again there is a need for a mix of oversight by politicians, civil servants and external experts. Ultimately politicians must be accountable, but it is important to require separation between politicians and the administration of the affairs of an individual to protect taxpayer confidentiality and to ensure that ministers will not be accused of meddling with the affairs of an individual, either to help or hinder.[23] This

---

21. Charles F. Manski, *Identification for Prediction and Decision*, 7 (Harvard University Press, 2007).
22. Charles F. Manski, *Public Policy in an Uncertain World*, 174 (Harvard University Press, 2013).
23. Christopher Wales, *The Implications of the O'Donnell Review for the Making of Tax Policy in the UK*, [2004] 5 Brit. Tax Rev. 543, 557.

can lead to difficult line-drawing when it comes to reviewing administration and learning the lessons of past cases, which are by definition concerned with the affairs of individuals.

A further area where oversight is needed is in relation to the discretion of revenue authorities. These authorities need to be able to use some discretion to make the tax system work, but this discretion must have limits.[24] Adding in oversight mechanisms can slow down administration and appear to create complexity, but it is part of the essential management framework for the tax system and a way of making the complexities more acceptable. In addition, revenue authorities can help to provide certainty where the complexity of the law appears to create confusion. This can be done by giving rulings or other forms of guidance, but this discretion to manage complexity also has to be the subject of careful procedures and oversight. This can be provided by the courts to some extent, but administrative frameworks will also be important in ensuring that the complexities are not only managed fairly but are perceived to be so managed. There is considerable concern in many quarters about giving revenue authorities too much discretion and so a careful line must be drawn that enables the revenue authority to exercise reasonable discretion in a way that is subject to controls and operates within the boundaries of a legal framework so that it is a genuine exercise of discretion rather than de facto law-making by the administration.

§16.04 THE UK INSTITUTIONAL APPROACH

[A] Tax Policy-Making in the UK

The conduct of tax policy-making in the UK has been the subject of criticism for many years and yet no radical reform of the parliamentary process has resulted.[25] However, there has been a gradual change, with new institutions created and old ones developed. In 2010 the new Coalition Government published a paper setting out a new approach to tax policy-making, with a key focus on simplicity.[26] This paper introduced the Office of Tax Simplification, a completely new body, with the aim of giving weight to simplicity alongside other policy objectives. The proposals in this paper also included better consultation and a framework for the introduction of new reliefs, given that reliefs are a major cause of complexity.

These promises for improvement came against a background of ever-increasing length of legislation, concerns about lack of proper consultation and relatively recent changes to the revenue authorities and the way policy is made within them.

---

24. These issues are discussed further in Chris Evans, Judith Freedman & Richard Krever (eds), *The Delicate Balance: Tax, Discretion and the Rule of Law* (IBFD Publications, 2011).
25. See references cited at above n. 13.
26. HMT & HMRC, *Tax policy making: a new approach* (June 2010), available at http://old.tax.org .uk/attach.pl/9358/10987/tax_policy_making%20discussdoc.pdf.

[1]   The Revenue Authorities: Role, Experience, 'Absorption' of Advice and Consultation

The employees of the revenue authorities (the civil servants) have a vital role to play in the absorption and analysis of the 'expertise of the experts'.[27] In the UK, the civil service has a proud history of talking truth unto ministers. The Civil Service Code requires civil servants to provide information and advice on the basis of the evidence, and take due account of expert and professional advice.[28] The difficulty is that the same Code requires that once decisions have been taken the civil servant must not frustrate the implementation of those decided policies. Whilst this must be correct, ultimately, there does need to be an opportunity for analysis and discussion before minds are made up, but it seems this does not always happen.

The less experienced the civil servant, the less likely that person is to be able to deter the making and announcement of the decision before due deliberation has taken place. All too often at consultation meetings, civil servants state that ministers are 'keen' on an idea, despite evident problems, and so the civil servants take the view that it is unlikely that they will be able to reshape the policy. The consultation process is thus relegated to the level of detail rather than fundamentals. Despite the fact that the consultation process has improved, and draft legislation for the Finance Bill is published earlier since 2011,[29] there are still cases where legislation comes as a surprise,[30] and even where there is consultation, it is not always open to consultees to question the fundamentals of the policy. Furthermore, the majority of consultees tend to be professional bodies, because they have the committee structures, mechanisms and knowledge to respond, and the larger professional firms and businesses. Comments from small business, academics and even NGOs, are much less frequent. Attempts are made to reach these groups through workshops and meetings, but once again the workshops are generally held in London, take several hours and are usually populated by representatives of professional firms and representative groups who have the resources to staff this. These consultees frequently make important and well-informed comments, but the consultation process can be limited in this way. Follow-up publications are sometimes circulated only to those who have attended the working groups, and this can act to cut down wider consultation also. There can be a perception of lobbying rather than consultation, despite the fact that the consultation is open to all.

---

27. Bacon & Hope, above n. 19.
28. Civil Service Code, paras 10 and 11 (version laid in Parliament on 11 November 2010), available at: http://civilservicecommission.independent.gov.uk/wp-content/uploads/2012/03/Civil%20 Service%20Code.pdf.
29. See HMT & HMRC, *Tax Consultation Framework*, published by the Coalition Government in March 2011, arising from its *Tax policy making* paper (HMT & HMRC, above n. 26) stating that the Government will engage interested parties on changes to tax policy and legislation at each key stage of developing and implementing the policy: see https://www.gov.uk/government/ uploads/system/uploads/attachment_data/file/89261/tax-consultation-framework.pdf. This does not mean that there will be consultation about what the policy should be.
30. For example, the highly complex diverted profits tax introduced in the 2015 Budget, just months before the May 2015 General Election, with very little opportunity for debate and no possibility of questioning the underlying policy.

In addition, there are private meetings between various groups and the revenue authorities. These have an important part to play but there is little doubt that they could amount to lobbying rather than consulting if not managed carefully by expert and knowledgeable civil servants.[31]

So, consultation is only useful if well handled. Some consultations become very bogged down in detail. Attempts to adopt simpler forms of drafting are particularly prone to being hijacked by objections that a case needs an exemption or should be covered for the avoidance of doubt.[32] Where a relief or exemption is being made available, there can be pressure to increase the thresholds for the relief or extend it in some other way.[33] This takes us back to the need for the civil servants to be well equipped to act as a bridge between the experts, other consultees and the politicians; otherwise consultation can be a cause of complexity.

The problems of tax policy-making have been exacerbated by the reorganization of the revenue departments following the recommendations of the O'Donnell Report which reviewed those departments,[34] as well as by a programme of cuts to the civil service as a result of budgetary constraints. An important aspect of this review was the decision that Her Majesty's Treasury (HMT) should have responsibility for all the policy work related to taxation, with Her Majesty's Revenue and Customs (HMRC), as a non-ministerial government department taking responsibility for operational work, including operational policy.[35] This part of the reorganization has been criticized as resulting in a single source approach to strategic policy advice, losing an important perspective from those with operational knowledge.[36] There is cooperation between HMRC and HMT on policy initiatives, but the lead is generally taken by HMT staff who, although very able, may have little experience of tax, will have no operational knowledge because of the need for operational detail to be confined to HMRC on confidentiality grounds, and may have moved from other parts of HMT or even other government departments. There is a culture of frequent movement in the UK civil service which is designed to bring new thinking to bear on problems, but which can lead to the importance of operational experience and knowledge being overlooked. This reorganization, combined with deep cuts to staffing for budgetary reasons, has

---

31. *Court rulings and lobbying help big firms pay less tax*, The Guardian (10 February 2009), http://www.theguardian.com/business/2009/feb/10/firms-lobbying-tax; Vanessa Houlder, *UK Treasury unveils avoidance reforms*, Financial Times (30 June 2011), http://www.ft.com/cms/s/0/f4068508-a298-11e0-83fc-00144feabdc0.html#axzz3VV0rrVNk. This covers the period of the Coalition Government and the Labour Government that preceded it, so is not a party-political point.
32. See Judith Freedman, *Improving (Not Perfecting) Tax Legislation: Rules and Principles Revisited*, [2010] 6 Brit. Tax Rev. 717, discussing the disguised interest legislation, which was initially intended to be principles-based legislation but became more complex following consultation.
33. See the discussion of the OTS below (§16.04[A][2]).
34. O'Donnell Review (Gus O'Donnell, chair), *Financing Britain's Future: Review of the Revenue Departments*, Cm 6163 (March 2004). For further discussion, see Tony Prosser, *The Economic Constitution*, 41ff and 90ff (Oxford University Press, 2014); Bowler, above n. 13.
35. This is designed to prevent intervention by ministers in decisions on the affairs of individual taxpayers: Prosser, above n. 34, 41ff and 90ff.
36. Wales, *The Implications of the O'Donnell Review for the Making of Tax Policy in the UK*, above n. 23, at 556.

seen a loss of many experienced staff and much of the institutional memory of those involved in tax policy-making has gone.[37] This may encourage 'blue-sky thinking' but that does not necessarily result in simplicity - on the contrary, it can result in legislation which contains predictable flaws that then need to be remedied by amendments. Even before the O'Donnell restructuring, there were problems with the revenue department staff having, as Lord Howe put it, 'unequalled but necessarily one sided experience'.[38] This has not been improved by the reorganization.

The situation following the O'Donnell reorganization makes the need for external expertise very great. This could be achieved, at least partially, through consultation, subject to the concerns discussed above. Secondments from the private sector and academia could also bring in expertise, although secondments from the 'Big Four' accountancy firms have attracted considerable criticism from the Public Accounts Committee (PAC) and others on the basis that they can create 'cosiness'.[39] To some extent this is unfair, and this expertise does need to be harnessed, but perceptions have to be taken seriously and the process handled with care. Thus, external expertise and experience need to be brought into tax policy-making, but the problems of lobbying and influence need to be dealt with by handling the 'expertise of the expert' with understanding and insight. This expertise needs to be absorbed and translated for use by government ministers, other politicians and the public. Pressures to create exemptions, reliefs and special cases need to be resisted unless a good case can be made out. Complexity in legislation can be resisted best by those with a clear sense of the objectives of that legislation and the fundamental underlying principles. Sensible use of expertise and removal of complexity go hand in hand. Only a well-trained, well-resourced and experienced civil service will be able to manage that process. They need the ability not only to absorb and translate the expert evidence and arguments in order to convey them to their political masters, but also to act as a buffer between Ministers on the one hand and the lobbyists on the other.

[2]   Office of Tax Simplification (OTS)

The failings in the system of leaving tax policy-making advice to the revenue authorities led to various proposals for setting up new bodies to engage in tax reform. Proposals have included a Parliamentary Select Committee on Taxation and a Tax Structure Review Programme answerable to Parliament.[40]

---

37. Evidence on the loss of experienced staff was given by the unions and others to the Treasury Select Committee and published in their Sixteenth Report, *Administration and Effectiveness of HM Revenue and Customs*, HC 731 (July 2011), and see recommendation in s. 2, at para. 27. See also James Alt, Ian Preston & Luke Sibieta, 'The Political Economy of Tax Policy', in *Mirrlees Review* 1204 (2010).
38. Lord Howe, above n. 13, at 119.
39. Gavin Hinks, *HMRC and Big Four Secondments*, Economia (15 March 2013), http://economia. icaew.com/business/march2013/the-big-four-secondments. One problem with secondments is the cost to the business or organization making the secondment. Inevitably it will fall to large firms to do this because smaller ones will not be able to afford this expense.
40. See Lord Howe, above n. 13; Tax Law Review Committee (Sir Alan Budd, chair), above n. 13.

The response of the Coalition Government to these concerns when it came to power was to create the OTS.[41] It is unclear at the time of writing whether the OTS will continue following the 2015 General Election, but many hope that it will do so in some form, although most consider that it will require greater resources and some reconfiguring to be of ongoing and sustainable value. It is rather soon to judge just how valuable the work of the OTS has been. It has commenced a debate and made some useful changes and proposals, but it has not been able to progress that debate as far as many would have liked.[42]

The first error was undoubtedly to call this organization the Office of Tax Simplification; an oversimplification of the problems in itself. Lord Howe has stated that a simplification banner would not be enough and he was correct.[43] In its very first project on small business taxation,[44] the OTS did go further than a pure simplification brief and recommended that the Chancellor should consider merger of tax and National Insurance contributions.[45] This has not been achieved, but the recommendation has been repeated in subsequent papers,[46] and a level of administrative merger is being pursued, which might lay the ground for bigger changes at some point. To an extent, the OTS has skilfully manoeuvred its way around the limitations under which it has had to work and has not refrained from referring to the need for fundamental changes, but on the whole these have not been within its remit.[47]

Such success as the OTS had had has been largely due to its personnel, including its Director, John Whiting, an experienced and widely supported appointment. But from the start there has been a lack of staff and funding, as pointed out by the PAC.[48] Much reliance is placed on secondees from HMRC and HM Treasury as well as from the tax professions. Perhaps more important is the fact that, although described as an

---

41. For more detail of its structure, see John Whiting, Jeremy Sherwood & Gareth Jones, *The Office of Tax Simplification and its Complexity Index*, this volume, §15.01. For critiques, see Sawyer, above n. 12; Judith Freedman, *Creating new UK institutions for tax governance and policy making: progress or confusion?*, [2013] 4 Brit. Tax Rev. 373.
42. For the OTS's own report of its achievements during the Coalition Government, see the summary issued on 27 March 2015, *OTS list of recommendations*, https://www.gov.uk/government/publications/ots-list-of-recommendations.
43. Lord Howe, above n. 13, at 123.
44. *OTS Framework Document* (2010), https://www.gov.uk/government/uploads/system/uploads/attachment_data/file/193545/ots_framework_document_jul10.pdf.
45. *OTS small business tax review: Final report, HMRC administration*, paras 7.35–7.37 (28 February 2012), https://www.gov.uk/government/publications/small-business-tax-review. The author was a member of a consultative committee advising the OTS on this project.
46. *OTS Employment Status report*, paras 10.47–10.50 (March 2015), available at: https://www.gov.uk/government/uploads/system/uploads/attachment_data/file/408608/OTS_Employment_Status_report.pdf.
47. *OTS Framework Document*, above n. 44; OTS Blog, 'Readout from the Office of Tax Simplification Workshop' (18 July 2013), https://taxsimplificationblog.files.wordpress.com/2013/07/workshop-readout1.pdf.
48. PAC, *Tax avoidance: the role of large accountancy firms*, HC 870 (26 April 2013), available at: http://www.publications.parliament.uk/pa/cm201213/cmselect/cmpubacc/870/870.pdf. See also the response of the OTS of 1 May 2013, https://www.gov.uk/government/uploads/system/uploads/attachment_data/file/199769/Letter_from_Rt_Hon_Michael_Jack_to_Margaret_Hodge_MP_Chairman_of_PAC.pdf.

'independent office of the Treasury',[49] the OTS is stated on its website to be part of HM Treasury. It has no formal constitution but is a creature of the Coalition agreement: nothing is to be found in statute. It can only investigate matters with agreement from the Chancellor. In these circumstances, it is not surprising to find the OTS looking for 'quick wins' in its reports, in order to persuade politicians that it should be supported as a continuing body. The OTS staff has had little option but to go along with this, but it has resulted in a good deal of 'tweaking' rather than fundamental change, although some useful changes have been made.

Two areas can be given as examples.[50] Having been unable to achieve a major review of small business taxation, the OTS proposed some relatively minor changes to the basis on which small unincorporated firms maintain their accounts and the way in which they can calculate tax deductible expenses.[51] A survey of small businesses suggested that they found some difficulty with expenses and accruals accounting, but the responses were far from convincing regarding the need for a reform of the law. The OTS proposed a limited provision for very small businesses, to relieve them from the burdens of accruals accounting as strictly required, even though many probably did not use accruals in any event. The problem was that by the time this reform had been processed by HMRC and HMT, the size limits for the cash basis had been increased as a result of various pressures, meaning that a number of anti- avoidance provisions and other complexities were seen to be necessary. Instead of seeing the cash basis as a simple change to reporting requirements, the HMRC and HM Treasury legislation went much further, actually using the scheme to change the basis of taxation, for example with limits on interest relief deductions.[52] The result was 'complification': twenty-four pages of new legislation, with unadvised taxpayers, who may have been using a cash basis anyway, now worse off because of the limitations introduced and with businesses which do have professional advice exposed to additional costs incurred as their advisers must advise which route is best for them.

The responsibility for this failure of the cash basis to simplify has been placed firmly at the door of HM Treasury and HMRC by commentators,[53] and implementation does seem to have gone awry. It is also the case, however, that the original idea was misconceived. Reforms proposed for micro-businesses are often hijacked by larger businesses in a form of threshold creep, and this was not unpredictable.[54] But the more

---

49. *OTS Framework Document*, above n. 44.
50. These are not the only projects undertaken by the OTS. See *OTS list of recommendations*, above n. 42.
51. *OTS Small business tax review: Final report - Simpler income tax for the smallest businesses* (February 2012), available at: https://www.gov.uk/government/uploads/system/uploads/attachment_data/file/199180/02_ots_small_business_tax_review_simpler_income_tax_280212.pdf.
52. *Finance Act 2013*, Sch. 4 amending *Income Tax (Trading and Other Income) Act 2005*, in particular s. 51A.
53. For example, Institute of Chartered Accountants in England & Wales (ICAEW), 'Cash Basis for Small Business: Comments submitted in February 2013 to HMRC', TAXREP 16/13 (ICAEWREP 20/13), http://www.icaew.com/en/technical/tax/tax-faculty/tax-faculty-representations/2013-tax-representations.
54. Freedman, *Why Taxing the Micro-business is Not Simple - A Cautionary Tale from the 'Old World'*, above n. 9.

fundamental problem is that this was a fiddling around the edges that should not have been attempted without being set firmly in the context of wider and more basic review. With no clear overarching design, there was a strong chance of something going wrong. As one ex-Parliamentary draftsman has put it:

> You start off designing a rowing boat and you end up trying to fly a Concorde and wonder why you have oars sticking out half way.[55]

This reform should not have been rushed to fit in with the political cycle. There was no particular need for quick reform other than the need to show something was being done for small businesses, because it was hard to do anything more fundamental. There was also a lack of accountability: the OTS felt that the implementation by HMT and HMRC was to blame, while the Government claimed to be following the advice of the OTS. Even had more fundamental change been proposed by the OTS, however, this would not have been successful without the political will to see it through. The overall result of this exercise was not simplification.

A second important example relates to tax reliefs. Despite a stated determination to reduce the number of reliefs, the Coalition Government ended its five-year term with more reliefs than when it started.[56] As the PAC stated:

> The [OTS] is grossly understaffed and has focused on abolishing tax rules that are no longer necessary, rather than more radical simplification. HM Treasury and HMRC should work together to make more radical progress in simplifying the UK's tax code, and should equip the [OTS] with the resources and influence it needs to help them do so.[57]

The management and scrutiny of tax reliefs is a topic which straddles the realm of tax policy-making and implementation scrutiny. At the moment it is being treated as a topic for scrutiny by the PAC,[58] but each relief needs to be considered in context as part of wider tax policy-making if any progress is to be made. Any exercise to cut down the number of reliefs from a list of all reliefs is bound to focus on those which have become unnecessary and unused. It is useful to tidy up the statute book, but this is not fundamental tax reform.

[3]   An Office of Tax Policy and New Joint Parliamentary Select Committee on Taxation?

Real change requires that the OTS or its equivalent is given greater powers, more independence and resources. Hopefully the OTS can evolve into a stronger and more independent institution, but this will require some bravery from politicians and more

---

55. Unpublished talk at Institute of Advanced Legal Studies, *Business Law Reform* conference, London 1992.
56. The *OTS final list of recommendations*, above n. 42, states that there were 1042 tax reliefs in November 2010 and 1140 in August 2014.
57. PAC, above n. 48, at 5.
58. PAC, *The effective management of tax reliefs*, HC892 (26 March 2015), http://www.publications .parliament.uk/pa/cm201415/cmselect/cmpubacc/892/892.pdf.

funding. The Office for Budget Responsibility (OBR) set up by the Coalition Government in 2010[59] shows that independence can be given even in areas of high sensitivity. An 'Office of Tax Policy' (OTP) would be a possibility.[60] It could not replace the political process, but it could act as a support for the civil servants whose everyday work takes them away from thinking about the structural issues of taxation. It would be a way of using expertise and absorbing it into political thinking. Such a body could perform a number of functions: investigating the structure of the tax system, proposing major reforms, taking up proposals from the revenue authorities and politicians (both government and opposition) and costing ideas put forward before they became too embedded in the political debate to change or dismiss them should that be necessary. It could also oversee drafting to ensure that the ideas were translated clearly into legislation. Politicians would be suspicious that such a body would interfere with the fact that tax is an essential part of the political debate, but the suggestion is not that the OTP would make policy, only that it would advise on policy. The ultimate decisions would always remain those of the politicians - the government of the day.

An Office of Taxpayer Responsibility has been proposed by Lord Gus O'Donnell, although in his version this would focus on vetting new policies put forward by government and perhaps the opposition.[61] The OTP proposed in this chapter would have wider powers than this because it would need to be able to initiate reforms, but the fact that Gus O'Donnell has proposed something not too far away from this should prevent it from being considered completely unviable.[62]

Staffing of such a body would need to come in part from secondments from the revenue authorities and private sector, since their expertise and experience will be

---

59. For further details on the role of the Office for Budget Responsibility, see HMT, *Charter for Budget Responsibility* (April 2011), https://www.gov.uk/government/publications/charter-for-budget-responsibility. The OBR scrutinizes HM Treasury's costing of tax measures but does not have any direct responsibility for tax design, though ideally comment on costing would feed into the design process. Suggestions that the OBR should also cost tax proposals from the Opposition parties in the run up to the General Election were discussed in 2014. The Chairman of the OBR, Robert Chote, did not consider this impossible but set out the difficulties in a letter to Andrew Tyrie MP, Chair of the Treasury Select Committee, on 15 January 2014. http://budgetresponsibility.org.uk/wordpress/docs/TSC_pre_election_costings1.pdf. The Labour party subsequently pressed for such costing but this was not agreed for the practical reasons set out in Chote's letter. It might be possible in a future election, but would require parties to put forward tax proposals very much earlier than usually done in an election: a positive advantage in the author's view, but one which might give the parties some campaigning difficulties.
60. Proposed by the author in *Creating new UK institutions for tax governance and policy making: progress or confusion?*, above n. 41, at 375–376.
61. Lord Gus O'Donnell, *UCL Inaugural Lecture: Building a Better Government*, 6 (April 2013), https://www.ucl.ac.uk/constitution-unit/events/inaugural_lecture_24042013.
62. Lord O'Donnell was the author of the O'Donnell Review (see above, n. 34) in his capacity as Cabinet Secretary, the most senior UK civil servant. This proposal has also been supported by the Association of Revenue and Customs, the trade union for senior tax officials: see http://blogs.mazars.com/letstalktax/files/2014/07/Tax-Transparency-The-Tax-Landscape-discussion-paper.pdf. Some note could also be taken of the New Zealand Generic Tax Policy Process and Tax Working Group, described in Sawyer, above n. 11. An 'Office of Tax Responsibility' has been proposed by activist Richard Murphy, but the focus of his institution is rather more on the Tax Gap than proposing fundamental reform and he would not permit secondments from the private sector. http://www.taxresearch.org.uk/Blog/2014/10/21/why-havent-we-got-an-office-for-tax-responsibility/.

needed, but there should also be staff qualified in other areas as necessary, with understanding of groups not always reached by consultation, including those with experience in various sectors of the taxpaying community such as those in the lower income tax group (where interaction with benefits must be considered), employee groups, the self-employed and small businesses. Academic expertise should also be engaged. It would be important, of course, to continue to have alternative academic and policy groupings that could express views that could be discussed by the OTP.[63]

The OTP would have to report to the Chancellor, since it is not possible for firm proposals for law reform to be dealt with in any other way, but both its proposals and any reports on the proposals of others could also be presented to a new Joint Parliamentary Select Committee on Taxation with membership drawn from both Houses, a suggestion with its origins in a possible reform put forward by Lord Howe and developed in the Budd report.[64] This would replace the current arrangement whereby the Parliamentary scrutiny that is given to tax reform comes only after the publication of proposals from the Economic Affairs Finance Bill Sub-Committee of the House of Lords. This Sub-Committee does good work but has very limited powers. The House of Commons Finance Bill Committee also reviews the Finance Bill but this debate is generally political rather than technical and there is very little time for proper discussion within the schedule of this Committee and no technical back-up or advice for non-ministerial members.[65]

[B] Scrutiny of Implementation and Administration in the UK

Various institutions exist in the UK for the scrutiny of implementation and tax administration, as opposed to tax policy-making. These might seem irrelevant in an article on tax simplification, and they will not all be catalogued here. However, the recent activities of the PAC cannot go unmentioned, since this committee has extended its reach considerably over the Coalition period and has pushed the boundaries of scrutiny to their limits and into areas that might be thought of as touching on policy. In addition, new institutions are being created which, to some extent, confuse the line between tax policy-making and governance, such as the panel established to assist in the application of the General Anti-abuse Rule (GAAR), the Assurance Commissioner appointed to monitor HMRC settlements with taxpayers and the independent reviewer set up to monitor aspects of the application of the Bank Code.

---

63. Sir Gus referred in his lecture (above n. 61, at 6) to the Institute for Fiscal Studies, saying that its conclusions on tax are accepted. This is rightly so, since it has an excellent track record, but a purely academic institution cannot have the level of responsibility and access to data that is required by an Office of Tax Policy. It would be healthy for the IFS to have an official counterpart in relation to tax design (the OBR already costs Government tax proposals, as previously explained in greater detail in above n. 59).
64. Lord Howe, above n. 13, at 120; Tax Law Review Committee (Sir Alan Budd, chair), above n. 13, at 1 (para. 7); Bowler, above n. 13, Executive Summary bullet point 2.
65. In an extreme version of this, the Finance Bill 2015 was passed in one afternoon in March 2015 with the May 2015 General Election imminent.

[1]   Parliamentary Committees

The PAC's terms of reference are to examine 'the accounts showing the appropriation of the sums granted to Parliament to meet the public expenditure'.[66] Under this head it must receive the accounts of HMRC via the Comptroller and Auditor General (C&AG),[67] to ascertain that adequate regulations and procedure have been framed to secure an effective check on the assessment, collection and proper allocation of revenue, and that they are being duly carried out.[68] The C&AG must examine the correctness of the sums brought to account and to report the results to the House of Commons. This is done through reports to the PAC[69] by the National Audit Office (NAO), a Parliamentary agency, of which the C&AG is the head.[70] The PAC can also commission the NAO to investigate and report to it on matters relating to whether expenditure has been properly incurred and its value for money.[71] Over the period of the Coalition Parliament it has done so on a variety of matters concerned with HMRC, including alleged 'sweetheart' deals with large business, tax avoidance and evasion and tax reliefs.[72] These investigations of whether HMRC is administering the tax system properly soon take the PAC into questions of whether the tax system is well-designed. It is hard to consider whether tax reliefs are being applied and monitored properly, for example, without discussing the question of whether those reliefs are desirable, because the examination involves consideration of the objectives of the relief. Similarly, discussions of whether cases of evasion and avoidance are being pursued with enough vigour bring further comments on the policy relating to the offences available, prosecutions and litigation. The PAC's report, marking the end of the 2010–2015 Coalition Parliament, recommends that HMRC should find new ways to tackle tax avoidance by multinational companies 'rather than waiting for the OECD's work to bear fruit', and that the number of tax reliefs should be 'radically' reduced.[73] The PAC has no power to

---

66. See Government Communication Service, 'Parliamentary committees', https://gcn.civilservice .gov.uk/guidance/how-to-guides/working-with-parliament/parliamentary-committees/.
67. An Officer of the House of Commons: National Audit Act 1983, s. 1(2).
68. Exchequer and Audit Departments Act 1921, s. 2.
69. See, for example, the PAC's inquiry of 2013–2014 drawing on the National Audit Office report, Her Majesty's Revenue and Customs 2013-14 Accounts: Report by the Comptroller and Auditor General (25 June 2014), http://www.parliament.uk/business/committees/committees-a-z/ commons-select/public-accounts-committee/inquiries/parliament-2010/hm-revenue--customs -accounts-2013-14/. For further information, see Patrick Dunleavy, Christopher Gilson, Simon Bastow & Jane Tinkler, The National Audit Office, the Public Accounts Committee and the Risk Landscape in UK Public Policy, Risk and Regulation Advisory Council Discussion Paper (October 2009), available at: http://eprints.lse.ac.uk/25785/.
70. http://www.nao.org.uk/about_us.aspx.
71. Prosser, above n. 34, at 53.
72. In the NAO report, Settling large tax disputes, HC 188, 6-10, 18-26 (14 June 2012) (http://www .nao.org.uk/report/settling-large-tax-disputes/), the head of the NAO concluded, on the basis of a report by Sir Andrew Park, a retired High Court judge, that the settlements reached by HMRC in five cases investigated were all 'reasonable' and successfully 'resolved multiple, long-outstanding tax issues'. However his report also confirmed the NAO's 'concerns about the processes by which the settlements were reached', and over poor communication with staff, which were considered to have undermined confidence in the settlements. The full list of NAO reports on HMRC can be found at http://www.nao.org.uk/search/hmrc/.
73. House of Commons PAC, Improving tax collection, HC 974, 5–6 (26 March 2015).

make binding recommendations, but it has influence and prestige and the support of the NAO, which gives it further weight.[74]

A further Parliamentary body that may assess the use of discretion by HMRC is the Treasury Select Committee.[75] This Committee is appointed by the House of Commons to examine the expenditure, administration and policy of a number of bodies, including HMRC. The Committee chooses its own subjects of inquiry, including the administration and effectiveness of HMRC.

There is a clear overlap between these two Committees and they have been engaged in noticeable territorial skirmishes during the period of the Coalition Government. In 2010 the House of Commons Standing Orders were amended to provide for election of select committee chairs[76] and this appears to have enhanced the authority of the chairs and made each of the posts a sought-after 'power base'. The Chair of the PAC, Margaret Hodge, has become a household name in the UK and beyond by pursuing tax issues and calling in the heads of global companies to appear before her Committee.[77] This, together with skilful use of the media and the current media and popular interest in taxation, has given the PAC considerable influence and there is little doubt that some of the recent developments in terms of tackling tax avoidance and evasion from the UK Government have been spurred on by this pressure. In this way, the strengthened parliamentary committee, although designed as a scrutiny body, can play a part in tax policy-making.

One difficulty with this is that the PAC covers a very wide range of topics besides taxation and has no formal advisers on taxation. It is advised by the NAO, which does important work on accounts and value for money audits, but which is not staffed as an expert tax advisory body. The NAO recognized this itself when it appointed Sir Andrew Park to assist on its work on settlements, since it did not have the expertise to do this.[78] Another limitation is that HMRC is (rightly) restricted from sharing information regarding the affairs of individual taxpayers with Members of Parliament and this leads to many tensions between the parliamentary committees and the HMRC officials, since they sometimes draw the line in different places.[79]

The parliamentary committees have an important part to play in scrutiny, but are not equipped to provide input into tax policy-making, nor should that be their role. If there was a properly advised and constituted Joint Committee of Parliament on Taxation Policy, working with an Office of Tax Policy, as suggested above, the PAC might feel it less necessary to expand its role to fill this vacuum and the NAO could

---

74. Prosser, above n. 34, at 132.
75. http://www.parliament.uk/business/committees/committees-a-z/commons-select/treasury-committee/.
76. Standing Orders of the House of Commons, Orders 122A-122C, http://www.publications. parliament.uk/pa/cm/cmstords.htm; cited in John Snape, *The Political Economy of Corporation Tax: Theory, Values and Law Reform*, 217 (Hart Publishing, 2011).
77. For further discussion of the rising importance of parliamentary committees, see Tom Shakespeare, *A Point of View: Do parliament's select committees wield too much power?*, BBC News Magazine (22 March 2015), http://www.bbc.co.uk/news/magazine-31961356.
78. See above n. 72.
79. Osita Mba, *Transparency and Accountability of Tax Administration in the UK: The Nature and Scope of Taxpayer Confidentiality*, [2012] 2 Brit. Tax Rev. 187.

focus on its role of assessing the accounts and value for money issues. Adding yet another institution might not seem to be a simplification, but streamlining the functions of the committees and allowing them to specialize could only be beneficial and would reduce complexity in the long run by promoting fundamental rather than reactive reform.

[2]   The GAAR Panel and Other New Institutions

In addition to these parliamentary committees, the period of the Coalition Government has seen the creation of the GAAR Advisory Panel,[80] a new Tax Assurance Commissioner and Tax Disputes Resolution Board to oversee settlements, in response to the PAC's criticisms of HMRC governance in this area,[81] and an independent reviewer for issues associated with the application of the Bank Code.[82] In each case, these institutions have a very specific role, which is not a policy-making function, but there is a sense in which they are exercising discretion in such as a way as to overlap with the tax policy-making function. In addition, none of these institutions is truly independent of HMRC and yet each one is supposed to be adding to public confidence and each one has a function that could have important policy implications. All three of these institutions are attempts to solve problems that would not arise were tax laws less complex and if fewer grey areas existed. The complexity of the law results, therefore, in proliferation of institutions. It may be that the institutions improve management and accountability in these cases, but the institutions themselves can also add to the costs and burdens of the system on taxpayers unless well designed.

The Tax Assurance Commissioner and Tax Disputes Resolution Board (TDRB) oversee settlements with taxpayers in sensitive cases and those with more than GBP 100 million in tax under consideration.[83] Given that the Litigation and Settlements Strategy governing whether there can be a settlement with a taxpayer[84] states that a dispute can only be resolved by settlement on a basis that is consistent with the law, it is clear that whether there can be a settlement is going to be an issue only where there is uncertainty. In deciding whether an agreement is acceptable or not, therefore, the Commissioners and the TDRB are, of necessity, involved in determining whether they believe there is uncertainty about the view of the law initially taken by HMRC. This new system of governance provides some protection to taxpayers and to the public generally that arrangements are not being reached without good reason, but there are

---

80. Discussed further in Freedman, *Creating new UK institutions for tax governance and policy making: progress or confusion?*, above n. 41, at 378–380.
81. See HMRC, *How we resolve Tax Disputes: The Tax Assurance Commissioner's annual report 2012-13*, 4-5 (2 July 2013), https://www.gov.uk/government/uploads/system/uploads/attachment_data/file/210246/3741_Tax_Assurance_AR_accessible.pdf. See also above n. 72.
82. Space prevents a thorough examination of the curious Bank Code and the independent reviewer here - for further details and discussion see Richard Collier, *Intentions, Banks, Politics and the Law: The UK Code of Practice on Taxation for Banks*, [2014] 4 Brit. Tax Rev. 478 at 496ff.
83. HMRC, *How we resolve Tax Disputes*, above n. 81.
84. HMRC, *Resolving tax disputes: Commentary on the litigation and settlement strategy*, 9 (November 2013), https://www.gov.uk/government/uploads/system/uploads/attachment_data/file/387770/Commentary_on_litigation.pdf.

questions about the fact that the system is operated entirely by HMRC Commissioners and employees and not by a genuinely independent body. As this involves individual taxpayers, the settlements are not subject to scrutiny by the PAC other than in general terms.[85] In addition, the need for this scrutiny may delay valid settlements and complicate the law in that sense.

The GAAR Panel is another example of an institution that has emerged to provide a framework to manage lack of certainty in tax law, but which might itself have become problematic. It was proposed by the Aaronson Study Group[86] on the GAAR as a forum for discussion to help mark out the place where the line should be drawn at which the GAAR should apply: the line between abuse and non-abusive transactions.[87] The Panel has now changed in membership form[88] and is being expected to take on tasks it was not initially intended to manage. In addition its composition has changed: in a bid to make the GAAR more acceptable to practitioners, the original design of the Panel, which involved having HMRC representation on it, was changed so that the body became a panel of external experts. This was the result of informal consultation which distorted the original intention.

The Panel has two functions. First, it opines on the non-statutory guidance around the GAAR - guidance that is recognized by statute but not given the force of statute and so is not binding. In practice this gives the Panel enormous influence over where the relevant lines are drawn, although the final say remains with the courts. This was initially intended to be undertaken together with HMRC: removal of the HMRC member appears on the surface to affect this function significantly, although HMRC can be expected to have their say informally.

The other function of the Panel is to give its opinion on the reasonableness of transactions (as defined in the GAAR legislation). This opinion is not binding on a court but must be taken into account by the court under the GAAR legislation. The Panel's role is not intended to be judicial, and the members are appointed by HMRC, so are not truly independent. Nevertheless, the removal of the HMRC member from this Panel during the translation of the proposal into legislation confuses the picture and emphasis on the decision of Panel members for the purposes of new provisions in some circumstances places a great strain on this new institution.[89] The resulting institution lies somewhere between a tax law-making body, a scrutiny body and, some would argue, despite HMRC denials, a judicial body.

The emergence of the institutions referred to in this section was the result of ad hoc reaction to problems rather than arising from full consideration and design. Institutions can offer a solution to tax policy and tax governance issues, but only if they

---

85. Although the NAO may review cases in more detail: see above n. 72.
86. For discussion by the Aaronson Study Group on the GAAR (of which the author was a member) on this issue, see *GAAR Study: Report by Graham Aaronson QC*, paras 6.8–6.9 (11 November 2011), http://webarchive.nationalarchives.gov.uk/20130321041222/http:/www.hm-treasury.gov.uk/d/gaar_final_report_111111.pdf.
87. *GAAR Study: Report by Graham Aaronson QC*, above n. 86, at para. 1.7 (vii).
88. *Finance Act 2013*, Part 5 and Sch. 43.
89. The *Finance Act 2014*, Part 4 provides for accelerated payments by taxpayers where two members of the Panel consider the transaction unreasonable within the terms of the GAAR.

are planned and conceptually coherent. It is not clear that the recent emergence and development of institutions in the UK tax arena have fully satisfied these criteria.

§16.05   CONCLUSION

Simplification of the tax system can never be the sole driver of reform. Some complexity will always be necessary in a complex world. Institutions have a role to play in helping to manage this complexity. Institutions can also improve tax systems and sometimes reduce complexity, but this simplification will only be achieved if the institutions are conceptually coherent with clear objectives.

It has been argued in this chapter that the formulation of tax policy objectives is a matter for politicians. Expertise is important but cannot be treated as uncontested, and policy-makers need an institutional structure which facilitates interrogation of the experts and absorption of their advice, as well as a wide range of other views. Scrutiny bodies and other institutions facilitating management are important but need a clear role. Like tax policy itself, institutions must be carefully designed. A proliferation of institutions can create their own complexity.

CHAPTER 17

Oversight Mechanisms and Administrative Responses to Tax Complexity in the United States

John Hasseldine[*]

§17.01 INTRODUCTION

The United States has, arguably, the most complex tax system in the world.[1] Not only is the volume of US income tax law impressively long, but technical aspects of the law add dramatically to its complexity.[2] Somewhat oddly, the length of the US tax law is not clear itself. However, it is estimated to be about 4 million words[3] (or roughly seven copies of Tolstoy's *War and Peace!*[4]). The National Taxpayer Advocate (NTA), in her 2010 Annual Report to the US Congress, highlighted that the most serious problem facing taxpayers – and the Internal Revenue Service (IRS) – is the complexity of the Internal Revenue Code (hereinafter referred to as 'the Code'). She lists four reasons for why tax reform is required in order to deal with complexity:[5]

---

[*] I am grateful for detailed and helpful comments from Michael D'Ascenzo, George Guttman, Nina Olson and participants at the Prato Conference on Tax Complexity on an earlier version of this chapter.
1. Victor Thuronyi, *Comparative Tax Law*, 17 (Kluwer, 2003).
2. Doug Barney, Daniel Tschopp & Steve Wells, *Tax Simplification through Readability: A Look at Tax Law Complexity*, 82(12) The CPA Journal 6 (December 2012).
3. National Taxpayer Advocate, *2012 Annual Report to Congress*, Vol. 1, 6, note 11 (2012).
4. See, for example, Kelly Phillips Erb, *Tax Code Hits Nearly 4 Million Words, Taxpayer Advocate Calls It Too Complicated*, Forbes (10 January 2013), available at: http://www.forbes.com/sites/kellyphillipserb/2013/01/10/tax-code-hits-nearly-4-million-words-taxpayer-advocate-calls-it-too-complicated/ (accessed on 9 November 2014).
5. National Taxpayer Advocate, *2010 Annual Report to Congress*, Vol. 1, 3–9 (2010).

(1) 'The Current Code Imposes Huge Compliance Burdens on Individual Taxpayers and Businesses'.

According to the IRS' own data, US taxpayers and firms spend 6.1 billion hours per year complying with the filing requirements of the Code. This figure excludes any additional time spent in dealing with IRS notices and audits. The IRS estimates that the compliance costs of the individual and corporate income tax requirements for 2008 were USD 163 billion – roughly 11% of aggregate income tax receipts. More recently, Marcuss et al. split this into a burden of at least USD 50 billion for individuals and at least USD 100 billion for businesses.[6]

(2) 'The Tax Code is Rife with Complexity and Special Tax Breaks, Helping Taxpayers Who Can Afford Expensive Tax Advice and Discriminating against Those Who Cannot'.

Tax complexity leads taxpayers to believe that they are unfairly paying more than others, which in turn, leads them to feel cynical if they believe that every other interest group, or other taxpayer, gets their own special tax break. The result of these narrow tax breaks is that voluntary tax compliance decreases. This finding is consistent with prior research investigating equity effects on tax compliance and other research on tax complexity.[7]

(3) 'Complexity Obscures Understanding and Creates a Sense of Distance Between Taxpayers and the Government, Resulting in Lower Rates of Voluntary Tax Compliance'.

As the Report notes, while few taxpayers would steal from a local charity, when taxpayers have a choice about reporting their income (e.g., cash income), compliance rates are very low. The NTA suggests there are two reasons for this. First, community members generally appreciate the role played by local organizations, but in contrast, few Americans understand where their tax dollars are spent, and how they benefit. Second, complexity results in taxpayers having little idea of how much they are paying and why. The NTA believes that this 'distance' between government and taxpayers must be addressed and that simplifying the Code is an important step.

(4) 'The Tax Code Is So Complex That the IRS Has Difficulty Administering It'.

The IRS is a large organization and, despite 90% of taxpayers relying on professional preparers or tax software, the IRS receives over 100 million calls per year. In fiscal years 2009 and 2010, it was unable to answer more than 25% of these and faces challenges in answering the more than 10 million pieces of taxpayer correspondence it receives each year.

Of course this list in itself leaves weighty issues to be grappled with – none of which are simple. For instance, how to measure compliance costs; the effect of

---

6. Rosemary Marcuss, George Contos, John Guyton, Patrick Langetieg, Allen Lerman, Susan Nelson, Brenda Schafer & Melissa Vigil, *Income Taxes and Compliance Costs: How Are They Related?*, 66(4) Nat'l Tax J. 833 (2013).

7. See Kate Krause, *Tax Complexity: Problem or Opportunity?*, 28(5) Pub. Fin. Rev. 395 (2000).

complexity on taxpayer compliance; how the US tax system could be reformed through piecemeal or large-scale policy reform to reduce complexity; whether the Code could be simplified by being rewritten, and so forth. This chapter sidesteps these issues[8] and focuses on addressing the NTA's fourth point in the list above, i.e., the difficulty that the IRS has in administering the Code. In particular, the focus is on oversight mechanisms of the IRS and the actions of these oversight mechanisms as they relate to tax complexity.

In an IMF paper,[9] Kidd and Crandall address just how difficult it can be to evaluate the performance of revenue authorities. As one example, they state that there can be many exogenous factors impacting on total revenue collections, such as, the economy in general, the quality of national statistics used, tax policy changes, regional growth trends, oil prices, population demographics, level of political commitment, and resources available.

Aside from any impact on revenue collections, there are other consequences of tax complexity – such as the growth in tax software and the use of professional tax preparers by individual taxpayers. Businesses also face greater compliance costs, and sometimes complexity can affect other areas – for example, financial reporting by large companies on Uncertain Tax Positions. With the passage in the US of the Foreign Account Tax Compliance Act (FATCA) in 2010,[10] these costs are even affecting non-US taxpayers in the form of foreign banks.[11]

This chapter proceeds as follows. As a starting point, §17.02 outlines a brief history of the Code, how US tax laws are made, sources of tax law and the IRS' administrative structure. Section §17.03 discusses the political framework surrounding taxes, drawing on the resources made available to the IRS, and noting salient facts from the 'Tea Party' scandal of 2013. Then §17.04 and §17.05 respectively discuss internal and external oversight of the IRS. Section §17.06 offers concluding remarks.

§17.02 HOW US TAX LAWS ARE MADE AND ADMINISTERED

[A] How Tax Laws Are Made in the US

Before 1939, US tax law provisions were contained in individual Revenue Acts enacted by Congress. The first codification was in 1939 and another took place in 1954. The Internal Revenue Code of 1986 however was not a recodification of the 1954 tax law. Apparently Congress felt that the changes made by the Tax Reform Act of 1986 were so substantial that a change in the Code title was in order. The Code has ballooned to

---

8. In addition, the complexity exhibited by, and caused by, differing state income tax systems is ignored here: see Joel Slemrod, *The Etiology of Tax Complexity: Evidence from U.S. State Income Tax Systems*, 33(3) Pub. Fin. Rev. 279 (2005).
9. Maureen Kidd & William Crandall, *Revenue Authorities: Issues and Problems in Evaluating Their Success*, IMF Working Paper WP/06/240 (International Monetary Fund, 2006).
10. Enacted as a part of the *Hiring Incentives to Restore Employment Act 2010* (US), 124 Stat. 71-118, amending the Internal Revenue Code.
11. See *Tax evasion: Dropping the bomb – America's fierce campaign against tax cheats is doing more harm than good*, The Economist, 61 (28 June 2014).

about 5,600 pages and, as noted previously, is estimated by the IRS to contain about 4 million words.

The last fundamental federal tax reform occurred in 1986. The process for tax legislation generally commences in the House of Representatives, specifically the House Ways and Means Committee. Once the proposed Bill is approved by the House it is sent to the Senate, and is considered by the Senate Finance Committee. Assuming approval by the House and the Senate, the Bill is sent to the President for approval or veto. If the versions approved by the House and the Senate differ, then a conference committee of representatives from the House and Senate work to resolve these differences. The Bill is subject to amendment at each stage of the process.

The process described so far excludes lobbying activity which is obviously present in practice and the Joint Committee on Taxation provides technical advice in the legislative process. Committee reports are an important source for ascertaining the intent of Congress when passing new tax laws. These are key for interpreting legislation, especially before regulations have been issued. For major tax legislation, the staff of the Joint Committee may prepare a general explanation of the Act. These are commonly known as the 'bluebooks' because of the colour of their covers. These detailed explanations can provide valuable guidance to tax advisers and taxpayers. The IRS will not accept 'bluebook' explanations as having legal effect but they are substantial authority for the purposes of the accuracy-related penalty.[12]

The Code is supreme Federal tax law, except in the following situations. First, when in direct conflict with a tax treaty, the law provides that whichever of the two was most recently passed will take precedence.[13] Second, the Code will not be supreme if the Supreme Court determines that a statutory provision is unconstitutional. In cases not involving constitutionality issues, Congress may override the Supreme Court by amending the Code. Taxpayers often have the impression that the Supreme Court always is the final word but this is not the case with the Internal Revenue Code.

[B]   Administrative Sources of Law

Administrative sources of tax law are either issued by the Treasury Department or the IRS. In respect of Treasury Department Regulations, under §7805(a) of the Code, Treasury has a duty to issue rules and regulations to explain and interpret the Code. Treasury Regulations carry considerable weight[14] and are important in tax compliance and, as they interpret the Code, they are arranged in the same manner as the Code but with a prefix indicating the type of tax to which they apply. There are several types of regulations, namely: Final, Proposed, and Temporary (which expire at the end of three years); Legislative regulations; Interpretative regulations; and Procedural regulations.

---

12. Notice 90-20, 1990-1 C.B. 328.
13. See, for example, Anthony Infanti, *Curtailing Tax Treaty Overrides: A Call to Action*, 62(4) U. Pitt. L. Rev. 677, 684, note 40 (2001).
14. For consideration of administrative practices and Treasury regulations in the force of law, see, for example, Kristin Hickman, *Unpacking the Force of Law*, 66(2) Vand. L. Rev. 465 (2013), and Mitchell Rogovin & Donald L. Korb, *The Four R's Revisited: Regulations, Rulings, Reliance, and Retroactivity in the 21st Century: A View From Within*, 46(3) Duq. L. Rev. 323 (2008).

Apart from Treasury Department regulations, the National Office of the IRS issues Revenue Rulings and Revenue Procedures as official pronouncements. These include Revenue Rulings (Rev. Rul.) which provide specific interpretations of the tax law and therefore do not carry the same legal force and effect as Regulations and Revenue Procedures (Rev. Proc.) which concern the internal management practices and procedures of the IRS. Both serve to provide guidance to both IRS personnel and taxpayers in handling routine tax matters.

Other remaining administrative pronouncements include:

(1) Treasury Decision (TD): issued by the Treasury Department to promulgate new Regulations, amend existing Regulations, or to announce Government positions on court decisions. Published in the Internal Revenue Bulletin (IRB).

(2) Technical Information Release (TIR): issued to announce the publication of various IRS pronouncements (e.g., Revenue Rulings, Revenue Procedures).

(3) Letter Ruling (Ltr Rul. or PLR): issued by National Office of IRS upon a taxpayer's request and describe how the IRS will treat a proposed transaction for tax purposes. In general, these apply only to taxpayers making the request but post-1984 rulings may be substantial authority for the purposes of avoiding accuracy-related penalties. The IRS must make letter rulings available for public inspection.

(4) Technical Advice Memorandum (TAM): issued by the National Office of IRS. TAMs resemble letter rulings, but they are issued in response to questions raised during audits.

[C] Judicial Sources of US Tax Law

After a taxpayer has exhausted remedies available within the IRS the dispute can be taken to the Federal courts. The matter is first considered by one of four courts of original jurisdiction (trial court) with appeals taken to the appropriate appellate court. The US Tax Court was established in 1942 and has nineteen judges, including one chief judge. If the amount in controversy is less than USD 50,000 on an annual basis, a taxpayer can have their case heard in the Small Cases Division, which is less formal than the regular Tax Court procedures – with taxpayers able to represent themselves.[15]

There is of course precedential value from court decisions. American law, following English common law, is frequently 'made' by judicial decisions. Under the doctrine of *stare decisis*, each decision has precedential value for future decisions with the same controlling set of facts.

---

15. William Hoffman, William Raabe, James Smith & David Maloney, *Corporations, Partnerships, Estates & Trusts*, 23 (36th ed., South-Western, 2012).

[D]   IRS Administrative Structure

In the late 1990s the IRS was deeply unpopular and Congressional hearings were held resulting in the Report of the National Commission on Restructuring the Internal Revenue Service.[16] Over fifteen years later, Hoffman notes[17] that the changes made under the IRS Restructuring and Reform Act (informally known as RRA '98) are being called into question as the IRS and its overseers face public and congressional alarm about deteriorating taxpayer service, alleged enforcement abuses in the Tax-Exempt and Government Entities Division, and questionable management and training decisions, not to mention many other considerable challenges. Further discussion on the difficult political environment facing the IRS is in the next section (§17.03).

The organizational structure of the IRS following RRA '98 was vastly altered from a geographical hierarchical form to a functional form. Aside from customary National Office shared services functions and divisional units on Research, Analysis and Statistics, Appeals, and Communication and Liaison, the major operating divisions are now Wage and Investment, Small Business and Self Employed, Large Business and International, and Tax Exempt/Government Entities.

§17.03   TAXES (AND THE FUNDING OF THEIR COLLECTION) IS 'POLITICAL'

[A]   The 'Tea Party Scandal'

In 2013, a scandal in the US erupted when a report was issued by the Treasury Inspector General for Tax Administration[18] which found that IRS employees in the Cincinnati office had targeted certain organizations' applications for tax-exempt status for heightened scrutiny. In particular, the employees singled out groups with 'Tea Party' or 'Patriot' in their names leading to long delays in clarification of the organizations' tax status under §501(c)(4) of the Code. A media maelstrom followed the report with accusations of a hidden political agenda extending all the way to the White House. In response, President Obama fired Steven Miller, the acting IRS Commissioner. Many committees held hearings on the issue including the Senate Finance Committee, the House Ways and Means Committee, the House Committee on Oversight and Government Reform, and the House Appropriations Subcommittee on Financial Services and General Government. A criminal investigation was launched by the FBI. Fall-out from the scandal continued into 2014 in a case brought by an activist group, Judicial Watch, against the IRS – where it transpired that hundreds of emails

---

16. National Commission on Restructuring the Internal Revenue Service (Bob Kerrey & Rob Portman, Co-Chairs), *A Vision for a New IRS: Report of the National Commission on Restructuring the Internal Revenue Service* (US Congress, 25 June 1997).
17. William Hoffman, *15 Years After RRA '98: Time to Re-restructure the IRS?*, 140(7) Tax Notes 647 (12 August 2013).
18. Treasury Inspector General for Tax Administration, *Inappropriate Criteria Were Used to Identify Tax-Exempt Applications for Review*, Report 2013-10-053 (14 May 2013).

sent by Lois Lerner, the IRS official in charge, had been lost in a computer crash and were not available to be produced.

The Tea Party Scandal raises many issues for the IRS including its use of administrative discretion,[19] the IRS' own legitimacy, likely reputational effects, and possible lasting damage to the tax system. Little reported in the media firestorm at the time was the fact that groups leaning to the political left were also subject to delay in clarification of their tax status under Code § 501(c)(4).

[B] IRS Budget

The IRS budget has been declining over the last four years even though President Obama has called for increases in the IRS budget. Congress reduced the IRS budget from approximately USD 12.1 billion for FY 2011 down to USD 10.95 billion for FY 2015. Provision of resources to the IRS is hugely political. For example, in July 2014, during Congressional debate, Rep. Bill Huizenga (R-Mich.) proposed a USD 788 million cut from the IRS' USD 5 billion tax enforcement budget, stating:

> The IRS has been targeting American taxpayers, as we've learned, for their political beliefs for the last four or five years .... During this period, a culture of shading the truth was fostered and developed by directors and administrators throughout the IRS..... Now this culture within the IRS has grown to one of stonewalling, double-talk and mistrust. It's up to Congress to use the power of the purse... to rein in the IRS and force them to conduct their analysis in an unbiased manner.[20]

This cut was voted by voice and has been reported as Republicans cutting the budget in response in part for the Tea Party scandal discussed above.[21] Democrats, normally supporters of the IRS' budget, were outvoted.

The IRS Advisory Council notes that the IRS is 'continually required to "do more with less" resources while operating in a complex ever changing environment'. While it seems likely that some efficiency gains have been made, and can be made, clearly these are extremely challenging times for the IRS and cutting the budget by more than USD 1 billion has led to evidence of declining performance as shown in a time series of key performance indicators obtained from the IRS Oversight Board's Taxpayer Attitude Surveys.[22]

---

19. Lily Kahng, *The IRS Tea Party Controversy and Administrative Discretion*, 99 Cornell L. Rev. Online 41 (September 2013).
20. The comments were shown on C-SPAN and cited by Pete Kasperowicz, *House Ravages IRS, Guts $1.1 Billion from Tax Enforcement Budget*, The Blaze (15 July 2014), available at: http://www .theblaze.com/stories/2014/07/15/house-ravages-irs-guts-1-1-billion-from-tax-enforcement-budget/ (accessed on 14 November 2014).
21. See, for example, Richard Rubin, *IRS Enforcement at Risk as Collections Drop 9% Amid Cuts*, Bloomberg News (18 September 2013), available at: http://www.bloomberg.com/news/2013-09-18/irs-enforcement-at-risk-as-collections-drop-9-amid-cuts.html (accessed on 9 November 2014).
22. IRS Oversight Board, *2013 Taxpayer Attitude Survey*, 9 (2014).

The New York Times in a July 2014 editorial suggests that funding is the *real* Internal Revenue scandal which will affect the ability of the IRS to enforce the Code and benefit 'the nation's highest-income taxpayers, many of whom donate generously to Republican politicians to keep their taxes low'.[23] Support for a realistic budget for the IRS is not restricted to 'IRS insiders', with the American Institute of Certified Public Accountants (AICPA) stating in a September 2013 letter to the House and Senate Appropriations Committee:

> The IRS needs sufficient operating funds to properly administer and enforce our complex tax laws, as well as provide assistance to taxpayers and their advisors ... a reduction in taxpayer service resources would negatively impact both taxpayers and our members alike.[24]

Chronic underfunding of the IRS has been highlighted by the NTA as a most serious problem. The NTA states that in fiscal year 2012, the IRS received around 125 million calls of which only about two in every three were answered by a live person, and each caller had to wait, on average, seventeen minutes to get through.[25] At year-end there was a backlog of over 1 million pieces of correspondence. Listed at number three under the section of 'Most Serious Problems', the report states:

> [T]he lack of sufficient funding is the sole or significant cause of many of the problems identified in this report. There are practical limits to how well the IRS can respond to tens of millions of telephone calls, more than 10 million letters, and hundreds of thousands of identity theft cases each year, as well as maintain robust tax-compliance programs including outreach and education, if it lacks adequate and educated personnel, technology, and other support.[26]

§17.04 INTERNAL ADMINISTRATIVE OVERSIGHT

It seems undeniable that the IRS itself understands that taxpayers face a very complex Code and that tax practice and administration takes place in an uncertain environment. Prior to discussing internal oversight, including Committee work and the work of the National Taxpayer Advocate, two of the initiatives the IRS has undertaken in relation to complexity are given as examples of this viewpoint.

[A]   Taxpayer Communications

In 2009, a Taxpayer Communications Taskgroup, within the Office of Taxpayer Correspondence, noted the problem of ineffective communications. For example, there were approximately 1,000 different types of notices and letters from 120 different

---

23. See New York Times Editorial Board, *The Real Internal Revenue Scandal*, New York Times (5 July 2014), available at: http://www.nytimes.com/2014/07/06/opinion/sunday/the-real-internal-revenue-scandal.html?_r = 0 (accessed on 9 November 2014).
24. Cited in IRS Oversight Board. *Annual Report to Congress 2013*. 4 (2014).
25. National Taxpayer Advocate, *2012 Annual Report to Congress*, above n. 3, Executive Summary, at 2.
26. National Taxpayer Advocate, *2012 Annual Report to Congress*, above n. 3, Vol. 1, at 34.

'Notice Authors' with 200 million pieces of correspondence sent annually from forty different systems, with a range of three to thirteen inserts sent with each notice. Problems with variability in content, style and format, erroneous correspondence, and a decentralized and fragmented approach were believed to lead to taxpayer confusion, and an unnecessary burden on taxpayers, and which did not always lead to consistent results.[27]

As an example, the initial 'Underreporter Notice', known as a CP2000 Notice, which is essentially a computer generated mismatch notice, required taxpayers to work through forty-two steps on the ten page Notice. The Taskgroup noted that while the tax environment is increasingly complex, taxpayers expect more 'plain language' communications. With a goal of improved clarity, accuracy, and effectiveness of written communications, the Taskgroup, working with external strategic branding consultants Siegel & Gale, has embarked on converting all notices and letters to plain language, which is expected to reduce the burden on taxpayers, reduce penalty and interest payments through faster resolution of issues, and improve taxpayer and practitioner satisfaction.[28] In terms of IRS outcomes, it is hoped this process will lead to faster resolution of taxpayer cases, improved taxpayer compliance, and cost savings achieved through postage and printing costs, reduced phone traffic, and increased process efficiencies.

[B]   IRS Research Conferences and Measurement of Compliance Costs

Each year, the IRS has held an annual research conference (now jointly with the Urban-Brookings Tax Policy Center) with the papers subsequently published in that year's IRS Research Bulletin and available on the IRS website.[29] A review of past conference programmes reveals several papers (co-)authored by IRS staff. Many of these papers address tax enforcement and compliance, (themselves linked to tax complexity), with others linked to the taxpayer perspective.

For example, a stream of work has been conducted within the IRS Office of Research on the topic of taxpayer burden and compliance costs, including, but not limited to, Contos et al. who estimate compliance costs for corporations and partnerships,[30] Beers et al. who establish that complexity influences voluntary compliance by

---

27. Jodi Patterson, *A plan for improving IRS written communications with taxpayers*, Presentation made by the Director, Taxpayer Communications Taskgroup (TACT) (30 October 2009), available at: http://www.centerforplainlanguage.org/downloads/2009_symposium/Patterson_Presentation_10-30-09.pdf (accessed on 10 November 2014).
28. See, for example, *Internal Revenue Service and Siegel + Gale Win ClearMark Grand Prize Award From the Center for Plain Language*, Bloomberg News (9 May 2011), available at: http://www.bloomberg.com/apps/news?pid = newsarchive&sid = aTpS74m3.eDM (accessed on 10 November 2014).
29. See, for example, the 2014 Internal Revenue Service – Tax Policy Center Research Conference, Advancing Tax Administration, held on 19 June 2014: http://www.irs.gov/uac/SOI-Tax-Stats-2014-IRS-TPC-Research-Conference (accessed on 10 November 2014).
30. George Contos, John Guyton, Patrick Langetieg, Allen H. Lerman & Susan Nelson, *Taxpayer Compliance Costs for Corporations and Partnerships: A New Look*, IRS Research Bulletin, New Research on Tax Administration: An IRS-TPC Conference, 3 (2012).

sole proprietors (and document differences between *high compliance v. low compliance* communities),[31] and Guyton and Hodge who examine compliance costs of IRS post-filing processes (i.e., amended returns, taxpayers with accounts receivable, audit cases, and appeal cases).[32]

[C]   IRS Committees

[1]   IRS Advisory Council

The IRS Advisory Council (IRSAC) serves as an advisory body to the Commissioner of Internal Revenue. In 2014, the Council has nineteen members with diverse and high-level backgrounds and is divided into four sub-groups: Wage and Investment, Small Business/Self Employed, Large Business and International, and the Office of Professional Responsibility. Issues requiring attention are reported annually by each sub-group and many of these pertain to reducing taxpayer burden, and more efficient and effective working practices.

Some of the more recent issues related to complexity include strategies to increase the use of online payment agreements,[33] risk assessment of large taxpayers,[34] provision of a central information source for taxpayers, particularly small business taxpayers, to understand their information reporting,[35] and filing requirements for the report of foreign bank and financial accounts – which were stated to be 'confusing and extremely overbroad'.[36]

[2]   Electronic Tax Administration Advisory Committee

The Electronic Tax Administration Advisory Committee (ETAAC), established pursuant to RRA '98, facilitates public discussion about electronic tax administration issues and provides a report to Congress each June on IRS progress in meeting goals for electronic filing of tax returns. An important IRS goal is to achieve an overall 80%

---

31. Tom Beers, Eric LoPresti & Eric San Juan, *Factors Influencing Voluntary Compliance by Sole Proprietors: Preliminary Survey Results*, IRS Research Bulletin, Tax Administration at the Centennial: An IRS-TPC Research Conference, 65 (2013).
32. John Guyton & Ronald Hodge, *The Compliance Costs of IRS Post-Filing Processes*, Paper presented at the 2014 IRS-TPC Research Conference, Advancing Tax Administration (19 June 2014).
33. Internal Revenue Service Advisory Council, *2013 Public Report*, Small Business/Self Employed Subgroup Report, 74 (20 November 2013).
34. Internal Revenue Service Advisory Council, *2013 Public Report*, above n. 33, Large Business and International Subgroup Report, 24. The IRSAC drew on tax administration experience in Australia and the UK in relation to this issue.
35. Internal Revenue Service Advisory Council, *2012 Public Report*, Small Business/Self Employed Subgroup Report, 75 (15 November 2012).
36. Internal Revenue Service Advisory Council, *2010 Public Report*, Small Business/Self-Employed Subgroup Report, 78 (17 November 2010).

electronic filing rate. While individual returns have been above 80% for three years, other return types mean that the overall e-filing rate is currently just under 75%.[37]

Progress has come through software technology and taxpayer access to general and specific tax information with the IRS now using some innovative approaches, e.g., virtual service delivery and social media (its 'IRS2Go' smartphone app released in 2011 has since exceeded 5.5 million downloads[38]). Challenges in this area include late legislation and the challenges posed by tax fraud and identity theft. Systems and technology requirements from two new areas of administration, the Patient Protection and Affordable Care Act (known as Obamacare) and the Foreign Account Tax Compliance Act, are also substantial.

[3] Information Reporting Program Advisory Committee

The Information Reporting Program Advisory Committee (IRPAC) was established in 1991 and works with the IRS to provide recommendations on a wide range of issues intended to improve information reporting and achieve fairness to taxpayers. It is split into four sub-groups, namely burden reduction, employee benefits and payroll, emerging compliance issues, and international reporting and withholding. Many of the Committee's reports[39] comprise detailed recommendations on technical practicalities of operating the IRS' information reporting programme.

§17.05 EXTERNAL ADMINISTRATIVE OVERSIGHT

[A] Taxpayer Advocate Service

Congress created the Taxpayer Advocate Service (TAS) to help individual and business taxpayers resolve problems that have not been resolved through normal IRS channels. TAS began life in 1979 as the Office of the Taxpayer Ombudsman to serve as the *primary advocate* within the IRS for taxpayers. After two interim organizational changes, following RRA '98, Congress renamed the 'Taxpayer Advocate' the 'National Taxpayer Advocate'. RRA '98 provided for Local Taxpayer Advocates to be located in each state, and mandated a reporting structure providing for these officials to report directly to the NTA – currently Ms. Nina Olson, who has held the post since 2001.

Under §7803(c)(2) of the Code, the Office of the Taxpayer Advocate has two principal statutory missions:

---

37. Electronic Tax Administration Advisory Committee, *Annual Report to Congress*, Publication 3415 (Rev 6-2014), 2 (June 2014).
38. Internal Revenue Service, *IRS2Go 4.0 Smartphone App Downloads Surpass 2.3 Million*, News Release (31 March 2014), available at: http://www.irs.gov/uac/Newsroom/IRS2Go-40-Smart phone-App-Downloads-Surpass-23-Million (accessed on 10 November 2014).
39. See http://www.irs.gov/Tax-Professionals/Information-Reporting-Program-Advisory-Commi ttee--(IRPAC)-Past-Briefing-Books.

(1) To assist taxpayers in resolving problems with the Internal Revenue Service (Case Advocacy).

(2) To identify areas in which groups of taxpayers are experiencing problems with the IRS and, to the extent possible, propose administrative or legislative changes to resolve or mitigate those problems (Systemic Advocacy).

Each year, two reports are made to Congress – independently of Treasury Department and IRS top management.[40] One is a forward-looking Objectives Report that details key issues, goals and activities of the TAS for the coming year. The second is an Annual Report to Congress which lists and explains at least twenty of the most serious problems encountered by taxpayers and facing the IRS. These include problems faced by vulnerable populations, problems causing taxpayer burden, problems relating to IRS enforcement and collection policies and practices, regulation of return preparers, etc. The report also documents legislative recommendations for Congress and details the most litigated issues. A second volume to the Annual Report includes TAS research and related studies, some of which are conducted in-house and some commissioned studies.

Ms. Olson as NTA has been a staunch advocate for greater fairness and less complexity in the tax system. Given the length of the NTA Annual Reports, it is difficult to do justice to every single area where complexity has been raised as a problem by the NTA, so the following examples are illustrative rather than comprehensive.

In her 2010 Annual Report, the number one most serious problem facing taxpayers – and the IRS – was listed as the complexity of the Code. The report suggests that tax reform is needed for the four primary reasons referred to previously (§17.01):[41]

(1) The Code imposes huge compliance burdens on individual taxpayers and businesses.

(2) The Code is rife with complexity and special tax breaks, helping taxpayers who can afford expensive tax advice and discriminating against those who cannot.

(3) Complexity obscures understanding and creates a sense of distance between taxpayers and the Government, resulting in lower rates of voluntary tax compliance.

(4) The Code is so complex that the IRS has difficulty administering it.

In the 2012 Annual Report, the complexity of the Code was again listed at number one. The Report re-visits the four reasons published in 2010, and further suggests the Code:[42]

---

40. See http://www.irs.gov/Advocate/Reports-to-Congress. This reporting relationship is the reason why discussion of the TAS is discussed in this section of the chapter under 'external administrative oversight', rather than in the preceding section (§17.04) – even though the TAS is housed within the IRS.
41. National Taxpayer Advocate, *2010 Annual Report to Congress*, above n. 5, Vol. 1, at 3–8.
42. National Taxpayer Advocate, *2012 Annual Report to Congress*, above n. 3, Vol. 1, at 3.

(5) Makes compliance difficult, requiring taxpayers to devote excessive time to preparing and filing their returns.

(6) Requires the significant majority of taxpayers to bear monetary costs to comply, as most taxpayers hire preparers and many other taxpayers purchase tax preparation software.

(7) Obscures comprehension, leaving many taxpayers unaware of how their taxes are computed and what rate of tax they pay.

(8) Facilitates tax avoidance by enabling sophisticated taxpayers to reduce their tax liabilities and by providing criminals with opportunities to commit tax fraud.

(9) Undermines trust in the system by creating an impression that many taxpayers are not compliant, thereby reducing the incentives that honest taxpayers feel to comply.

(10) Generates tens of millions of telephone calls to the IRS each year, overburdening the agency and compromising its ability to provide high-quality taxpayer service.

The NTA makes several observations/recommendations for Congress. She states that there is a widespread view that 'special interests' are one of the biggest roadblocks to comprehensive tax reform, although she notes that tax expenditures passed into law, and which benefit millions of taxpayers, now total more than USD 1 trillion each year. Simply put, tax reform requires a trade-off between tax rates and tax breaks. It is then suggested that a programmatic zero-based budgeting approach might assist Congress in deciding which tax breaks and IRS-administered social programmes to retain and which to eliminate.

The 2012 Report suggests that prior NTA recommendations to simplify parts of the Code should be considered. These are listed as:

(1) repeal of the Alternative Minimum Tax for individuals;

(2) consolidation of the family status provisions;

(3) improve other provisions relating to taxation of the family unit (e.g., 'kiddie tax' rules);

(4) consolidate education savings tax incentives;

(5) consolidate retirement savings tax incentives;

(6) simplify worker classification determinations to minimize employee versus independent contractor disputes;

(7) eliminate (or reduce) procedural incentives for lawmakers to enact tax sunsets;

(8) eliminate (or simplify) phase-outs; and

(9) streamline the penalty regime.

Finally, while the need for corporate tax reform is acknowledged, the NTA maintains that individual income tax reform should be given a higher priority as corporate tax reform alone will not eliminate any of the complexity that most American taxpayers currently experience. This is due to a population of only 2.3 million C

Corporations taxed at the entity level, compared to 140 million individual tax returns filed in 2011, with a further 32 million pass-through entities.[43]

[B]   IRS Oversight Board

Following RRA '98, the IRS Oversight Board (IRSOB) was established to 'oversee the IRS in its administration, management, conduct, direction, and supervision of the execution and application of the internal revenue laws or related statutes and tax conventions to which the United States is a party'.[44] IRSOB has statutory responsibilities to review and approve strategic plans of the IRS; review IRS operational functions; review the selection, evaluation and compensation of IRS senior executives; review and approve the budget request of the IRS prepared by the Commissioner; and to review and approve plans for major reorganizations.

The 2013 Annual Report to Congress (released in March 2014) contains a message in relation to the findings of the Treasury Inspector General for Tax Administration in May 2013 as to the treatment of certain organizations applying for tax-exempt status and the resulting political controversy (see §17.03[A] above). Linked to the earlier section on the IRS Budget, the Board noted that, while it appreciates concerns relating to inappropriate spending of IRS funds, it 'believes under-funding the IRS only punishes America's taxpayers and endangers the fiscal health' of the country.[45]

Aside from providing progress updates with key performance measures, reporting the outcomes at Nationwide Tax Forums and other IRSOB meetings, IRSOB provides Congress with separate reports on electronic filing, Budget recommendations, and the results of its annual Taxpayer Attitude Survey.

The 2013 Annual Report documents several complexity/burden reduction initiatives that have been introduced or expanded. First, the IRS simplified a complex home office deduction by providing eligible taxpayers with a simple deduction capped at USD 1,500 per year, reducing small business' paperwork and record-keeping requirements. Second, the IRS streamlined their instalment agreements through its 'Fresh Start' programme to help eligible taxpayers catch up on back taxes (which must be less than USD 50,000 and paid off within six years). Third, the IRS announced it will continue to test the expansion of its Volunteer Income Tax Assistance (VITA) programme, often facilitated on university campuses, to individual taxpayers who file a Schedule C providing the business expenses are less than USD 25,000. Some of these taxpayers may not fully understand the tax-related requirements of running a small business and are less likely to employ a professional tax preparer. Lastly, when telephoning a toll-free IRS, taxpayers can choose to use a temporary PIN number so they will not be asked to repeat the same identifying information when transferred to another customer service representative – although unfortunately, telephone wait times have increased over the last five years. This is counter-balanced by a trend for increased accuracy

---

43. National Taxpayer Advocate, *2012 Annual Report to Congress*, above n. 3, Vol. 1, at 21.
44. 26 US Code §7802.
45. IRS Oversight Board, *Annual Report to Congress 2013*, above n. 24, at 3.

rates, suggesting employees provide excellent assistance but more staff are needed to keep up with demand from the public.

[C] Government Accountability Office

The Comptroller General heads the Government Accountability Office (GAO), a supreme audit institution – similar to the National Audit Office in the UK. One of the GAO's strategic objectives is to analyse the US Government's fiscal condition and ways of addressing current and projected fiscal gaps. Two specific goals are to contribute to Congressional deliberations on tax policy (Performance Goal 3.1.4) and to identify opportunities to reduce the tax gap by improving taxpayer voluntary compliance and the IRS' ability to pursue non-compliance (Performance Goal 3.1.5).[46]

In addressing the tax gap, key efforts listed in GAO's strategic plan are to:

(1) Identify potential improvements to IRS taxpayer service, such as easier tax return filing; faster refund processing; and more informative telephone, website, and written communications.
(2) Identify opportunities to improve the IRS' enforcement programmes in light of a changing US and international economy, evolving technology, and the tax gap.
(3) Identify opportunities to leverage paid preparers, tax preparation software companies, and information return reporters to ensure timely, accurate filing of tax returns.
(4) Evaluate the IRS' efforts to modernize its expenditure plans and its information system.
(5) Assess the IRS' efforts to improve planning, resource allocations, and evaluation of operations, including using research and data to enhance compliance programmes.

GAO reports are often 'commissioned' by members of Congress or, less frequently, made at their own instigation. GAO releases their reports on to their website[47] with some reports being fairly narrow and technical and others broader in outlook. Two respective examples are Report GAO-14-652R on 'Tax Policy: Differences in Definitions and Rules in the Tax Code' (18 July 2014) and Report GAO-11-747T on 'Tax Gap: Complexity and Taxpayer Compliance' (2011).

[D] Treasury Inspector General for Tax Administration

The TIGTA provides independent oversight of IRS activities, the IRS Oversight Board, and the IRS office of Chief Counsel. While located within the Department of the

---

46. United States Government Accountability Office, *Serving the Congress and the Nation: Strategic Plan 2014-2019*, 169 (2014).
47. See http://www.gao.gov/index.html.

Treasury and reporting to the Secretary of the Treasury and to Congress, it functions independently from all other offices. TIGTA provides audit, investigative and inspection and evaluation services, with 2013 seeing a report of inappropriate use of taxpayer dollars at IRS training meetings and conference – but with the most high-profile case being Report 2013-10-053[48] – leading to the 'Tea Party scandal' discussed earlier (see §17.03[A] above).

Key areas for TIGTA at present are security for taxpayer data and employees, tax compliance efficiencies and cost savings. Although dealing with complexity is not specifically mentioned in TIGTA's most recent Annual Report,[49] it is implicit in its goal of making recommendations that the IRS will accept and which will then promote protection of taxpayers' rights and entitlements, cost savings and more efficient use of resources.

§17.06   CONCLUDING REMARKS

Professor Surrey investigated the problem of tax complexity in the US and his pioneering article discussed the causes of complexity, the Code, and the inevitability of complex detail and the problem of the effective management of that detail.[50] Much of what he had to say forty-five years ago still rings true today. D'Ascenzo has noted that finding good measures of effectiveness is not easy and all performance indicators have their limitations and weaknesses.[51] The purpose of this chapter, however, is not to evaluate the performance of the IRS, but rather to take a 'macro' view of efforts in the US to seek tax simplification. The chapter has briefly outlined the current tax environment in the US and highlighted issues of IRS funding and the difficulties created in a politically-divided approach to that funding of the process of tax administration and collection. Colloquially, with decreasing resources and increasing demands being placed on it – the IRS, in this author's words, finds itself 'between a rock and a hard place'.

It is incorrect to say that there is no effort being made to simplify the US tax system. Some initiatives are internal and within the IRS – with examples being written communications to taxpayers, form design, and other initiatives. There are also constructive efforts being made by external agencies – notably the NTA, TIGTA, the IRS Oversight Board and the GAO. Even this list does not include contributions made by professional associations such as the AICPA and the American Bar Association.

It is difficult to evaluate the oversight and governance mechanisms of the IRS. For example, in terms of the various IRS Committees discussed in §17.04[C], it is the IRS which makes appointments to these committees, and the IRS may/may not listen to,

---

48. Treasury Inspector General for Tax Administration, *Inappropriate Criteria Were Used to Identify Tax-Exempt Applications for Review*, Report 2013-10-053, above n. 18.
49. Treasury Inspector General for Tax Administration, *Semiannual Report to Congress, October 1, 2013 – March 31, 2014*.
50. Stanley Surrey, *Complexity and the Internal Revenue Code: The Problem of the Management of Tax Detail*, 34(4) Law & Contemp. Probs. 673 (1969).
51. Michael D'Ascenzo, *Sustaining Good Practice Tax Administration*, 4(1) J. Australasian Tax Teachers' Ass'n 25 (2009).

and/or implement, their recommendations. In terms of 'external' oversight, as discussed in §17.05, these oversight bodies have vastly different resources. The GAO has less than 20 professional staff working on tax administration issues, whereas TIGTA has over 2,000 staff.

One oversight body that has received some critical comment is the IRSOB (see §17.05[B]). Hoffman notes that the Oversight Board was originally meant to serve as a governing board similar to a corporate board with external members.[52] The original report leading to RRA '98 envisaged an oversight body charged with the appointment, performance evaluation and compensation of senior IRS executives. However, given that the IRSOB is a nine member part-time board, and is down to two private-life members at the time of writing, there is currently limited scope for the Board to have greater authority and influence over the actions, performance and behaviour of the IRS.

It is interesting to note that there is no specific office or formal body in the US dedicated to dealing with tax simplification (e.g., as with the Office of Tax Simplification in the UK[53]). In making cross-Atlantic comparisons, while Freedman[54] has raised concerns with tax institutions in the UK, it would seem that similar conclusions might be reached in the US: that knee-jerk responses should be avoided and deliberation and care be taken when designing, implementing and funding oversight institutions; to do otherwise risks creating even more complexity as D'Ascenzo points out.[55] In conclusion, whether the highly charged atmosphere that exists in US politics, when tax reform, tax administration and funding are under discussion, leads one to feel optimistic or pessimistic on the prognosis for change and improvement may simply depend on one's mood and whether your glass appears to be half-full or half-empty.

---

52. See Hoffman, above n. 17.
53. See John Whiting, Jeremy Sherwood & Gareth Jones, *The OTS and its Complexity Index*, this volume.
54. Judith Freedman, *Creating new UK institutions for tax governance and policy making: Progress or confusion?*, [2013] 4 Brit. Tax Rev. 373; also Judith Freedman, *Managing Tax Complexity: The Institutional Framework for Tax Policy-Making and Oversight*, this volume.
55. Michael D'Ascenzo, *Pathways for Tax Policy and Administration: Institutions and Simplicity – An Australian Perspective*, this volume.

CHAPTER 18

Pathways for Tax Policy and Administration: Institutions and Simplicity – An Australian Perspective

Michael D'Ascenzo

§18.01 INTRODUCTION

In some jurisdictions specific institutions have been established to focus on ways in which the tax system can be made simpler for taxpayers. For example, the UK's Office of Tax Simplification is one such institution. In Australia there has been a lot of rhetoric about simplicity but what is simple is often dependent on the perspective of the user.

One thing is clear, efforts to increase tax simplicity and to reduce complexity are worthy goals because a simpler system reduces the dead weight of compliance costs and influences higher levels of voluntary compliance with the tax system. However, simplicity is not an overriding objective and needs to be weighed against other policies directed at improving the wellbeing of the community. Often the political nature of tax policy development results in simplicity taking a back seat where there is disagreement with the policy settings.

In this context it is useful, therefore, to ponder whether existing institutions could be improved, or whether new institutions could make a positive difference in driving a simplification agenda or more generally in developing and administering an optimal tax system. The purpose of this chapter is to consider possible pathways for tax policy development and administration, with a focus on institutions and simplicity.

§18.02 EQUITY, EFFICIENCY AND SIMPLICITY

Three traditional benchmarks for tax policy are equity, efficiency and simplicity. The antonym of simplicity is complexity.

Unfortunately, the objectives of equity, efficiency and simplicity are not always aligned and, in policy development, trade-offs between these criteria are often necessary. Given that trade-offs are inherently a feature of policy development, questions arise as to how relevant values are to be ascribed to conflicting objectives and who should be responsible for those choices? These are considerations relevant in assessing the institutional arrangements that could support sound tax policy development and administration. For example, who should 'make the call' on policy decisions; who advises the decision-maker; who should be reviewing the policy behind the legislation in a thorough and radical way; how are the outcomes to be progressed to implementation; and how do we ensure that the legislative intent is being administered in a proper and effective way?

While low compliance costs are one aspect of an optimal tax system, simplification for some merely means lower taxes. It is indicative of this that following the Tax Forum in Australia in October 2011 involving representatives of a range of public and private organizations and interests,[1] the then Treasurer announced the establishment of a Business Tax Working Group to look at how the taxation system could 'best help businesses respond to the pressures of a changing economy'.[2] No consensus could be found by the Working Group among the business community as to base-broadening savings that could be made to compensate for the revenue costs associated with the reduction in the corporate tax rate favoured by the Working Group.[3]

Realpolitik suggests that when the choice is between equity and simplicity, the default setting is usually in favour of equity where that outcome reduces the overall tax that would otherwise be payable by the constituents or influential segments of the economy.

§18.03   WHOSE ROLE IS IT TO 'MAKE THE CALL' ON TAX POLICY?

One would have thought that in democracies it is the elected government's role to 'make the call' on tax policy, but other options and new approaches have recently been mooted. For example, in 2013 the Institute of Chartered Accountants in Australia (ICAA) proposed an economic policy platform with an emphasis on locking-in a stronger and more robust public policy-making process.[4]

The ICAA's recommendations include: developing processes to deal with the short-term demands of the 'round the clock' news cycle on decision-making; investing in and enhancing the roles of the Productivity Commission and Council of Australian Governments (COAG) to bridge the gap in policy momentum caused by the three-year

---

1. See http://www.treasury.gov.au/Policy-Topics/Taxation/Tax-Forum.
2. See http://www.treasury.gov.au/Policy-Topics/Taxation/BTWG.
3. Business Tax Working Group, *Final Report*, iii (1 November 2012).
4. Institute of Chartered Accountants in Australia, *Future[inc]: Developing a Plan for Australia's Prosperity* (April 2013); and *Future[inc]:An economic policy platform for the next term of government* (June 2013). The Institute also considers that a simplified small business entity tax regime is one pathway to streamlining and reducing regulation and red tape. In addition, the ICAA recommends minimizing 'marginal tax rate inequities' which would translate to less progressivity in the tax system.

electoral cycle as well as crossing the boundaries between State and federal jurisdictions; creating an effective role for policy think tanks, operating outside the political sphere; and enhancing programmes to bring public and private sector experts together.

In terms of simplicity, three of the Institute's areas of focus have particular relevance. The first relates to fiscal sustainability – with an expanded goods and services tax (GST) system as a component of Australia's tax mix. The clear intention is to secure a revenue base to supplement declining returns from the corporate sector. Nevertheless, reducing exemptions in the GST law would make the system simpler.

The second focus area is on reducing red tape. In response the present Government has developed a deregulation agenda focusing on the public sector,[5] including reporting on deregulation outcomes by public sector departments. The Institute's primary recommendation is the removal of inefficient taxes levied by Australia's sub-national (State) governments. This would have simplicity as well as efficiency benefits. However, it remains the case that the constitutional boundaries in the Australian federation present significant challenges, with a workable tax-transfer system perhaps being the single greatest point of contention.[6]

The third focus area relates to productivity and includes potential roles in tax policy development for the Productivity Commission and COAG.

More recently, Ernst & Young has published what it considers to be the case for an Australian Tax Reform Commission.[7] The proposal is that the Commission be the Government's research and advisory body on tax reform; that it be a statutory authority; and that it take over some of the responsibilities currently performed by the Board of Taxation, the Treasury and the Australian Taxation Office (ATO), without impinging on the Government's ultimate decision-making authority. This is a bold recommendation. However it does require a little more clarity on the specific roles and accountabilities of the proposed Commission, so as to ensure no duplication or fuzziness in responsibilities.

Others such as former federal Opposition Leader and current member of Australia's Tax and Transfer Policy Institute John Hewson have taken the notion further by arguing for an independent permanent tax commission as an institution to go beyond government. However, Hewson is sketchy on the details of his model:

> At one level it could be empowered to provide fiercely independent advice to governments as to the key elements of a reform package... – a productivity commission-type role. At the other extreme, it could be truly independent of government... – an RBA [Reserve Bank of Australia] -type role.[8]

---

5. The agenda in relation to the public sector is set out on the Department of the Prime Minister and Cabinet website:http://www.dpmc.gov.au/office-deregulation/whole-government-deregulation-agenda. See also, generally: http://www.cuttingredtape.gov.au/.
6. See Australian Government, *Reform of the Federation White Paper: A Federation for Our Future, Issues Paper 1*, 30-37, 46-53 (September 2014).
7. Ernst & Young, *Tax Reform: A Better Way - The Case for an Australian Tax Reform Commission* (2014).
8. John Hewson, *The Politics of Tax Reform in Australia*, 1(3) Asia & Pac. Pol'y Stud. 590, 599 (2014).

§18.04   WHAT IS AT THE HEART OF TAX COMPLEXITY?

This brings us to the question of what is at the heart of complexity, what does simplicity mean? Evans and Tran-Nam have noted different shades of complexity, including:[9]

(1) Policy complexity that arises because of the choice of policy by the policy maker.
(2) Statutory complexity that is the result of the way the tax laws are drafted.
(3) Administrative complexity that applies to the rules and practices of the administration.
(4) Compliance complexity that arises from the tax computation and tax planning behaviour of tax professionals and taxpayers.

In addition, tax authorities that do not apply the rule of law give rise to complexity in the form of uncertainty as to how the laws will be administered.

Accordingly, simplification could mean different things to different people, with responses aimed at different shades of complexity. For example:

(1) Making the tax system structurally simpler. This could include broadening the tax base and removing choices. This is a task often made difficult because of equity considerations. Simplification could also include minimizing changes to the tax system, but note, however, calls for annual amendment bills[10] and the positive feedback associated with taxpayer-friendly measures, even where they add to compliance costs.[11]
(2) Making the laws simpler through improvements in the drafting process. This could involve greater emphasis on user-based design,[12] tri-partite design teams,[13] and less 'black letter' law.[14] However principle-based drafting is

---

9. Chris Evans & Binh Tran-Nam, *Towards the Development of a Tax System Complexity Index*, 35(3) Fiscal Stud. 341 (2014).
10. Ernst & Young, above n. 7, at 26.
11. See, for example, the 1999 small business capital gains tax concessions which introduced choices and increased compliance costs. A 2005 review of the provisions by the Board of Taxation in this context nevertheless found that introduction of the concessions had 'had a positive impact on the availability of concessions under the CGT system for eligible small business entities': Board of Taxation, *A Post-implementation Review of the Quality and Effectiveness of the Small Business Capital Gains Tax Concessions in Division 152 of the Income Tax Assessment Act 1997*, 9 (2005).
12. See, for example, the discussion of consultation processes in Board of Taxation, *Improving Australia's Tax Consultation System* (2007), and Board of Taxation, *Post-implementation Review of the Tax Design Panel Recommendations* (2011).
13. Tax Design Review Panel, *Better Tax Design and Implementation*, 25 (2008). See also Board of Taxation, *Government Consultation with the Community in the Development of Taxation Legislation* (2002); Neil Warren, *Tax: Facts Fiction and Reform*, Australian Tax Research Foundation Research Study 41, Ch. 5 (2004).
14. Daniel Lovric, *Principles-based drafting: experiences from tax drafting*, [2010] 3 The Loophole 16, available at: http://www.opc.gov.au/calc/docs/Loophole/Loophole_Dec10.pdf (accessed on 12 November 2014); Duncan Bentley, *Tax law drafting: the principled method* (Editorial), 14(1) Revenue L.J. 1 (2004).

often criticized for producing uncertainty, and as Krever[15] notes legislation is in any event subject to judicial traditions such as the literal interpretation of tax statutes.[16]

(3) One way of lowering compliance costs is by shifting them onto the tax administration or to a sector in the community (e.g., to employers in relation to PAYG withholding). However, information relevant for the assessment process may be known only by the taxpayer and so it may be more efficient to retain certain responsibilities with the taxpayer. In addition, where a tax authority is under-resourced, shifting the burden can make administration more difficult, and provide an incentive for non-compliance.[17]

Moreover there is also an international dimension to complexity:

What we confront instead is considerable complexity in the evolution, and the political interests, associated with international tax arrangements. Countries of residence may have a long run interest in sustaining BEPS [Base Erosion and Profit Shifting].[18]

§18.05 THE WORLD IS COMPLEX AND THERE MAY BE NO PANACEA

Tax is part of a network of global, social and economic systems that are interconnected, non-linear, interdependent, and evolving. Over the next decade drivers such as borderless commerce and digital technologies will create new tensions, opportunities and balance points. Public expectations of the tax system will continue to evolve, with the public voice becoming increasingly enabled by new channels and information sources. In such an environment perceptions of complexity are likely to intensify.

The perception already exists that the level of tax complexity in Australia is excessive.[19] The tax system is the outcome of a political process, and the federal nature of the Australian political system adds further complications. Moreover, as Krever observed, Treasury may have tended at times to provide government with piecemeal responses to issues but this has often been done in recognition of government's concerns over electoral risks inherent in a three-year term of office.[20]

Nevertheless the problems of complexity are not new and efforts have been made to simplify the tax system and its administration. For example, in 1996 the Office of Regulation Review within the Productivity Commission recognized the large number of underlying causes for tax complexity including the increasingly complex nature of

---

15. Richard Krever, *Taming Complexity in Australian Income Tax*, 25(4) Syd. L. Rev. 467, 476–480 (2003).
16. See, for example, the decision of Australia's High Court in *Alcan (NT) Alumina Pty. Ltd. v. Commissioner of Territory Revenue (Northern Territory)* [2009] HCA 41; 239 CLR 27 at 46–47.
17. John Hasseldine, *Oversight Mechanisms and Administrative Responses to Tax Complexity in the United States*, this volume, §17.03[B].
18. Greg Smith, *Tax Avoidance: An Economic Policy Perspective*, paper presented at the Tax Avoidance in the 21st Century conference, Melbourne Law School, 17 May 2013.
19. Federal Commissioner of Taxation, *Annual Report 2011-12*, 10 (2012).
20. Krever, above n. 15, at 486.

economic activity as well as the ad hoc development of the tax law over time.[21] It noted that government efforts to reduce compliance costs had at that time generally been limited primarily to the ATO undertaking a number of initiatives such as the simplification of forms including the use of plain English, electronic lodgement of returns, and telephone support for taxpayers to mask tax system complexity.

A major government-sponsored initiative at the time was the Tax Law Improvement Project (TLIP). The Productivity Commission considered that the Tax Law Improvement Project was at best only a partial solution. The intended rewrite of the tax law in plainer English, incorporating purpose clauses and a dictionary, ran out of steam over time, leaving Australia with the *Income Tax Assessment Act 1936* and the *Income Tax Assessment Act 1997*, as well as a range of other relevant legislation such as the *Taxation Administration Act 1953*. In my opinion one of the reasons why TLIP was only a partial solution is that any confusion that existed in the interpretation of particular provisions under the existing law was retained in the new law. In other words, as a general rule policy issues were not clarified when the law was rewritten – lending weight to the proposition that simplification requires a thorough review of the underlying policy.[22]

§18.06   NEW INSTITUTIONS: 'PROGRESS OR CONFUSION?'

Given the current focus on the pathways for tax policy development and implementation it is appropriate to ask whether existing, new or proposed institutions are or would be fit for purpose and well designed, or whether new institutions would be reactions to particular issues?[23] Freedman points out that new institutions are dependent on the quality of the appointees; they are often subject to resourcing constraints; and they have layered expectations imposed upon them that make them prone to failure.

No doubt very careful attention is needed in designing new institutional arrangements. In particular, their responsibilities and accountabilities need to be mapped against the activities of other players in the field to ensure that there is no duplication. If the new institution operates with part-time appointees, we need to ask ourselves whether they would be able to develop a coherent blueprint for the future tax system. Just as importantly, would they be able to maintain that vision against the short-term priorities or the long-term direction of the government of the day?

In Australia broader reviews of the tax system have typically been conducted by government-initiated processes which conclude with a report to the government.[24] An

---

21. Office of Regulation Review, *Compliance Costs of Taxation in Australia* (1996).
22. Judith Freedman, *Creating new UK institutions for tax governance and policy making: progress or confusion?*, [2013] 4 Brit. Tax Rev. 373.
23. Freedman, above n. 22.
24. For example, the 'Asprey Review' of 1975 (see Taxation Review Committee (Justice K. Asprey, chair), *Full Report* (31 January 1975)), the 1998 'A New Tax System' (ANTS) proposals (see Australian Treasury (circulated by Hon. P. Costello, Treasurer), *Tax Reform: not a new tax, a new tax system* (August 1998)), the 1999 'Ralph Review' (Review of Business Taxation (J. Ralph, chair), *A Tax System Redesigned: More certain, equitable and durable* (July 1999)), the 2002-03 Review of International Taxation Arrangements (RITA) (Board of Taxation, *International*

issue with such reviews is the question of who should or is in a position to champion the longevity of their recommendations. This is a question that is being asked in respect of the recommendations made in relation to Australia's Future Tax System Review.[25]

In addition, what role would the new institution play if its package of reform is 'cherry-picked' as a result of the political process? If there is full-time staffing of the new institution, we must ask the question, 'are we just establishing another bureaucracy?'. How do we ensure that new institutions are bi-partisan and operate in the national interest? If existing institutions are already playing in that space, should we first ask whether the existing process could be improved?

For example, in the sphere of tax administration, the establishment of an Inspector-General of Taxation (IGOT) in Australia in 2003 virtually duplicated the powers in relation to taxation of the Commonwealth Ombudsman. The vast majority of responses in the consultation process thought there should be an IGOT, notwithstanding existing scrutiny mechanisms such as the Commonwealth Ombudsman and the Australian National Audit Office.[26] Only recently has it been proposed to reduce the obvious overlap of responsibilities between the IGOT and the Ombudsman.[27]

Any new institution's fit within the Westminster concept of responsible government is an important consideration. It also raises issues about whose role it would be to do what, and who would be accountable to whom for doing so? For example, Freedman raises these concerns regarding the standing of the UK General Anti-Avoidance Rule (GAAR) Panel as a quasi-judicial body.[28] She points out that the partial implementation of the Office of Tax Simplification and of the GAAR Panel did not reflect their original intent. The UK GAAR Panel was intended to be administrative, much like the ATO's GAAR Panel, but the consultative responses were strongly in favour of independence from Her Majesty's Revenue and Customs (HMRC). As well as raising constitutional issues in the Panel's quasi-judicial role, such an approach limits HMRC's independence in administering the UK tax laws. It would be interesting to see whether this extra step in the assessment process reduces the application of the GAAR in circumstances where it might otherwise have been reasonably arguable.[29]

Taxation: A Report to the Treasurer (2003)), and the 2009 Australia's Future Tax System Review ('Henry Review' or AFTS Review) (Australia's Future Tax System Review Panel (Dr K. Henry, chair), *Australia's future tax system: Report to the Treasurer* (December 2009)).

25. See Australia's Future Tax System Review Panel, above n. 24.
26. Inspector-General of Taxation, *Annual Report 2003-04*, Overview (2004).
27. In its 2014 Budget, the government announced a proposed transfer of the Ombudsman's tax complaint handling role to the IGOT: Australian Treasury, *Portfolio Budget Statements 2014-15*, Treasury, 281 (2014).
28. Freedman, above n. 22, at 378–379.
29. In the course of a Senate Economics Committee inquiry in Australia into the ATO in relation to allegations made in a television broadcast (Channel Nine's *Sunday* programme, 31 May and 7 June 1998), the Committee commented that as a general rule it behoves the tax authority to pursue substantial matters where there is a reasonably arguable position, so as to protect the interests of the broader community. The Senate Economics Committee's 9 March 2000 Report found the allegations made in the programme to have been without substance: http://www.aph.gov.au/Parliamentary_Business/Committees/Senate/Economics/Completed%20inquiries/1999-02/ato/report/contents (accessed on 12 November 2014).

One source of complexity which is seldom discussed is the multitude of institutions, whose responsibilities overlap and who are subject to different degrees of accountability. In a political environment who should government listen to if there are conflicting recommendations? Which recommendations should take priority? Who ensures that the various ad hoc recommendations are aligned with a coherent tax or administrative structure? Who does the costings on proposed measures? And who reviews the institutions? All these issues are layered on the direct and opportunity costs associated with the servicing of each institution.

§18.07   THE PROS AND CONS OF INDEPENDENCE AND CONSULTATION

A matter on which I am currently ambivalent is the need for independence in policy development – notwithstanding the element of independence implicitly being a positive factor in many of the suggestions for change.[30] Independence from the government, the Treasury, HMRC, the Internal Revenue Service (IRS) or the ATO always seems to be a winner in consultative processes. While I have always championed consultation, consultative responses do not always articulate fairly the pros and cons of competing viewpoints. Nor do they necessarily lead to simpler solutions, even though I strongly believe that user-based design processes can make things simpler. For example, they do not work well where self- or vested interest, or a disappointing lack of trust (possibly unfounded) in the existing institutions holds sway.

In Australia, the Review of Aspects of Income Tax Self-Assessment conducted by the Treasury in 2004 provides an example of added complexity to address issues that were to a substantial degree perceived rather than real. For example, the changes to the ruling system including the establishment of a binding oral ruling system[31] added size to the Act, but have largely been otiose. In a similar vein the shorter periods of review now make it more difficult for taxpayers to ascertain what review period they now fall into, and distorted the symmetry that had previously existed.[32]

Another example is the so-called simplification of the small business capital gains tax concessions which introduced choices as to the methodology that could be used in calculating the tax payable (see §18.04 above), thereby generally increasing compliance costs as each method is tested for the preferred outcome.

§18.08   THE ROLE OF AN ELECTED GOVERNMENT

On the topic of independence, it can be argued that tax policy is already an increasingly contested debate. In Australia ministerial responsibility for tax policy lies with the Treasurer. However, as Heferen, Mitchell and Amalo point out, reform, research and

---

30. See, for example, the discussion of the role of independence in various reviews in Chris Evans, *Reviewing the Reviews: A Comparison of Recent Tax Reviews in Australia, the United Kingdom and New Zealand or 'A Funny Thing Happened on the Way to the Forum'*, 14(2) J. Austl. Tax'n 146, 155–158.
31. See *Taxation Administration Act 1953* (Cth.), Sch. 1, Div. 360, effective 1 January 2006.
32. *Income Tax Assessment Act 1936* (Cth.), s. 170(1).

policy options are generated by a multitude of sources including electoral parties, Senate and Parliamentary inquiries, academics, think tanks, lobby groups, tax representatives and the media.[33]

Heferen, Mitchell and Amalo add that the bulk of tax policy is developed and evaluated during the Budget process. They refer to Treasury as the government's principal adviser on tax policy. However, the ambit of that role remains unclear. For example, it is not explicit whether Treasury sees its role as bringing together all the threads relevant to the development of sound tax policy, including the intelligence drawn from research, consultation and international tax law developments so as to formulate a blueprint for the future tax system. Such a blueprint could guide its advice to government. In my opinion there would be merit in Treasury articulating its position in this regard.

No doubt the sufficiency of resources may be one barrier to evidence-based policy-making. On the other hand it could be that the AFTS Review (§18.06 above) is that blueprint for the Australian Treasury. If the latter is the case it is difficult for commentators to express the AFTS Review vision in one simple and unifying statement which might facilitate its translation into practical policy outcomes.[34] Moreover, the Review was precluded by its terms of reference from considering the rate or base of the GST.

Heferen, Mitchell and Amalo also argue that tax debates concern trade-offs between different values and priorities and so tax policy-making appropriately sits with elected officials.[35] They go on to note that successive governments have introduced a range of innovative institutions and practices aimed at improving the quality of tax policy-making in Australia including greater involvement of the private sector, extensive consultations and accountability mechanisms.

Evans has observed that independence can be a 'double-edged sword', leaving the institution to '"think the unthinkable" and to make proposals that may take the debate outside institutional comfort zones', but that this freedom may not translate to legislative outcomes.[36] One benefit of independence however is the ability to socialize new ideas with the general public, an outcome that would not be open to Treasury unless sanctioned by the government. This freedom could justify a review of current arrangements but alternatives should in my opinion be harmonious with the concept of responsible government and the wide traditional role of Treasury.

§18.09   COMPLEXITY AND ADMINISTRATION

As Hasseldine notes, the US may have one of the most complex tax system in the world.[37] The law is voluminous and the technical aspects of the law add to its complexity. Reasons for this include the importance of compromise in the legislative

---

33. Robert Heferen, Nicole Mitchell & Ian Amalo, *Tax Policy Formulation in Australia*, Canadian Tax Foundation Tax Policy Roundtable, Ottawa, 2013 (also [2013] 2 Econ. Round-up 1).
34. Evans, above n. 30, at 175.
35. Heferen, Mitchell & Amalo, above n. 33.
36. Evans, above n. 30, at 156.
37. Hasseldine, *Oversight Mechanisms and Administrative Responses to Tax Complexity in the United States*, this volume, §17.01.

process and the existence of special tax breaks. As with other tax systems, there is also a need to take into account temporal as well as international dimensions of the tax law, including treaties. Layered over all of this are regulations, rulings, and guidance materials as well as judicial precedents. The result is that most modern tax systems become daunting for many individuals and small businesses. The Australian tax system is no exception.

It may be that there are simpler ways to base the share of tax that is to be paid by entities coming within the definition of a taxpayer for a particular jurisdiction. However, looking at things just from the perspective of Australia's current income tax system, that system is based on a realized legal or accounting construction of income. The point to be made is that 'accounting' is complex for many individuals and businesses, even without the overlay of legal concepts; and mandatory record-keeping imposes further costs. This being the case, it is likely that the growth of software packages and the use of tax agents (often referred to as indicators of complexity) actually reduces the compliance burden across the economy, especially where an entity's financial dealings are themselves complex.[38]

The introduction of simplified accounting regimes in some countries is recognition by policy-makers that accounting, particularly accruals accounting, is difficult for many. Ironically, in Australia most tax agents preferred to keep their small business clients on an accruals footing, and, following consultation with the tax profession, changes were made to the legislation to allow deductions for certain pre-paid expenses.[39]

The ATO has for a long time worked closely with software developers on the premise that software packages could make tax compliance easier and cheaper (if opportunity costs are taken into account) for taxpayers. While the ATO has undertaken many initiatives to make the system easier, cheaper and more personalized for taxpayers,[40] including a focus on compliance costs in its *2006–2007 Taxation Statistics*, three more fundamental changes rely on digital developments.

The first is the tax agent portal which revolutionized the practices of tax agents, making them more efficient (and reducing their costs). These savings could then be passed on to their clients in a competitive market.

The second is the prefilling of the returns of individuals. This has been made possible in recent years by the ability of the ATO to obtain third party data in digital form, together with the upgrade to the ATO's IT systems which allows that information

---

38. Joel Slemrod, 'Complexity in the Australian Tax and Transfer System', in *Melbourne Institute – Australia's Future Tax and Transfer Policy Conference: Proceedings of a Conference* 257, 260 (Melbourne Institute of Applied Economic and Social Research, 2010).

39. See the small business rules for immediate deduction of certain prepayments introduced into s. 82KZM of the *Income Tax Assessment Act 1936* (Cth.) from 2001 under the 'simplified tax system' (STS) proposals of the Ralph Review (see above n. 24). Compulsory cash accounting under the STS was removed in 2005: John Tretola, *The Simplified Tax System – Has It Simplified Tax At All and, If So, Should It Be Extended?*, 17(1) Revenue L.J. 1, 6 (2007).

40. ATO, *Making it Easier, Cheaper and More Personalised for Taxpayers*, released in hardcopy in each of the years 2003-2004, 2004-2005, 2005-2006, 2006-2007, 2007-2008, and see now 'Building Confidence', which includes 'fostering willing compliance through improved services': https://www.ato.gov.au/printfriendly.aspx?url=/general/building-confidence/.

and data contained in the ATO's core processing system to be used to pre-populate tax returns. For individual taxpayers (with simple affairs) this allows a 'tick and flick' approach to their annual tax return obligations.

The third is the championing of standard business reporting (SBR), together with its taxonomy which harmonizes definitions across a range of legislation.[41] SBR allows businesses to prefill reporting to government from their SBR-enabled digital record-keeping systems. The Australian Business Number provides a single unique identifier for business which, together with the authentication solution 'AUSkey', enables efficient digital communication and transactions between businesses and government. Moreover, it represents infrastructure that could (subject to government decisions) be used for efficient business-to-business dealings.

§18.10 RESOURCING ISSUES

As discussed previously (§18.04), Hasseldine has argued that a consequence of chronic underfunding in the US is that the ability of the IRS to mask complexity for taxpayers is diminished.[42] No doubt the chronic lack of funding has affected the IRS' ability to carry out its functions effectively and efficiently. For example, it was not able to answer more than 25% of its calls in 2009 and 2010.[43] If that had occurred in Australia the public outcry might have prompted the establishment of yet another institution, or at least a range of parliamentary or other reviews.

Tax authorities that put the taxpayer at the heart of their administration seek to influence simplicity both in the legislative design and in the processes, services and products that impact on taxpayers. Where necessary, they seek to mask complexity through the services and tools they provide (e.g., websites, call centres, assistance visits, research tools, calculators and decision trees). Importantly, they invest for the future, and the ATO's Change Program was at the centre of enabling the ATO to respond to the contemporary needs and demands of taxpayers.[44] For example the ATO's client relation management system, introduced as part of the Change Program, allowed the ATO to better respond to the 10 million calls it receives each year.

The importance of the Change Program to future possibilities cannot be overstated. This point is highlighted by the difficulties many tax authorities face to adapt their antiquated IT systems to contemporary needs. If the tax authority is underfunded, it is not able to invest for the future, impacting on both its services and its compliance strategies.

---

41. Australian Federal Commissioner of Taxation (Michael D'Ascenzo), *Promoting tax excellence – an essential ingredient for a prosperous community*, Curtin University Taxation Seminar, 30 October 2012, 3–4, available at: https://www.ato.gov.au/Media-centre/Speeches/Commissioner/Promoting-tax-excellence---an-essential-ingredient-for-a-prosperous-community/ (accessed on 13 November 2014). See also Federal Commissioner of Taxation, *Annual Report 2011-12*, above n. 19, at 104.
42. Hasseldine, *Oversight Mechanisms and Administrative Responses to Tax Complexity in the United States*, this volume, §17.03[B].
43. National Taxpayer Advocate, *2010 Annual Report to Congress*, Vol. 1, 8 (2010).
44. Federal Commissioner of Taxation, *Annual Report 2011-12*, above n. 19, at 9 and 127.

§18.11   DANGERS IN EXAGGERATED CRITICISM

Returning specifically to the IRS, their 1993 Business Vision was a sophisticated blueprint for improvements in service and compliance.[45] In my opinion, the processes leading to the Report of the National Commission on Restructuring the IRS[46] in 1997 and its aftermath[47] diminished the confidence of the IRS in terms of thought leadership.

One might ponder how the recent 'Tea Party Scandal' has impacted on the IRS, noting that: '[l]ittle reported in the media firestorm at the time was the fact that groups leaning to the political left were also subject to delay in clarification of their tax status under [the Code]'.[48]

The damage in reputation and trust, and to the confidence of the administration, as well as the opportunity costs of such reviews, can severely dent the effectiveness of a tax authority. Even if the criticism proves to be misdirected or disproportionate, the damage often has already been done. An example in the Australian context was the many reviews undertaken in the early 2000s by Parliament and other institutions into mass-marketed agricultural tax avoidance schemes.[49] After many years the ATO was largely vindicated, with the main criticism being that it could have acted earlier.

While oversight and scrutiny are an integral part of tax administration, there is room for trust in the bona fides of world-class tax administrations.[50] More generally, lack of trust in government institutions can be corrosive in democratic societies.

§18.12   EXTERNAL OVERSIGHT AND REVIEW BODIES

It is not uncommon to find numerous review bodies and other tax-related institutions in developed countries. Checks and balances are important to the legitimacy of the tax system and its administration. In terms of external oversight, many tax-related

---

45. Internal Revenue Service, *Strategic Business Plan FY 1993 and Beyond*, (September 1992).
46. National Commission on Restructuring the Internal Revenue Service, *A Vision for a New IRS* (25 June 1997).
47. *Internal Revenue Service Restructuring and Reform Act of 1998*.
48. Hasseldine, *Oversight Mechanisms and Administrative Responses to Tax Complexity in the United States*, this volume, §17.03[A].
49. Senate Economics Reference Committee, *Inquiry into Mass Marketed Tax Effective Schemes and Investor Protection, Interim Report* (June 2001); *Second Report* (September 2001); and *Final Report* (February 2002); Taxation Ombudsman, *The ATO and Budplan* (June 1999); and *The ATO and Main Camp* (January 2001); Australian National Audit Office, *The Australian Taxation Office's Management of Aggressive Tax Planning* (January 2004); Inspector-General of Taxation, *Review of the Remission of the General Interest Charge for Groups of Taxpayers in Dispute with the Tax Office* (November 2004).
50. The ATO has been recognized globally as a leading tax administration. See, for example, Inspector-General of Taxation, *Annual Report 2004-05*, 4 (2005) (commenting in relation to meetings with senior revenue and other officials overseas that '[i]t was very interesting to note the high regard the Australian Tax Office is held in by other revenue agencies'); John Hasseldine, *Study into: 'Best Practice' in Tax Administration*, Consultancy Report for the National Audit Office (UK), 5 (15 October 2007) ('[a]necdotally, the Australian Tax Office is perceived as one of the leading tax agencies in the world'); and see the global recognition of the ATO as a leader in tax administration referred to in Federal Commissioner of Taxation, *Annual Report 2009-10*, 187 (2010), and *Annual Report 2010-11: Recognizing Our Centenary*, 142–147 (2011).

institutions often find their counterparts in other jurisdictions. For example, the National Taxpayer Advocate in the US has similarities with the Ombudsman and the IGOT in Australia, although the IGOT legislation in Australia had envisaged an independent reviewer rather than a taxpayer advocate.

In addition there is extensive Parliamentary scrutiny in Australia as there is in many other countries. As well as the Senate Economics Committee, the House of Representatives Standing Committee on Tax and Revenue conduct public hearings on the administration of the tax system.[51]

There can be no argument against extensive scrutiny of a tax administration and, as a general rule, such reviews are to be welcomed. However, it is disappointing if proceedings are used for political purposes, or when unsubstantiated concerns give rise to a 'feeding frenzy' that is disproportionate or even misplaced.

In the legislative space, Australia's Senate performs a house of review function through its committees, particularly the Senate Standing Committee on Economics in relation to taxation. The House of Representatives Standing Committee on Tax and Revenue also looks at both policy and administration.

In addition there is a requirement for regulatory impact statements from responsible departments to inform legislative decisions. There may be room to improve their contribution to 'taming complexity' and minimizing compliance costs.

Under their protocol, Treasury and the ATO are engaged in integrated tax design.[52] Post-implementation reviews on tax policy are sometimes conducted by the Board of Taxation.

Australia also has a Tax Issues Entry System (TIES) to identify small 'p' legislative and administrative policy issues relating to the care and maintenance of the tax system. In theory this should help address minor sources of complexity. However, notwithstanding marketing of TIES by Treasury and the ATO, relatively few matters have been raised through that mechanism. Often the suggestions made require more fundamental changes to the tax system.

Since the early 2000s consultation has formed an integral part of the tax design process. Most consultation starts after the government has a policy objective in mind (e.g., following the release of an initial discussion paper), but there have been recommendations to start the consultation process as early as possible in the policy design phase.[53]

---

51. See House of Representatives Standing Committee on Tax and Revenue, *2013 Annual Report of the Australian Taxation Office: First Report* (March 2014). The Joint Committee of Public Accounts and Audit has also carried out a public scrutiny role in relation to the tax administration: see, for example, Joint Committee of Public Accounts and Audit, *Report 426: Ninth biannual hearing with the Commissioner of Taxation* (23 November 2011); and *Report 434: Annual Public Hearing with the Commissioner of Taxation - 2012* (November 2012).

52. See currently *Treasury and the Australian Taxation Office – Tax and Superannuation Protocol* (10 September 2012), https://www.ato.gov.au/General/New-legislation/In-detail/ATO---Treasury-protocols/ATO---Treasury-protocol/.

53. Board of Taxation, *Improving Australia's Tax Consultation System*, above n. 12, at 16: 'New Zealand, Germany, Sweden and Norway use external expertise in different forms and structures quite early in the policy development process. They believe this assists government and officials to get a better view of what needs to be achieved and how government decisions may be

The Parliamentary Budget Office established in 2011 is a relatively new independent body whose function is to provide non-partisan analysis of the budget cycle, fiscal policy and the financial implications of the proposals. In addition, the 2013–2014 Federal Budget provided funding for the establishment of the Tax and Transfer Policy Institute (see §18.03 above) as a centre for research into the tax and transfer system, an initiative recommended by the Henry Review.[54] It is too early to say whether these developments will promote a simplification agenda.

As mentioned (§18.06 above), Australia has a history of major tax reviews. History suggests that there is often a long gestation period for substantial changes to the tax law. Non-government institutions could facilitate change by championing measures proposed in these reviews. However it is important that these institutions are non-partisan and are committed to the national interest.[55]

§18.13   CONCLUSION

It seems to me that any system will be subject to the criticism, even by those benefiting from fundamental changes, that it is complex, under one or other of the shades of complexity. New processes and new institutions may be of assistance but there is no guarantee. Moreover, if new approaches and the role of new institutions are not well thought-out, they could themselves be a source of complexity.

Consultation and wide engagement in the process of policy development are positive ingredients to sustainable tax reform, but that involvement, in whatever form it takes, must start from a commitment to the national interest.

New or existing tax-related institutions, private or public, independent or not, can play a role in informing government as to tax reform options. In my opinion it is important that Treasury or some other public sector institution has a formal role to take into account the wide range of views, research and intelligence so as to develop and maintain a sense of what might be considered an optimal tax system for Australia. On one hand Treasury would be well placed to influence government decision-making. On the other hand, an independent institution may be better placed to socialize possible changes to the tax system amongst the wider community. Given an appropriate level of role clarification by government, there would be substantial scope for a strategic partnership to achieve tax reform over time.

Ultimately however, under Australia's system of responsible government, and in the context of parliamentary and constitutional requirements, tax policy decisions should be made by the democratically-elected Government.

Adequate resourcing of new or existing institutions (such as Treasury and the ATO) will also be necessary to achieve quality outcomes in policy development,

---

implemented'; Board of Taxation, *Post-implementation Review of the Tax Design Panel Recommendations*, above n. 12, at 22–34.
54. Henry Review, above n. 24, Pt. 2, Vol. 2 at 722.
55. Board of Taxation, *Improving Australia's Tax Consultation System*, above n. 12, at 17: 'Some other countries (particularly New Zealand) have shown that given the right conditions, stakeholders are prepared to place a higher priority on national or community interests than their own self or sectional interests'.

implementation, administration and review. The administration in particular should play an important role in masking complexity for taxpayers.

Tax has political, social and economic dimensions. Even with major tax reform, simplification is unlikely to be the overriding criterion for change. Nevertheless if an absolutely simple tax system in all its shades cannot be realized, simplification and the masking of complexity remain worthy goals.

CHAPTER 19

Simplified Small Business Tax Regimes in Developing Countries: Empirical Evidence of Use and Abuse

Jacqueline Coolidge & Fatih Yılmaz[*]

§19.01 INTRODUCTION

Broadly speaking, the goal of simplified tax regimes for micro, small, and medium enterprises (MSMEs) in most developing countries is to facilitate voluntary tax compliance and provide access for small businesses to the benefits of (more) formalization. One important instrument to pursue this objective is the introduction of simplified (presumptive) tax regimes for micro and small enterprises. In practice, there have been many different approaches to presumptive taxation, with the exact design of such regimes generally differing from country to country. There are, however, two broad types of simplified regimes that are relatively common in the developing world:

(1) A very simple lump sum or fixed amount tax (sometimes called a 'patent'), usually targeted at micro-enterprises, the owners of which are often illiterate or semi-literate.

---

[*] This chapter is based on research supported by the World Bank Trade and Competitiveness Global Practice. The findings and views published are those of the authors and should not be attributed to the International Finance Corporation (IFC), World Bank, Multilateral Investment Guarantee Agency (MIGA), or any other affiliated organizations. Nor do any of the conclusions represent official policy of the World Bank or of its Executive Directors or the countries they represent. The authors wish to thank Joenn Khoo for valuable editorial assistance, Michael Engelschalk and Jan Loeprick for helpful advice and inputs, and the participants of the Prato Symposium on Tax Complexity (September 2014) for helpful feedback. All remaining errors remain the responsibility of the authors.

(2) A presumptive profit tax or single tax (replacing a number of other taxes) based on turnover, either with a percentage rate on turnover or a presumptive per cent reduction of turnover for expenses and a standard profit tax rate on the estimated 'profit'.

Over time, we have seen that the specific country-level results of MSME taxation reform vary, depending on the design characteristics of the regime, but also its application. In some countries, firms remain deterred from formalization by perceived excessive tax burdens, compliance costs and risks (including risks of punishment for real or alleged non-compliance); in other countries, the bigger problem appears to be that firms using a simplified regime may be deterred from 'graduating' because of overly generous conditions of the MSME regimes. The main purpose of the research set out in this chapter is to contribute to the discussion on the use of presumptive tax instruments by examining evidence on their use, abuse, and related experiences with enforcement.

The World Bank Group's Trade and Competitiveness department has carried out tax perception and compliance cost surveys (TPCCSs) in over a dozen countries. This chapter presents a systematic analysis of reported experiences and perceptions of taxes by MSMEs using survey-based estimates of the effects of presumptive regimes on their decisions to use such regimes (among those eligible for it) or to abuse them (among those using it while self-reporting firm characteristics, such as turnover levels, that should make them ineligible).

Descriptive summaries of the TPCCS findings regarding the use (and abuse) of simplified/presumptive regimes have been completed for the following countries: Yemen, Ukraine, Burundi, Albania, South Africa, and Nepal. The country reports analyse data on the use and abuse of simplified regimes in these countries, along with data on firm characteristics (size, sector, location, legal form, etc.).[1]

While the surveys all promised anonymity to the respondents (and followed strong protocols to fulfil that obligation), not all respondents have full confidence in such promises. A certain proportion of them (which probably varies across countries) provide either no responses to certain 'sensitive' questions or give answers that might not be accurate.[2] The initial analysis in this chapter provides direct evidence for frequent abuse of fixed tax regimes in some, but not necessarily in all, countries analysed. The findings are based on self-reported information, principally regarding businesses that have reported to have turnover above the legal threshold of eligibility for the fixed tax regime that nevertheless also report having been registered for such regimes during the year of the survey.

---

1. For a fuller description of the surveys, see Jacqueline Coolidge, *Findings of tax compliance cost surveys in developing countries*, 10(2) eJournal of Tax Research 250 (2012). The surveys were all of at least several hundred active business taxpayers, based on a stratified sample from the relevant tax authority. More detailed draft country reports are available from the authors on request.
2. Additional analysis shows, however, that few respondents are strategic enough to be consistent in their non-frank answers across a range of related questions.

§19.02   USE AND ABUSE OF PRESUMPTIVE REGIMES

All the countries included in this study had some kind of presumptive regime at the time a tax compliance cost survey was conducted. These are briefly summarized by category of regime in Table 19.1.

Table 19.1   Availability of Presumptive Regimes

Country (Year of Survey)	Fixed Tax Regime	Turnover Tax or Simplified Accounting	Comments
Yemen (2007)	Yes	Turnover tax	Eligibility for fixed tax regime based on reported inability to keep books; fixed tax liability based on negotiations, turnover tax regime barely used
Ukraine (2007)	Yes	Turnover tax	Fixed tax regime accessible for sole proprietors only
Burundi (2010)	Yes	Simplified accounting	Simplified accounting barely used at time of survey
Nepal (2010)	Yes	No	Presumptive flat tax used by all eligible
South Africa (2011)	No	Turnover tax	Turnover tax introduced in 2008, with low take-up rates; used only by small proportion of those eligible
Albania (2012)	Yes	Simplified accounting	Simplified accounting regime threshold (LEK 8 million) higher than VAT threshold (LEK 5 Million). Fixed tax for businesses with turnover below LEK 2 Million

Fixed tax regimes tend to be very popular. They typically offer both attractive rates and minimal compliance costs. However, actual turnover levels and thus eligibility of businesses tend to be hard to monitor. Although a well-designed fixed tax regime should usually be targeted toward poverty-level illiterate or semi-literate owners of micro-enterprises, the survey responses suggest that, in practice, such regimes are often used by small or even medium-sized businesses such that participation in the general tax regime risks being eroded. In some transitional and developing countries, such regimes may have initially been introduced in part to minimize the burden on relatively low-capacity tax administrations facing a rapid growth of the MSME segment. Once in place, they become very popular among a large number of constituents, and may be politically difficult to remove,[3] even when the original rationale for introducing them has partly lost importance (e.g., tax administrations have been strengthened, most business owners are sufficiently literate and numerate to at least report revenues and be taxed on that basis, and poverty is relatively low). Figures 19.1 and 19.2 provide data on literacy rates and poverty in the countries covered in this analysis.

Figure 19.1   Adult Literacy Rates

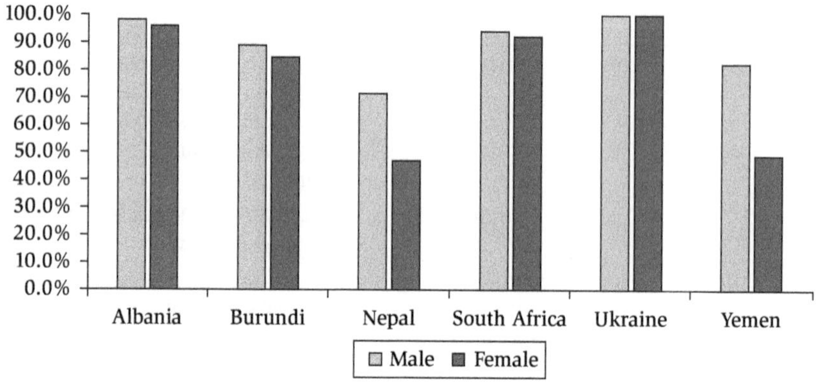

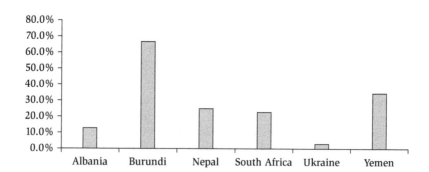

Source: World Bank World Development Indicators (various years 2008–2012).

Figure 19.2   Poverty Headcount Ratio at National Poverty Line (% of Population)

Source: World Bank World Development Indicators (various years 2008–2012).

3. Michael Engelschalk, 'Creating a Favorable Tax Environment for Small Business', in James Alm, Jorge Martinez-Vazquez & Sally Wallace (eds), *Taxing the Hard-to-tax: Lessons from Theory and Practice* 275 (Elsevier, 2004); Richard M. Bird, Jorge Martinez-Vazquez & Benno Torgler, *Tax Effort in Developing Countries and High Income Countries: The Impact of Corruption, Voice and Accountability*, 38(1) Econ. Analysis & Pol'y 55 (2008).

Poorly designed fixed tax regimes tend to involve one or more of the following features:

(1) Inappropriate threshold definition (e.g., higher than necessary to protect poverty-level, illiterate or semi-literate micro-enterprises).
(2) Very low tax burden for presumptive taxpayers (in terms of amount of tax payment as a proportion of income).
(3) Weak enforcement (e.g., little effort or low effectiveness in identifying and dealing with abusers).

Poorly designed turnover tax regimes, by contrast, tend to suffer from a lack of popularity. While less subject to potential abuse, they may fail to encourage formalization or graduation from fixed tax regimes in countries where both are available.

The tax compliance cost surveys (TCCS) data provide illustrations of these problems, as described further in this chapter.

§19.03   SIMPLIFIED TAX REGIMES IN YEMEN, 2007

In Yemen, the great majority of business taxpayers used presumptive regimes before enactment of a new tax code in 2010. The regimes are summarized in Table 19.2.

Table 19.2   Tax Regimes in Yemen, 2007

Tax	Description
Statutory Tax Regime (STR)	A tax regime through which businesses file and/or pay taxes based on their accounts. This regime applies to businesses which meet the following criteria: – Has a Tax ID Number and a Tax Card – Maintains regular books – Files and pays taxes based on its accounts
Estimation Tax Regime (ETR) and Percentage of Turnover Tax Regime (PTR)	Tax regimes through which businesses file and/or pay taxes based on estimates by the Tax Authority. This regime applies to businesses, which maintain some accounts or supporting documents but do not maintain regular accounts (as required by the statutory regime).
Fixed Amount Tax Regime (FTR)	A simplified tax regime through which businesses pay a fixed amount of income tax every year. The amount is increased annually for all businesses under this regime by a fixed percentage. The Chairman of the Tax Authority is authorized to decide on the annual increase percentage. This regime applies to the smallest businesses, which do not maintain any accounts or supporting documents.

Source: IFC, *Yemen Tax Cost of Compliance Survey* (unpublished manuscript, 2008).

About 94% of survey respondents in Yemen paid their taxes under the Fixed Tax Regime (FTR), which was originally targeted at micro businesses lacking the capacity to comply with book-keeping requirements. The vague definition of the system threshold was in contradiction to international good practice in that it offered an overly generous alternative to enforcing tax accounting obligations. De facto, in Yemen, the presumptive system was available to businesses – regardless of their size – that were not *willing* to comply with the requirement of the general tax regime.[4] Figure 19.3, shows the distribution of taxpayers in Yemen using the various regimes available in 2007, according to their legal eligibility to use the fixed tax regime. It reveals that almost half of the FTR population did not meet the system eligibility criteria and should have been taxed based on the turnover (ETR or PTR) or the statutory tax regime. In fact, based on responses to the survey conducted in 2007, the majority of businesses in Yemen (about 53%) reported at least basic book-keeping and therefore should not have been eligible to use the FTR.

Figure 19.3   Eligibility and Use of Fixed Tax Regime in Yemen, 2007
(Per Cent of Firms Reporting Using Each Type of Regime and Reported
Capability to Keep Books of Account)

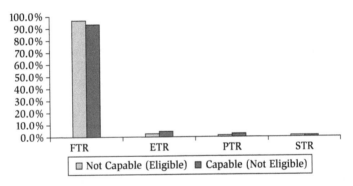

The amount of tax to be paid was usually established on the basis of 'negotiations' between tax officials and the business, and thereafter increased every year on the basis of general inflation and assumed business growth. Not surprisingly, corruption in the 'negotiations' was allegedly widespread, and the policy encouraged businesses to report that they did not keep books, even if they did.

The FTR allowed businesses to make very small official payments (estimated at an average of about 3% of turnover). The only 'reporting burden' was a visit from the tax official (including bribes to be allowed to stay out of the statutory regime in the majority of cases).

---

4. The only exceptions were importers and enterprises with government contracts, which were required to use the STR.

Given the perverse incentive structure for businesses and tax officials, enforcement efforts of the tax administration seem not to have focused on the abuse of the fixed tax regime (see Table 19.3).

Table 19.3 Correlation between Tax Regime and Visits by Tax Officials, Yemen

ALL MSMEs (obs = 842)	Not Eligible for FTR (obs = 494)	Eligible for FTR (obs = 348)
STR 0.0948	STR 0.0805	FTR -0.1094
FTR -0.0885	SME 0.0114	
PTR 0.0581	FTR* -0.0588	
ETR 0.0013		

FTR*: ABUSE of 'Fixed Tax Regime', STR: Statutory Tax Regime, FTR: Fixed Tax Regime, PTR: Percentage Tax Regime, and ETR: Estimated Tax Regime. Simplified regimes for SME (PTR or ETR).

A large majority (87% of survey respondents) reported being visited by tax officials (on average three to four times per year). A simple correlation coefficient analysis shows that a significant negative relationship exists between the probability of being visited by tax officials and paying taxes under FTR, as shown in Table 19.3.[5] This means firms paying tax under FTR were less likely to be audited relative to other regimes. In principle, such an approach would be in line with international good practice to focus audit activities on larger businesses with higher revenue importance. This is no longer the case, however, when the abuse of the presumptive regime is obvious; measures should be taken to detect businesses abusing the presumptive regime and transfer them to the standard regime. The high level of abuse of the FTR suggests that the frequent inspections of fixed tax payers, while probably increasing the compliance burden for businesses (e.g., in the form of informal payments), were not very effective in deterring abuse of that regime, and thus the survey data provide evidence that the base for the STR was probably significantly eroded.

A new MSME tax regime enacted in Yemen in 2008 after the IFC survey changed the eligibility criteria to more objective indicators based on turnover and number of employees.

§19.04 SIMPLIFIED TAX REGIMES IN UKRAINE, 2007

In contrast to the situation in Yemen, simplified tax regimes in Ukraine provide very clear criteria for taxpayer segmentation and eligibility to use one of the several presumptive approaches offered. Options for simplified taxation differ somewhat between legal entities and sole proprietors. For companies (legal entities) there were two main presumptive regimes available as alternatives to the regular profit tax at the time of the survey: the Unified Tax (UT) regime and the Fixed Agricultural Tax (FAT,

---

5. At least at the 90% level.

for agricultural producers, processors, and fishery firms). Firms with a turnover under UAH 1 million (about USD 150,000) and fewer than fifty workers were eligible for UT, while firms with over 75% of their turnover from agricultural production could qualify for the FAT, assessed based on the area of land and which substituted for profit tax, land tax, and municipal tax (see Table 19.4).

Table 19.4   Presumptive Tax Regimes for Legal Entities in Ukraine (2007)

Regime	Unified Tax (6)	Unified Tax (10)	Fixed Agric. Tax
Key provisions	Turnover tax of 6% substituting for profit tax	Turnover tax of 10% substituting for profit tax and VAT	Based on land area, substituting for profit tax, land tax and municipal tax
Eligibility	Under UAH 1 million turnover; fewer than fifty employees	Under UAH 1 million turnover; fewer than fifty employees	Over 75% of turnover from agricultural production
Proportion of firms using the regime (remainder use regular regime)	8%	26%	10%

Source: IFC, *The Costs of Tax Compliance in Ukraine* (2009).

Very different from the situation in Yemen, the take-up rates of the presumptive regimes for legal (incorporated) entities in Ukraine are rather modest, with about 56% of entities paying regular tax, 26% paying UT(10) (substituting for both profit tax and VAT), 8% paying UT(6) (substituting for profit tax only), and 10% paying FAT. Looking only at the non-agricultural sector, about 60% of businesses were eligible for the UT regime. Of those that were *not* eligible for it, 87% correctly used the regular tax regime, but 13% abused the UT.[6] Among those that *were* eligible for UT, over 50% nevertheless opted to use the regular regime, while 37% paid UT(10) and the remaining 10% paid UT(6) (see Figure 19.4 and Table 19.5). However, there is also the possibility that some proportion of respondents under-reported their turnover in the survey.[7] It is not clear what factors cause the limited popularity of presumptive taxation among legal entities in Ukraine (one possible explanation is that small firms

---

6. However, there is also evidence that many businesses use other ploys such as contracting of 'sole proprietors' instead of employees or splitting up a business into two or more entities in order to qualify for the presumptive regime (IFC, *The Costs of Tax Compliance in Ukraine*, 88 (2009), available at: http://www.ifc.org/wps/wcm/connect/725f0b804b5f7ae59f06bf6eac26e1c2/UTC CS_eng.pdf?MOD = AJPERES&CACHEID = 725f0b804b5f7ae59f06bf6eac26e1c2 (accessed on 19 November 2014)); see also OECD, *Ukraine: Economic Assessment*, OECD Economic Surveys Vol. 2007/16, Annex 2.A2 (OECD, 2007).
7. The survey asked respondents about their perceptions about under-reporting of turnover for tax purposes among 'businesses like yours'. Only about 40% of respondents answered the question at all. Among those who answered, the overall average estimate was about 74% total income was

applying the standard tax regime may have better access to larger businesses in the VAT system; many retailers may also find the regular regime preferable as their margins are often tighter than those in the manufacturing and service industries).

Figure 19.4   Eligibility for UT and Usage of Tax Regimes

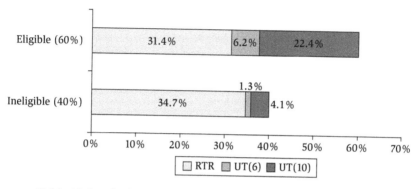

Table 19.5   Eligibility for UT versus Participation, Ukraine, %

	Eligibility	Participation			
		RTR	UT(6)	UT(10)	Total
Not Eligible	40.0	86.7	3.2	10.2	100.0
Eligible	60.0	52.3	10.4	37.3	100.0
Total	**100.0**	**66.1**	**7.5**	**26.5**	**100.0**

RTR: Regular tax regime. UT(6): Unified tax regime, pay 6% turnover tax rate, excluding VAT. UT(10): Pay 10% turnover tax rate, including VAT.

Findings are substantially different for non-incorporated small businesses. Sole Proprietors (SPs) in Ukraine could pay taxes under the regular tax regime, the UT (as described above) or the fixed tax regime (FTR), or simple patent fees. The turnover threshold for SPs was UAH 500,000 (about USD 75,000) and ten workers for the UT, and the payment was not determined as a percentage of turnover but levied as a simple flat amount between UAH 20–200 per month, which substituted for both profit tax and VAT. The FTR was for SPs with turnover up to UAH 119,000 and up to five workers. The payment was between UAH 20–100 per month, but required many visits to the municipal authorities per year to renew the patent (see Table 19.6).

reported for tax purposes. To the extent that some respondents might have been worried about possible lack of confidentiality of their answers, they might have also under-reported their turnover in the survey.

Table 19.6   Presumptive Tax Regimes for Sole Proprietors in Ukraine (2007)

Regime	Unified Tax	Patent (FTR)
Key provisions	Flat amount between UAH 20–200 per month depending on sector and location; substitutes for profit tax and VAT	Flat amount between UAH 20–100/month depending on sector & location; substitutes for profit tax & VAT; requires more visits
Eligibility	Under UAH 500,000 turnover and ten or fewer workers	Under UAH 119,000 and five or fewer workers
Proportion of sole proprietors using the regime (remainder use regular regime)	73%	20%

Of the SPs who participated in the survey, only 7% used the regular tax regime, 73% paid UT, and 20% used the FTR.[8] There is apparently less self-reported abuse of the simplified tax regimes among sole proprietors. About 98% of firms in the sample were eligible for UT and 70% were eligible for FTR, according to their reported annual turnover level. Only about 1.8% of firms not eligible for UTR reported using it, while 2.3% of businesses who reported turnover above the FTR eligibility threshold operated in the regime (See Table 19.7). Only about 28% of SPs that were eligible for both UT and FTR used the latter, which may reflect the compliance costs associated with getting multiple renewals of the patent each year. As mentioned above for legal entities, it is possible that some proportion of sole proprietors under-reported their turnover in the survey.

Table 19.7   Tax Regimes Used by Sole Proprietors in Ukraine*

Tax Regime	Regular	UTR	FTR
Eligibility	100%	98%	70%
Use	7%	73%	20%
Abuse	n.a.	2%	2%

* Eligibility and Use are percentage of all sole proprietors; while Abuse is percentage of firms not eligible for the regime but using it.

The analysis above suggests that the thresholds for use of the FTR, which in principle was supposed to be a micro regime, was probably higher than it needed to be. With 70% of sole proprietors eligible to use both the UT and the FTR, a choice was

---

8. Although the survey of legal enterprises in Ukraine was based on a stratified random sample of active business taxpayers, the survey of sole proprietors was a convenience sample and not necessarily representative of the full population.

introduced for most non-incorporated businesses to select one of two presumptive regimes, which did not even differ fundamentally in their design. Such a possibility to pick the regime that provides the most advantages to the taxpayer is neither necessary nor desirable. In Ukraine, it led to the dwindling importance of the FTR. Indeed, with the similarity of both regimes and the fact that neither illiteracy nor severe poverty are common problems in Ukraine, one could question the rationale for offering a fixed tax even for the true micro business segment.

Looking at the actual use and abuse of the regimes, relatively few interviewed sole proprietors provided direct evidence of substantial abuse in the form of under-reporting income to the tax administration to operate in the simplified regimes (rates of abuse for legal entities were somewhat higher); however, one would of course suspect that survey respondents may have under-reported their income in the survey as well. On the other hand, there is evidence that businesses in Ukraine found other mechanisms for tax evasion (as noted above). In addition, the difference in tax treatment probably incentivized many business owners to opt for operations as sole proprietors. The continuously high growth rate of non-incorporated businesses compared to incorporated businesses also points in this direction. Such decisions do not necessarily constitute abuse, but the incentives to use the simplified regimes probably distort decision-making about the choice of legal form for a business.

Table 19.8   Inspected at Least Once in 2007 by Tax Regime, Ukraine

Visit	Overall	RTR	UTR[6]	UTR[10]	FATR
No	38.7	33.8	30.3	55.3	28.6
Yes	61.3	66.2	69.7	44.7	71.4
Total	**100.0**	**100.0**			

RTR: Regular tax regime. UT(6): Unified tax regime, pay 6% turnover tax rate, excluding VAT. UT(10): Pay 10% average tax rate, including VAT. FATR: Fixed agricultural tax.

On the inspection side, some analogies between the situation in Yemen and the situation in Ukraine can be observed with regard to both a high level of inspection of presumptive taxpayers and a relatively weak targeting of system abuse risks. Inspections of legal entities in Ukraine were relatively high at over 60% (including 'desk audits' that did not involve a visit to the businesses), but those in the RTR, UT(6), and the FAT were targeted at higher rates than those using UT(10). While these findings in principle reflect an appropriate audit focus on taxpayers in the VAT system, the survey results do not show any evidence that those abusing UT(10) were inspected at rates higher than those legitimately using it, suggesting that the authorities had not developed an effective strategy for targeting abuse of the UT (see Table 19.8).

A relatively smaller number of SPs faced inspection, at 29% (which is still very high compared to developed countries and suggests an inefficient allocation of resources). As expected, those paying regular income tax (which tended to be relatively larger) were more likely to face an inspection (about one-third) than those paying UTR or FTR (roughly one-fifth).[9]

Overall the survey results suggest that tax inspections in Ukraine were probably not effective in deterring abuse of the simplified regimes available to MSMEs in the country.

§19.05   SIMPLIFIED TAX REGIMES IN BURUNDI, 2010

In Burundi in 2010 (before major tax reforms were enacted), there were two presumptive tax regimes available to MSMEs: a 'Simplified Tax Regime' (STR) for small businesses (offering only a slight reduction in reporting requirements) and a 'Fixed Tax Regime' (FTR) for micro businesses, available only to individual entrepreneurs with turnover up to BF 15 million (about USD 12,000) in the services and accommodation sectors and BF 20 million (about USD 16,000) in all other sectors (mostly trade and manufacturing). However, because of the low attractiveness of the simplified regime, its take-up rate was less than 1% of the taxpayer population, and taxpayers either decided to directly apply the regular tax regime or move into the FTR for micro businesses (See Table 19.9).

Table 19.9   Simplified Tax Regimes in Burundi (2010)

Tax Regime	Fixed Tax Regime	Simplified Regime
Key provisions	Fixed amount depending on sector and location	Slightly Reduced reporting requirements, same rates and base as profit tax
Eligibility	Turnover up to BDI 15 million (services) or up to BDI 20 million (trade and manufacturing)	Businesses below VAT threshold (BDI 100 million)
Proportion of businesses using the regime (remainder use regular regime)	50%	(less than 0.5%)

Source: IFC, *Rapport: Le Coût de la Mise en Conformité avec la Réglementation Fiscale du Secteur Formel et la Perception de la Fiscalité par le Secteur Informel au Burundi* (2012).

About 50% of active formal businesses in Burundi paid FTR, 20% paid profit tax only, and 29% paid both profit tax and VAT. However, only about 36% of all businesses were actually eligible to pay FTR. Looking at the survey data in more detail, it appears that 27% of firms that were ineligible to use the FTR nevertheless reported using it, which is equivalent to 17% of all active business taxpayers. Among all firms that reported a turnover level below the FTR eligibility threshold, 92% used the regime and

---

9. Although the survey of Sole Proprietors in Ukraine was not a scientific sample, the distribution appeared close to that of the relevant population.

the remainder paid in the regular tax regime (see Figure 19.5). There was no mechanism available for micro businesses to advance to a truly simplified small business tax regime before entering the general tax regime, creating obvious disincentives for micro business growth and development.

Figure 19.5   Fixed Tax Regime Usage (Yes or No) by Eligibility in Burundi

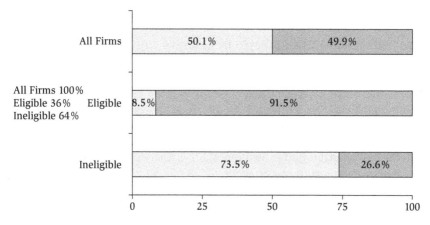

Looking at approaches to counteract the frequent abuse of the FTR, the survey shows that overall, about one-third of businesses reported that they had been subject to inspection, with those in the regular regime (mostly relatively larger businesses) being more likely to be inspected than those in FTR. Again, similar to the situation in Ukraine, this is an appropriate inspection focus in principle. Also, as a positive element of the inspection-target strategy, among FTR payers, those abusing the regime faced a somewhat higher inspection level (35.1%) than those taxpayers legitimately using the FTR (24.2%). More questionable, however, is the effectiveness of the audit strategy, given that the higher audit probability for businesses not eligible to use the FTR does not appear to act as a deterrent against system abuse (see Table 19.10).

Table 19.10   FTR Usage and Inspection, by Eligibility for FTR, Burundi, %

Inspection	All Firms	Ineligible		Eligible	
		No	Yes	No	Yes
Not Inspected	68.0%	62.8%	64.9%	82.3%	75.9%
Inspected	32.0%	37.2%	35.1%	17.7%	24.2%
Total	**100.0%**				

Thus in Burundi, although there was a clear reason to offer the FTR, there was evidence of abuse of that regime by businesses too large to be eligible, while enforcement failed to either identify or deter such abuse. The 'simplified' regime was barely used, as it offered only a slight reduction in reporting requirements. A new MSME regime enacted in 2012 created a turnover tax targeted at small businesses, allowing micro-enterprises to continue to pay the fixed tax (administered by the local level). This case shows that the negative effects of base erosion may occur even in a situation where the threshold of the micro business regime has been set appropriately. It demonstrates that presumptive regime abuse may not only be driven, like in Yemen, by an unclear setting of the system threshold and weak enforcement, but also by the lack of a suitable simplified small business regime, leading to taxpayers artificially migrating downwards into the micro regime and staying there longer than appropriate.

§19.06   SIMPLIFIED TAX REGIMES IN ALBANIA, 2012

In Albania, there were three different tax regimes available to small firms in 2012 when the survey data were collected. These were the Regular Tax Regime (RTR), a Small business (Simplified) Tax Regime (STR) and finally, a Fixed amount Tax Regime (FTR). Annual turnover was the only eligibility criterion for all the regimes. Firms with annual turnover of not more than ALL 2 million (roughly USD 20,000) were eligible for FTR; firms with annual turnover between ALL 2–8 million were eligible for STR and finally, firms with annual turnover above ALL 8 million were required to apply the standard tax regime. A major weakness of small business taxation in Albania was that presumptive regimes were not appropriately coordinated with the VAT regime, as firms with turnover above ALL 5 million were required to also register and file for value added tax (VAT).[10]

Table 19.11   Business Tax Regimes in Albania (2012)

Regime	Fixed Tax Regime	Simplified Tax Regime, without VAT Registration	Simplified Tax Regime, with VAT Registration
Key Provisions	Fixed amount	Simplified accounting and reduced tax rate on profit; no need to account or remit VAT	Simplified accounting and reduced tax rate on profit
Eligibility	Under ALL 2 million	ALL 2–5 million	ALL 5–8 million
Proportion of businesses using the regime*	58%	19%	6%

* Remainder are in Regular Tax Regime
Source: IFC, *Albania Tax Compliance Cost Survey Report* (unpublished, 2012).

---

10. There was an exception for independent professions (like doctors, dentists, architects, lawyers, accountants, consultants, etc.) for which VAT registration was mandatory irrespective of actual turnover.

Micro firms having annual turnover of up to ALL 2 million could pay a fixed amount under the FTR. For small businesses, the STR offered certain simplifications in tax accounting procedures and a reduced tax rate of 10% of net income. In practice, firms anticipating that they might generate an annual turnover of less than ALL 2 million could initially register as FTR payers. If, however, the realized turnover ended up being above the FTR threshold, the firm was required to move to the STR. Businesses in the general tax regime were required to pay profit tax on a quarterly or monthly basis and were liable to keep full accounting records (based on national accounting standards or international financial reporting standards).

Figure 19.6 presents the actual use of each tax regime among Albanian firms in 2012. It shows that 99% of all firms that reported a turnover under ALL 2 million in the survey and thus were eligible for FTR actually used the regime (57% of the total taxpayer population). Similarly, almost all businesses (99%) reporting a turnover above the threshold of presumptive regimes, which therefore were eligible for neither FTR nor STR, actually complied with the requirements of the general tax regime. The striking finding in the Albanian case is the interest of businesses above the micro business level to avail themselves of the micro business tax regime whenever possible: a large majority (92.3%) of the firms that reported turnover for the year between ALL 2–8 million signed up for both STR and FTR during the year (presumably starting with FTR and only switching to STR after they went over ALL 2 million) – instead of starting out with STR from the outset. About 3% of the firms in this group (or 0.75% of the overall population) actually paid tax under only STR, and the remaining 1.8% and 2.6% of these firms paid tax either only under FTR or RTR. This implies that most firms initially paid fixed tax, and as their realized turnovers exceeded ALL 2 million at some point in the fiscal year, they adjusted their tax bills accordingly by the difference between STR tax bill and prepaid fixed tax. Overall, these figures do not provide direct evidence of abuse of regimes in the country, but perceptions of evasion (i.e., perceptions about amounts of revenue reported for tax purposes in 'firms similar to yours') suggest abuses may be quite substantial.[11]

---

11. Asked about under-reporting of income for tax purposes among 'businesses like yours' in the survey, the average estimate was about two-thirds, and it is possible that some respondents also under-reported their turnover in the survey, in which case abuse rates might be somewhat higher.

Figure 19.6   Tax Regime Usage by Eligibility in Albania (Percent of Firms)

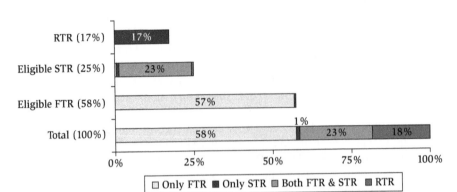

Overall, a large majority (86% of firms in the country) were inspected in the last two years (2011–2012), including both planned and unplanned inspections. The vast majority (96%) of the inspections were relatively short (under two days) and focused on relatively minor issues such as 'control of proper usage of cash registers', 'short fiscal visits on different issues' and 'control of insurance contributions and employment income taxes' rather than comprehensive audits (see Figure 19.7). Micro firms (mostly using FTR) were least likely to face a 'full audit' (about 20% of them within a two-year period) and the medium/large businesses mostly using RTR were relatively more likely to face such an audit.

Figure 19.7   Incidence of Tax Inspection by Type of Inspection and Size of Business

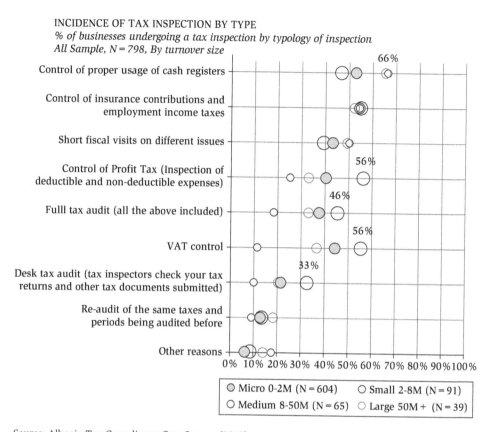

INCIDENCE OF TAX INSPECTION BY TYPE
% of businesses undergoing a tax inspection by typology of inspection
All Sample, N = 798, By turnover size

Source: Albania Tax Compliance Cost Survey (2013).

On the one hand, the overall incidence of inspection was relatively high. On the other hand, the targeting of different types of inspection toward different size firms appears appropriate.

Figure 19.8   Inspections by Tax Regime, %

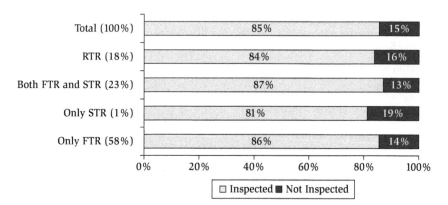

Overall, firms that were inspected at all were visited an average of eight times in the aforementioned two years. Firms that paid tax under only FTR reported 7.7 visits and firms that were under RTR also recorded a similar number, 7.2. However, firms that were under both FTR and PTR were visited more frequently, 8.9 times in the previous two years. A simple mean comparison test (for the difference between these averages and the mean of the overall sample) shows that the differences are not significant, except the difference between 'Both FTR & PTR' and the overall sample, which is marginally significantly different than zero.[12]

As was the case with Ukraine, illiteracy is not a significant issue in Albania. A major source of the challenges in enforcing tax compliance in Albania is the misalignment of incentives across the government agencies: local government implements the FTR and loses revenue when businesses graduate to the RTR, administered centrally.

§19.07   SIMPLIFIED TAX REGIME IN NEPAL, 2011

In Nepal, a presumptive (Patent) Tax Regime (PTR) was available as of 2011 for micro firms with turnover under NPR 2 million (about USD 20,000),[13] which was also the VAT threshold. Those using the PTR paid a fixed amount of NPR 3,500 in municipalities or NPR 1,250 in areas outside municipalities. It was possible to voluntarily register for VAT and still pay the patent in lieu of profit tax (see Table 19.12). Essentially, all businesses eligible for the PTR used it, while about 12% of businesses below the PTR/VAT threshold voluntarily signed up for VAT.

---

12. At 90% significance level.
13. Also taxi owner-drivers, truck owner-drivers, and owners of public vehicles.

Table 19.12   Business Tax Regimes in Nepal (2011)

Regime	PTR
Key provisions	NPR 3,500 in municipalities
	NPR 1,250 outside municipalities
Eligibility (main criteria)	Turnover under NPR 2 million
Proportion of firms under PTR/VAT threshold (remainder required to pay regular income tax)	About 86%

Source: IFC, *Nepal Tax Compliance Cost Survey Report* (2012), https://www.wbginvestmentclimate .org/publications/loader.cfm?csModule = security/getfile&pageid = 33942.

On the basis of turnover as reported in the survey, it appears that over a quarter (26%) of businesses above the threshold had not registered for VAT, as required by law (see Figure 19.9).

Figure 19.9   VAT Registration Status by Annual Turnover in Comparison to PTR/VAT Threshold

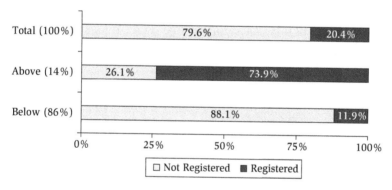

Inspections in Nepal were more likely for businesses above the PTR/VAT threshold. While about 40% of all businesses faced an inspection in 2011, about 36% of those below the threshold were inspected at least once, while 60% of those above the threshold were inspected (and 12% were inspected three or more times during the year) (see Figure 19.10). However, there was almost no difference in perceptions about the legitimacy (or lack thereof) of tax inspections between those above and below the threshold: only about 40% were perceived to be for 'legitimate reasons ... to deter tax evasion'.

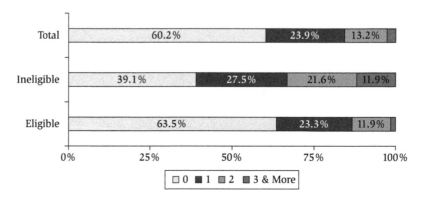

Figure 19.10   Number of Inspections by PTR Eligibility, %

§19.08   SIMPLIFIED TAX REGIME IN SOUTH AFRICA, 2011

In South Africa, before 2008, all businesses paid regular income tax without any simplified or presumptive regime. As of 2008, a new voluntary Turnover Tax (TT) for businesses under R 1 million (about USD 125,000) was introduced, with progressive marginal rate bands ranging from zero to 7%.[14] By most accounts, take-up of the new regime was lower than expected. A survey of small business taxpayers (those with turnover under R 14 million) was undertaken by researchers at the University of Pretoria with the cooperation of the South Africa Revenue Service (SARS). It was estimated that almost 70% of small businesses were eligible for the TT, but only about 2%–3% of small firms registered for it or were using it (see Table 19.13).

Table 19.13   Simplified Tax Regime for Micro-Enterprises in South Africa

Regime	Turnover Tax
Key Provisions	Progressive rates ranging from 0% for turnover under R 150,000 to a marginal rate of 7% for turnover greater than R 750,000
Eligibility	Businesses owned directly by individuals (natural persons) with turnover less than R 1 million, excluding professional services
Proportion of small businesses eligible for the regime/using the regime	About 70%/about 3%

Source: Sharon Smulders, Madeleine Stiglingh, Riel Franzsen & Lizelle Fletcher, *Tax compliance costs for the small business sector in South Africa – establishing a baseline*, 10(2) eJournal of Tax Research, 184 (2012).

---

14. Other restrictions about sector and ownership narrowed the field of eligible businesses some-what.

In South Africa as of 2011, there was considerable evidence of confusion and lack of information about the TT regime (as well as other small business tax concessions, such as the ability to expense certain capital investments in the year of purchase). Asked in the survey about whether they were 'eligible for any tax concessions', only 12% responded 'Yes' and 42% responded 'Unsure/Don't know' (see Figure 19.11).

Figure 19.11   Firms' Self-Reported Eligibility for Tax Concessions

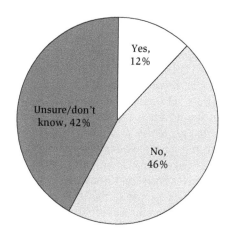

Asked more specifically about usage of the TT, about 3.2% of small businesses reported in the survey that they used it in 2011, while SARS' data on registrations showed about 3.8% of respondents were registered for it. The majority of the discrepancies are more likely due to confusion on the part of the survey respondents than misuse of the actual regimes.[15]

On the one hand, only about 1.3% of businesses seemed to be abusing the TT (i.e., using the TT while reporting annual turnover in the survey over R 1 million). On the other hand, as a proportion of TT users, this accounts for up to 18%. While other countries showed a pattern of ineffective inspections (in terms of catching abusers of simplified regimes by those not eligible for them), and a habit of trying to inspect all businesses on a regular basis, regardless of size, South Africa had already established a risk-based audit system by the mid-1990s. On the basis of previous survey evidence,[16] inspections of small businesses in South Africa were relatively rare and usually took

---

15. There was no overlap between the two groups in the survey so the overall estimate is 7% of small businesses.
16. World Bank, *South Africa - Tax Compliance Burden for Small Businesses: A Survey of Tax Practitioners*, Working Paper 58813 (2007); available at http://www-wds.worldbank.org/ext ernal/default/WDSContentServer/WDSP/IB/2011/01/06/000334955_20110106030819/Render ed/PDF/588130WP0FIAS110BOX353820B01PUBLIC1.pdf.

place for less than 5% of such businesses per year. However, it may become necessary to put somewhat more effort into identifying businesses that might be under-declaring turnover either to avoid mandatory VAT registration or to register for TT (especially businesses with a relatively high profit margin, such as those in service sectors).

§19.09   CONCLUSIONS

The cases presented in this chapter provide empirical evidence for a number of problems associated with simplified regimes for MSMEs. While the general framework remains sound (i.e., allowing low-capacity, poverty-level micro-enterprises to pay a small fixed amount of tax without a requirement for keeping books; and allowing small businesses to pay a simplified tax based on their turnover while requiring them to show at least minimal books), the surveys analysed show that abuse of these regimes (especially fixed tax) appears substantial. On the other hand, measures designed to mitigate abuse may (as in South Africa) add to the complexity of the regimes and may thereby deter businesses that genuinely would be eligible for them.

Albania and Ukraine still have fixed tax regimes that appear to be unnecessary from the point of view of taxpayer capacity and are used by businesses that can, and arguably should, be paying taxes based on turnover, if not profits. The survey data on self-reported turnover suggest that abuse of the UTR in Ukraine is at least 13%. The figure for Albania is less than 2%, but the self-reported turnover is itself likely to reflect the high levels of under-reporting perceived among 'businesses like yours'. Yemen had a regime with overly generous features and inappropriate criteria for inclusion. While designed explicitly for illiterate entrepreneurs, it simply encouraged almost all businesses to declare that they could not carry out book-keeping. It also had the highest rate of estimated abuse, at almost 50%. Burundi's regime offered a fixed tax for micro-enterprises that may have been appropriately designed and targeted, but the 'simplified' regime intended for small businesses was only slightly simpler than the regular regime, and was rarely utilized. Its estimated rate of abuse was about one-third of those using the regime. Nepal's regime appears to be abused by at least one-quarter of those in it. In South Africa, where barely 7% of businesses use the turnover tax (compared to almost 70% that should be eligible), abuse by those in the regime might be as high as 18% (see Table 19.14). Note that in any given country, some eligible businesses use it and some might opt for the regular regime; some who are using the regime are eligible for it and others may be abusing it.

Table 19.14 Summary of Estimates of Use and Abuse of Simplified Regimes

Country	Type of Simplified Regime	% of all Firms That Are Eligible for the Regime	Use (% of all Businesses)	Use (% of Those Eligible for the Regime)	Estimated Abuse (% of All Businesses)	Estimated Abuse (% of those Using the Regime)
Yemen	FTR	47%	94%	202%	47%	48%
Ukraine (non-agricu-ltural companies)	UT	60%	34%	29%	5%	16%
Burundi	FTR	36%	50%	92%	14%	34%
Albania	FTR	58%	58%	98%	< 2% *	< 1%*
Nepal	Exemption from mandatory VAT	86%	80%	88%	4% *	26%*
South Africa (MSME)	TT	69%	7%	8%	1%	18%

* Abuse of FTR in Albania and Nepal is probably substantially higher taking into account average estimated levels of under-reporting turnover.

With regard to enforcement, the survey evidence suggests that the tax regimes in all evaluated countries failed to put in place risk-management strategies targeted at abuse of the fixed tax regimes.

In terms of the *policy implications*, in theory, it has been well-accepted that presumptive taxation should be designed to address the highest priority problems of taxing MSMEs in developing and transition countries, and that these priorities are likely to change as countries grow and capacity improves (both in the public and the private sectors). As such, simplified tax regimes should be reformed periodically to ensure that they continue to address priority needs under changing circumstances. Surveys of small businesses focusing on education levels, book-keeping practices, use of bank accounts, and estimates of cash flow (including both the business side and household side of small, cash-based, family-run businesses) may help inform the key parameters of simplified regimes.

The data from Burundi, Nepal, and Yemen (and arguably Albania and Ukraine) suggest that a fixed tax regime may be causing significant damage in erosion of the base for regular and/or turnover-based tax, which would need to be taken into account in a cost-benefit analysis of these regimes. At the same time, the findings suggest that the use of risk-based audit should be expanded to include the risk of abuse of the presumptive regimes and to encourage (or compel, if necessary) more graduation into regimes that require at least basic book-keeping. However, regular Risk Based Audit

(RBA), to the extent that it relies on third-party data (e.g., comparisons of tax returns between companies, data from customs, data from the financial sector) is likely to under-estimate the risks of evasion through under-reporting of cash transactions, which are very common among small businesses. In these cases, it may be helpful to identify objective indicators of the size of a business that are correlated with turnover but also easy to measure and verify (e.g., square metres of floor space of a business, numbers of employees, value of fixed assets, value of inventory, etc.), which could then help in selection of audit targets.

The data from Burundi, Nepal, and Yemen suggest a continuing need for a fixed tax regime for micro-enterprises, as many such businesses are apparently unable to practice book-keeping (e.g., adult literacy rates under 90%, in some cases significantly) and have net incomes at or near the poverty threshold. Even for these countries, however, it may be beneficial to place more emphasis on the design of simplified regimes appropriate for small businesses yielding incomes above poverty levels. Such businesses should be required to keep basic books (e.g., reports of daily sales) and to pay tax based on turnover. Thresholds should be set taking into account correlations between turnover, on the one hand, and literacy and (roughly) estimated net income, on the other. The thresholds should be revised periodically to keep them in line with their target population. Small businesses should be offered training in basic book-keeping and preparation of simple tax returns and other aspects of realistic tax compliance.

The case of South Africa illustrates the need for targeted outreach and education campaigns aimed at micro-enterprises, so that they can gain a better understanding of the options available to them. The emphasis in South Africa has arguably been too heavily in favour of 'deterrence' of businesses that might be ineligible to use the regime, such that most businesses are afraid to apply for it. Instead of encouraging micro-enterprises that are engaged in retail and services (such as taxi drivers and hairdressers), it presents a long list of criteria that renders certain businesses ineligible. While it is both understandable and reasonable to exclude professional services and subsidiaries of corporations or trusts from registering for the turnover tax, SARS' information has probably dwelt too heavily on the topic of ineligibility and not sufficiently on informing and encouraging eligible small businesses about the opportunity and benefits of the TT.

More broadly, it appears that, in many cases, 'simplified' regimes that require book-keeping tend to be perceived as still overly complex and therefore unpopular, and require more encouragement; while 'patent' or fixed tax regimes tend to be overly popular, prone to abuse, and need to be made more restricted.

Index

SERIES ON INTERNATIONAL TAXATION

1. Alberto Xavier, *The Taxation of Foreign Investment in Brazil*, 1980 (ISBN 90-200-0582-0).
2. Hugh J. Ault & Albert J. Rädler, *The German Corporation Tax Law with 1980 Amendments*, 1981 (ISBN 90-200-0642-8).
3. Paul R. McDaniel & Hugh J. Ault, *Introduction to United States International Taxation*, 1981 (ISBN 90-6544-004-6).
4. Albert J. Rädler, *German Transfer Pricing/Prix de Transfer en Allemagne*, 1984 (ISBN 90-6544-143-3).
5. Paul R. McDaniel & Stanley S. Surrey, *International Aspects of Tax Expenditures: A Comparative Study*, 1985 (ISBN 90-654-4163-8).
6. Kees van Raad, *Nondiscrimination in International Tax Law*, 1986 (ISBN 90-6544-266-9).
7. Sijbren Cnossen (ed.), *Tax Coordination in the European Community*, 1987 (ISBN 90-6544-272-3).
8. Ben Terra, *Sales Taxation. The Case of Value Added Tax in the European Community*, 1989 (ISBN 90-6544-381-9).
9. Rutsel S.J. Martha, *The Jurisdiction to Tax in International Law: Theory and Practice of Legislative Fiscal Jurisdiction*, 1989 (ISBN 90-654-4416-5).
10. Paul R. McDaniel & Hugh J. Ault, *Introduction to United States International Taxation* (3rd revised edition), 1989 (ISBN 90-6544-423-8).
11. Manuel Pires, *International Juridicial Double Taxation of Income*, 1989 (ISBN 90-6544-426-2).
12. A.H.M. Daniels, *Issues in International Partnership Taxation*, 1991 (ISBN 90-654-4577-3).
13. Arvid A. Skaar, *Permanent Establishment: Erosion of a Tax Treaty Principle*, 1992 (ISBN 90-6544-594-3).
14. Cyrille David & Geerten M.M. Michielse (eds), *Tax Treatment of Financial Instruments*, 1996 (ISBN 90-654-4666-4).
15. Herbert H. Alpert & Kees van Raad (eds), *Essays on International Taxation*, 1993 (ISBN 90-654-4781-4).
16. Wolfgang Gassner, Michael Lang & Eduard Lechner (eds), *Tax Treaties and EC Law*, 1997 (ISBN 90-411-0680-4).
17. Glória Teixeira, *Taxing Corporate Profits in the EU*, 1997 (ISBN 90-411-0703-7).
18. Michael Lang et al. (eds), *Multilateral Tax Treaties*, 1998 (ISBN 90-411-0704-5).
19. Stef van Weeghel, *The Improper Use of Tax Treaties*, 1998 (ISBN 90-411-0737-1).
20. Klaus Vogel (ed.), *Interpretation of Tax Law and Treaties and Transfer Pricing in Japan and Germany*, 1998 (ISBN 90-411-9655-2).
21. Bertil Wiman (ed.), *International Studies in Taxation: Law and Economics; Liber Amicorum Leif Mutén*, 1999 (ISBN 90-411-9692-7).
22. Alfonso J. Martín Jiménez, *Towards Corporate Tax Harmonization in the European Community*, 1999 (ISBN 90-411-9690-0).

23. Ramon J. Jeffery, *The Impact of State Sovereignty on Global Trade and International Taxation*, 1999 (ISBN 90-411-9703-6).

24. A.J. Easson, *Taxation of Foreign Direct Investment*, 1999 (ISBN 90-411-9741-9).

25. Marjaana Helminen, *The Dividend Concept in International Tax Law: Dividend Payments Between Corporate Entities*, 1999 (ISBN 90-411-9765-6).

26. Paul Kirchhof, Moris Lehner, Kees van Raad, Arndt Raupach & Michael-Rodi (eds), *International and Comparative Taxation: Essays in Honour of Klaus Vogel*, 2002 (ISBN 90-411-9841-5).

27. Krister Andersson, Peter Melz & Christer Silfverberg (eds), *Liber Amicorum Sven-Olof Lodin*, 2001 (ISBN 90-411-9850-4).

28. Juan Martín Jovanovich, *Customs Valuation and Transfer Pricing: Is It Possible to Harmonize Customs and Tax Rules?*, 2002 (ISBN 90-411-9888-1).

29. Stefano Simontacchi, *Taxation of Capital Gains under the OECD Model Convention: With Special Regard to Immovable Property*, 2007 (ISBN 978-90-411-2549-1).

30. Michael Lang, Josef Schuch, & Claus Staringer (eds), *Tax Treaty Law and EC Law*, 2007 (ISBN 978-90-411-2629-0).

31. Duncan Bentley, *Taxpayers' Rights: Theory Origin and Implementation*, 2007 (ISBN 978-90-411-2650-4).

32. Sergio André Rocha, *Interpretation of Double Taxation Conventions: General Theory and Brazilian Perspective*, 2008 (ISBN 978-90-411-2822-5).

33. Robert F. van Brederode, *Systems of General Sales Taxation: Theory, Policy and Practice*, 2009 (ISBN 978-90-411-2832-4).

34. John G. Head & Richard Krever (eds), *Tax Reform in the 21st Century: A Volume in Memory of Richard Musgrave*, 2009 (ISBN 978-90-411-2829-4).

35. Jens Wittendorff, *Transfer Pricing and the Arm's Length Principle in International Tax Law*, 2010 (ISBN 978-90-411-3270-3).

36. Marjaana Helminen, *The International Tax Law Concept of Dividend*, 2010 (ISBN 978-90-411-3206-2).

37. Robert F. van Brederode (ed.), *Immovable Property under VAT: A Comparative Global Analysis*, 2011 (ISBN 978-90-411-3126-3).

38. Dennis Weber & Stef van Weeghel, *The 2010 OECD Updates: Model Tax Convention & Transfer Pricing Guidelines - A Critical Review*, 2011 (ISBN 978-90-411-3812-5).

39. Yariv Brauner & Martin James Mcmahon, Jr. (eds), *The Proper Tax Base: Structural Fairness from an International and Comparative Perspective— Essays in Honour of Paul McDaniel*, 2012 (ISBN 978-90-411-3286-4).

40. Robert F. van Brederode (ed.), *Science, Technology and Taxation*, 2012 (ISBN 978-90-411-3125-6).

41. Oskar Henkow, *The VAT/GST Treatment of Public Bodies*, 2013 (ISBN 978-90-411-4663-2).

42. Jean Schaffner, *How Fixed Is a Permanent Establishment?*, 2013 (ISBN 978-90-411-4662-5).

43. Miguel Correia, *Taxation of Corporate Groups*, 2013 (ISBN 978-90-411-4841-4).
44. Veronika Daurer, *Tax Treaties and Developing Countries*, 2014 (ISBN 978-90-411-4982-4).
45. Claire Micheau, *State Aid, Subsidy and Tax Incentives under EU and WTO Law*, 2014 (ISBN 978-90-411-4555-0).
46. Robert F. van Brederode & Richard Krever (eds), *Legal Interpretation of Tax Law*, 2014 (ISBN 978-90-411-4945-9).
47. Radhakishan Rawal, *Taxation of Cross-border Services*, 2014 (ISBN 978-90-411-4947-3).
48. João Dácio Rolim, *Proportionality and Fair Taxation*, 2014 (ISBN 978-90-411-5838-3).
49. Paulo Rosenblatt, *General Anti-avoidance Rules for Major Developing Countries*, 2015 (ISBN 978-90-411-5839-0).
50. Gaspar Lopes Dias V.S., *Tax Arbitrage through Cross-Border Financial Engineering*, 2015 (ISBN 978-90-411-5875-8).
51. Geerten M.M. Michielse & Victor Thuronyi (eds), *Tax Design Issues Worldwide*, 2015 (ISBN 978-90-411-5610-5).
52. Oktavia Weidmann, *Taxation of Derivatives*, 2015 (ISBN 978-90-411-5977-9).
53. Chris Evans, Richard Krever & Peter Mellor (eds), *Tax Simplification*, 2015 (ISBN 978-90-411-5976-2).